The Shape of Utopia

BUELL CENTER BOOKS IN THE HISTORY
AND THEORY OF AMERICAN ARCHITECTURE

REINHOLD MARTIN, SERIES EDITOR

The Temple Hoyne Buell Center for the Study of American Architecture at Columbia University was founded in 1982. Its mission is to advance the interdisciplinary study of American architecture, urbanism, and landscape. The Buell Center sponsors research projects, workshops, public programs, publications, and awards.

The Temple Hoyne
Buell Center
for the Study of
American Architecture

The Shape of Utopia

The Architecture of Radical Reform
in Nineteenth-Century America

IRENE CHENG

University of Minnesota Press
Minneapolis
London

Portions of chapter 1 were published in "Race and Architectural Geometry: Thomas Jefferson's Octagons," *J19: The Journal of Nineteenth-Century Americanists* 3, no. 1 (Spring 2015): 121–30; copyright 2015 C19: The Society of Nineteenth-Century Americanists, published by University of Pennsylvania Press; and as "The Racial Geometry of the Nation," in *Race and Vision in the Nineteenth-Century United States,* ed. Shirley R. Samuels (Lanham, Md.: Lexington Books, Rowman and Littlefield, 2019).

Copyright 2023 by the Regents of the University of Minnesota

All rights reserved. No part of this publication may be reproduced, stored in a retrieval system, or transmitted, in any form or by any means, electronic, mechanical, photocopying, recording, or otherwise, without the prior written permission of the publisher.

Published by the University of Minnesota Press
111 Third Avenue South, Suite 290
Minneapolis, MN 55401-2520
http://www.upress.umn.edu

ISBN 978-1-5179-0745-7 (hc)
ISBN 978-1-5179-0746-4 (pb)

A Cataloging-in-Publication record for this book is available from the Library of Congress.

Printed in the United States of America on acid-free paper

The University of Minnesota is an equal-opportunity educator and employer.

30 29 28 27 26 25 24 23   10 9 8 7 6 5 4 3 2 1

CONTENTS

INTRODUCTION
The Visual Rhetoric of Reform   1

CHAPTER 1
Antinomies of American Utopia   29
Thomas Jefferson's Grids and Octagons

CHAPTER 2
The Visual Rhetoric of Equality   57
The Land Reformers' Grid

CHAPTER 3
Cultivating the Liberal Self   95
Orson Fowler's Octagon House

CHAPTER 4
Picturing Sociality without Socialism   133
The Kansas Vegetarian Octagon Colony

CHAPTER 5
Toward More Transparent Representation   165
The Hexagonal "Anarchist" City of Josiah Warren

CHAPTER 6
Models, Machines, and Manifestations   195
The Spiritualists' Circular Utopias

EPILOGUE
The Afterlife of Geometric Utopianism   243

Acknowledgments   261
Notes   265
Selected Bibliography   301
Index   339

INTRODUCTION

The Visual Rhetoric of Reform

In the spring of 1856, a group of emigrants from the eastern United States embarked on an unlikely venture: the establishment of an antislavery vegetarian colony in the newly organized Kansas Territory. The passage of the Kansas–Nebraska Act opened the region, which the federal government had promised to Indigenous people as a permanent home only twenty years earlier, to encroachment by an unruly array of squatters, speculators, and railroad interests, while also transforming it into the main battleground in the fierce national debate over the extension of slavery into the West. Pro- and antislavery settlers flooded into the territory in hopes of winning it to their column—in most cases, motivated more by hunger for land and profit than by their convictions about slavery. Amid this fractious environment, the founder of the vegetarian colony, an Englishman named Henry Clubb, wrote that he hoped to carve out "one tract of land on this fair earth free from the stain of habitual bloodshed . . . where the birds shall fill the air with melody without fear or trembling."[1]

In addition to its curious and contradictory convergence of dietary and moral–political reform commitments, the colony was distinct for its unusual design, which its creator called "the octagon plan of settlement." The prospectus for the colony prominently featured an eye-catching diagram depicting eight wedge-shaped lots arranged radially around a central park and building (Figure I.1). Engraved in stark white lines on a black background, the eight-sided plan lent an iconic visual identity to the project. The text of the prospectus offered only a cursory explanation for the colony's geometric organization. Among the benefits cited were that the centralized, graduated arrangement of private lots would help to equalize property values and enable residents to live in close community. With its measured scale and precise legend, the diagram lent a sense of concreteness and credibility to what might otherwise have appeared a hopelessly quixotic experiment. Remarkably, some eighty families purchased shares in the enterprise; the first group arrived in Kansas in May 1856. Less surprising, the full plan was never constructed, and the colony disappeared within a few months of its establishment.

2   Introduction

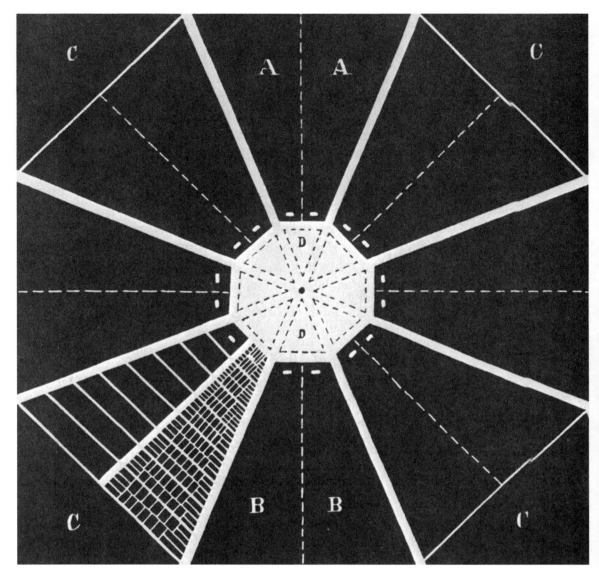

FIGURE I.1. The octagon plan of settlement. Prospectus for the Octagon Settlement Company, 1856. Courtesy Kansas State Historical Society.

Eccentric as this episode may seem, the vegetarian octagon colony was not an isolated episode but part of a larger constellation of projects that I call "geometric utopias"—architectural and urban-scale plans set apart by their distinct shapes and promoted by creators who believed that such communities would help bring about individual and social regeneration. These projects emerged in the United States in the middle decades of the nineteenth century, when a confluence of religious millennialism, volatility in the developing market economy, technological upheaval, territorial expansion, and tensions over slavery spawned an atmosphere of social ferment and an efflorescence of communitarian social experimentation. During this period, known among historians as the first age of reform, advocates of temperance, antislavery, women's rights, pacifism, socialism, vegetarianism, water cures, free love, and other causes large and small sought to remake U.S. society.[2] They did so through both "moral suasion" and the creation of model communities that would serve as seedbeds for a new world. More than one hundred communitarian societies were founded in the half century before the Civil War.[3] Ralph Waldo Emerson captured the atmosphere of optimism bordering on fanaticism when he wrote to his friend Thomas Carlyle in 1840: "We are all a little wild here with numberless projects of social reform. Not a reading man but has a draft of a new community in his waistcoat pocket. . . . One man renounces the use of animal food; and another of coin; and another of domestic hired service; and another of the State; and on the whole we have a commendable share of reason and hope."[4] Another prominent writer described the time as "most emphatically an age of experiments."[5]

Although only a handful of the "drafts" referenced by Emerson featured geometric architectural or urban plans, those that did constitute a distinct strain within the corpus of nineteenth-century utopianism. This book centers on five sets of schemes that were put forward from 1840 through 1873: the vegetarian settlement described above, a gridded township and eight-sided republican village proposed by labor radicals, an octagon house design published by a phrenologist, a hexagonal city plan presented by America's first home-grown anarchist, and a series of oval and circular buildings envisioned by spiritualists intent on creating more harmonious spaces of dwelling and commerce (Figure I.2). Common to all these plans is that they were created not by professional architects or urban designers but by self-styled reformers, men who were veterans of Fourierism and Owenism and were enmeshed in the spheres of radical reform centered in New York, Boston, Philadelphia, and Cincinnati. All of these creators believed that by designing a better house or city they could help strengthen individual bodies or usher in a more equitable society. Their designs were published in pamphlets or reform newspapers, bespeaking their rootedness in the medium and networks of popular print and raising the possibility that *how* these utopians spoke to audiences was as important as *what* they were proposing. And, without exception, all of the designs were ephemeral or never realized.

Failed Utopias

Given the transience of geometric utopias, it is easy to surmise why they have attracted little scholarly attention. The five examples discussed here are, for the most part, more marginal, more eccentric, and shorter-lived than the communities examined in Dolores Hayden's now-classic book *Seven American Utopias,* which explores the architecture of groups such as the Shakers, Mormons, and Fourierists.[6] They also lack the architectural virtuosity of the beautifully rendered utopian drawings of professional architects like Claude-Nicolas Ledoux or Étienne-Louis Boullée. Geometric utopias thus have often fallen into the cracks between academic disciplines. On the one hand, some of their creators—men like the phrenologist Orson Fowler and the

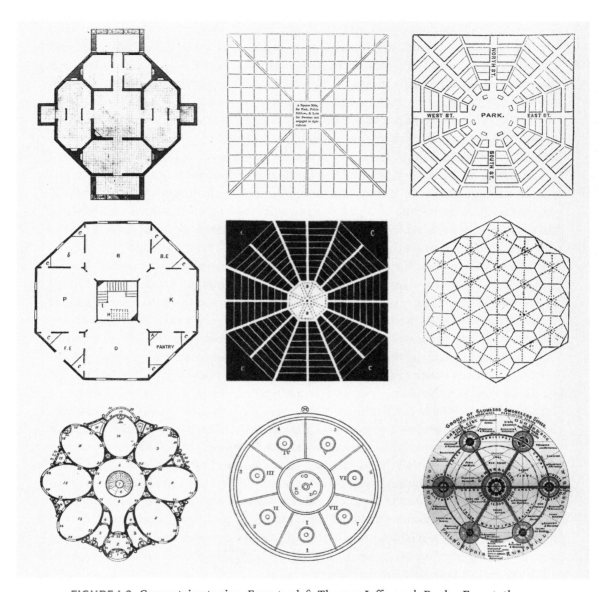

FIGURE I.2. Geometric utopias. *From top left:* Thomas Jefferson's Poplar Forest; the National Reform Association's republican township grid and village plans; Orson Fowler's octagon house; the Octagon Settlement Company's plan for a Kansas colony; Josiah Warren's hexagonal city; the spiritualists' home of harmony and institution of equitable commerce; and Ebenezer Howard's plan of a garden city.

early anarchist Josiah Warren—are familiar to political and cultural historians, but these same scholars have tended to gloss over the reformers' drawings and diagrams as peripheral diversions. On the other hand, architectural historians have frequently regarded such amateur designs as too crude to merit scrutiny. As one architectural critic dismissively wrote in a survey of utopian designs across three centuries, nineteenth-century utopian movements informed by utilitarianism and other reform ideologies failed to attract any "first-class architectural talent" and thus the designs these movements produced tend to be "unduly mechanical" and "naïve," "wear[ing] a look of either strenuous philanthropy or equally strenuous self-help."[7] For historians, the geometric utopias are too speculative and marginal; for architectural scholars, they are too unsophisticated to sustain serious interest.

A more significant factor in the scholarly neglect of geometric utopias has been the sharp historical, and historiographic, turn against nineteenth-century reform and utopianism in recent years. Within the field of U.S. history, the pendulum has swung over the past century from accounts that posited early nineteenth-century reformers (especially abolitionists and women's rights advocates) as naive but well-meaning forerunners of liberal progressivism to more recent interpretations that emphasize their self-righteousness, paternalism, social control, and class and racial domination.[8] Another critique of nineteenth-century utopianism has focused on its complicity with U.S. settler colonialism and the ideology of "manifest destiny." As was true of the Kansas vegetarian colony, new communities were often proposed for development on the putatively "vacant" lands of the West—that is, on lands only recently expropriated from and, in many instances, still occupied by Indigenous people. There is, of course, a long tradition of Europeans looking to the American continents as Edenic sites for regenerating society, while ignoring or erasing the region's Indigenous inhabitants. Thomas More's eponymous narrative of 1516 was itself partially inspired by recent European incursions into the so-called New World.[9] As several scholars have observed, utopianism and settler colonialism are structurally homogeneous. Both rely on the idea of seceding from one society and founding a new model to be replicated on terra nullius.[10] Utopianism and colonialism are also historically intertwined in the context of the United States. Beginning in the eighteenth century, proposals for producing a more egalitarian U.S. society frequently relied on granting cheap or free land (that is, Indigenous land) to white working-class men. White men's utopia thus depended directly on Indigenous dispossession.

These critiques of nineteenth-century reform and utopianism are paralleled in the post–World War II historiography of utopian architecture. Once lauded as visionary, the idea that redesigning the physical form of buildings or cities could lead to revolutionary changes in society has come to be seen in many quarters as, at best, overly optimistic or, at worst, authoritarian. Historians have critiqued the distinct forms of utopian plans from the nineteenth through the twentieth centuries—ranging from rectangular villages of harmony to cruciform towers—as extravagant, rigid, idealistic, and hubristic, and as ultimately contributing to the failure of those projects.[11] As Antoine Picon has pointed out, such postwar condemnations of utopianism in architecture often conflate nineteenth-century communal visions with twentieth-century architectural modernism.[12] As a result, the banner of anti-utopianism has become a veil for attacking modernism as such—the dream of building new, technologically advanced, rational dwellings, factories, and cities for the masses, whether the working classes of Europe and America or colonial subjects abroad—and consigning it to the dustbin of failures along with nineteenth-century utopian socialism

6   Introduction

and twentieth-century state socialism. These critiques demand that we be wary of schemes in which one group imposes its own doctrinaire vision of social order and beauty on others, or in which utopia for some is built on the expropriation of land, resources, and labor from others.

A corollary of the negative assessment of utopia is the conclusion that it is a mistake to imagine that social reform can be carried out through architecture—specifically through architectural form, defined here as the visible shape and organization of the parts of a building or city.[13] Just as Marx and Engels condemned the utopian socialists of their day for trying to invent solutions to social problems out of their own heads, recent critics of utopia assert that it is naive to imagine that complex social problems can be magically resolved through the design of a better city or dwelling.[14] Much of the post–World War II scholarship on architectural utopias is informed by a suspicion of rapprochements between architectural formalism and politics. Colin Rowe and Fred Koetter, for example, condemn utopianism of the grand, architectural, tabula rasa variety, advocating instead that architects work with and within existing urban conditions.[15] Even those sympathetic to utopianism or communitarianism have been critical of excessive formalism. Hayden concludes in her study of American utopias that processes of organizing and building should take precedence over form and "odd architecture."[16]

Yet those who aim to dispel the idea that architectural form can have sociopolitical efficacy frequently remain trapped within the logic of reformers' own justifications— that is, within what we might call a "functionalist-intentional fallacy." In justifying their plans, nineteenth-century utopians almost invariably relied on functionalist arguments, contending that particular ways of organizing space would have specific effects on individual bodies or the social collectivity. In rationalizing the shape of the vegetarian octagon colony, for example, Clubb cited the equal proximity of all residences to the central public octagon building. Thus, the layout of the city would literally enact egalitarian conditions while also ensuring that settlers would enjoy the benefits of sociality and proximity to neighbors, which would bolster their vegetarian commitments. Such instrumental explanations were shaped by a strong current of environmental determinism within nineteenth-century reform. This was the belief that architecture and landscape could not only represent their inhabitants (the traditional view of architectural expression) but also literally mold individuals' bodies and minds by controlling sight, sound, and movement.[17] With roots in Enlightenment sensationalist and utilitarian theory, faith in environmental determinism would lead many late eighteenth- and nineteenth-century reformers to lavish inordinate attention on the physical designs of all kinds of spaces, from asylums to houses to gardens, as part of their efforts to improve both individual bodies and society at large. The best-known manifestation of such views was the English reformer Jeremy Bentham's design in the 1790s for a panopticon prison (Figure I.3), which featured a central guard tower surrounded by a circular array of cells. The idea was that this arrangement would induce the specter of near-constant surveillance and thereby teach the prisoners to practice self-discipline, which would lead to the reform of their character.[18] Both

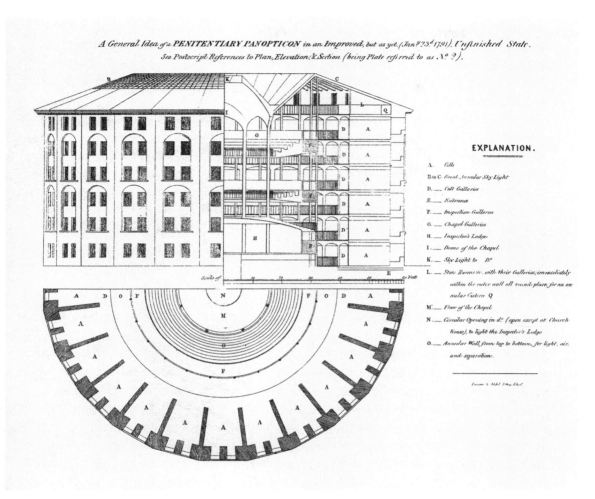

FIGURE I.3. Jeremy Bentham, composite plan, elevation, and section of a panopticon prison, drawn by Willey Reveley, 1791. From *The Works of Jeremy Bentham,* volume 4, 1968.

the geometric utopias that purported to offer greater freedom and the carceral spaces intended to do just the opposite relied on similar ideas about the power of architecture and urban design to produce direct effects on human subjects.[19]

When we accept utopians' functionalist claims at face value, it is easy, and entirely justifiable, to conclude that their plans did not succeed. Clubb's eight-sided city did not bring about the peaceful end of slavery, much less flesh-eating; octagon houses failed to produce stronger, healthier bodies. Yet focusing solely on *what* the plans purported to do, rather than on *how* reformers made their claims, puts too much weight on their intentions. Observers (then and now) have often reflexively assumed that the plans were simple transcriptions of their designers' ideas, intended—with more or less plausibility—to be realized if circumstances allowed. However, this leaves out questions about how these images circulated and what precise effects they were imagined to have on viewers. Lost, in other words, are the communicative, cognitive, and affective dimensions of the images within a printed public sphere.[20] In this book, I argue that utopian plans were not simply technical blueprints to be executed; they were also, and perhaps more importantly, rhetorical images transmitted within a public sphere (or a dissenting counterpublic sphere) of print.[21] Alongside sentimental novels, pamphlets, oral lectures, pictorial wood engravings, medallions, and stereoscopes, printed diagrams were one discursive medium that nineteenth-century utopians deployed to promote their viewpoints and to prod their fellow Americans to work toward alternative arrangements of society. Geometric utopians hoped that in addition to documenting designs and ideas, their diagrams, in concert with these other media, could represent critiques of the prevailing order, conjure communities of supporters, and thus advance the realization of a more just and harmonious world.[22]

Geometric Utopias in Print

To understand geometric utopias' broader discursive role, we need to view them from within the visual and political ecologies of the mid-nineteenth-century United States and, specifically, to consider their emergence within an expanded mass illustrated print culture. Pictures of geometric utopias were printed in pamphlets, passed out on street corners, and sold in phrenological museums. They contributed to a dense semiotic environment of printed texts that included street signs, newspapers, currency, and political broadsides.[23] In the first half of the nineteenth century, innovations such as mechanized papermaking, the steam-powered printing press, lowered postage rates for periodicals, and expanded transportation networks made printed materials more widely accessible than ever before.[24] The advent of stereotyping and lithography allowed for the inclusion of increasing numbers of pictures in this printed matter, and images flooded the market, adorning evangelical tracts, children's educational materials, sheet music, and more. In the words of Amy K. DeFalco Lippert, a veritable "pictorial revolution" was taking place. As she argues, pictures were not just ornamental additions to printed texts but crucial means through which nineteenth-century Americans could represent the rapidly changing world and themselves as modern subjects.[25]

Much of the recent research on nineteenth-century visual culture has focused on newly introduced media like photography, which exploded onto the world scene when Louis-Jacques-Mandé Daguerre published his invention of the photographic process in 1839. Photography was deemed revolutionary for its supposed ability to capture unvarnished reality and also its capacity for mechanical reproduction (albeit initially requiring remediation through wood engraving or lithography).[26] Other scholars of nineteenth-century visual culture have explored how phenomena such as panoramas, urban illumination, department stores, and world's fairs, as well as new techniques of observing and seeing, helped produce a culture of mass spectacle, centered in cities like New York and Paris but thoroughly global in purview.[27] Taken all together, this research affirms that the era's new abundance of images and scopic experiences was a defining element of modernity.

But the emphasis on photography and spectacle in visual-cultural studies has obscured humbler, less obviously innovative forms of imagery, such as the plan diagrams and other pictures explored in this book. Before the Civil War, working- and middle-class Americans were as likely to encounter woodcut or wood-engraved illustrations as they were to come across daguerreotypes or lithographs.[28] Thomas Leonard has observed that printed pictures, particularly on political themes, were relatively scarce before the Civil War. American newspaper editors tended to recycle engravings, often relying on specimen books rather than commissioning new illustrations: "Pictures waited for events to happen. The dangling man lived in the printer's case until summoned for execution stories."[29] Before 1860, most Americans' exposure to printed images would have been in the form of "low-fidelity" pictures in letter sheets, chapbooks, almanacs, illustrated Bibles, children's primers, antislavery or temperance tracts, and how-to manuals.[30] Many of these images were didactic or rhetorical in nature: their purpose was to enlighten and to persuade. As historians like David Paul Nord and David Morgan have demonstrated, evangelical groups were instrumental in creating the first American visual mass media, facilitating the transition from a culture premised on orality to a culture of print. Organizations like the American Tract Society printed and distributed vast numbers of illustrated pamphlets, almanacs, periodicals, and Bibles as part of their campaigns of mass conversion.[31] By the 1820s, the ATS had built centralized publishing operations that deployed the newest technologies to print more than five million tracts annually (at a time when the United States contained about three million households). The tract societies also developed extensive systems of colportage involving networks of volunteers and auxiliaries.[32] Pictures were an integral part of the organizations' printed materials. An 1824 report by the Boston branch of the ATS explained the rationale for including "cuts," or illustrations, in its publications: "for the sake of rendering them more attractive and acceptable in their external appearance, and of exciting interest in their concerns."[33] Evangelicals believed that images would draw readers' attention and help their books and pamphlets compete with the enticements of secular illustrated print materials.[34]

By the 1830s, reformers of other stripes were adopting the evangelicals' media-savvy techniques. Temperance and antislavery advocates printed tracts with vignettes showing the evil effects of drunkenness and the horrors of slavery.[35] The American Anti-Slavery Society's pamphlets and almanacs frequently included engravings of enslaved women being viciously flogged or of children being torn from their parents, all intended to arouse sympathy—to speak, via the eye, to the heart as much as to the mind (Figure I.4). As numerous scholars have observed, illustrated "scenes of subjection" often reinforced the abjection and eroticization of enslaved Black bodies for white audiences, rendering Black people as objects of sympathy rather than fully empowered subjects.[36] Antislavery images fed a culture of sentimentalism in which novelists and reformers aimed to link emotion to action. As Radiclani Clytus points

FIGURE I.4. Antislavery woodcut from *The American Anti-Slavery Almanac for 1840*. Courtesy Johns Hopkins University Sheridan Libraries / Archive.org.

out, for the task of speaking to the heart, images were seen as having a more direct power than words.[37] In an 1836 essay titled "Pictorials," published in an antislavery journal, a writer observed:

> Engravings are employed to enforce arguments, to illustrate facts, to give an energy to language, and life to the form of words, to bring before the "mind's eye" more vividly than the arbitrary signs of the Alphabet can, the reality of things of which we speak.—They are used to bring home to the bosom of the reader a full conception of the wrongs and sufferings of his fellow-men, that he may *look on* them as well as *read of* them, and that he may feel as though he were among them and of them, an eye-witness and partaker of their woes.[38]

Many utopians of the 1830s and 1840s also subscribed to the belief that engravings could convey ideas more clearly than "the arbitrary signs of the Alphabet," and included pictures in their treatises. Like the antislavery advocates, the utopians sought to conjure images in the "mind's eye," to help readers mentally manifest the intangible, whether it was a feeling of injustice over the present economic system or the promise of a society not yet in existence. Pictures of utopia operated in a decidedly different affective register than antislavery images, however. Rather than aiming for readers' hearts, the utopians' engravings were intended to produce rational anticipation of an improved society to come. The best-known communitarians of the day were the French and British visionaries Charles Fourier and Robert Owen, who attracted significant numbers of followers in the United States, including several who

FIGURE I.5. Robert Owen's New Harmony, Indiana, from the *Co-Operative Magazine and Monthly Herald,* January 1826. Courtesy Indiana State Library.

would go on to become geometric utopians. Both men formulated grand architectural visions for their cooperative communities, modeled in Owen's case on collegiate quadrangles and in Fourier's on the Palace of Versailles. Published representations of their architectural projects often featured painterly, bird's-eye, perspective views rich with detail, drawn by professional architects and engravers. A wood engraving of Robert Owen's New Harmony community from 1826 shows a quadrangle bounded by buildings with steep repetitive gables, set amid manicured farm fields in a pastoral river valley (Figure I.5). This was a projection only: New Harmony never remotely resembled this idealized vision, since Owen reused the buildings of an existing Rappite community. The images of Fourier's phalanstery and Owen's New Harmony adopted the conventions of picturesque and panoramic landscape representation, presenting comprehensive and detailed views. Beholders could literally see the new social world before their eyes, as these depictions left relatively little to the imagination.[39]

Compared to the sentimental pictorial vignettes of the evangelicals and the temperance and antislavery advocates, as well as the aspirational architectural renderings presented by Fourier and Owen, the midcentury American geometric utopians' plan diagrams were notably spare and abstract. Although they occasionally deployed perspectival renderings, the geometric utopians favored inexpensively printed, black-and-white, wood-engraved plan views that highlighted their schemes' distinct geometric shapes but little more. This raises the question of why geometric utopian reformers limited themselves to such reticent plans. Would more elaborate images not have enabled them to better attract the attention of potential followers? The most obvious explanations are cost and skill. Simple geometries were easier to draft and to reproduce. As I discuss in chapter 2, close inspection of published geometric utopias reveals that plans were sometimes not even engraved but instead laid out with standard pieces of printer's rule. That is, they were typeset, composed rather than drawn. Still, many of the geometric utopians were printers; they had access to and occasionally deployed other modes of representation, such as figurative emblems and cartoons. Frugality or lack of skill therefore cannot entirely explain their representational choices. We need to search further to illuminate why these reformers considered such starkly simple diagrams of geometric architecture to be an effective means of conveying their ideas. At the core of this study are two questions: Why did mid-nineteenth-century reformers turn to geometric plans as part of their campaigns for social transformation? And what visual associations, what rhetorical and cognitive effects, did they imagine these drawings would evoke?

Diagrams as Visual Rhetoric

As alluded to above, many reformers believed illustrations had a unique power to sway viewers by cutting through the printed word and speaking directly to hearts and minds; that is, images performed a unique persuasive, or rhetorical, role. Scholars have defined "visual rhetoric" as images that carry within them "some potential for activation—that is, an explicit or implicit intent to produce an alteration of viewpoint or action on the viewer."[40] Yet observing that pictures were rhetorical is not enough, for it is clear that the images the reformers deployed were different in format from the ones used by evangelicals or antislavery advocates. In contrast to images directed toward arousing readers' sense of "sympathy" and a culture of sentiment, the diagrams preferred by utopians aimed at stimulating more arid affects—such as a sense of order, rationality, and feasibility.

Diagrams share certain formal characteristics: they tend to be abstract, reductive representations composed primarily of lines and outlines, sometimes supplemented with notations keyed to explanatory captions. In the semiotician Charles Peirce's triadic categorization of signs, diagrams are *icons* (signs that visually resemble their referents) while also having some attributes of *indices* (signs that denote their objects by having a literal relation to them) and *symbols* (signs that have an arbitrary or customary relation to their referents).[41] Thus they have the picture-like quality of icons while also exhibiting a degree of abstraction—a severe reduction of detail—that can render them into symbols. They are often instrumental drawings, tools for mediating

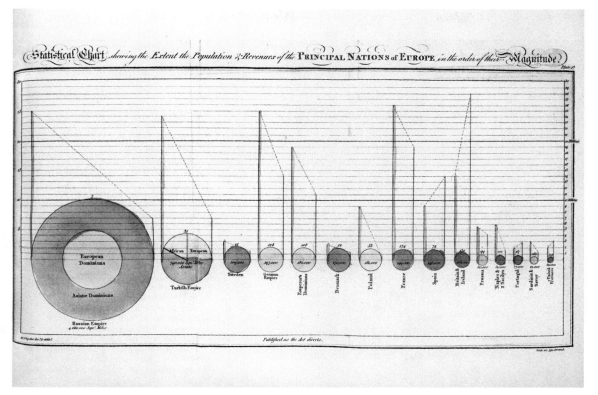

FIGURE I.6. Diagram of extent, population, and revenues of the principal nations of Europe. From William Playfair, *Statistical Breviary*, 1801.

thought or the translation from concept to physical realization. As John Bender and Michael Marrinan recount, diagrams gained popularity in the seventeenth century as media to represent a range of complex scientific processes and machines, reaching a high point of innovation in the illustrated plates of Denis Diderot and Jean le Rond d'Alembert's *Encyclopédie,* published in 1751–66, and in William Playfair's pictorial statistical atlases, with their innovative graphical techniques for representing information, beginning in the 1780s (Figure I.6).[42] These diagrams derived their power from the Enlightenment belief that vision was superior to verbal communication as a means of transmitting and acquiring knowledge—an idea that continued to hold sway in the nineteenth century.[43] While images in general were thought to be clearer than words, diagrams, in particular, were deemed an especially objective and efficient form of representation. In the nineteenth-century United States, diagrams proliferated in popular print, especially in geometry textbooks, surveying manuals, mechanical guides, and didactic texts—literature that the geometric utopians, many of them polymathic inventors and artisans, would have been steeped in. The popularity of diagrams reflected what the historian Neil Harris has called an "operational aesthetic" that fed nineteenth-century Americans' appetite to see and understand how systems work.[44] In the early nineteenth century, pedagogues like Heinrich Pestalozzi

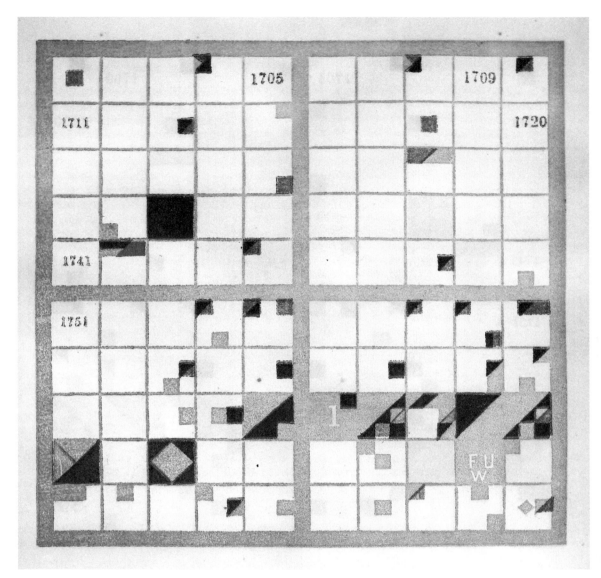

FIGURE I.7. Mnemonic grid for learning history. From Elizabeth Palmer Peabody, *Chronological History of the United States, Arranged with Plates on Bem's Principle*, 1856. Courtesy Library of Congress / Archive.org.

and Elizabeth Peabody pioneered the use of visual aids, and especially diagrams, in primary education (Figure I.7). As a lecturer at the American Institute of Instruction explained in 1833, visual illustrations offer a form of proof superior to that provided by verbal descriptions or memory, especially when the goal is to teach abstract concepts. Underscoring the connection between images and rhetoric, he explained that instruction through pictures "substitutes the assurance of demonstration for the blind assent of the will."[45]

Throughout this book, I contend that these qualities of diagrams—their association with clarity and proof ("the assurance of demonstration"), their simultaneous legibility and abstraction, and their instrumental nature—made them especially attractive to reformers as vehicles of visual rhetoric. This overarching thesis is supported by three subsidiary arguments. First, although diagrams appear objective and rational, their meanings and affects are historically specific, emerging from a rich world of visual-cultural references, and these meanings and affects changed over time. In order to operate effectively as rhetoric, diagrams had to be both familiar and different from existing pictures, taking advantage of preexisting associations while being unique enough to connote something new. In the late eighteenth century, geometric diagrams were associated with mathematical proofs and astronomical illustrations. Writers such as Alexander Hamilton were quick to use the association of mathematics with certainty and self-evidence to rhetorical effect. In *Federalist* No. 31, for example, he began his argument for the national government's power of taxation with a lengthy rumination on geometry. Just as in geometry there are "primary truths, or first principles" that, "antecedent to all reflection or combination, command the assent of the mind," so, too, he reasoned, in the spheres of ethics and politics there are propositions "so obvious in themselves, and so agreeable to the natural and unsophisticated dictates of common sense, that they challenge the assent of a sound and unbiased mind, with a degree of force and conviction almost equally irresistible."[46] But whereas Hamilton merely referenced geometry metaphorically, political rhetoric of the nineteenth century sometimes featured actual geometric diagrams. Over the course of the century, diagrams expanded beyond their origins in mathematics and were increasingly associated with technical and machine drawings, which purported to offer transparent, unbiased depictions of the objects being represented.[47] Diagrams thus began to have connotations of technical realizability, objectivity, and transparency. This association with transparency made the diagram a fitting vehicle for reformers of the period who critiqued the government and the emerging market economy as being excessively mediated and obscure, with power relegated to phantom representatives in distant legislatures and to economic "middlemen" and bankers. Many geometric utopians linked their calls for more direct forms of markets and government (or even the abolition of government) with a desire for transparent representation across a range of realms, including language and notation. The literary scholar Kevin Gilmartin has observed that English working-class radicals in this period favored simple, descriptive literary representations not out of an "obtuse empiricism" but out of a desire "to strip away accumulated layers of corruption and mediation."[48] Finally, many diagrams, including patent drawings and architectural and urban plans, were understood as instrumental images whose function was to translate designs into material reality. The American geometric utopians' diagrams thus connoted the feasibility of their plans. They also manifested a radical artisans' aesthetic that understood and represented the world as a complicated but comprehensible machine, capable of being limned in the lucid straight lines of a diagram. These shifting cultural valences of the geometric diagram—from an earlier association with mathematical proof to later connotations of semiotic transparency and mechanical constructability—contributed to its appeal as a medium of political persuasion. Diagrams could make the reformers' radical ideas appear clear, rational, objective, self-evident, and realizable.

Second, geometric utopias also functioned as eidetic representations, or "cognitive maps," of present and future social relations. They were not simply projections of a future state of society, as is often assumed; they were also "counterimages" of the present, offered as diagnoses of the existing system. As abstract images that leave out details in favor of a legible overall organization or pattern, diagrams were especially well suited to making visible structural social conditions and relations that might otherwise remain elusive or invisible. I borrow the term "cognitive map" from Fredric Jameson, who has argued that in the dense and extended network of relations of late capitalism it becomes increasingly difficult for individuals to imagine the totality of such relations and to find a point of orientation for political action.[49] This problem of visibility was also felt earlier, during the period of industrial capitalism's emergence, and geometric utopians were among a number of nineteenth-century Americans who sought to make visible, and therefore comprehensible, the new system of political economy *as* a system.[50] Some critics of capitalism turned to cartoon diagrams, as in T. Wharton Collens's "Monogram of Political Economy," published in 1876, depicting capitalism as a system of pipes and cisterns channeling a flow of liquid (Figure I.8). The image shows a looped circuit, with the majority of capital's benefits being siphoned off for profit, rent, usury, and taxes, with only a small amount going to the subsistence of the laborer. While geometric utopians also occasionally made use of such figurative diagrams, I would argue that at least some of their architectural and urban plans also functioned as a mode of cognitive mapping. For instance, in the 1840s, a group of labor radicals co-opted the Jeffersonian land ordinance grid, which was commonly understood as an instrumental diagram for converting public land into private property, and made it into a visual symbol of a more egalitarian distribution of land and wealth (while still conveniently obscuring that the land had been taken from Indians). They turned the symmetrical grid into an icon of equality premised on individualism and division, a contrast to the existing vastly unequal distribution of land, which a previous workingman radical had represented in an asymmetrically divided square diagram. Thus, the visual representation of the grid could function simultaneously as a diagnosis of present conditions and an image of the future. These attempts to theorize and represent society as a system justify the inclusion of the geometric utopians among the ranks of the earliest sociologists—those who sought to understand the fundamental principles structuring society and to prescribe improved systems.[51]

Finally, I contend that utopian diagrams produced unintended and ambivalent effects. Geometric utopians may have sought, by borrowing the visual language of Enlightenment rationality and technical transparency, to make their fantastical social ideas seem plausible and practicable and to evoke a world rendered systematic and orderly. But it is the nature of images to generate effects and readings that exceed their creators' intentions. This is perhaps especially true of the diagram, with its re-

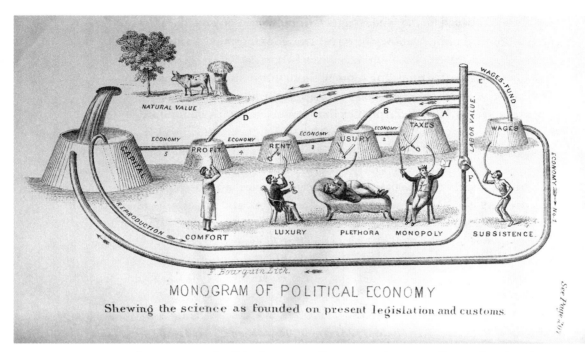

FIGURE I.8. "Monogram of Political Economy." From T. Wharton Collens, *The Eden of Labor,* 1876. Courtesy American Antiquarian Society.

ductive abstract language of lines. Bender and Marrinan suggest that the defining characteristic of the diagram is that it is a "working object," a medium that gives rise to new understandings, new perceptions of "correlations neither rooted in direct experience nor verifiable by the sense." Unlike a closed, replete representation such as a realistic still life, the diagram encourages multiple perspectives and invites viewers to use their own active powers of observation and connection. "Diagrams de-naturalize things in order to open up spaces for creative misuse."[52] The diagram can thus be related to Marshall McLuhan's distinction between "cool" and "hot" media. Hot media like photography and film, McLuhan claims, are high-definition, "well filled with data," and therefore require less participation from the audience, whereas cool media like cartoons and television provide comparatively little sensory information and therefore require completion by the audience.[53] In McLuhan's terms, a diagram is a form of cool media. This open-endedness of the diagram is also evoked by Gilles Deleuze's definition of the abstract social diagram as something "highly unstable or fluid," containing within itself "certain relatively free or unbound points, points of creativity, change and resistance."[54] Deleuze is speaking of conceptual rather than literal social cartographies, but the metaphor nevertheless is apt, indicating the inherent semiotic openness of drawn diagrams and their capacity to reveal emergent social formations.

For some viewers, the diagrammatic pictures of nineteenth-century geometric utopias may appear as caricatures of rationality, as depictions of reason pushed to mythic and absurd forms. The vegetarian octagon colony is a case in point: the excessive formalism of its graphically arresting cobweb image could easily seem to be far removed from the fractious and violent social conflicts that the colony's creator hoped to address. At nearly the same moment and within miles of where Clubb was establishing his vegetarian abolitionist paradise, pro- and antislavery groups were engaging in a series of bloody skirmishes that would eventually contribute to the outbreak of war. Meanwhile, both sides were embroiled in perpetual conflicts with the Osage, Cherokee, and other Indigenous occupants of federally designated reservations that white settlers—Clubb's colonists included—were in the process of preemptively and illegally occupying. The octagons, hexagons, circles, and grids that geometric utopians drew so neatly could appear complete, closed, and ill equipped to deal with the conflicts and contradictions of nineteenth-century U.S. society. In the chapters that follow, I consider both the occlusions and the violence that geometric utopias perpetrated, as well as another possibility: while the abstraction of the geometric utopias might appear static and blindered, their very spareness also arguably made them more malleable and open to interpretation.[55] As one 1833 writer observed, in "outline figures, or mere diagrams, . . . the imagination of the beholder is required to supply all except the general feature of the object delineated."[56] The land reformers behind the National Reform Association explicitly hoped that their grid diagrams would enable readers to "*carry out in their own minds* the consequences that would result from [these] schemes."[57] At least some utopians saw their plans as intentionally minimalist scaffolds that could accommodate future experimentation and change while leaving room for readers' own imaginations.

These three hypotheses about the aesthetic-political effects of nineteenth-century geometric utopians' plans suggest that to understand these images we must go well beyond a functionalist view of architecture's capacity to reform bodies and society. Whether performing as visual rhetoric to help win audiences over to new and sometimes radical ideas, offering cognitive maps of social conditions, or producing other contradictory and unanticipated readings in spectators, these plans manifested the ramified ways that visual representations could articulate sociopolitical ideas and contribute to movements for change.

Reformers, Radicals, Utopians

The geometric utopians were part of a coherent if unnamed movement. Their architectural and urban imaginings were informed by shared ideas about the power of diagrams as tools of political persuasion and ideation. All were active members of a reform milieu—what was then called a "sisterhood of reforms"—linked through media networks centered in the northeastern United States. Many of the similarities in the shapes of their utopias can be attributed to specific cross-influences and borrowings. Like others in their orbit, these men agreed on many of the most divisive issues of their day: they were uniformly opposed to slavery (while, like many abolitionists, harboring racial prejudices), advocated women's rights, and believed that broad social improvement must entail changes to basic practices and systems such as spelling, pedagogy, and diet. While several of the reformers opposed the type of U.S. imperialism represented by the Mexican–American War, all of them essentially operated within a settler colonial worldview that presumed the ready availability of land on which to build their new, improved dwellings and cities. Their vision of a more just society therefore depended on past and ongoing cessions of Indian land to white possession while disavowing that foundational violence.[58]

Nevertheless, the geometric utopians diverged significantly in their visions of an improved U.S. society, and these differences turned on their attitudes toward the emerging market economy and, especially, the ethos of competitive individualism that the market was helping to foster. Over the first half of the nineteenth century, American society transformed from an economy rooted in family farming and small-scale workshops to a modern market economy increasingly based on mechanized manufacturing and globe-spanning geographies of resource extraction, production, trade, and consumption, exemplified in the global cotton economy.[59] The new market economy ushered in ever more brutal modes of enslavement and forced labor in the South and the growth of wage labor in the North, as well as new institutions of finance and credit. These changes rendered older paths to autonomy and assumptions about value unstable. Throughout the nineteenth century, a series of economic "panics," or downturns, each bringing on "hard times" marked by high unemployment and bankruptcies, reinforced for many white Americans that their fates were not entirely in their own hands—they were subject to larger forces beyond their control (a fact that Indigenous people and enslaved African Americans knew all too well). As the market economy grew, some Americans responded by turning to a new liberal ideology emphasizing individual rights and competitive self-interest, which displaced an older republican ethos, with its view of independent, virtuous citizens working to cultivate the common good.[60] The cultural-philosophical corollary to liberalism was the "individualism" and "self-reliance" preached by Emerson. Other Americans became critics of the market system, pointing out that it gave unfair advantages to an idle "aristocracy" possessed of wealth and power while doing little for those who labored with their hands. Theories explaining political economy and society began to proliferate alongside proposed remedies. A variety of socialisms, in particular, arose to critique a capitalist market that exalted selfish interest and competition, and to advocate systemic remedies based in cooperation, association, and the "union of interests." Orestes Brownson, a leading reformer in the 1840s, argued that the evil of inequality was "not merely individual in its character. . . . [It] is inherent in all our social arrangements, and cannot be cured without a radical change of those arrangements."[61] Yet in the early nineteenth century, few countenanced the kind of state socialism that would be advocated at the end of the century. The prevailing consensus among Americans was that government should be small. "The best government is that which governs least," John O'Sullivan penned in 1837, words that would be echoed by Henry David Thoreau more than a decade later (and that resonate for some still today).[62] At a time when many believed the primary function of government was negative—to prevent any one group "from infringing on the rights of other men"—many reformers advocated measures such as the decentralization of government and banking and broader distribution of public land (never mind that the latter was an example of massive state intervention dependent on genocidal state violence).[63] Above all, radical critics of the existing order turned to "association," the formation of small experimental communities, as the best avenue for crafting a more cooperative, more socially minded, and less individualist society. In these small communities, people would receive benefits corresponding with their labor and could experiment with new forms of economic exchange based on mutual benefit rather than competition.[64]

Each of the geometric utopians discussed in this book can be interpreted as staking a definable position on this central problem of how to reconcile individual freedom with concerns for equality and the collective good in a capitalist society. Whether or not they used the labels "liberal," "republican," or "socialist," all of these thinkers adopted positions that could be allied with one or more of these now-identifiable ideologies. Some, like the phrenologist Orson Fowler, fully embraced the new ethos of self-interest and individual advancement. Fowler's octagon can be read as a symptomatic middle-class response to the new age: he marketed it as an invention intended to help working-class and middling white men compete in the "age of go-ahead."[65] Other geometric utopians, such as the ex-Owenite Josiah Warren, were intensely critical of the new society's betrayal of republican equality and sought to create more just economic systems, though still on individualistic principles. While many of these positions anticipated and aligned with political ideologies identifiable today, it is worth remembering David Brion Davis's admonition that terms such as "conservative," "liberal," and "radical" are inadequate to classify nineteenth-century reformers.[66] Similarly, the historical sociologist Craig Calhoun has cautioned against retrospectively applying a contemporary right–left continuum onto nineteenth-century political movements, since radicalism during the period was often informed by the defense of tradition and religion.[67]

Relatedly, I use the terms "reformer," "radical," and "utopian" somewhat interchangeably in this book, but it is important to draw some distinctions.[68] Of the three words, "reformer" was the one most frequently employed by mid-nineteenth-century Americans themselves to describe advocates of myriad campaigns for social improvement, including antislavery campaigns for social improvement such as the ten-hour workday, temperance, particular dietary regimens, water cures, world peace, new orthographies, spiritualism, free homesteads, free love, and women's rights. The term "radical" was often used as a modifier of "reformer," indicating a more extreme or revolutionary position, one that addressed the roots or origins of a problem. Unlike in England, where "Radicals" referred to members of a specific political party, only a few American reformers embraced the denomination. The words "ultraist" and "ultraism" were also applied, mostly pejoratively, to reformers seen as pushing principles to an unreasonable extreme. More recently, some historians of nineteenth-century reform have drawn a distinction between "radicals," who advocated far-reaching structural transformations of society, and moral reformers, who sought to improve individuals or ameliorate existing social, economic, and political arrangements.[69] While important, such delineations are extremely blurry when applied to this period, since even those who pushed for seemingly minor reforms (for example, the adoption of shorthand) often projected that the changes they proposed would have earthshaking consequences. And causes that are today widely seen as conservative and moralistic (such as temperance) also attracted self-defined radicals; for example, William Lloyd Garrison, the fiery abolitionist who condemned the U.S. Constitution as a pro-slavery pact, was also an advocate of temperance (and, early on, colonization). Finally, the label "utopian" was rarely used by nineteenth-century reformers themselves (one notable exception being Warren, who embraced the term enough to found a community in Ohio called Utopia). This is not surprising: "utopian" was often wielded as an epithet hinting at an unrealizable fantasy or distraction from more effective courses of political action. My reasons for resurrecting the label "utopian" are several. First, I want to retain a sense of the comprehensiveness of nineteenth-century reformers—their interest in the wholesale transformation of society's arrangements, which stemmed from their sense that society and its structures were still in formation and thus malleable. Second, I use the term to connect my work with a rich tradition of interdisciplinary utopian studies, historiography, and theorization, both broadly speaking and specifically in relation to nineteenth-century radical reform. This body of work encompasses the writing of architectural historians like Dolores Hayden and Anthony Vidler, historians of American communitarianism such as Arthur Bestor and Carl Guarneri, and theorists ranging from Karl Marx to Ernst Bloch to José Esteban Muñoz. Finally, I want to challenge traditional dismissals of utopianism as antipolitical by suggesting that we need to reconsider the political value of utopian imaginings. This book contests the notion that radical imagination and practical politics were antithetical. In this way, it offers a perhaps oblique contribution to recent historical research that attempts to recuperate or reconstruct a critical form of architectural utopianism.[70]

The five sets of projects at the core of this book are "minor" by most historical measures, humble descendants of better-known utopian plans like Owen's New Harmony and Fourier's phalanstery. The geometric utopians were neither leading statesmen nor architects, neither anonymous vernacular builders nor visionary artists, neither "typical" representatives of their time nor enlightened geniuses. Like most nineteenth-century reformers, the geometric utopians tended to be middle-class or lower-middle-class rather than working-class. Some could be counted among the new breed of individuals—often former ministers—who made their livings through a combination of lecturing and writing on reform subjects. Others identified as the kinds of mechanics and skilled craftsmen who constituted an "artisan" class in the early republic and were part of an emerging urban "middle class" by the mid-nineteenth century.[71] All of the main protagonists in this book are white and male. Women were members of utopian communities and in some cases planned new settlements (Fanny Wright's Nashoba colony is a principal example).[72] And numerous African Americans participated in quasi-utopian internal and external colonization schemes, as well as attempts to form self-sufficient communities of freed-people from the 1820s onward, sometimes carried out under the patronage of white benefactors.[73] (One of the most unusual was Davis Bend, Mississippi, a plantation owned by Joseph Davis, brother of Jefferson Davis, who came under the sway of Robert Owen in the 1820s and transformed his plantation along Owenite principles. By the 1870s, Davis Bend became a Black-owned community that was the third-largest cotton producer in the state.)[74] However, none of these utopian schemes, to my knowledge, adopted geometric plans, a fact that strongly suggests the circumscription of geometric utopianism's appeal to white middle- and lower-middle-class men residing in the strongholds of reform in the Northeast. These men were the main constituencies of the intersecting cultures of artisan republicanism, village Enlightenment, mechanical and technical learning, millennialist extremism, printing, and socialism that commingled to produce the particular aesthetic-political formation that was geometric utopianism. While utopianism (expansively defined in the Blochian sense as a wish for a better, different world) may be a near-universal impulse, the utopian longings of different people took divergent forms.[75] Before the Civil War, enslaved Black people were more likely to dream of escape, insurrection, *marronage,* and emancipation, or of engaging in quotidian activities like stealing away—what Saidiya Hartman describes as the "pedestrian practices [that] illuminate inchoate and utopian expressions of freedom"—than of newfangled house designs or systems of land division.[76] During Reconstruction, emancipated African Americans advocated for their due portions of land, only to be foiled when federal policy shifted to restore plantations to their original owners.[77] Indigenous people, dispossessed of ancestral lands and repeatedly forced by the U.S. government to move beyond the frontier of white settlement, did not enjoy the assurance of stable territorial sovereignty that would make it worthwhile for them to envision new forms of architecture. Moreover, many Native people eschewed the goals of land subdivision and individual ownership that were the raison d'être for many urban schemes of the period. Geometric utopianism thus appealed primarily to only a subset of nineteenth-century Americans: those armed with the tool of the printing press, interested in scripting the terms of individual ownership and communal relations through spatial diagrams, and able to indulge in what Susan Buck-Morss has called the "narcissistic illusion . . . that one can (re)create the world according to plan."[78] It is important to highlight the specificities of culture, power, and privilege that led some individuals to engage in such formalized and stationary modes of utopian speculation.

Geometric Utopias: Residual and Emergent

There is a temptation to fit the story of geometric utopias into the standard narrative of early nineteenth-century communitarianism, to conclude that it surged in the 1830s and 1840s during a period of economic upheaval and millennial perfectionism, declined in the 1850s as the debate over slavery's expansion consumed the national consciousness, and was extinguished by the Civil War.[79] Yet this "rise and fall" (or per-

Introduction   23

haps "flash in the pan") narrative fails to capture the nuances of geometric utopianism as a cultural formation, including the ways it drew on eighteenth-century cultural symbols and structures of feeling, crystallized as a phenomenon, and then continued to reverberate into the twentieth century. A more useful framework is Raymond Williams's notion of residual, dominant, and emergent elements of culture. Williams defines the residual as comprising cultural elements "formed in the past, but . . . still active in the cultural process, not only and often not at all as an element of the past, but as an effective element of the present." The residual, he notes, "may have an alternative or even oppositional relation to the dominant culture."[80] A prime example is the idea of rural community: this was a residual element of an earlier historical period, yet by the nineteenth century it could act as an alternative or oppositional idea to urban industrial capitalism. In contrast, "emergent" cultural forms encompass new meanings, values, and practices created in opposition to the prevailing culture yet prone to being incorporated into the dominant culture.[81] Williams offers the example of the English radical popular press, which was later incorporated into the mainstream press.

Williams's categories of residual, dominant, and emergent are useful for understanding the historical evolution of geometric utopianism. The structures of feeling that led to the appearance of geometric utopianism were in many ways residues of the eighteenth-century world—a fusion of Enlightenment rationality, belief in a Newtonian cosmic order, neoclassical aesthetics, and republican agrarian ideology—adapted in the nineteenth century to make sense of the new market economy. The workingmen who composed the first American geometric utopias looked explicitly to the ideas of Thomas Jefferson to develop their worldviews, their critique of the capitalist market, and their visual vocabulary. I therefore begin this book with a chapter exploring Jefferson's vision of an extended agrarian republic and the land ordinance grid that he helped craft in 1785. In many ways Jefferson set the precedent for deploying geometry to enact a disposition of land linked to a political vision of settler colonial democracy. He prefigured later geometric utopians in another more surprising way, however, for he was also an originator of the idea of the octagonal house, a freestanding, self-contained, and autonomous dwelling fit for an ideal, white liberal subject. In chapter 1, I read Jefferson's grid and octagon, field and figure, as two halves of a latent spatiopolitical program, premised on the conjoining of egalitarianism and liberal individualism, that would set the terms for later geometric utopias.

By the early decades of the nineteenth century, the land ordinance grid would come to be seen mainly as a utilitarian instrument for the commodification and sale of land. But in 1844, a group of New York workingmen led by George Henry Evans appropriated the grid, by now a dominant and residual form, as an emblem of their movement calling for the federal government to provide free homesteads for workers, or "land for the landless." Chapter 2 explores how Evans's group, the National Reform Association, deployed the images of a square, gridded township and an octagonal republican village to help galvanize workers around the vision of a more egalitarian society that could redeem the promises of the founding era. One appeal of the grid as a rhetorical emblem was its association with mathematical proofs and scientific principles.

If the land reformers' geometric utopia grew out of an eighteenth-century artisan and republican view of the world, then Orson Fowler, best known as one of nineteenth-century America's leading popular phrenologists, adapted the land reformers' ideas to the dominant ideology of nineteenth-century liberalism. Building on the National Reformers' call for "land for the landless," Fowler proposed a way to provide "homes for the homeless." In his book *A Home for All,* he presented an octagonal house as an efficient, improved dwelling type that could enable all Americans to attain economic independence and physical and emotional health. The eight-sided house would be a tool for creating an autonomous liberal subject capable of navigating the competitive urban market economy. In chapter 3, I explore Fowler's development of a functionalist logic that imagined the house as capable of literally shaping the minds and bodies of its inhabitants. Drawing on the aesthetics of technical manuals and popular entertainment, Fowler's functional house aesthetic was a pointed rejoinder to the sentimental ideas about architectural character and expression being promoted by contemporary pattern book writers like Andrew Jackson Downing.

Fowler's book was concerned primarily with how *individuals* could use the octagon mode of building to get ahead. In 1856, one of the phrenologist's associates, a vegetarian English immigrant named Henry Clubb, combined the octagon idea with the land reformers' earlier urban and territorial schemes to create a utopia with an ostensibly more radical and socially oriented ambition: a vegetarian, antislavery octagonal city. The story of this ill-fated enterprise is the subject of chapter 4, and it provides an occasion to think about how geometric utopians' diagrammatic images communicated in comparison to the sensational visual practices of other radical and reform movements of the day, especially the antislavery movement.

The tensions between individual and community also preoccupied the subject of chapter 5: Josiah Warren, often described as the first American anarchist, included a plan for a hexagonal city in his book *Practical Applications of the Elementary Principles of "True Civilization."* Published in 1873, at the end of his life, the book is somewhat anachronistic since it is mostly a summation of his pre–Civil War reform work and ideas. Hence it presents a wrinkle in the chronological order of this book, but placing Warren here allows me to demonstrate the indebtedness of his hexagonal plan to the earlier geometric utopias while also laying out aspects of his broader thought that influenced another scheme from the 1850s, elucidated in chapter 6. Warren was a former Owenite who turned against socialism and toward a starkly individualistic model of society that would foster a more "equitable commerce"—a market economy without exploitation. I relate Warren's hexagonal plan to his theories of language and representation, as manifested in his interest in the reform of spelling and musical notation, as well as his work as an inventor and printer. Warren believed that diagrammatic images could cut through the obfuscation of words and politics and help to create the kind of unmediated, direct democracy and economy that he and other, later anarchists advocated as a remedy for social inequality and conflict.

Warren's ideas about fostering a more "equitable commerce" found adherents in an unexpected place in the 1850s, among a group of spiritualists based in Boston and western New York State, who gave his ideas a metaphysical twist. Under the guidance of voices from the spirit world, a circle around the Boston-based medium John Murray Spear produced diagrams of several buildings, including a "heavenized" marketplace and several "harmonial homes." Spear and his followers believed a circular architecture featuring whispering galleries, pneumatic tubes, and a rarefied atmosphere could help transform commercial exchange into an exalted, spiritual experience and ultimately usher in a more harmonious world. In chapter 6, I argue that while the spiritualists' utopia might seem to represent a fanciful, apolitical, inward withdrawal from social conflicts, this turn to the spirit world, a harmonious realm said to exist parallel to the earthly one, can also be interpreted as a desire for a more immanent, even magical, social transformation than the one seemingly possible through more normative political avenues.

While a "rise and fall" narrative of geometric utopias could easily conclude that they mostly disappeared after the Civil War, a casualty of the corporate, technocratic, industrial capitalist society that was ascendent by the end of the century, afterimages of geometric utopianism continued to appear at the turn of the twentieth century. In the Epilogue, I take up the case of the English reformer Ebenezer Howard's garden city, first published in 1898, as just such an apparition. One of the most influential urban planning ideas of the twentieth century, the garden city is today remembered as the model that launched a thousand suburbs, an emergent idea that became a dominant cultural formation. Often forgotten are its origins in Howard's involvement with various radical movements, including socialism, land nationalization, shorthand, and spiritualism—in other words, the residual spawning grounds of nineteenth-century geometric utopianism. The story of the garden city, and especially Howard's extraordinary diagrams, offers a final opportunity to consider the possibilities and the limits of geometric diagrams as media for galvanizing social change.

The Political Aesthetics of Geometric Utopias

What appears at first glance to be most utopian about these nineteenth-century geometric utopias is their seemingly misplaced faith in form. In focusing on the shapes (or, more precisely, images of the shapes) in these plans, this book contends that there is more to these pictures of utopia—with their strange combination of extravagance and reduction, fantasy and abstraction—than naive workingmen's functionalism. Indeed, the geometric utopias evince the ways that functionalism, rationality, simplicity, clarity, and symmetry were *aesthetic* qualities, deployed (sometimes in exaggerated form) to advance not entirely self-evident conclusions: that property should be equally divided or that a house could help maximize one's health and wealth. I use the term "aesthetic" in the broad sense outlined by Williams in his *Keywords*; that is, to indicate emphasis on visual appearance and effect, as well as that which seems to exceed the practical or utilitarian.[82] But I also mean "aesthetic" in its narrower sense of being concerned with the "fine" or "beautiful." In classical aesthetics, symmetry and roundness were associated with beauty because these attributes supposedly evoked the perfection of the universe and God's creation. So, too, in mid-nineteenth-century America, a perfectly equal grid or a symmetrical house composed of oval forms could connote a harmonious and equitable social world, a cosmos in universal concordance. But I also employ the term "aesthetic" to hint at a latent avant-gardism in the work of the geometric utopians, which we can see in their use of starkly reduced forms to arrest attention, to "shock." Like later modernists, the nineteenth-century utopians deployed radically Platonic and spare geometric plans to communicate that the world they envisioned would be new, a departure from the status quo. The geometric utopians also borrowed and modified ready-made visual languages from the worlds of art, architecture, urban design, mathematics, science, technology, and popular culture to give form to their critiques of society and to persuade audiences of proposed alternative configurations of their worlds, all while generating unexpected and sometimes ambivalent readings.

Thinking about the aesthetic dimensions of nineteenth-century utopian plans compels us to reconceive how architecture can be political (that is, not only through function but also as symbolic images), as well as how all politics may have an aesthetic dimension. Politics entails struggles between different ideologies or systems of belief over the distribution of power and resources in a society. Within a democracy, such struggles are not just waged through words and verbal arguments but are also shaped by styles, symbols, visual forms, and utopian imaginings. Within U.S. history, scholars looking to signs, symbols, festivals, and rhetoric have spurred a cultural turn in political history.[83] Discussions of the aesthetic aspect of politics inevitably raise the specter of what Walter Benjamin calls the "aestheticization of politics," exemplified in its most troubling form in fascism, with its orchestrated mass rallies and glorification of power and violence. Critiques of the aestheticization of politics have sometimes been applied to utopianism. On the one hand, historians have seen utopianism, the positing of perfect societies, as an evasion of politics. On the other hand, critics have accused utopians of confusing political states and communities with works of art, of trying to reshape society according to aesthetic ideals such as perfection, closure, clarity, and organicism at the expense of sociopolitical ends such as justice, redistribution, equality, liberty, and recognition of difference.[84]

Claiming an aesthetic dimension to politics, however, is very different from conflating art and politics, form and content, or reducing one to the other. This book does not argue that images of utopian architecture could ever subsume or replace political struggle and negotiation. Instead, it explores the possibility that utopian images can be a part of political praxis and debate. Politics consists not simply of rational, verbal argument in an idealized public sphere (in the classic Habermasian formulation), or of decisions negotiated in presidential offices and parliamentary chambers, but also of popular, mass-mediated images, symbols, and rituals that operate on rational *and* affective levels. Such aesthetic practices have been essential to modern social movements. They contribute to a social imaginary: the ideas, significations, figures, and symbols that individuals and groups employ to make sense of the world, to make arguments about it, and to motivate themselves and others to act on those beliefs.[85] On these terms, geometric utopias enabled at least some Americans in the nineteenth century to interrogate their world critically and visualize its hidden structure so that they could begin to remake it. While the buildings and cities discussed in the following pages were circumscribed by predispositions of race, culture, and empire, perhaps it is still possible to glean something from these experiments, both from their ambitions and their errors.

CHAPTER 1

Antinomies of American Utopia
Thomas Jefferson's Grids and Octagons

In 1844, when leaders of New York's early labor movement printed the plan of a square, gridded "Rural Republican Township" in their newspaper the *Working Man's Advocate,* illustrating a proposal to give every citizen a free share of the public lands, they credited the idea to the long-buried Thomas Jefferson. For good measure, the workingmen included on the same page an engraving of the third president surmounted by a halo of stars, along with the text of the Declaration of Independence (Figure 1.1). It is thus no exaggeration to say that at least some nineteenth-century reformers regarded Jefferson as a kind of patron saint in whose footsteps they were following. To modern eyes, this juxtaposition of the images of Jefferson and the township grid—the latter based on the survey system that he helped to formulate for the Land Ordinance of 1785—may seem unsurprising. But for workingmen in the post-Jacksonian era, resurrecting the words of the Declaration of Independence and yoking them to an image of the grid was a pointed tactic of recuperation and appropriation. In transforming the meaning of the gridded township from its prevailing sense as a pragmatic instrument of land division and sale to a symbol of egalitarianism, the land reformers were positing an association between geometric form and political ideal that was incipient but not explicitly articulated in Jefferson's own writings.

What the workingmen may not have known was that Jefferson's embryonic democratic spatial imagination encompassed not one but two shapes: not just the territorial grid but also, at a smaller architectural scale, the octagon, a figure that proliferated in his sketches for various kinds of buildings, especially private houses. These two geometries—grid and octagon, field and figure—were two halves of a latent, multivalent spatiopolitical program. Both were intimately related to Jefferson's broader vision of an expansionist empire composed of individual, independent freehold farmers. Though he himself never explicitly merged the two shapes, it is not difficult to imagine the result if he had: a sprawling American territory divided into identical square

FIGURE 1.1. Front page of the *Working Man's Advocate*, May 18, 1844. Courtesy American Antiquarian Society.

homesteads, each containing a freestanding, eight-sided farmhouse sheltering a self-sufficient white household. Thus joined together, octagon and grid could serve as a fitting visual allegory for the resolution of one of the fundamental ideological conflicts of the early republic, a problem that continues to confound American society to this day: how to meld individual freedom with the collective good. Central to the solution that Jefferson came up with was land—specifically the reorganization and conversion of western territory (that is, Indian land) into the privatized domains of white settlers.

Embedded in Jefferson's spatial politics was a nascent belief that spatial geometry could not just symbolize but actually help to bring about the ideal political society. On the one hand, the territorial grid would be a literal instrument to effect the transfer and distribution of land, wealth, and power, and to realize a more direct and egalitarian democracy. On the other hand, in his octagonal architectural designs, Jefferson wrestled with shifting theories about how architecture, especially that of the house, could both represent and help produce a liberal subject through the choreography of sound, movement, and especially vision.

Jefferson's geometric utopianism was embryonic in multiple senses, however. First, unlike those of later projectors, his theory of how geometry would shape an ideal polity was not fully articulated. His view of spatial geometry straddled eighteenth-century aesthetic modalities—namely, humanist classicism and an emergent sensationalism—and the functionalist logics of the nineteenth century. In Jefferson's work, the former predominated in his approach to architecture, while the latter were applied to the seemingly pragmatic project of territorial organization. Second, Jefferson's geometric figures never entered the public imagination as symbols concretely associated with political ideas. In his lifetime, images of the land ordinance grid appeared in maps, surveying manuals, and land offices, but they remained largely ensconced in their immediate, technical uses rather than circulating as visual icons tethered to political rhetoric. And representations of his octagonal houses were not widely known at all, apart from a few picturesque renderings of Monticello. Eight-sided architecture was something experienced in private among a circle of Virginia gentry (and their enslaved cohabitants), rather than in the public sphere through printed images, as it would be in the nineteenth century. Thus, while seeds of geometric utopian ideas can be traced to Jefferson's work, they did not germinate until the workingmen's recuperation of his grid in the mid-nineteenth century.

Finally, it might be said that Jefferson's utopianism was stillborn, because despite his rhetorical references to the equality of "all men," what he ultimately envisioned was a republic of white yeomen in which the "independence" of a few relied on the labor of enslaved people and on the violent expropriation of land from Indigenous people. The redistribution of land as property was central to an egalitarian democracy. Jefferson's vision thus rested fundamentally on the conversion of Indian lands into white farms, "conquest into cultivation: empire into equality," as Walter Johnson has put it.[1] Grid and octagon together constituted not only an incipient geometric utopia but also a technology of abstraction that advanced the processes of settler colonialism and the commodification of land. The clarity of the diagram thus belied the intrinsic and intractable contradictions within what Jefferson paradoxically called an "empire for liberty."[2]

"Dividing and Subdividing": Jefferson's Grids

The basic history of the rectangular survey system is familiar. In 1784, the Continental Congress, confronted with a crushing war debt and pressure from squatters and speculators eager to settle the Northwest Territory, tasked Jefferson with leading committees to devise methods for establishing new states and for enabling the expedient sale of public lands.[3] The answers Jefferson proposed to both problems involved a series of precisely nested grids. The Northwest would be "scientifically" divided into states along lines of longitude and latitude, subdivided into townships, and divided again into square 640-acre sections prior to sale. These general principles were codified in the Land Ordinances of 1784 and 1785 (though slightly modified from Jefferson's original conception), resulting in a rectangular land survey system that would profoundly shape the landscape of the American West (Figure 1.2). Although the system

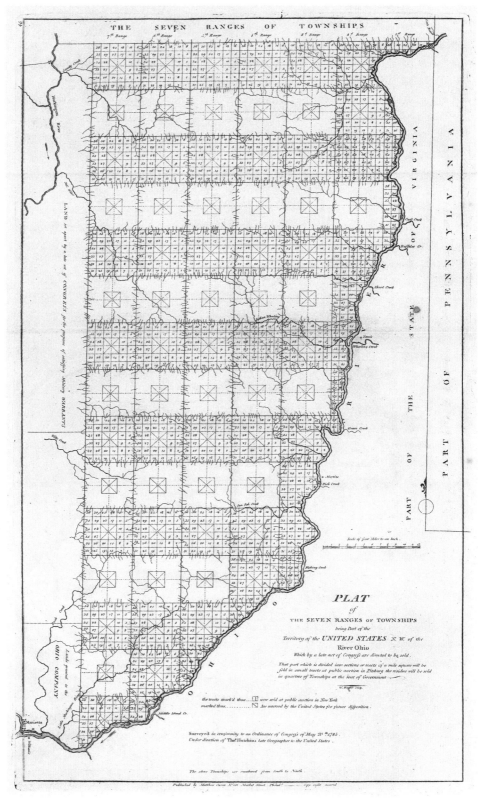

FIGURE 1.2. Plat of the Seven Ranges, showing Congress's scheme of selling land in alternating whole townships and individual lots. From *Carey's General Atlas,* 1811. Courtesy David Rumsey Map Collection, David Rumsey Map Center, Stanford Libraries.

was intended to address immediate and pragmatic problems, Jefferson himself saw his task in utopian terms. In coming up with the state and land survey grids, he was drawing an orderly blueprint not only for the western territories but also for the future of the republic itself. As Drew McCoy has argued, whereas James Madison saw the future of the nation in terms of development through time, Jefferson emphasized expansion through space.[4]

In designing that spatial future, Jefferson saw an opportunity to apply Enlightenment principles of rationality and order to territorial organization. Just as later French republicans would propose new calendars, territorial divisions, and measurement systems in the wake of revolution, Jefferson conceived of a decimal system for subdividing the Northwest into "hundreds," a unit that he based on the geophysically derived geographical mile rather than more conventional English measures.[5] Congress ultimately modified Jefferson's grid, opting for more traditional "townships" rather than his proposed "hundreds." Still, the essence of the grid's severe rationalization remained. To this day, few sights better convey the idea of human-engineered abstraction dominating the earth than an aerial view of the Midwest, where in places the grid stretches to the horizon, determining the courses of roads and the shapes of agricultural fields and towns, in blithe disregard of bodies of water, mountains, and other topographical features.[6]

The effects of the land survey system were profound for other reasons as well. The Jeffersonian grid was a key tool in the process by which a vast terrain occupied by Indigenous people for millennia was converted into the private property of white settlers over just a few hundred years. Since most Indigenous people did not conceive of land as alienable property before their encounter with Europeans, this process of dispossession was double-edged. As Robert Nichols argues, settlers had to simultaneously turn land into property (something capable of being possessed) and assert their own exclusive rights of possession.[7] This helps to explain the shifting and contradictory ways in which white men assumed ownership over land throughout the eighteenth century: sometimes resorting to brute seizure and theft, at other times negotiating nominally legal treaties and sales. In many instances, Indigenous people were accorded "rights" to the lands they inhabited, but only the rights to sell, not to possess the land or to continue living there.[8] As even Jefferson acknowledged in private, many of the Indian land sales were executed "with the price in one hand and the sword in the other."[9] The rectangular survey specified in the land ordinances was a critical technology for carrying out this process of transmutation and dispossession.[10] At the time Jefferson was designing the grid system for the Northwest Territory, ownership of the land was still actively being fought over by the United States and various Indigenous nations, including the Wyandot, Shawnee, Miami, and Six Nations. Only with the signing of the Treaty of Greenville in 1795 following a decade-long war did the Indians cede their remaining territories in Ohio to the federal government, opening the way for the accelerated sale of land to white speculators and settlers. As Brenna Bhandar observes, the acts of surveying the land and representing it in abstract geometric form "effaced preexisting ways of knowing and using the land" and instead rendered land into a fungible commodity, something capable of being owned and alienated.[11]

To the members of Congress who passed the land ordinance, the grid was an instrument for the expedient sale of land and the raising of badly needed funds. Federalists such as Alexander Hamilton favored selling off the land in large parcels of 640 acres or more, a policy designed to favor wealthy speculators and landholders. Jefferson, in contrast, favored smaller parcels set at prices accessible to individual farmers, a position that reflected his belief that both landed wealth and political power should be more broadly distributed. Although Jefferson never explicitly connected the dots from the figure of the land grid to his vision of a more egalitarian democracy, it was precisely this association that the nineteenth-century land reformers would extrapolate and amplify.

Throughout his life, Jefferson saw a link between the geometry of territorial organization and the nature of democracy. In the debates about the size of the new western states that preceded the passage of the land ordinance, he advocated dividing the Northwest into a relatively tight grid, proposing nine small states (given idealistic names like Sylvania and Polypotamia) in the space where Congress eventually delineated five.[12] The approximate boundaries of these proposed states can be seen in a map copied by David Hartley in 1784 or 1785 from an original sketch by Jefferson (Figure 1.3). Jefferson followed Montesquieu in believing that republicanism was best undertaken in small states with relatively homogeneous populations bound by shared interests and customs. In such states, he asserted, citizens were well positioned to engage in "inergetic" self-government.[13] In contrast, Madison argued that large states with greater diversity of viewpoints and even competing factions were desirable to prevent one political party (or one class) from dominating.[14] Jefferson's ideal democracy was smaller-scale, local, and decentralized. As a member of Virginia's state legislature in the 1770s, he had proposed subdividing counties into "hundreds" for the purpose of organizing local primary schools.[15] Forty years later, in a letter to Virginia state senator Joseph Cabell, he again advocated spreading power across a "gradation of authorities" from national to state to county to "ward" levels—a distribution he described as a kind of geometric process: "It is by *dividing and subdividing* these republics from the great national one down through all its subordinations, until it ends in the administration of every man's farm by himself; by placing under every one what his own eye may superintend, that all will be done for the best."[16] He further explained that the subdivision of political states into smaller units would enable more direct citizen participation in government, which in turn would be a bulwark against autocracy:

> Where every man is a sharer in the direction of his ward-republic, or of some of the higher ones, and feels that he is a participator in the government of affairs, not merely at an election one day in the year, but every day; when there shall not be a man in the State who will not be a member of some one of its councils, great or small, he will let the heart be torn out of his body sooner than his power be wrested from him by a Caesar or a Bonaparte.[17]

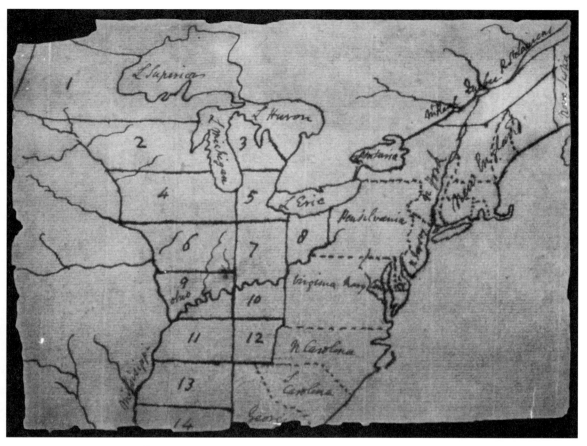

FIGURE 1.3. Jefferson–Hartley map showing Jefferson's proposed division of new states, drawn by David Hartley, 1784 or 1785. Courtesy William L. Clements Library, University of Michigan.

Jefferson's preference for small political units, whether "hundreds" or "ward-republics," stemmed not from an abstract idea but from a concrete vision of democracy as a daily praxis, carried out in geographical space. Active citizens were those who lived close enough to the town hall to participate vigorously and to mobilize quickly when the occasion called for it. Jefferson recalled how the townships of New England—models for his ward-republics—had organized so effectively against his Embargo Act of 1807, generating a "momentum" that made him feel "the foundations of the government shaken under my feet." He contrasted this with the large counties of the South and West, where many citizens' political voices were muted because "the distances are too great for the good people and the industrious generally to attend" public meetings.[18] A generation later, Jefferson's vision of local democracy would find an echo in the land reformers' proposals for octagonal republican villages in which every citizen would be within walking distance of the town hall.

Another of Jefferson's ideas that the land reformers took up concerned the connection between the distribution of political power and the dispersal of economic power.

Republican political theory held that the small landowning farmer was the ideal citizen, since those who owned their own means of livelihood were more independent and less subject to coercion than those who did not. "Cultivators of the earth are the most valuable citizens," Jefferson wrote in a letter to John Jay. "They are the most vigorous, the most independent, the most virtuous."[19] (Writing from an Indigenous perspective, Roxanne Dunbar-Ortiz has called Jefferson's yeoman farmers "the foot soldiers of empire.")[20] Although Jefferson's exaltation of farmers has often been caricatured as a symptom of his regressive pastoralism, it is important to recall the links he imagined between farming, property ownership, and democratic politics. As a legislator in Virginia in the 1770s, Jefferson proposed several policies intended to widen property ownership; these included giving every landless white man fifty acres of free public land and abolishing entail and primogeniture laws that favored preserving large estates intact upon inheritance. Reflecting on how the new United States could avoid the concentration of landed wealth found in Europe, which he had witnessed firsthand in France, Jefferson wrote to Madison in 1785: "I am conscious that an equal division of property is impracticable. But the consequences of this enormous inequality producing so much misery to the bulk of mankind, legislators cannot invent too many devices for subdividing property, only taking care to let their subdivisions go hand in hand with the natural affections of the human mind."[21]

Scholars interested in interpreting Jefferson as a "radical" rather than a Lockean liberal have pointed to this passage as an example of his openness to using policies like inheritance law or progressive taxation to effect the "subdivision"—that is, the wider distribution—of property.[22] As Staughton Lynd and Richard Matthews have argued, Jefferson went as far as to assert here (and in other writings) that property ownership is a matter of social convention and agreement rather than natural right, even suggesting that such agreements must be reconceived and rewritten by every generation. As he wrote to Madison in 1789, "The earth belongs in usufruct to the living; . . . the dead have neither powers nor rights over it." Benefits like inheritance therefore are not "natural rights" but determined by "a law of the society," and such laws "naturally expire" with each generation, or every nineteen years.[23] In the next decades, these embryonic ideas would be taken up enthusiastically by workingmen radicals. Adopting the ideas of not only Jefferson but also Thomas Paine, Thomas Spence, and other eighteenth-century radicals, the workingmen would repeat the idea that the "earth belongs in usufruct to the living" and that it is incumbent on each generation to determine anew how property and power should be justly distributed. What both the workingmen and Jefferson and Paine omitted, however, was that the land whose division and distribution would furnish the material basis for white men's equality first had to be taken from Indigenous people.[24]

The Image of the Grid in Early America

A few historians, following an influential reading by Hannah Arendt, have interpreted Jefferson's vision of "ward-republics" as a pyramid, in which power rises up from below.[25] But I would contend that the grid is the more apt figure: more than mere metaphor, it was the spatial technology that would enable Jefferson's "dividing and subdividing" of the republic into its smallest unit, the individual freehold farm, which would be the substrate for his ideal democratic republic. Jefferson himself, notably, never connected the dots between the land grid and his vision of more widely distributed political and economic power. One reason for this may have been the grid's nascent status as an identifiable figure. Strange as it may sound, the grid was invisible to many early Americans. No illustration of it appeared in the Land Ordinance of 1785, for example. The text of the law merely stated that surveyors would "divide the said territory into townships of six miles square, by lines running due north and south, and others crossing these at right angles, as near as may be," with further specific instructions for how the survey would be conducted. In the ordinance, the grid was described as a process—the act of laying out imaginary lines in real space and matching those to an abstracted, drawn representation. Surveyors were to indicate the locations of boundary lines on-site by carving chaps on trees; then they drew the lines onto plats to be submitted to a geographer, who would submit them to the board of treasury, which would in turn transmit copies to the states for the purpose of enabling property sales. Historians such as Hildegard Johnson have noted the surprising absence of comments on the rectangular survey system in travel narratives, newspapers, diaries, and correspondence from the early nineteenth century.[26] Writing about land sales of the time, Johnson remarks, "It is doubtful that buyers were impressed by a checkerboard pattern on township plats in government or railroad land offices; 'checkerboard' did not seem to be part of the vocabulary of contemporary writers."[27]

Most Americans at the turn of the century were, of course, familiar with the image of the grid if not the word, from cadastral survey maps and city plats as well as everyday objects like quilts and windowpanes.[28] But grids do not seem to have had the visual iconicity to merit their own term. Indeed, the word "grid" did not come into use until sometime after 1839, perhaps in relation to new "gridiron" cities like New York.[29] In the early republic, those wishing to refer to a pattern of regularly spaced lines crossing each other at perpendicular angles would instead have used the term "chequerboard" or "chessboard."[30] Jefferson himself preferred the former. In 1793, he wrote to an associate requesting a copy of the Seven Ranges township map, saying he had only a "conjectural" "large chequer-board map" of the area.[31] Later, when he designed a gridded city with alternating building lots, he described the town as laid out like a "chequer board," with the "black squares" to be built up and the "white squares" remaining unbuilt and landscaped with trees (Figure 1.4). (He believed this low-density arrangement would help to guard against the threats of both yellow fever and fire, and would make the atmosphere of the town more like "that of the country.")[32] Elsewhere, Jefferson described coordinate paper, which he discovered while living in France in the 1780s, to the scientist David Rittenhouse in terms that indicate its novelty: "I send for your acceptance some sheets of drawing-paper, which being laid off in squares representing feet or what you please, saves the necessity of using the rule and dividers in all rectangular draughts."[33] The grid's dominant association clearly was with utility and convenience. Coordinate paper, a "chequer-board" town plan, and the rectangular land survey were expedient ways to accomplish specific pragmatic ends. In

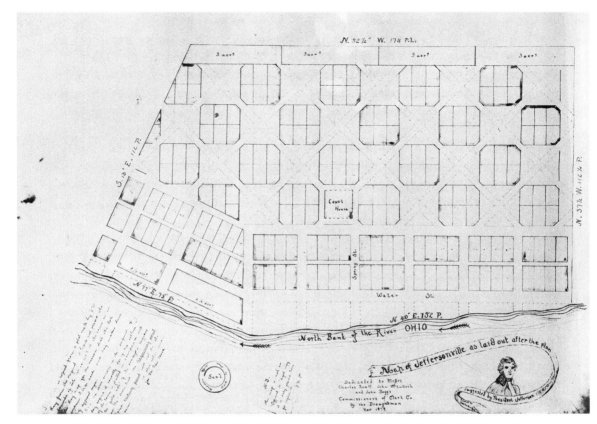

FIGURE 1.4. Plan of Jeffersonville, Indiana, 1802 (drawn 1879), showing Jefferson's idea for a "chequer board town." From John Reps, *The Making of Urban America: A History of City Planning in the United States,* 1965.

1807, New York City's commissioners of streets and roads also cited cheapness and convenience as the best reasons for choosing "rectilinear and rectangular streets" over the embellishments of "circles, ovals, and stars" in laying out the gridiron of the city.[34] It was perhaps this bare utilitarianism that rendered the land grid apparently unremarkable to Americans.

Even from the scant evidence, it is possible to distinguish two distinct ways that the grid was imagined within Jefferson's own oeuvre as grid maker: on the one hand, as a network of perpendicular lines drawn over a piece of ground (as in the land ordinance text) and, on the other, as an arrangement of square shapes (as in his chequerboard towns). The first tended to be used at the cartographic scale; the second was deployed at the more zoomed-in scale of the town plan. One concept entailed laying out lines to divide abstract space; the other imagined composing solid units into larger assemblages. The grid therefore carried connotations of both division and association: both the recursive division of land into ever smaller units, ending in individually owned plots, and, conversely, the recombination of these unit squares into civic groupings such as Jefferson's ideal "ward-republics." In other words, the grid simultaneously embodied liberal connotations of delineating individual property, a radical implication of division and distribution, and a democratic valence of assembly. Whether drawn as lines or as squares, as divisions or as aggregations, the grid's meaning was still somewhat ambiguous and open at this moment in U.S. history, awaiting semiotic recoding by later generations.

Jefferson's Octagons

If the grid was Jefferson's designated figure for shaping the polity at a territorial scale, the octagon was his favored device for housing its constituent citizens at an architectural scale. As an architect, Jefferson was obsessed with octagons. The figure's telltale 135-degree angles appear again and again in his drawings, materializing in the form of single bows; double, triple, and quadruple projections; and freestanding volumes. He used the octagon for myriad programs, including a chapel, a courthouse, an observatory, and a prison. Above all, he used it in his designs for private dwellings, including his own houses and several residences he designed for friends and neighbors.

Architectural historians have interpreted Jefferson's octagons in several ways: as the products of specific European architectural influences, as reflections of his love of light and air and his fondness for mathematics, and even as "maternal allusions."[35] Rather than focusing on his motivations, however, my task here is to understand Jefferson's octagonal houses through the backward prism of the mid-nineteenth-century fashion for octagonal houses (the subject of chapter 3). In contrast to the case of the workingmen land reformers, who were inspired by the land ordinance grid, there is no evidence that the originator of the octagon house fad, a phrenologist named Orson Fowler, knew of Jefferson's earlier designs. Nevertheless, we can glimpse in Jefferson's architecture prefigurations of Fowler's argument that the house could produce a particular kind of subject (stronger, healthier, adapted to the capitalist market). Jefferson, too, imagined a link between geometric buildings and the formation of subjects, specifically the autonomous, private, property-owning, "free" man conjured by political theorists like John Locke and invoked in Jefferson's own writings. Between Jefferson's time and Fowler's, this liberal ideal of subjectivity emerged and solidified as older republican ideas about the necessary interconnection between individual interest and public good gave way to an ideology of competitive individualism and self-interest.[36] Simultaneously, ideas about how architecture relates to human subjects evolved as well, from older ideas about classical representation via analogy to newer aesthetic theories that stressed architecture's capacity to direct sensations like sound and sight, which led eventually to the belief that buildings could almost literally reform subjects.

As an avid reader of architectural treatises, Jefferson imbibed several distinct ideas about how architecture relates to human subjects that directly informed his choice of octagonal geometric forms. From Palladio and other classical authorities, Jefferson gleaned the idea of geometry embodying the harmonies of an orderly universe. Indeed, his earliest known octagonal design, for a chapel in Williamsburg, around 1778 (Figure 1.5), was based on Palladio's circular Temple of Vesta (Figure 1.6).[37]

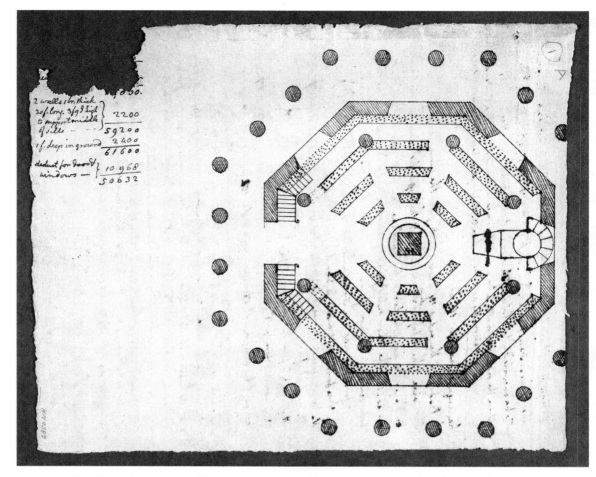

FIGURE 1.5. Thomas Jefferson, Design of a Chapel, on the model of the Temple of Vesta, circa 1778. Pen and ink, 6¼ × 7½ inches. Courtesy Huntington Library, San Marino, California, HM 9387 N419r.

In the classical tradition, the round forms of buildings evoked the divine harmony of the universe. Geometric attributes like symmetry and proportion manifested the resonances between architecture, heavenly bodies, and the human figure, a view given iconic expression in the image of Vitruvian man inscribed within a circle (Figure 1.7).[38] By Jefferson's time, however, such images of human figures embodying universal proportions and beauty were undercut by widespread belief in the essential inequality of the human races, an inequality seen to apply not only to moral and physical traits but also to aesthetic ones. In *Notes on the State of Virginia,* for example, Jefferson wrote that white bodies had "a more elegant symmetry of form" than Black bodies.[39] Such statements point to the intertwining of race and aesthetics in the late eighteenth century, as well as the prejudices embedded in physiognomic metaphors in architecture.[40]

For Jefferson, octagonal architecture embodied the rationality of mathematics

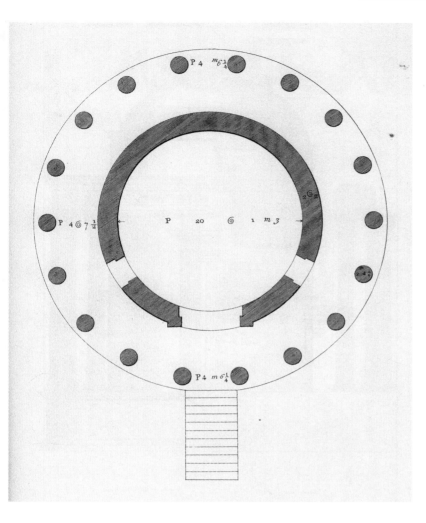

FIGURE 1.6. Temple of Vesta. From Andrea Palladio, *The Four Books of Architecture,* 1715 edition, Book IV, Plate 38.

at the same time it affirmed classical canons of beauty signifying an orderly universe. That Jefferson understood the eight-sided features in his buildings as exercises in mathematical reasoning is evidenced by his sketches for the octagonal bows at Monticello, in which he approached the task of drawing these architectural elements like a geometric proof (Figure 1.8). Like Locke, who advocated mathematical learning as "a way to settle in the mind a habit of reasoning closely and in train," Jefferson linked mathematical education to the cultivation of a rational and virtuous body of citizens, writing in 1818 that training in "the mathematical and physical sciences" would help to "develop the reasoning faculties of our youth, enlarge their minds, cultivate their morals, and instill into them the precepts of virtue and order."[41] But despite his generally egalitarian beliefs about education, he did not deem all Americans equally fit to enjoy the edifying effects of mathematical instruction, and he wrote disparagingly of African Americans' capacity to learn geometry: "One could scarcely be found capable of tracing and comprehending the investigations of Euclid."[42] Following

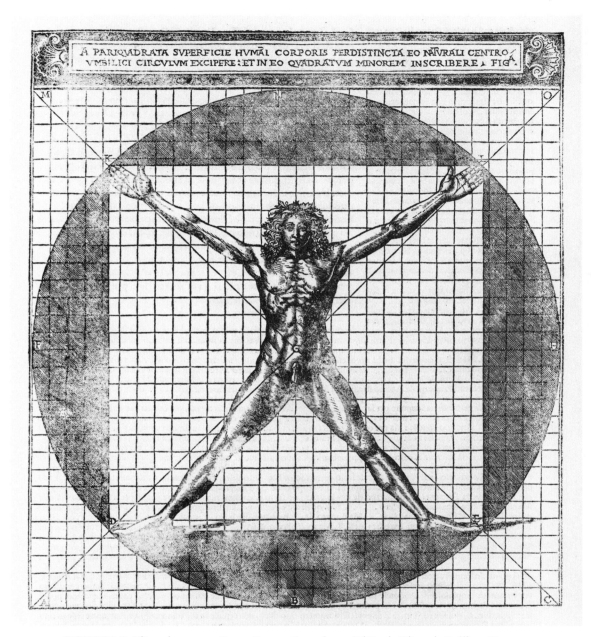

FIGURE 1.7. Vitruvian man. From Cesare Cesariano, *Di Lucio Vitruvio Pollione De architectura,* 1521. Courtesy Library of Congress, Rare Book and Special Collections Division.

Jefferson's logic linking citizenship with reason, a people who lacked the capacity to reason geometrically could, by extension, be excluded from the corpus of rational democratic citizens.

Jefferson's octagons were also informed by a third, newer, and more modern understanding of the relationship between architecture and its human subjects, one centered on the sensory effects of aesthetic forms.[43] Under the influence of English sen-

Antinomies of American Utopia 43

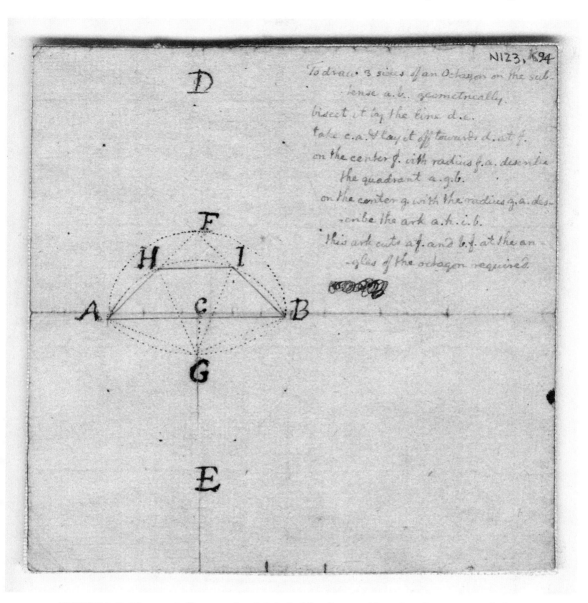

FIGURE 1.8. Thomas Jefferson, sketch labeled "to draw 3 sides of an Octagon . . . ," circa 1771. Collection of the Massachusetts Historical Society, N123, K94.

sationalist philosophy, which posited a mind shaped through sensory perception of the exterior world, architects and aesthetic theorists in eighteenth-century England began to focus on the effects of geometric forms on the perceiving subject. The view of architecture as a practice in the manipulation of perception can be found in the book that was likely a direct source for many of Jefferson's eight-sided figures, Robert Morris's *Select Architecture* (1755).[44] Of the fifty plates in the book, nine feature octagonal shapes, most in connection with garden follies and country houses. Morris described the eight-sided elements in his architecture primarily in perceptual terms, as objects meant to be viewed both from without and from within. In his notes on an octagonal pavilion, he explained: "A Building of this Kind would be an Object seen at a Distance" and would contribute to creating "a new Succession of pleasing Images" in the landscape.[45]

Octagons were not just objects to be seen but also objects to enable seeing—they were optical devices, in a sense. Morris characterized one house as best suited for a hill, "where an agreeable Prospect may be had." Its "many Windows" were designed to enable "more easy obtaining [of] a Variety of Views" (Figure 1.9).[46] The new perceptual approach to architecture had a political dimension. Within architecture, sensationalist theory was most prominently manifested in picturesque designs of houses and gardens for landed estates in England. This picturesque landscape aesthetic emerged from a historic shift in landownership patterns, from feudal arrangements that provided common land for peasants' use to the growing enclosure and privatization of land. As landownership became consolidated, displaced rural workers migrated to cities, eventually becoming the surplus labor force for factories. Meanwhile, estate owners created extensive pleasure gardens whose winding paths and expanses of rolling green lawn exuded a vision of rural ease and naturalism.[47] This aesthetic of "territorial aristocracy," defined by a grand house set off by a landscape with "square miles of conspicuous waste," migrated from English manors to Virginian plantations in the eighteenth century.[48] Octagonal architecture was a product of this new aesthetics of territorial possession. Eight-sided forms at such Anglo-American country estates were often associated with garden follies and hunting lodges, with spaces of retreat that allowed owners to look out over privatized and domesticated landscapes.[49] The power to see was linked inextricably with the power of ownership. The English author Henry Wotton wrote of something he called a "royalty of Sight" in a dictum that was reprinted frequently in the eighteenth century. In Wotton's words: "For as there is a Lordship (as it were) of the Feet, wherein a Man walketh with much Pleasure about the Limits of his own Possessions, so there is a Lordship likewise of the Eye, which being a Ranging, and Imperious (I had almost said) Usurping Sense, cannot indure to be Circumscribed within a small Space, but must be satisfied both with Extent, and variety."[50] Wotton's evocation of a "lordship of the eye"—a "ranging," "imperious," and "usurping" sense, engaged in surveying one's possessions—makes clear the link between picturesque perception and the power of owning a piece of land. The octagon was an aesthetic technology that enabled this visual sovereignty, a sovereignty that, in the context of eighteenth-century Virginia, was available only to what Bhandar describes as the Lockean "self-possessed, proprietorial subject"—the white settler landowner.[51]

THE OCTAGONAL HOUSE AS PROTOTYPE

All of these connotations of the octagon—as a harmonious figure mirroring the order of the universe, a shape constructed through the exercise of mathematical reason, and a spatial form enabling visual surveillance and a sense of possessive sovereignty over

FIGURE 1.9. Robert Morris, "A pavillion intended to terminate the Boundaries of a Garden . . ." In the text, Morris explains, "I made so many Windows in it, for the more easy obtaining a Variety of views." From Robert Morris, *Select Architecture,* 1755.

FIGURE 1.10. Thomas Jefferson, Monticello, west elevation of second version. Drawing by Robert Mills, 1803. Collection of the Massachusetts Historical Society, N154, K155.

its surroundings—converged in Jefferson's deployment of eight-sided motifs in his architecture. The octagonal dome at the center of his self-designed house, Monticello, gave the building a sense of proportion, symmetry, and physiognomy, akin to the head of the human body (Figure 1.10). His "octagon theorem" sketch evinced the pleasure he took in the mathematical construction of the figure. But the few hints we find in firsthand accounts of Jefferson's architectural octagons indicate that their main appeal for him lay in the sensory experiences they afforded: a combination of the feeling of optical mastery over his surroundings and the enjoyment of being in spaces that were unusually bright, especially by eighteenth-century Virginian standards.[52] Jefferson sited Monticello on the top of a hill so that he could step outside his house and easily survey the plantation below. And he designed the eight-sided projection of the central parlor so that its five tall windows and double door faced onto the large main lawn, providing him with an immediate view of an expansive domesticated landscape. Whereas the typical bows in English pattern books were three-sided, Jefferson's in the first Monticello were five-sided, yielding spaces suffused with light and air and permitting even more unfettered visual access to the exterior (Figures 1.11 and 1.12).

Jefferson was so enamored of octagons that over the years his designs for houses frequently included eight-sided forms on the model of the first Monticello.[53] The parti of a rectangular house with a central projecting octagonal parlor appeared again and again in Jefferson's oeuvre. He deployed variations on it in a house that he de-

Antinomies of American Utopia 47

FIGURE 1.11. Thomas Jefferson, Monticello, the octagonal parlor. Copyright Thomas Jefferson Foundation at Monticello.

signed for his friend James Barbour, as well as a Governor's House in Virginia (Figures 1.13–1.16). One of Jefferson's Albemarle County neighbors recounted a conversation with the third president: "As you predicted he was for giving you Octagons. They were charming. They gave you a semi-circle of light and air."[54] Jefferson seems to have regarded the house with an octagonal projection as something of a prototype. Hugh Howard has called the house with octagonal bow "a paradigm for Jefferson's agrarian ideal."[55]

Yet if Jefferson did imagine the house with an octagonal projection as a kind of prototypical home for his ideal farmer-citizen, we must also note that none of the houses he designed were for yeomen engaged in the day-to-day labors of the farm. Rather, the houses were for wealthy plantation owners who relied on enslaved African Americans to perform the backbreaking word of cultivation. In this context, octagonal architectural forms, which afforded British lords a "royalty of sight," must have reinforced a sense of surveillance and domination by the plantation master over his human chattel. Peter Fossett, a slave born at Monticello, recalled Jefferson "looking through his telescope to see how the work was progressing over at Pan Top, one

48 *Antinomies of American Utopia*

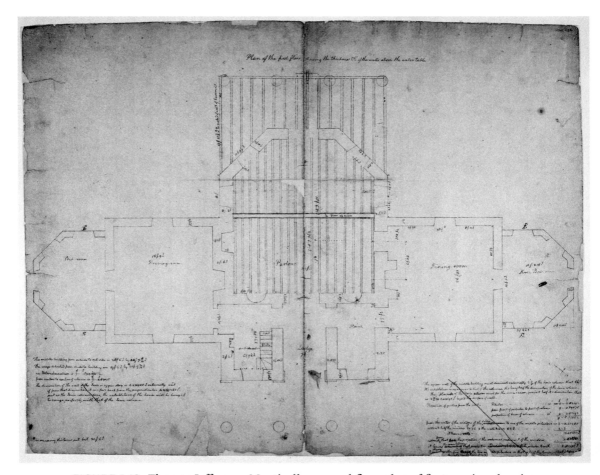

FIGURE 1.12. Thomas Jefferson, Monticello, ground-floor plan of first version showing octagonal additions, 1771. Collection of the Massachusetts Historical Society, N49, K24.

of his plantations." Another African American man who was involved in building the University of Virginia remembered Jefferson standing and watching "we alls at work through his spyglass."[56] Yet it is also important to recognize that such oversight was not absolute. Scholars believe that the enslaved laborers at Monticello enjoyed a relatively high degree of freedom from supervision.[57] As Dell Upton has pointed out, enslaved people often had more liberty of movement through the private spaces within plantation houses than did lower-class white visitors.[58] The enslaved inhabitants of Monticello also had access to the site's imperial views. Isaac Jefferson, an enslaved blacksmith there, would later recall the breathtaking view from the mountaintop: "From Monticello you can see mountains all round as far as the eye can reach."[59] Thus, while the octagon was a figure that symbolically and spatially subtended a white landowner's sense of sovereignty, it also produced occasions when the correlation of experience, subjectivity, and power could be reconfigured, if only momentarily.

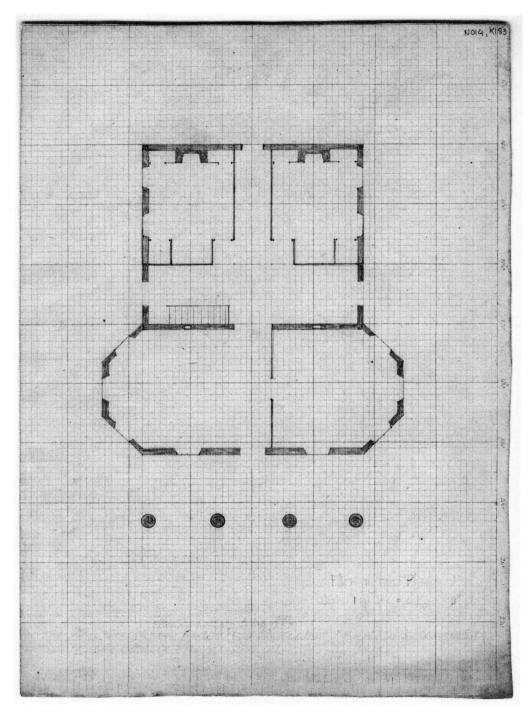

FIGURE 1.13. Thomas Jefferson, plan of Farmington, a house for George Divers, 1802 or earlier. Collection of the Massachusetts Historical Society, N14, K183.

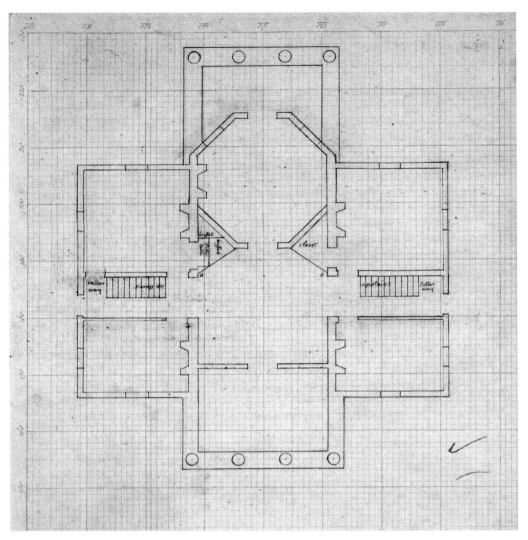

FIGURE 1.14. Thomas Jefferson, plan of Barboursville, a house for James Barbour, 1817. Collection of the Massachusetts Historical Society, N5, K206.

PRIVACY AND PUBLICITY

Architectural octagons were the devices that enabled the owners of Jefferson's houses to exercise visual sovereignty over their property, both landed and human. But paradoxically, they also became sites where that mastery was sometimes undermined, since the power to see out also entailed a threatening susceptibility to being seen. The windowed octagonal bow's inherent openness counteracted Jefferson's desire for his house to be a private retreat, where he could escape the pressures of public life. In the first decade of the nineteenth century, Monticello increasingly attracted guests, both invited and uninvited. The public was now literally perched outside Jefferson's bedroom window, producing an uncomfortable blurring of his public and private

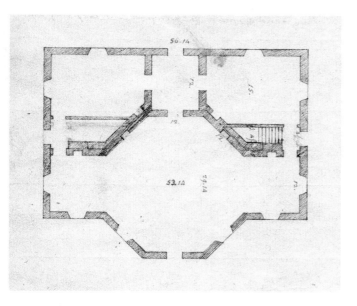

FIGURE 1.15. Thomas Jefferson, study plan for Governor's House in Richmond, Virginia, 1780. Collection of the Massachusetts Historical Society, N283, K104.

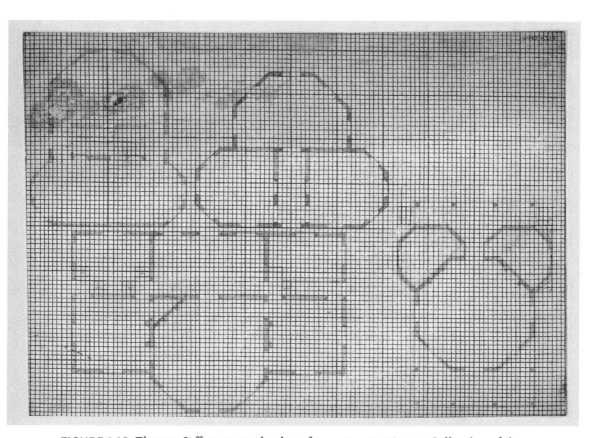

FIGURE 1.16. Thomas Jefferson, study plans for a retreat, 1789–94. Collection of the Massachusetts Historical Society, N490, K217.

FIGURE 1.17. Porticles outside Jefferson's bedroom at Monticello, first installed in 1809. Copyright Thomas Jefferson Foundation at Monticello.

spaces.[60] Jefferson was an ardent subscriber to the republican tradition that regarded politics as a temporary duty, a public service but also a kind of performance, to be followed by a retreat to private life. Already, in his early thirties, he had written of his desire to "withdraw . . . totally from the public stage and pass the rest of my days in domestic ease and tranquility."[61] But privacy and publicity were not so easy to separate. Perhaps in response to the intrusions on his domestic life at Monticello, Jefferson in 1806 ordered the construction of what he termed "porticles" or "Venetian porches" outside his bedroom and library windows; these boxes made of wooden adjustable louvers enclosed the south terraces, creating two semioutdoor spaces sheltered from prying eyes (Figure 1.17). Ironically, the Venetian blinds Jefferson deployed to counter the excessive exposure at Monticello were the same devices Jeremy Bentham had recently proposed using in his circular panopticon prison to shield the prison warden at the center of the structure from the eyes of prisoners. Jefferson himself had designed an octagonal prison in 1797, for which he suggested using wooden blinds to allow

Antinomies of American Utopia 53

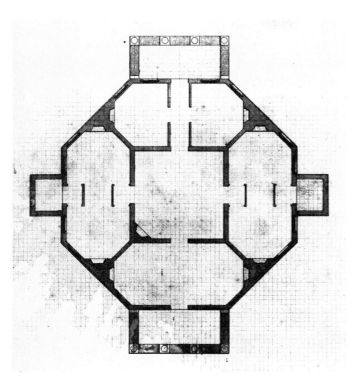

FIGURE 1.18. Thomas Jefferson, plan of Poplar Forest, undated. Drawn by John Neilson. Thomas Jefferson Papers, Albert and Shirley Small Special Collections Library, University of Virginia, N-350.

passage of air but not sight, an idea possibly influenced by Bentham.[62] Liberty and confinement could sometimes involve the same architectural instruments.

Confronted with the paradox of the octagon—the way its openness could lead to overexposure—Jefferson tried again. In search of refuge from his "public" home, he began in the 1800s to design a private retreat at Poplar Forest (Figure 1.18). A simple octagon in plan, the house possessed the geometric purity of a mathematical theorem.[63] Its central dining room was a perfect twenty-foot cube, illuminated only from above by a skylight.[64] Here again, Jefferson was interested in using octagons to create visual links to the outdoors. The primary public space was an elongated octagonal parlor with two windows and a door opening onto an elevated covered porch, with no direct access to the ground (Figure 1.19). Jefferson could walk out onto the porch and gaze out at his property but not actually walk out onto the land. In other words, vision was primary. The self-possessed, free individual could indulge the dream of a rational, enlightened self able to see all, yet free from prying eyes and a judging public—a panoptic fantasy of an eye whose gaze cannot be returned.

Yet here, too, some of the contradictions and complications of the myth of liberal subjectivity reared their heads, revealing themselves in architectural form. These tensions manifested themselves in the section of the house, which contrasted with the geometric clarity of the plan. Although Jefferson imagined Poplar Forest as a space where he could dwell in solitude, at least one enslaved person usually accompanied

FIGURE 1.19. Thomas Jefferson, Poplar Forest, Bedford, Virginia. Courtesy Library of Congress, Historic American Buildings Survey.

him during his stays there. As at Monticello, he regraded the surrounding land so that the two-story house would appear as a more modest one-story structure from the front facade, and he relegated the living and working quarters of enslaved people to the level below the main living area, out of sight. In his initial plan for Poplar Forest, Jefferson—perhaps inordinately absorbed with the ideal geometry of his design— neglected to include stairs connecting the living spaces above and the work spaces below. After construction began, he asked his builder to add the stairs, acknowledging, if grudgingly, the interdependence of freedom and enslaved labor.[65] This "lapse" was not a fluke but indicative of a fundamental tension in Jefferson's house designs. As Dell Upton has insightfully argued, Jefferson subscribed to the republican mythology of the citizen as a kind of "hermit" (upright, independent, incorruptible), and he employed a variety of architectural and technological devices at Monticello to buttress this self-image of independent existence. Besides suppressing the enslaved people's working quarters in below-grade dependencies, he concealed the family rooms in a hidden second story and used dumbwaiters and other devices to minimize the presence of enslaved people in his private spaces (Figure 1.20).[66] As Upton writes: "Visually Jefferson's house claims that the home of many people, white and black, is the home of one man. A man surrounded by family and enslaved workers represented himself as a hermit alone on his mountain."[67]

FIGURE 1.20. Thomas Jefferson, Monticello, view of south service wing. Jefferson designed the house so that the spaces where enslaved people lived and worked would not be visible from the front of the house. Courtesy Library of Congress, Historic American Buildings Survey.

The Image of the Octagon

At the beginning of the nineteenth century, Monticello—always a communal site but imagined by Jefferson as a private one—became more of a public house than its owner wanted. But in another sense it remained more private than many less eminent houses just a few decades later. For unlike George Washington's home, Mount Vernon, images of which were widely reproduced in the popular press, Monticello was depicted in illustrations with relative rarity.[68] Jefferson's octagons, with their nascent connotations of individual sovereignty enacted through architectural geometry, remained a largely private preoccupation. The gentleman architect never explicitly articulated the idea that a house's shape could help fashion a particular kind of enlightened, republican settler subject, just as he did not overtly link the geometry of the land ordinance grid with his beliefs about widening the distribution of property and power. It was not until the land reformers began printing the image of a square township in their tracts and newspapers that the grid would become yoked firmly to a radical political program. And not until Orson Fowler published his popular treatise in 1848 would octagon houses take off as a nationwide trend. In other words, it was not until these geometric figures met the printing press that they would gain their use as political-rhetorical images. Nevertheless, Jefferson's twin obsessions with grids and octagons contained the germs of many of the ideas and contradictions that would inform later geometric utopias. Among these were the ideas that the key to a more egalitarian democracy was the reorganization of land and its transmutation to private property (which made the white men's utopia dependent on Indigenous dispossession), that geometric spatial forms could be instruments for fashioning an ideal self and polity, and that possessive individualism and equality could be harmonized and reconciled. In the decades to come, these themes would continue to influence, as well as constrain, the imaginations of later utopians.

CHAPTER 2

The Visual Rhetoric of Equality
The Land Reformers' Grid

Thomas Jefferson hoped that his land survey grid would help produce an "empire for liberty," an extensive nation of independent freehold farmers. But fifty years later, those ideological dimensions of the land ordinance survey had largely faded from view, as the grid came to be regarded primarily as a pragmatic instrument for selling public land to private interests or, from a different perspective, turning Indian land into white-owned property. Jerome Higgins, the author of a popular nineteenth-century surveying manual, expressed the prevailing wisdom when he wrote that the grid system "was originated for land-parceling for sale, and it has answered the purpose."[1]

This dominant understanding of the grid was momentarily interrupted in 1844, when the National Reform Association, a radical workingmen's group based in New York City, began featuring an image of a gridded township in its pamphlets and newspaper, alongside calls for a new solution for the growing inequality between capitalists and workers in American society: "land for the landless." Angry over a rising market economy in which a privileged few were gaining wealth at the expense of a majority of downtrodden and dependent laborers, the land reformers turned to the idea of western land as a safety valve. They argued that if each landless individual in the United States received a free share of the public domain, all workers would be in a position either to gain independence as freehold farmers or to negotiate higher wages in workshops and factories. Articulating a key precept of settler colonial ideology, the reformers claimed that free land was not a gift but a right. As the group exhorted the public in an 1845 handbill titled *Vote Yourself a Farm* (Figure 2.1):

> Are you an American citizen? Then you are a joint-owner of the Public Lands. . . .
>
> Are you tired of slavery—of drudging for others—of poverty and its attendant miseries? Then, *Vote yourself a Farm.*
>
> Are you endowed with reason? Then you must know that your right to life

necessarily includes the right to a place to live in—the right to a home. Assert this right, so long denied mankind by feudal robbers and their attorneys. *Vote yourself a Farm.*[2]

Drawing on the classical rhetorical technique of symploce (repeating phrases at the beginnings and ends of successive sentences for emphasis), this appeal reprises several key elements of white northern labor ideology of this period: the Enlightenment rhetoric of "reason" and "rights," the idea of white workers' oppression as a form of wage "slavery" comparable to chattel slavery, and the vilification of large landholders and monopolists as "feudal robbers." The handbill's central imperative, "Vote yourself a farm," signals the movement's core status as a political campaign in an age of expanded white male suffrage.

Printed on the back of the handbill were two drawings whose sobriety belied the fiery verbal rhetoric on the front: a diagram of a six-mile-square township gridded into 140 family-size farms—modeled on the Jeffersonian land ordinance grid—and a plan of the concentric octagonal republican village that would lie at the center of each township (Figure 2.2). Appearing repeatedly in the National Reformers' handbills, pamphlets, almanac, and newspaper the *Working Man's Advocate* (later retitled *Young America*) throughout the 1840s, the two images would become symbols for the workingmen's call for a radical redistribution of land and wealth in the mid-1840s. As the National Reformer Lewis Masquerier put it with hardly a trace of hyperbole, these "diagrams of a township and village . . . are the most important divisions for the social relations of man."[3]

The Grid as Instrument and Image

Why did the workingmen include these diagrams in their appeals? What kind of work were the drawings intended to do? The township and village plans were not exactly blueprints: there is no evidence that the National Reform Association ever seriously set out to launch a township or village on these models.[4] But neither were they merely graphic illustrations of workingmen's egalitarian ideals, as historians are wont to treat them.[5] The plans' existence remained a paper one, a fact that is reinforced when we look more closely at the printed artifact. Scrutinizing the township grid, we see regular breaks in the vertical lines at the intersections with the horizontals and diagonals, suggesting that it was likely composed using standard printer's rules (the metal specimens used to create divider lines) rather than engraved (Figures 2.3 and 2.4). In other words, it was composed in a printshop, not drawn or surveyed. This is not surprising, considering that many of the leaders of the National Reform Association were printers by trade. Their grid was an artifact of print, visually similar to but fundamentally different from the gridded drawings that U.S. government surveyors sketched in the field, with a Gunter's chain in hand, and sent back to the General Land Office. Despite its straightforward technical appearance, the National Reformers' grid was a printed fiction, unmoored from any precise referential or representational relationship to a particular piece of land.

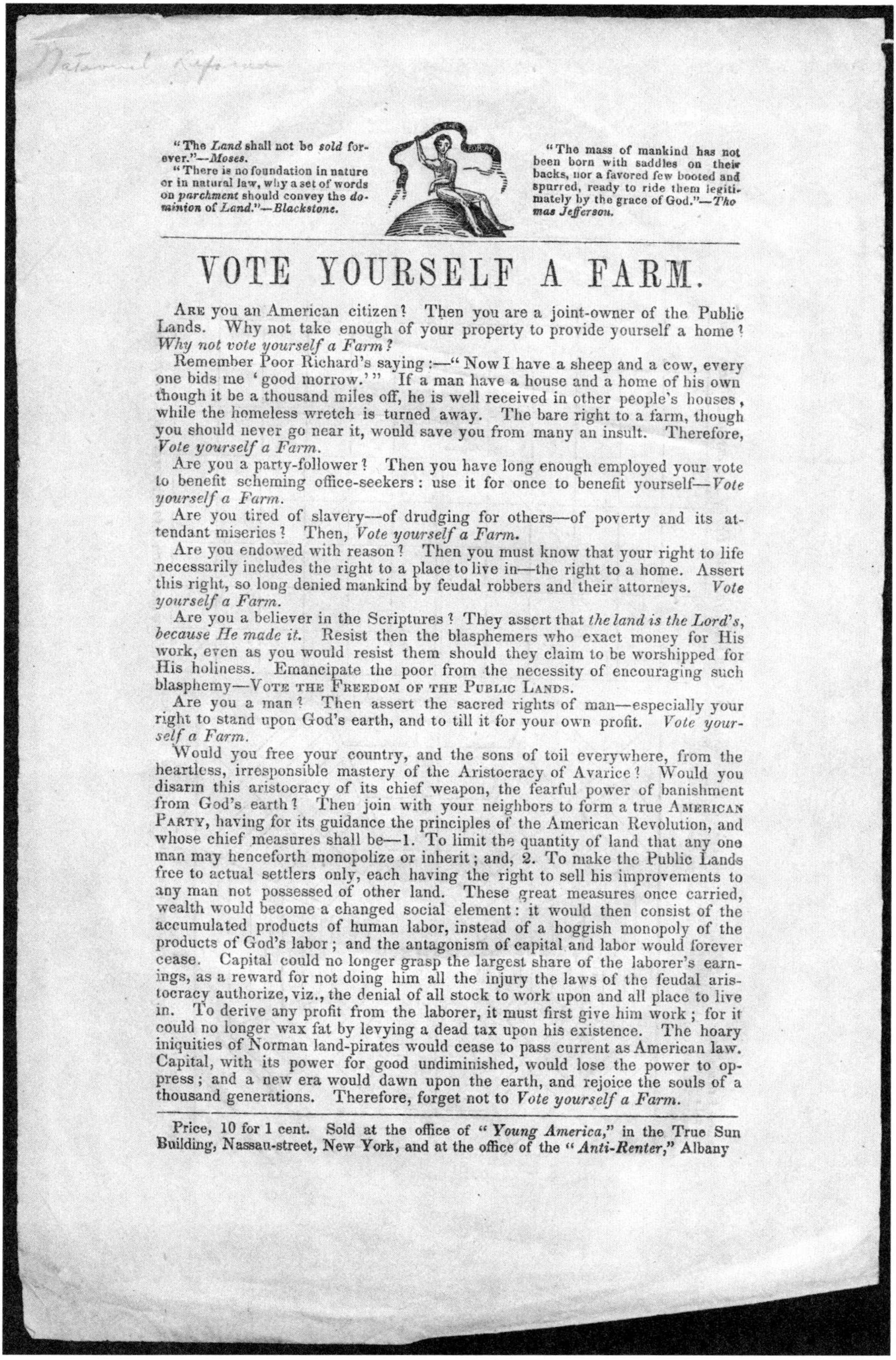

"The *Land* shall not be *sold* forever."—*Moses.*
"There is no foundation in nature or in natural law, why a set of words on *parchment* should convey the *dominion of Land.*"—*Blackstone.*

"The mass of mankind has not been born with saddles on their backs, nor a favored few booted and spurred, ready to ride them legitimately by the grace of God."—*Thomas Jefferson.*

VOTE YOURSELF A FARM.

ARE you an American citizen? Then you are a joint-owner of the Public Lands. Why not take enough of your property to provide yourself a home? *Why not vote yourself a Farm?*

Remember Poor Richard's saying :—" Now I have a sheep and a cow, every one bids me 'good morrow.'" If a man have a house and a home of his own though it be a thousand miles off, he is well received in other people's houses, while the homeless wretch is turned away. The bare right to a farm, though you should never go near it, would save you from many an insult. Therefore, *Vote yourself a Farm.*

Are you a party-follower? Then you have long enough employed your vote to benefit scheming office-seekers: use it for once to benefit yourself—*Vote yourself a Farm.*

Are you tired of slavery—of drudging for others—of poverty and its attendant miseries? Then, *Vote yourself a Farm.*

Are you endowed with reason? Then you must know that your right to life necessarily includes the right to a place to live in—the right to a home. Assert this right, so long denied mankind by feudal robbers and their attorneys. *Vote yourself a Farm.*

Are you a believer in the Scriptures? They assert that *the land is the Lord's, because He made it.* Resist then the blasphemers who exact money for His work, even as you would resist them should they claim to be worshipped for His holiness. Emancipate the poor from the necessity of encouraging such blasphemy—VOTE THE FREEDOM OF THE PUBLIC LANDS.

Are you a man? Then assert the sacred rights of man—especially your right to stand upon God's earth, and to till it for your own profit. *Vote yourself a Farm.*

Would you free your country, and the sons of toil everywhere, from the heartless, irresponsible mastery of the Aristocracy of Avarice? Would you disarm this aristocracy of its chief weapon, the fearful power of banishment from God's earth? Then join with your neighbors to form a true AMERICAN PARTY, having for its guidance the principles of the American Revolution, and whose chief measures shall be—1. To limit the quantity of land that any one man may henceforth monopolize or inherit; and, 2. To make the Public Lands free to actual settlers only, each having the right to sell his improvements to any man not possessed of other land. These great measures once carried, wealth would become a changed social element: it would then consist of the accumulated products of human labor, instead of a hoggish monopoly of the products of God's labor; and the antagonism of capital and labor would forever cease. Capital could no longer grasp the largest share of the laborer's earnings, as a reward for not doing him all the injury the laws of the feudal aristocracy authorize, viz., the denial of all stock to work upon and all place to live in. To derive any profit from the laborer, it must first give him work; for it could no longer wax fat by levying a dead tax upon his existence. The hoary iniquities of Norman land-pirates would cease to pass current as American law. Capital, with its power for good undiminished, would lose the power to oppress; and a new era would dawn upon the earth, and rejoice the souls of a thousand generations. Therefore, forget not to *Vote yourself a Farm.*

Price, 10 for 1 cent. Sold at the office of "*Young America,*" in the True Sun Building, Nassau-street, New York, and at the office of the "*Anti-Renter,*" Albany

FIGURE 2.1. National Reform Association, *Vote Yourself a Farm,* 1845 (front). Courtesy Gerrit Smith Pamphlets and Broadsides, Special Collections Research Center, Syracuse University Libraries.

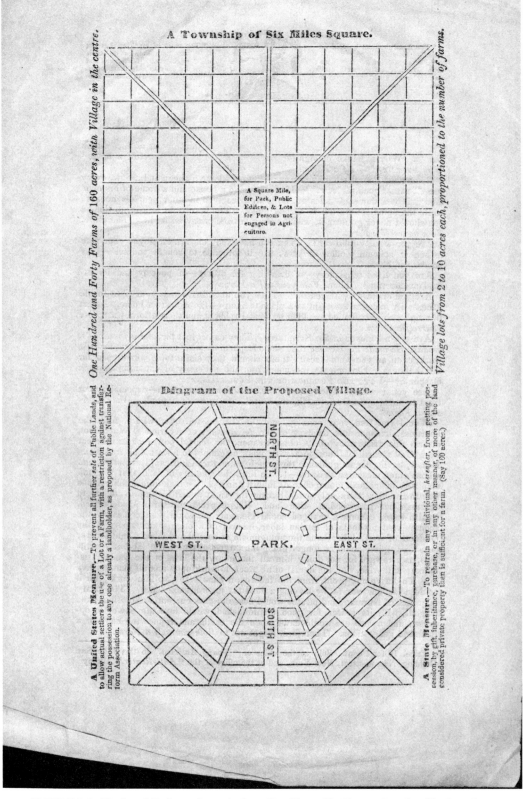

FIGURE 2.2. National Reform Association, *Vote Yourself a Farm,* 1845 (back), showing the group's republican township and village plan. Courtesy Gerrit Smith Pamphlets and Broadsides, Special Collections Research Center, Syracuse University Libraries.

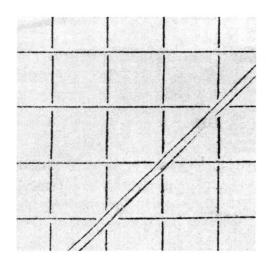

FIGURE 2.3. Detail of National Reform Association, *Vote Yourself a Farm,* 1845 (back). Courtesy Gerrit Smith Pamphlets and Broadsides, Special Collections Research Center, Syracuse University Libraries.

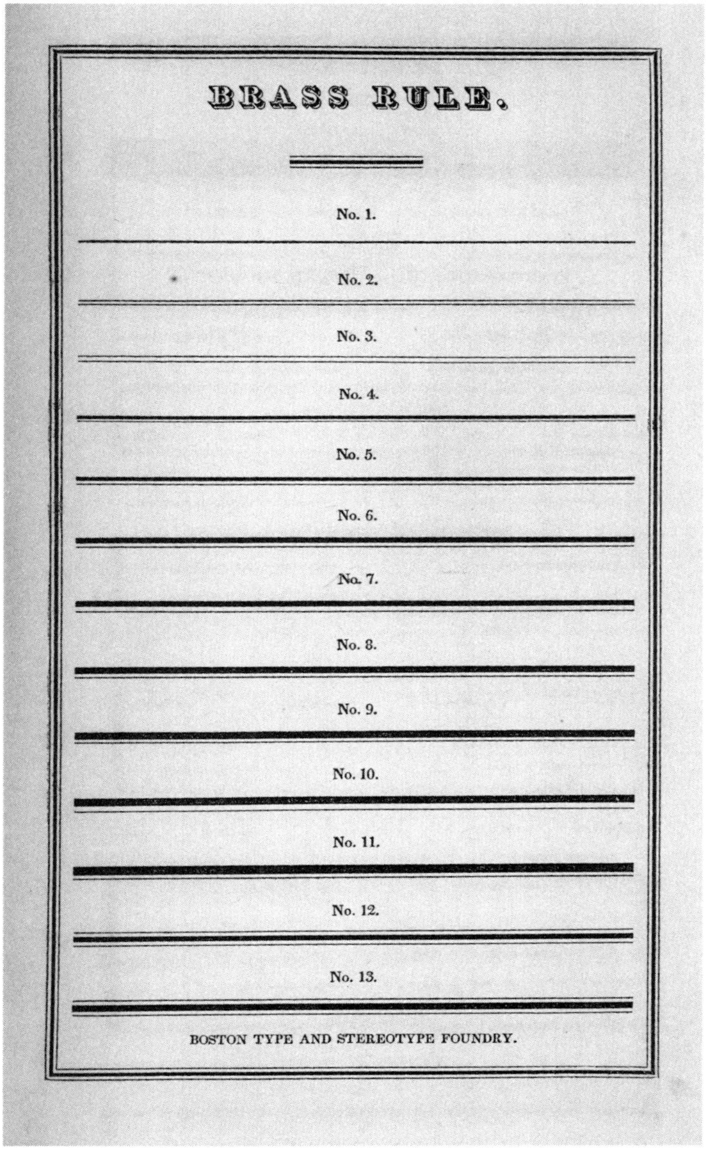

FIGURE 2.4. Sample lines printed with brass rule, used by printers to create lines. From *Specimen of Printing Types from the Boston Type & Stereotype Foundry,* 1832. Courtesy Library of Congress / Archive.org.

This fact is important when we consider the significance of the land reformers' deployment of the grid. Within the literatures of U.S. history and geography, the land survey grid has most often been portrayed as a technical instrument for converting Indigenous land into private property, for imposing Enlightenment rationality and abstraction on the land, or for advancing democratic egalitarianism. In other words, the grid (and its derivatives) can be variously read as a tool of capitalist commodification and settler colonialism, a symptom of rationality run amok, or a democratic symbol.[6] In this chapter, I draw on all of these interpretations to understand the significance of the land reformers' diagrams. At the same time, I explore another dimension of the images that has received far less attention—namely, their mobilization as visual-political rhetoric. I argue that the township and village diagrams were critical elements of the workingmen's general strategy of political "agitation" through which they sought to "address and disturb the immediate interests of men and parties."[7] If in 1785 Congress had reasoned that land first had to be surveyed in order to be sold, Masquerier cleverly reworked this conventional wisdom: "That each man and association may demand their due proportion of the earth, it must be regularly surveyed."[8] Notably, the rationale for surveying was not that it aided in delineating or distributing shares of land but that it allowed persons and collectives to "demand" their due. That is, the purpose of the grid was to facilitate a political claim. The National Reformers did little if any surveying or settling of townships. Instead, what they did was print the image of the grid, again and again, as part of an organized campaign to win supporters, with the ultimate goal of swaying their political representatives to enact new land policies. Given their circulation in both the "virtual" public sphere of print and the "actual" public space of the street, the workingmen's representations of township and village offer perhaps the earliest instance of geometric plans being deployed as part of a campaign of popular political persuasion.

Focusing on the land reformers' diagrams as forms of visual-political rhetoric allows us to expand beyond the functionalist and symbolic interpretations that have dominated scholarly interpretations of the grid as a spatial figure, whether at the scale of the territory or the city. In this chapter I home in on the political-rhetorical dimensions of the grid as a printed image—the effects it was intended or imagined to have on readers—rather than on what the grid did when it was enacted on the land, or what it meant as a symbol. Unpacking the land reformers' rhetorical use of the grid offers a more nuanced understanding of not only this particular diagram but also the visual culture of the nineteenth-century labor movement. Despite a proliferation of excellent studies on the visual representation of labor and work during this period, relatively little research has examined how workingmen themselves deployed images as part of their activism.[9] By reading the grid as part of an expanded constellation of nineteenth-century visual references and practices—a world that included emblems, geometric proofs, pedagogical grids, and maps—we gain a more complex understanding of not just *what* the land reformers' images meant but also *how* they produced those meanings. We can also begin perhaps to see the grid as a more polysemic and overdetermined symbol than it at first appears.

Labor, Land, and Equality: The Land Reform Movement

The turn to land reform marked a distinct shift in strategy in the early labor movement.[10] The late 1820s saw the birth of the first labor unions in cities like New York, Boston, and Philadelphia—a response to the upheavals brought on by the market revolution, which entailed a shift in the urban economy from an older workshop system based in small shops, skilled labor, and apprenticeship to a manufacturing economy increasingly reliant on mechanization, capitalization, and immigrant, female, and child wage workers.[11] Beginning in 1819, a series of economic "panics" and depressions led to widespread bankruptcies and unemployment, reinforcing for workingmen a sense of vulnerability to market forces beyond their control. Out of these volatile conditions emerged a number of sharp analyses and critiques of the industrial capitalist economy and of the growing concentration of wealth and inequality in U.S. society.[12] The urban laborers who advanced this new thinking adopted a strident producerist rhetoric that posited labor as the true source of wealth and decried speculators, capitalists, merchants, and other "nonproducers" who idly built wealth off the honest toil of others. In the prevailing "cursed system of splendid misery and squalid wretchedness," two of the movement's leaders pointed out, "those who produce the most are allowed to consume the least."[13] Throughout the 1830s, the unions grew stronger, organizing strikes for higher wages and the ten-hour workday, and forming a short-lived political party, the Working Men's Party.

The Panic of 1837 and subsequent severe economic depression effectively decimated this first wave of labor radicalism. George Henry Evans (1805–1856), who had been active in the Working Men's Party and as an editor and publisher of labor and free-thought newspapers, found himself mired in debt and retreated to a farm in New Jersey for several years. In 1844, he returned to New York City with a new strategy. He now saw western land, rather than higher wages or a shorter workday, as the key to remedying unjust economic relations.[14] Gathering some of his old Working Men's Party colleagues in the back of a printshop, he formed the National Reform Association to advance three main proposals: a homestead policy granting free land for the use of settlers not already possessed of land, the exclusion of land from seizure for debt (or what today we might call a ban on foreclosures), and—most controversial—a limit to the amount of land that any individual could hold. The Homestead Act passed by Congress in 1862 would codify the first of these proposals but exclude the more radical elements.

In formulating their positions, the National Reformers consciously revived two older ideas, the labor theory of property and the safety valve theory, adapting and radicalizing both for their own ends. At the core of the original colonization of the Americas as well as westward U.S. expansion was the idea that applying labor to land (by, for example, farming it) conferred a right of ownership. This labor theory of property was given systematic articulation in the seventeenth century by John Locke. In *Two Treatises of Government* (1689), Locke wrote that the earth in its original state was given to mankind in common. "In the beginning," he wrote, "All the world was

America." Men, however, could claim dominion over portions of land by applying their labor to nature and thereby "improving" it: "Whatsoever then [Man] removes out of the State that Nature hath provided, and left it in, he hath mixed his *Labour* with it, and joyned to it something that is his own, and thereby makes it his *Property*."[15] This Lockean doctrine, combined with the self-serving theory of America as terra nullius (empty land belonging to no one), was used by the English and Europeans in the seventeenth and eighteenth centuries to justify their colonization of the American continent and their disregard for Indian sovereignty. English settlers in America adopted Locke's ideas to formulate a "labor theory of empire," which posited that the costs and risks they assumed in settling a new territory gave them a "natural" right to the land, as well as political rights.[16] In the early nineteenth century, as the original colonies became more densely populated, land-hungry white speculators and settlers pressured the U.S. government into opening western land (much of it designated as Indian Territory) for purchase and settlement. To rationalize these policies, they revived the Lockean labor theory of property alongside the falsehood that Indians did not engage in sedentary farming, but rather exercised only a "precarious and transient occupancy," and therefore did not own the land.[17] In reality, the federal government, acting at the behest of settlers, was the one making Indian occupancy precarious if not impossible. Throughout the nineteenth century, the United States practiced a policy of effectively clearing Native Americans from western lands through brutal measures like the 1830 Indian Removal Act, while simultaneously transferring the land to settlers via increasingly generous land sale policies.[18] The 1841 Preemption Act, for example, granted settlers the legal right to claim a 160-acre piece of public land and later purchase it at a price of $1.25 per acre if they "improved" it by plowing or building a cabin. The labor theory of property helps explain how a group of New York workingmen came to espouse a settler colonial ideology of land. In one context, the notion of labor as the true source of value enabled them to argue for the rights of artisans and workingmen against idle capitalists. In another context, it allowed them to claim that they had a more legitimate right to land than did absentee speculators and putatively nomadic Indians.

Yet the workingmen also pushed the Lockean theory of property in more radical directions—for example, emphasizing the part of the theory that held that the earth was originally the inheritance of all. From this they extrapolated a universal "natural right" to land, drawing further inspiration from the writing of eighteenth-century thinkers such as Thomas Paine and Thomas Spence, "Ricardian socialist" economists such as John Gray, the early nineteenth-century radicals Cornelius Blatchly and Langton Byllesby, and even Native American thinkers.[19] The masthead of the *Working Man's Advocate* included a quotation from the British economist John Gray stating, "The earth is the habitation, the natural inheritance of all mankind of ages present and to come: a habitation belonging to no man in particular but to every man; and one in which *all* have an *equal* right to dwell," as well as a quotation attributed to the Sauk leader Black Hawk: "My reason teaches me that *land cannot be sold*. The Great Spirit gave it to his children to lie upon, and cultivate, as far as is necessary for their subsistence; and so long as they occupy and cultivate it, they have the right to the soil—but if they voluntarily leave it, then any other people have a right to settle upon it. Nothing can be sold, but such things as can be carried away."[20] If land was meant to be owned by no one but shared by all, then it logically followed that an individual's "right" to the land was one of usufruct (the right to use it in one's lifetime only) rather than outright ownership. Such ideas were remarkably radical for the challenge they posed to the foundations of private property ownership. In the contemporary press, the land reformers were often accused of promoting dangerously "agrarian" ideas—a term that harked back to ancient Rome and connoted the forced redistribution of landed property and, more generally, "hostility to existing property-institutions, and a determination, if possible, to subvert them."[21] In the nineteenth century, "agrarian" elicited approximately the same opprobrium that the word "socialist" inspires today.[22] While the National Reformers embraced the accusation of agrarianism and were careful to phrase their rhetoric as support for a right to the use of public land rather than outright ownership, few pursued the radical implications of their insistence on a collective inheritance to their most extreme ends. As an 1859 writer pointed out, most in the Working Men's Party did not support wholesale socialism "for the plain reason, that most workingmen were property owners themselves."[23] Notably, while the National Reformers cited Native American ideas about collective landownership, the apocryphal passage they selected from Black Hawk could also be interpreted to justify white men's occupation and "right" to the soil once the Indians had "voluntarily" left it. Thus, while they flirted with the rhetoric of collective ownership of land, in their policies the National Reformers hewed to the principles of individual use and cultivation that subtended justifications for settler colonialism.

Another eighteenth-century concept that Evans and company reworked and mobilized was the notion of the West as a safety valve for urban workers.[24] As early as 1755, Benjamin Franklin had voiced the idea that cheap western lands could help siphon off excess urban labor, keeping wages high in cities and preventing unrest. Similarly, Jefferson wrote in 1805 that the availability of western lands reduced American urban workers' risk of exploitation and degradation, especially as compared with the situation in Europe: "As yet our manufacturers are as much at their ease, as independent and moral as our agricultural inhabitants, and they will continue so as long as there are vacant lands for them to resort to; because whenever it shall be attempted by the other classes to reduce them to the minimum of subsistence, they will quit their trades and go to laboring the earth."[25] The workingmen took up the safety valve theory, but they reworked the idea for the context of an industrial market society, emphasizing not only the traditional republican ideas about the economic independence afforded by land but also the argument that urban artisans would be in a stronger negotiating position in the struggle between capital and labor if they owned land.[26] A two-part cartoon published by the land reform leader Thomas Devyr vividly illustrates the workingmen's radicalized version of the safety valve premise (Figure 2.5).[27] (Although the cartoon was not published until 1882, at the end of Devyr's career, it accurately reflects the land reformers' rhetoric in the 1840s.) Employing the classical rhetorical technique of antithesis, the cartoon contrasts two scenes. The first, depicting the world without land reform, shows a group of workers confronting a factory owner over wages. The owner insists on a pittance of a wage—eighty cents a day—which drives the workers to a variety of fates, as depicted on the left side of the image: tramping, begging, prison, and the poorhouse. Lest any readers miss the point, two figures are portrayed falling off a cliff into a chasm labeled "Eternity" with the word "suicide" hovering ominously above. In the second scene, showing a society with free homesteads, workers stand their ground against the factory owner, because behind them is the alternative: their choice of forty-acre farm tracts. The cartoon illustrates the land reformers' claim that the availability of the option of a homestead would strengthen urban workers' ability to negotiate for higher wages and thus avoid poverty, misery, and worse.

Evans's and other labor reformers' shift from their earlier trade union politics to the safety valve solution of free homesteads could be interpreted as an evasive knight's move, one that paralleled the contemporaneous shift in the English Chartist movement toward land as a solution for working-class empowerment.[28] Although the National Reformers saw their goals as practical and achievable, land reform could also be characterized as a typically utopian approach to social problems like poverty and economic injustice, symptomized by the impulse to locate the solutions to intractable problems elsewhere, in an imagined tabula rasa. As William Channing explained, in a quotation that was included in the masthead of the *Working Man's Advocate* in 1844, "The remedy I propose for the increasing pauperism of the United States, and of New York, in particular, is the location of the poor on the lands of the far west, which would not only afford permanent relief to our unhappy brethren, but would restore that self-respect and honorable principle inseparable from citizenship."[29] Like contemporary advocates of African colonization, the National Reformers proposed that the ills created by capitalism could be transferred someplace else.[30]

The problem, of course, was that the "elsewhere" that the land reformers proposed to subdivide and redistribute was not empty land but territory that the federal government and individual settlers had acquired, seized, and stolen from Native Americans in innumerable acts of legal and extralegal dispossession since the seventeenth century. The land reform movement coincided with a period of aggressive U.S. expansion that included the annexation of Texas in 1845, the acquisition of what became the Oregon Territory in 1846, and the Mexican–American War in 1848, which resulted in the conquest of California and New Mexico. Evans was critical of U.S. territorial expansion and the unfair expropriation of Indian lands. He opposed the war with Mexico and the annexation of Texas (positions that were not universally shared by his fellow land reformers), and he criticized the campaign against the Seminoles in Florida and the removal of the Cherokees from Georgia.[31] Yet the National Reformers also tended to blame the existing system of public land sales for instigating the "business of cheating or bullying the Indians out of their lands."[32] They suggested that land reform would be a panacea for the problem of white–Indian relations, arguing that eliminating land speculation—by reducing minimum lot sizes, making land free, and

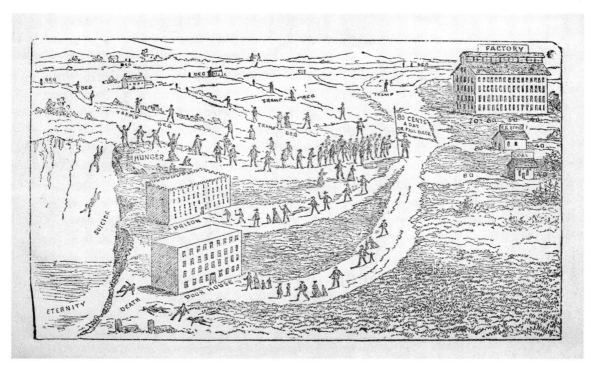

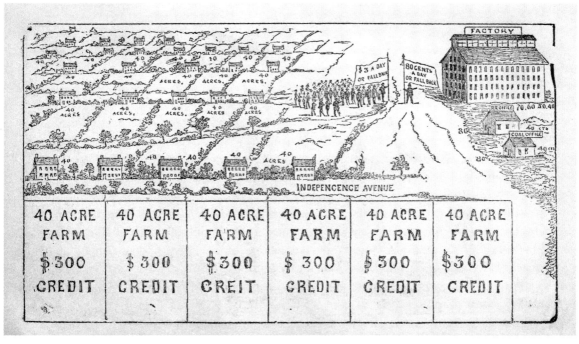

FIGURE 2.5. Two-part cartoon illustrating the workingmen's belief in free land as a safety valve for urban labor conflict. From Thomas Devyr, *The Odd Book of the Nineteenth Century,* 1882. Courtesy University of California Libraries / Archive.org.

restricting public land sales to settlers only—would curtail white demand for land. They asserted that "the strongest motives to encroachments by Whites on the rights of the Indians would be done away with by prohibiting *speculation* in land," and naively suggested that "the danger of Indian aggressions would be materially lessened if our people only took possession of land enough for their use."[33] The land reformers further argued, as Jefferson had, that Indians could choose to assimilate to the Anglo-American property regime by claiming their own homesteads along with other landless Americans. As Shelley Streeby has cogently pointed out, this fantasy of peaceful coexistence between Indians and white Americans depended on naturalizing white liberal ideas of property and assumed that Native Americans would happily be converted to farming isolated plots of land.[34] The National Reformers' rhetoric sometimes revealed deeply racist beliefs underlying their assimilationist policies. One land reformer writing in *Young America* accused the Indians along the western boundary of Missouri of "loafing upon far more than their equal portion of the soil" and argued that the National Reformers' principle of giving land only to actual settlers should apply to Indians "as well as to their loafing non-producing Anglo-Saxon brethren." The writer concluded, "If philanthropy cannot reclaim these incorrigible Indians and other non-producers by Land Reform measures, let them become extinct."[35] Such ideas underscore the fact that, while the land reformers' utopia was nominally universal, it was at core a white settler colonial project. Though the reformers often proclaimed that the right to land was possessed by men and women of all races, their proposed solution to capitalism's contradictions nevertheless rested on the past (and perhaps ongoing) transfer of Indian-inhabited lands to individual and predominantly white settlers.[36]

A Paradise of Rural Cities

Building on the safety valve ideology and the labor theory of property, the National Reformers developed a platform advocating free homesteads for actual settlers. Their organizing efforts were largely focused on advancing this platform by winning converts and petitioning Congress rather than on laying plans for a new society. On balance, the workingmen did not engage much in utopian projection, and their notions of the new farms and cities that laborers might one day settle were never more than vague sketches. In printing the diagrams of the republican township and village plans, the land reformers' stated purpose was simple: "That our readers may have a distinct idea of what these modern disciples of the Jeffersonian school are aiming at, and that they may be the better enabled to carry out in their own minds the consequences that would result from their schemes."[37]

Yet digging into the land reformers' writings reveals that at least some workingmen did have more developed ideas of what society would be like after land reform, and how the land grid and village plan would help shape civic and economic life. Lewis Masquerier, for example, the Kentucky-born, ex-Owenite printer responsible for the republican village design, envisioned a future "paradise of rural cities."[38] This oxymoronic phrase exemplifies the land reformers' paradoxical stances as urban workingmen advocating for rural settlement. The land reformers generally followed the Jeffersonian tradition in seeing the countryside as an environment of health and prosperity and the city as a site of misery and squalor, conditions that emanated from the latter's status as the seat of the capitalist economy. Evans voiced a common view when he wrote, "I am of Jefferson's opinion, that great cities are great nuisances, and that there ought to be a considerable vacant space between all houses."[39] Masquerier, too, contrasted "the independent, self-employed freemen tilling their rural farms and homes in a health-giving and odorous atmosphere and the toil-worn tenant-housed hireling of the great crammed cities, amid the putrid gases and fetid slums, obliged to subsist upon the musty articles of diet vended at the huckster's stalls."[40] However, Masquerier and his colleagues were also city-dwelling mechanics at a time when the eastern United States was undergoing rapid industrialization and urbanization. They recognized the interdependence of country and city, and of agricultural, manufacturing, and commercial pursuits, as an essential aspect of a market economy. Their plans therefore attempted to balance the rural and the urban—prefiguring later utopian schemes such as Ebenezer Howard's garden city and Frank Lloyd Wright's Broadacre City.[41]

In recalibrating the relationship of country and city, the land reformers modified the original land ordinance grid in subtle but significant ways. Believing that the original public land policy, with its large section size of 640 acres, favored speculators, the National Reformers divided their grid into quarter sections, and they anticipated further subdivisions as the population grew, down to lot sizes as small as 10 acres.[42] In advocating for land to be subdivided into smaller parcels and distributed for free to landless settlers, they were following through on Jefferson's intuition that "legislators cannot invent too many devices for subdividing property."[43] For the workingmen, a smaller grid spelled a more egalitarian society.

Another way that the land reformers attempted to balance country and city was through the introduction of a "republican village" at the center of each thirty-six-square-mile township. Represented initially as a blank square in the middle of the grid, the village was later fleshed out with its own plan: an octagon within a square, centered on a thirty-acre public space, with eight radial avenues intersecting a series of concentric streets (Figures 2.2 and 2.6). Credited to Masquerier, the design of the republican village plan at first glance seems to be related to a group of "cobweb" and "pinwheel" cities that appeared in the northwest United States during the early nineteenth century. Examples include Circleville, Ohio, laid out in 1810 by Daniel Dreisbach; Perryopolis, Pennsylvania, platted in 1814; and Marienville, Pennsylvania, planned around 1841 (Figures 2.7 and 2.8).[44] According to John Reps, these towns were vernacular versions of European Renaissance and baroque circular cities such as Palmanova and Grammichele, Italy; Christopher Wren's plan for London; and, more proximately, Pierre Charles L'Enfant's plan for Washington, D.C.[45] In the case of Circleville, which features a plan quite similar to Masquerier's, the planner took his inspiration from the circular Hopewell mounds on the site.[46] But Reps speculates that the majority of nineteenth-century American designers of cobweb-plan cities simply

70   The Visual Rhetoric of Equality

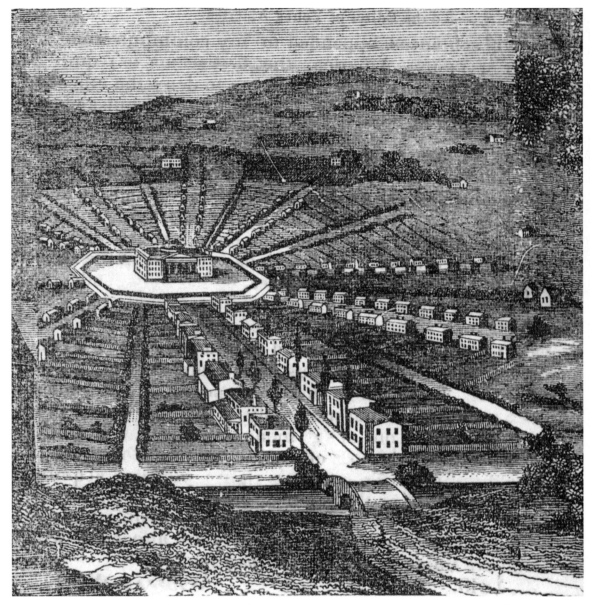

FIGURE 2.6. Aerial perspective of republican village, included with a National Reform Association petition sent to the U.S. Senate in 1852. Courtesy Center for Legislative Archives, National Archives.

wanted to "create something different from the ordinary grid pattern."[47] These plans conveyed the sense of a polity with a grander raison d'être, distinct from the typical western U.S. city platted into a rectangular grid for economy and expedience. Another precedent that Masquerier may well have seen is a plan for a home colony published by Robert Owen in 1841 featuring a square version of his New Harmony quadrangle, with a courtyard that combined radial and concentric circular walkways with winding picturesque paths (Figure 2.9).[48]

The Visual Rhetoric of Equality   71

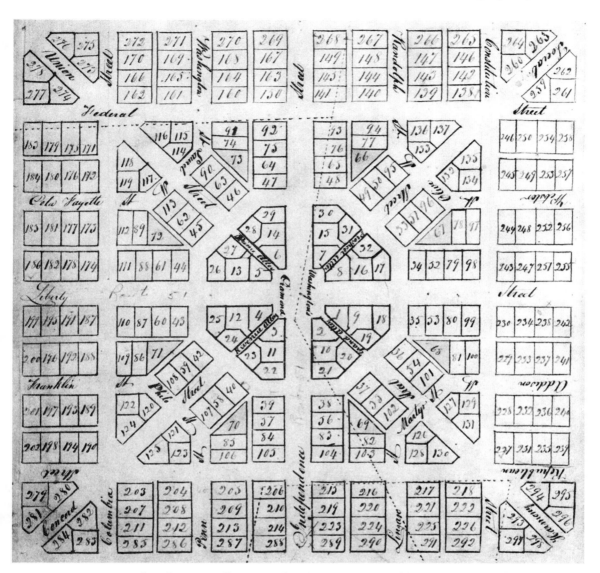

FIGURE 2.7. Plat of Perryopolis, Pennsylvania, 1814. Surveyed by William E. Griffith. Courtesy Madalyn Linderman.

Urban theorists have observed that inserting a central element into a grid introduces "hierarchies into the isotropic order of the grid," potentially undercutting its egalitarian symbolism.[49] Masquerier attempted to obviate the hierarchy of the central arrangement by making lots that were farther from the center larger, which he believed would help equalize their values.[50] But his main motivations for introducing the village were twofold. First, a village would enable a smoothly functioning economy in which agricultural and manufacturing needs would be balanced. Farmers would have markets "almost at their own doors" without having to pay "city rents," while avoiding the problems of exploitation, scarcity, and oversupply created by speculators and middlemen.[51] Masquerier specified that each National Reform village would include a

FIGURE 2.8. Bird's-eye view of Circleville, Ohio, as it was in 1836, drawn from memory in 1870 by G. W. Wittich. Courtesy Library of Congress, Geography and Map Division.

"town mart" where surplus products would be exchanged on the "equitable principle of equal time of labor for labor."[52] The labor exchange idea was likely adopted from Owen and from Masquerier's friend Josiah Warren, whose theories of "equitable commerce" are discussed in detail in chapters 5 and 6.[53] Masquerier imagined that, over time, a network of "rural cities" would predominate in the landscape, linked by diagonal roads. "City populations would diminish gradually," and rural areas would become more "compactly settled, making less roads and bridges necessary, and giving greater facilities of education."[54]

A second rationale that the land reformers cited for the central republican village was that it would promote political equality and participation. In contrast to Renaissance and baroque centralized cities, where a geometric plan was often the sign of a strong central authority, the land reformers' plan was intended to promote a vision of distributed democracy similar to Jefferson's vision of ward-republics. Masquerier explained that his "rural republican villages" would be sites where citizens could engage in face-to-face deliberations. Public amenities would be centrally located to ensure that every inhabitant was within an hour's walk from the seat of government and business, and could therefore partake equally in civic life:

> Every man can meet in Township Hall, and by direct speech and vote, declare his consent to a brief statement of all the laws proposed, and send it round to all the other Townships, so that a committee meeting at the capital may digest these briefs of laws, enacted by a majority of the townships in a State, into a well written form and send it back to the people to be confirmed, amended,

FIGURE 2.9. Robert Owen, plan of a home colony, from *A Development of the Principles and Plans on which to Establish Self-Supporting Home Colonies* [. . .], 1841.

or rejected. Thus honest legislation, for the first time in the history of man, will be done by the people themselves.[55]

Masquerier even drew up a state constitution for his proposed democratic system, one that placed the bulk of power in township assemblies composed of all citizens, with minimal roles for the judicial and executive branches.[56] This preference for local, direct governance was an inheritance of eighteenth-century republicanism, which tended to associate powerful centralized governments with corruption. The workingmen were generally hostile to the American political system, which they saw as controlled by the wealthy. "Government has always been, through all ages, the greatest scoundrel in a nation," wrote Masquerier.[57] Like most nineteenth-century reformers, the workingmen believed that the solutions to social problems lay not with the state but in individual or communitarian action. The republican village offered an alternative spatial vision of a form of governance in which decision-making power would be distributed and would flow from the bottom upward.

The Workingmen's Visual Politics

Masquerier may have envisioned a utopian future in which citizens of his octagonal republican village would walk to their local town hall and engage in democratic deliberation, but in the near term, he, like other National Reform leaders, accepted that the path to adoption of land reform policies lay in electoral and legislative campaigning. The day-to-day focus of land reform activity thus was not the settling of townships but rather the work of persuasion: penning articles and letters to editors, publishing newspapers and almanacs, handing out leaflets on street corners, holding weekly ward meetings indoors and outdoors, giving lengthy speeches, sending petitions to Congress, and even engaging in the occasional agitprop. In 1846, Masquerier suggested following the example of the English Chartists and submitting to Congress a "mammoth petition," so large it could "barely [be] rolled through the door of the Capitol."[58] The workingmen's campaign tactics included an attention to the visual that encompassed the space of the street. In April 1844, for example, a supporter produced a "transparency" (probably something like a magic lantern slide) of the masthead of the *Working Man's Advocate* and brought it to a National Reform Association meeting in the Third Ward. In addition to the masthead's usual drawing of a man sitting atop the globe, the transparency included the slogan "Freedom of the Public Land" at the top and the notice "The National Reformers meet here this evening" at the bottom. The transparency reportedly "attracted a numerous crowd of admirers and gave *fits* to two or three land speculators who happened to be passing by."[59] The workingmen's images participated in a vibrant activist culture that played out on the streets and in public lecture halls, at indoor and outdoor meetings, conventions, banquets, public demonstrations, and even infiltrations of hostile spaces such as middle-class parks or rival groups' meetings.[60]

The printed images of grid and octagon must be understood as part of this broader visual politics. The National Reformers' initial motivation for using illustrations was undoubtedly the same as that of the many newspaper editors and pamphleteers in the period who began to incorporate pictures in their publications: the simple desire to capture readers' attention. An advertisement for the *Vote Yourself a Farm* pamphlet printed in the *National Reform Almanac for 1849* shows that it was priced at twenty cents for a hundred. The ad describes the pamphlet as containing "diagrams" and as a "pithy production . . . suitable for distributing gratuitously on steamboats and at public meetings, and well calculated to induce people to think on their right to the soil when they would otherwise be thinking of far less important measures."[61] Pictures were selling points, intended to capture the attention of unsuspecting ship passengers and people preoccupied with their daily lives or in a "state of distraction." Illustrations integrated into cheap printed matter were still something of a novelty. As was typical of newspapers of the time, the vast majority of issues of the *Working Man's Advocate* and *Young America* featured few if any illustrations apart from the occasional tiny cut. To provide graphic interest, early nineteenth-century editors and printers frequently resorted to typographic devices such as display (or fat-face) fonts; small cuts of pointing fingers, ships, stagecoaches, and runaway slaves; and iteration copy (repetition of the same phrase multiple times for graphic effect).[62] The township grid was just such a typographically constructed image, deploying the ready tools of print to stand out from the dense columns of tiny type. The tactic apparently was effective. The township diagram was frequently reprinted, not only in the movement's own literature but also in other newspapers; on occasion, readers even requested that it be republished.[63]

The land reformers hoped that the township and village diagrams would do more than just draw attention, however. They anticipated that the images would allow readers "to carry out in their own minds the consequences that would result from their schemes." But just how would this visual inducement to imagination occur, especially considering the reductive, matter-of-fact quality of the diagrams? Answering this question requires reading the images in their historical visual-cultural contexts, the universe of representational and signifying practices in which they circulated. It requires understanding the diagrams' relations to at least four contemporaneous types of representation—emblems, proofs, maps, and systems—each of which offered a distinct political affect to the grid and village plans.

The Grid as Emblem

When the image of the township grid first appeared in the *Working Man's Advocate* in March 1844, it was buried on the second page, sandwiched within a narrow column of type, about three inches wide. But as the township grid became a recurring feature in the newspaper, it gained prominence: it seems that the land reformers over time experimented with the rhetorical power of the image and how to wield it. In July, it appeared on the front page, just below an illustrated masthead, next to a portrait of Jefferson surmounted by a halo of clouds and stars (Figure 1.1). The appearance of the republican township grid side by side with the portrait of Jefferson not only underscores the land reformers' calculated adoption of Jefferson as a predecessor but also highlights how they deployed the grid alongside, and in relation to, other kinds of visual-cultural forms. The inclusion of Jefferson's portrait, for example, reflects the continuing prominence of public portraiture and physiognomy in American culture. From the late eighteenth to the early nineteenth century, portraits and busts of "great men," public portrait galleries, silhouettes, and wax figures proliferated in American visual culture. Portrait representations were thought to communicate exemplary character and civic virtue, attributes that would rub off on viewers.[64] The

FIGURE 2.10. Benjamin Franklin, *Join or Die*, political cartoon exhorting the British colonists in America to unite together against the French and their Indigenous allies. Published in the *Pennsylvania Gazette*, May 9, 1754. Courtesy Library of Congress.

juxtaposition of the grid and Jefferson's portrait seems to have been calculated to lend some of the prestige of the latter to the land reformers' plan.

Yet there is more to the apposition of these images than a bid for endorsement by association. Looking more closely at Jefferson's portrait, we can recognize that it takes the form of an emblem, and that it appears below another emblem, the newspaper's masthead.[65] A genre of representation originating in the sixteenth century, emblems were traditionally defined as having three parts that together represented a complex idea: an enigmatic image *(pictura),* a motto *(inscriptio),* and an epigram *(subscriptio).*[66] In the *Working Man's Advocate,* the juxtaposition of Jefferson's haloed portrait, the words "all men are created equal" in script, and the motto "Si Monumentum quaeris, circumspice" (His country is his monument) conforms to this definition. By the late eighteenth century, the descendants of emblems included political cartoons such as Franklin's engraving of a snake cut into several parts, accompanied by the words "Join, or Die" (Figure 2.10).[67] Emblems—now more loosely defined as symbolic pictures representing abstract concepts, with or without accompanying text—proliferated in the early republic in the form of liberty trees and poles, eagles, and bells, as well as in transatlantic artisan and labor culture. In the 1820s, the New York City–based General Trades' Union, following the practice of British trade unions, revived the image of the arm and hammer in its literature and banners (Figure 2.11).[68] The masthead of the *Working Man's Advocate* was also an emblem. It featured an image of an unclothed man sitting atop the globe, with one hand pointed down toward the sphere below and the other upraised, holding a banner reading "For me, for thee, for all" (Figure 2.12). The image conveyed that the earth "belonged" to all human beings equally and that every man could be a "master" of the globe and its resources.

By the nineteenth century, such emblems thus came to function as political symbols that drew "imagined communities" together.[69] They were identifiable and familiar icons around which semianonymous audiences gathered and to which they

The Visual Rhetoric of Equality 77

FIGURE 2.11. Arm and hammer emblem, published in the New York General Trades' Union newspaper *The Union,* 1836.

FIGURE 2.12. Detail, masthead for the *Working Man's Advocate,* 1844. Courtesy American Antiquarian Society.

attached emotions—belonging, pride, belief in shared goals or values. Bucking the conventional association of pictures with greater clarity than words could provide, emblems made for effective political symbols precisely because their meanings were simultaneously enigmatic and definite. As E. H. Gombrich observes in discussing the visual icons of the French Revolution, a "penumbra of vagueness" surrounds the most successful symbols.[70] At the same time, to perform effectively as political rhetoric in the context of a mass democracy, such images had to be much more widely legible than their early modern predecessors.[71] Emblem-logos like the masthead of the *Working Man's Advocate* and the grid had to enable expedient delivery of messages

FIGURE 2.13. Detail, new masthead for *Young America*, introduced in July 1847. Courtesy American Antiquarian Society.

that were still vague enough to draw together communities of viewers whose precise individual viewpoints might differ.

We can witness how the National Reformers calibrated this combination of ambiguous and precise signification in the evolution of their newspaper's masthead. In the original version, the figure on the globe was discernibly white and male, yet his nudity evoked the Enlightenment tropes of the state of nature and "universal man." In July 1847, the newspaper introduced a new version in which a man, now clothed in short jacket and trousers, stood atop the globe holding a shovel (Figure 2.13). The editors explained that the woodcut of this new image had been left anonymously at the newspaper's office with a note suggesting that it replace the old illustration. The editors expressed their appreciation for the contribution, adding, "The original design was to show that man in a state of nature had an equal and universal right to the soil. The demonstration of that proposition our artist thinks, no doubt, is henceforth superfluous, and he designs to show that the right is inalienable, and that a civilization that does not secure it as such is no longer to be tolerated."[72] In the shift from the nude to the clothed figure, the allegorical scope of the image was significantly narrowed. No longer did it depict "universal man" claiming an "equal right to the soil." Now it clearly portrayed a mid-nineteenth-century white American working- or middle-class man taking aim at a particular polity (the United States) that had not granted him his "inalienable" right. Moreover, rather than sitting atop a globe, the new figurehead now stood holding a shovel inserted into the globe—a reference to the workingmen's self-serving subscription to the labor theory of property, which held that "improving" or cultivating a piece of land conferred the right of possession. The new masthead thus projected a shift in ideology from Enlightenment universalism to a more specific liberal rhetoric centered on the rights of particular individuals in a particular place.[73]

If the workingmen's masthead conveyed a tension between Enlightenment universalism and liberal individualism, then the same could be said of the grid as political emblem. It embodied the contradictory meanings inherited from Jefferson's time, tensions that persisted within the workingmen's rhetoric. While some readers could look upon it and see a symbol of egalitarianism, others could interpret it as an icon of individual white settlers' putative right to a private plot of land. The emblem held these tensions momentarily in abeyance by presenting a single, succinct, and coherent image around which people of varying viewpoints could gather.

The Grid as Proof

As an emblem, the workingmen's grid conjured unity through a calculated mixture of ambiguity and clarity. But read in another context, the grid could be interpreted as presenting a different epistemological affect: that of conveying absolute certainty or proof. As we saw in chapter 1, geometric diagrams had long been associated with mathematical ratiocination and demonstration. In the eighteenth century, the geometric proof was considered the apex of rationality and truth, such that philosophers and statesmen often referred to it when they wanted to assert the incontrovertibility or "self-evidence" of their (often not at all self-evident) points. In the context of fractious debates over the drafting and passage of the Constitution, for example, both Federalists and Anti-Federalists fretted about the limits of language for conveying clearly what the document intended. "Where is the man who can see through the constitution to its effects?" one Anti-Federalist wrote. "The constitution of a wise and free people, ought to be as evident to simple reason, as the letters of our alphabet."[74] To address these anxieties about language, writers such as James Madison sometimes resorted to mathematical metaphors, dropping references to Euclid and Newton in their attempts to convince readers of their points.[75] Madison was even mocked by one critic for attempting to explain the meaning of the Constitution "by MATHEMATICAL demonstration, and . . . to prove its *right angular* construction." His next recourse, the writer opined, would be to "CONIC SECTIONS, by which he will be enabled . . . to discover the *many windings* of his favorite system."[76]

This association of mathematical diagrams with proof and reason continued in the nineteenth century. Influential educational reformers such as the Swiss pedagogue Johann Heinrich Pestalozzi argued that learning is most effectively accomplished through firsthand experience of objects or, when direct contact is not possible, through visual illustrations and diagrams. Pestalozzi proposed a series of gridded diagrams for teaching arithmetic to children (Figure 2.14). The transcendentalist educational reformer Elizabeth Palmer Peabody also advocated the use of colored grids as mnemonic devices for learning history (Figure I.7).[77] According to Peabody, the key to retention is "placing" facts within an orderly spatial matrix—a need well served by the regular form of the grid.

Given the grid's promotion in reform schoolbooks as an effective way to organize, show, and transmit information, perhaps it was only a matter of time before it appeared in a political manifesto. One example that is especially relevant to the land

FIGURE 2.14. Pestalozzian mathematical diagram. From Joseph Neef, *Sketch of a Plan of Education*, 1808.

reformers' grid, and that would certainly have been known to them, comes from the labor radical Thomas Skidmore's 1829 book *The Rights of Man to Property!* Born into a poor Connecticut family in 1790, Skidmore had been a prominent voice in the Working Men's Party. He and Evans were rivals for control of the party in 1829, with Skidmore leading a more radical faction.[78] Like many of the subjects in this study, Skidmore was a self-taught tinkerer and machinist who experimented with papermaking, gunpowder production, telescopes, and the reform of society. In *The Rights of Man to Property!* he condemned the contemporary distribution of wealth in society because it originated in innumerable acts of theft and dispossession. "No man has any just and true title to any possessions at all . . . they are in fact, possessions growing out of injustice, perpetrated by all governments, from time immemorial."[79] Because these original illegitimate seizures (what Marx called "primitive accumulations") were compounded generation after generation through inheritance, Skidmore concluded that the contemporary distribution of landed property was unlawful. Accordingly, he argued that all possessions should be transferred to the state and then reapportioned equally to all adult citizens in a new "general division." Individuals could subsequently augment their allotments in their lifetimes through labor, but upon death their property would revert to the state. In conceiving of land as a collective resource, Skidmore pushed the principles of communal ownership of property and usufruct to their logical and most extreme conclusion, something that most later land reformers avoided. At least one historian has called *The Rights of Man to Property!* "the most thoroughgoing 'agrarian' tract ever produced by an American."[80]

To prove the unfairness of the existing system of property distribution and inheritance, Skidmore resorted to a thought experiment that he illustrated with three diagrams (Figure 2.15). The first took the form of a large square representing "the surface of the globe"; this, he explained, corresponded to an original state in which all property was "one wide common; a wilderness" that "belongs to all equally." "Let this undivided common be represented by the following diagram, in the shape of a square, since shape is immaterial, denoted by the letters, A, B, C, D."[81] He then presented a second square, subdivided into one hundred equal squares, evincing an alternative "original and primary" condition in which property was divided equally. Under such circumstances, Skidmore held, the majority could collectively decide how to distribute the land and under what terms it should be held. Toward the end of the tract, he included a third and final square diagram, divided into four unequal portions. In this scenario, he explained, the owners of larger tracts would be able to collect rents from their properties, accumulating wealth unfairly. He reasoned that all such accumulation and subsequent transfers of real estate, whether through sale or inheritance, were invalid. This scenario, he added, resembled the unfair colonial-era distribution of land in New York State.[82] Thus, the first square showed property as it was theoretically conceived by Locke and others, the second showed Skidmore's radical egalitarian system, and the third was a diagram of unequal property relations as they existed.

Skidmore explained his reasons for including these geometric images by referring to the association between mathematics and proof: "Conclusive, against the propriety or justice of the power of making wills, as this [verbal] train of reasoning will probably appear to the candid reader, the subject is still capable of a *more rigid, and, as it were, a mathematical mode of treatment; such that no man, after having understood it, can possibly have a moment's hesitation in renouncing it forever.*"[83] In optimistically asserting that the grid diagrams would furnish sure proof, doing away with any hesitation viewers might have about his radical proposal to collectivize and redistribute property, Skidmore was drawing on the long association between mathematics and epistemological certainty. Richard Whately, author of popular nineteenth-century treatises on

logic and rhetoric, offered this explanation for why mathematical proofs furnished such compelling models for logic: "In the longest demonstration, the Mathematical teacher seems only to lead us to make use of our own stores, and point out to us how much we had already admitted." Similarly, "in the case of many Ethical propositions, we assent at first hearing, though perhaps we had never heard or thought of the proposition before."[84] In other words, such arguments produced quick agreement because they built on listeners' or readers' existing beliefs or already accepted premises. By including literal geometric diagrams, Skidmore was not so much engaging in actual deductive reasoning as he was deploying a rhetorical technique, playing to his readers' associations of gridded diagrams with demonstrative geometric and pedagogical images, as well as reinforcing their view of themselves as subjects capable of ratiocination.

Skidmore presented his diagrams as a form of proof. But they did something else—a task that is both challenging and critical for all social movements: they trans-

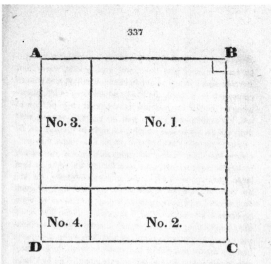

FIGURE 2.15. Diagrams illustrating three different property arrangements: an undivided common, equally divided, and unequally divided. From Thomas Skidmore, *The Rights of Man to Property!*, 1829. Courtesy Library of Congress / Archive.org.

formed concepts as inherently abstract as economic inequality and property into concrete images. They made social abstractions tangible. In a simple graphic form, the three grids allowed readers to picture the disposition of property as it was, as it is, and as it should be. Pier Vittorio Aureli has observed that a territorial grid is never simply a form; it is "an abstraction of social relationships as property relationships," a point that Skidmore's diagrams manifest perfectly.[85] By adopting the highly abridged language of the geometric diagram, Skidmore offered early nineteenth-century Americans a tangible way to glimpse social relationships, to *see* inequality, as well as equality, and furthermore to regard both the diagnosis and the solution as self-evident. Fifteen years later, when the National Reformers revived the figure of the grid in calling for their own redistributive scheme (albeit one less radical than Skidmore's), that figure, in addition to carrying residual associations with proof and with propositions that only had to be seen to be embraced, furnished a concrete image of egalitarianism.

The Grid as Geographic System

Beyond performing as emblems and proofs, the National Reformers' township and village diagrams were related to a third kind of visual figure: the geodetic grid of modern European geography. Like many nineteenth-century Americans, Masquerier, the land reformer who devised the octagonal republican village plan, had an avid interest in geography.[86] In 1847, he published a twelve-page pamphlet titled *A Scientific Division and Nomenclature of the Earth, and Particularly the Territory of the United States into States, Counties, Townships, Farms and Lots; for Promoting the Equality, Individuality, and Inalienableness of Man's Right to Sovereignty, Life, Labor and Domain, While at the Same Time It Constitutes a Scientific Geography of the Earth: Also a Constitution for Nebrashevil or Any Other State.* This remarkable tract makes clear that the township and village were synecdoches for a comprehensive proposal to rationalize and reorder the globe using the grid as a fundamental organizing structure. Extending the logic of the Land Ordinance of 1785 beyond the boundaries of the United States, Masquerier proposed dividing the entire earth into 380 square states, each exactly 7 degrees high and 7 degrees wide. These would be subdivided into counties, each 18 miles square and containing nine townships, themselves subdivided into 160-acre farmsteads. A republican village would be at the center of each township (Figure 2.16).[87] Thus, the entire earth would be organized into a series of recursively nested squares. As part of his geography, Masquerier also invented a "scientific" system for naming the states, counties, and villages. Perhaps taking a cue from the Linnaean system of binomial nomenclature for organisms and plants, Masquerier's system entailed selecting the name of a prominent object in a state (the majority of his examples were Indigenous toponyms and terms), cutting off the last syllable, and appending, according to a fixed rule set, two suffixes (derived primarily from French, Spanish, Latin, and Anglo-Saxon terms for towns and numbers). Within each state, counties would be named according to a system that transposed their numerical order, starting with the southeast corner, into letters.[88] For example, the first state west of Missouri would be named Nebrashevil, after Nebraska (the Siouan name for the Platte River), and its first county Wuwushe (the syllable "wu" deriving from "one"), followed by Wutushe, and ending with Twetweshe.[89] Within each county, townships would be named according to their geographical locations: Norwestownship, Northtownship, Noreastownship, and so on. Masquerier illustrated his plan with a series of gridded diagrams at scales from the continental to the county level (Figures 2.17 and 2.18).

Masquerier believed that developing a clear system of land division and naming would obviate some of the conflicts common in the process of settlement. By setting out county and township boundaries, locations, and names methodically and transparently in advance, the system would "cut off all that speculation and dissention in settling county boundaries and seats so prevalent in new states."[90] In a sense this was simply an extension of the rationale for the original rectilinear survey system. Congress had believed a transparent system would help clarify land titles, avoid the chaos engendered by colonial-era land disputes, and provide a lucid framework for

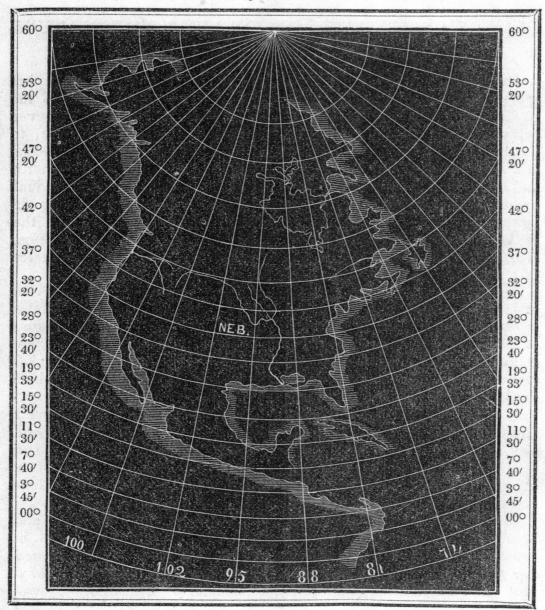

FIGURE 2.16. Image of scientifically gridded globe. From Lewis Masquerier, *A Scientific Division and Nomenclature of the Earth* [...], 1847. Courtesy Rare Book and Manuscript Library, Columbia Seligman 1847A M38.

Specimen of a scientific Geography of names of the Shires and Villes for the south east fourth of the proposed State of Nebrashevil, embracing the Platte and Kanzas river vallies.

Teteshe,	Tenishe	Teatshe	Teseshe	Tesishe	Tefishe	Tefoshe	Tethreshe	Tetushe	Tewushe
TETEVILÓPOLIS	Tenivil	Teatvil	Tesevil,	Tesivil	Tefivi.	Tefovil	Tethrevil	Tetuvil	Tewuvil,
Niteshe	Ninishe	Niatshe	Niseshe	Nisishe	Nifishe	Nifoshe	Nithreshe	Nitushe	Niwushe
Nitevil.	Ninivil	Niatvil,	Nisevil,	Nisivil,	Nifivil,	Nifovil,	Nithrevil	Nituvil,	Niwuvil,
Atteshe	Atnishe	Atatshe	Atseshe	Atsishe	Atfishe	Atfoshe	Atthreshe	Attushe	Atwushe
Attevil,	Atnivil,	Atatvil,	Atsevil,	Atsivil,	Atfivil,	Atfovil,	Atthrevil	Attuvil,	Atwuvil,
Seteshe	Senishe	Seatshe	Seseshe	Sesishe	Sefishe	Sefoshe	Sethreshe	Setushe	Sewushe
Setevil	Senivil.	Seatvil	Sesevil.	Sesivil,	Sefivil	Sefovil	Sethrevil	Setuvil,	Sewuvil,
Siteshe	Sinishe	Siatshe	Siseshe	Sisishe	Sifishe	Sifoshe	Sithreshe	Situshe	Siwushe
Sitevil,	Sinivil	Siatvil,	Sisevil,	Sisivil,	Sifivil.	Sifovil,	Sithrevil,	Situvil,	Siwuvil,
Fiteshe	Finishe	Fiatshe	Fiseshe	Fisishe	Fifishe	Fifoshe	Fithreshe	Fitushe	Fiwushe
Fitevil,	Finivil,	Fiatvil,	Fisevil,	Fisivil,	Fifivil,	Fifovil,	Fithrevil.	Fituvil,	Fiwuvil,
Foteshe	Fonishe	Foatshe	Foseshe	Fosishe	Fofishe	Fofoshe	Fothreshe	Fotushe	Fowushe
Fotevil.	Fonivil.	Foatvil.	Fosevil,	Fosivil.	Fofivil,	Fofovil	Fothrevil,	Fotuvil,	Fowuvil,
Th'teshe	Th'nishe	Th'atshe	Th's'sh'	Th'sish'	Th'fish	Th'fosh'	Th'th'she	Th'tushe	Threwushe
Th'etevil	Thr'nivil	Th'atvil	Th'sevil	Th'sivi	Th'fivil,	Thefovil	Thr'th'vil	Thr'tuvil	Threwuvil
Tuteshe	Tunishe	Tuatshe	Tuseshe	Tusishe	Tufishe	Tufoshe	T'thr'she	Tutushe	Tuwushe
Tutevil,	Tunivil,	Tuatvil	Tusevil,	Tusivil,	Tufivil.	Tufovil.	Tuthrevil	Tutuvil,	Tuwuvil,
Wuteshe	Wunish'	Wuatsh	Wusesh	Wusish	Wufish	Wutosh	Wuth'she	Wutushe	Wuwushe
Wutevil,	Wunivil,	Wuatvil	Wusevil	Wusivil	Wufivil	Wufovil	Wuthr'vil	Wutuvil,	Wuwuvil,

FIGURE 2.17. System for dividing and naming shires and villes within the hypothetical state of Nebrashevil. From Lewis Masquerier, *A Scientific Division and Nomenclature of the Earth* [. . .], 1847. Courtesy Rare Book and Manuscript Library, Columbia Seligman 1847A M38.

the expansion of the republic. Masquerier's belief that a clear and logical system could prevent political conflict reflected an assumption shared by many reformers of his generation: that political problems frequently stemmed from verbal misunderstandings and the ambiguity of language, such as disputes over the textual descriptions common in colonial plats or the names of new cities. This belief in the linguistic origins of political conflict gave rise to a vigorous language and spelling reform movement beginning in the late eighteenth century. Like several of the geometric utopians discussed in this book, Masquerier himself developed a simplified alphabet that he hoped would make literacy more widely accessible and would facilitate communica-

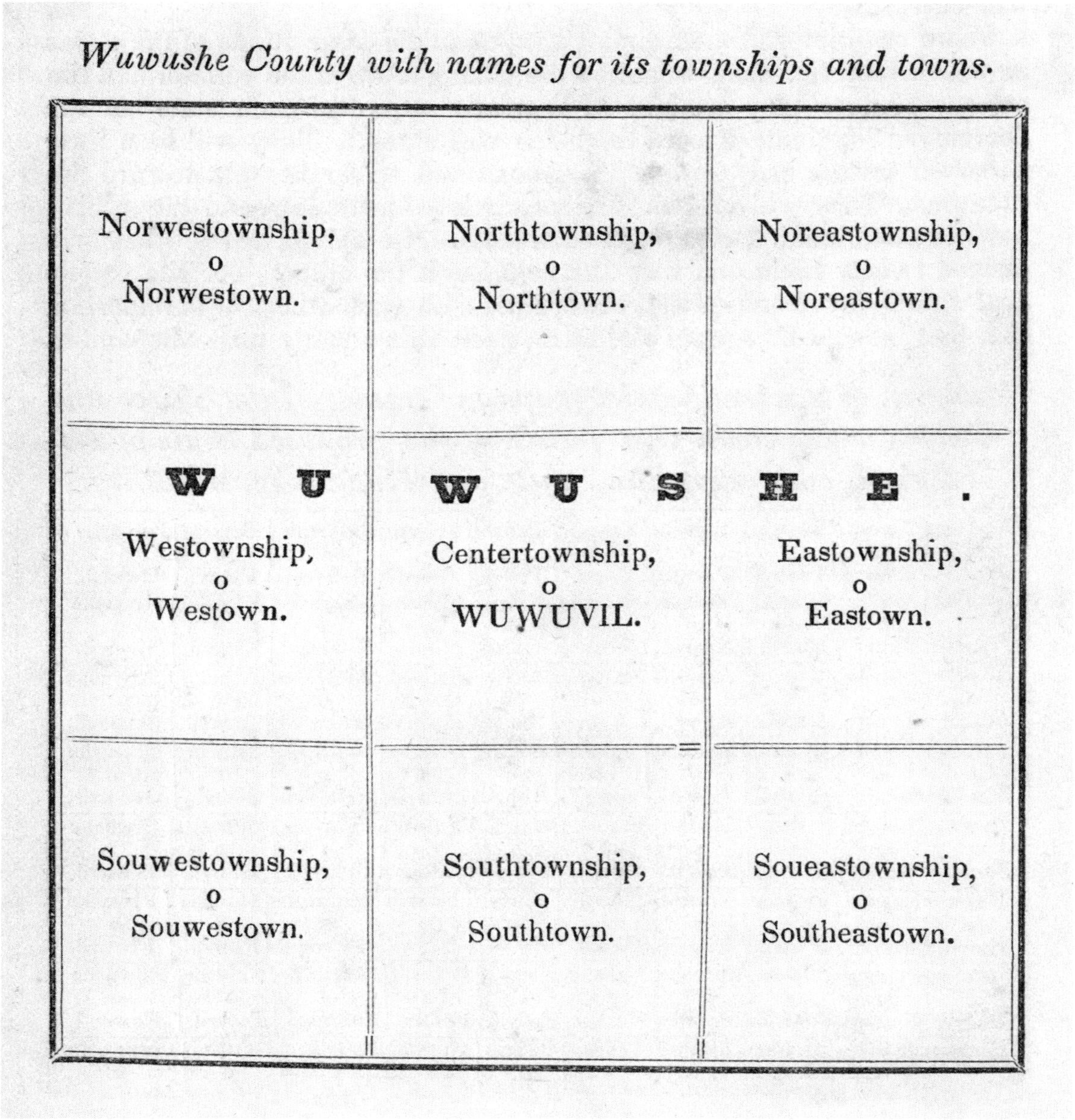

Wuwushe County with names for its townships and towns.

Norwestownship, o Norwestown.	Northtownship, o Northtown.	Noreastownship, o Noreastown.
W U Westownship, o Westown.	**W U S H E .** Centertownship, o WUWUVIL.	Eastownship, o Eastown.
Souwestownship, o Souwestown.	Southtownship, o Southtown.	Soueastownship, o Southeastown.

FIGURE 2.18. System for naming townships in a hypothetical county. From Lewis Masquerier, *A Scientific Division and Nomenclature of the Earth* [. . .], 1847. Courtesy Rare Book and Manuscript Library, Columbia Seligman 1847A M38.

tion between individuals of different nations.[91] Certain of its value, not only to his own generation but also to future ones, he even had this reformed alphabet engraved on his tombstone (Figure 2.19). I address the relationship of geometric utopianism to semiotic utopianism at greater length in chapter 5. For now, I merely wish to point out the convergence of impulses toward overhauling all kinds of structural systems—of

FIGURE 2.19. Reformed alphabet engraved on Lewis Masquerier's tombstone in the Cypress Hill Cemetery, Brooklyn, New York. Photograph by author.

language, of geography, of urban organization—that was an undercurrent of early nineteenth-century radical reform.

Masquerier's "scientific geography" betrayed an Enlightenment zeal for abstract systems and order that made Jefferson's land ordinance plan appear modest. Like the earlier survey system, the Brooklyn printer's proposed geographic organization ignored natural topography, watersheds, existing political boundaries, and human settlement patterns. But it went further, treating land not just as terra incognita or tabula rasa but as a blank page imprinted with lines and letters.[92] Untethered from the physical earth and from those who inhabited it, the gridded map became an abstraction, a world rendered cognizable simply through the setting of some lines and type on a page.

That historians of imperialism and geography regard maps and grids as twin tools of colonial conquest has become a commonplace. "As much as guns and warships, maps have been weapons of imperialism," J. B. Harley writes.[93] So, too, the grid as planning device has been deployed by settler colonizers from the Romans to the Spanish, reaching its largest-scale application with the U.S. government's surveying of the entire western half of the nation into squares as part of the process of transferring Indigenous land to white settlers. Masquerier's proposal for a scientific geography is also susceptible to this imperial critique. His system would have completely obliterated Indigenous patterns of land tenure and sovereignty while also overwriting Indigenous place-names with new toponyms.[94] Masquerier's imperialism, however, was less that of a jingoistic expansionist than that of a myopic Enlightenment universalist. His pamphlet included a conic projection map of North America with no national boundaries—just a continental outline with a few major rivers indicated, all overlaid by a net of longitude and latitude lines. On the one hand, we can read this image as affirming U.S. hemispheric territorial ambitions in light of the Monroe Doctrine and the recent Mexican–American War. (In the text Masquerier suggested that all the unsettled public lands of the United States and Mexico should be surveyed, and that this would soon lead to the addition of fifteen new states to the union.) On the other hand, given his avowed preference for local government, Masquerier may have imagined a distant future in which the scale of the nation-state would be bypassed entirely in favor of a new world order based primarily in states and their subdivisions. The overall keynote of Masquerier's plan was less American aggrandizement than the goal of guaranteeing the putatively universal rights of all human beings. "Let them invite every landless American, Mexican, Indian, White or Black Slave throughout the earth to claim his right to an equal, individual and inalienable homestead upon these lands," he wrote.[95] All were nominally welcome in this "new civilization" in the "era of equality," so long as they agreed to take up a square plot within Masquerier's compulsively gridded world. Yet, as discussed above, this rhetorical universalism obscured assimilationist violence and a fundamental disregard for Indigenous sovereignty. Masquerier's imagined blank page was in fact land already inhabited by Indigenous people and the terrain of much violence and struggle that even the most rational cartography could not resolve.

The Diagram of Society

Masquerier's obsession with reforming the conventions of spelling and geography was symptomatic of a broader characteristic of nineteenth-century utopianism and reform: a belief that social reform must be systematic and structural, because society itself was a complex but decipherable system. The 1828 edition of Noah Webster's *American Dictionary of the English Language* defined "system" as an "assemblage of things adjusted into a regular whole; or a whole plan or scheme consisting of many parts connected in such a manner as to create a chain of mutual dependencies." Just as the orbits of disparate planets were governed by universal laws of gravitation, so, too, reformers approached society as a system with rules of operation. The origins of these ideas lay in the work of late Enlightenment thinkers such as the Marquis de Condorcet and Jeremy Bentham, who sought to apply the principles of Newtonian science to ethics and social reform. These social philosophers looked for the root causes of poverty, crime, and inequality and developed institutions and programs for individual and social transformation.[96] Nineteenth-century European utopians such as Charles Fourier, Robert Owen, and Henri de Saint-Simon continued these efforts to understand and reshape what Owen called the "system of society." Opposing the dominant view that poverty was the result of individual moral failings, Owen coined what would become a kind of mantra of nineteenth-century reform: "The character of man is formed for him, and not by him."[97] This idea lay at the crux of reformers' belief that human behavior was molded by larger social forces and institutions that could be reshaped and improved. Owen and his followers codified his doctrine of the social determinants of an individual's character (including forces such as parents, educators, religion, class, profession, and institutions of poverty) in a concentric circular figure resembling a Copernican diagram of a heliocentric solar system (Figure 2.20). Masquerier subscribed wholeheartedly to the Owenite view of human nature and social-environmental determinism, as his writings from the 1830s and 1840s make clear.[98] Like several other geometric utopians, he saw society's present operations as determined by explicable external causes. One only had to be able to see and understand the system to diagnose its ills and prescribe a solution, which would inevitably take the form of a new and better system. In his book *Sociology,* Masquerier presented an entire classificatory schema for "rights" and "wrongs," modeled on natural philosophy and divided into orders, genera, and species. Correctly schematizing human beings' natural rights and social evils was a first step to effecting remedies. This systemic orientation toward reform explains why historians of sociology have sometimes cited Masquerier, along with Warren, Owen, and Fourier, as a pioneer of the discipline. Indeed, the origins of modern social science are inseparable from nineteenth-century utopianism.[99]

In trying to develop a "science of society," reformers like Owen and Masquerier borrowed not just the language and classificatory logics of natural science but also some of its representational methods, including diagrams of various forms. Diagrams, with their capacity to illustrate relationships among multiple entities, were especially well suited for representing systems, whether natural/physical or social. Rather than

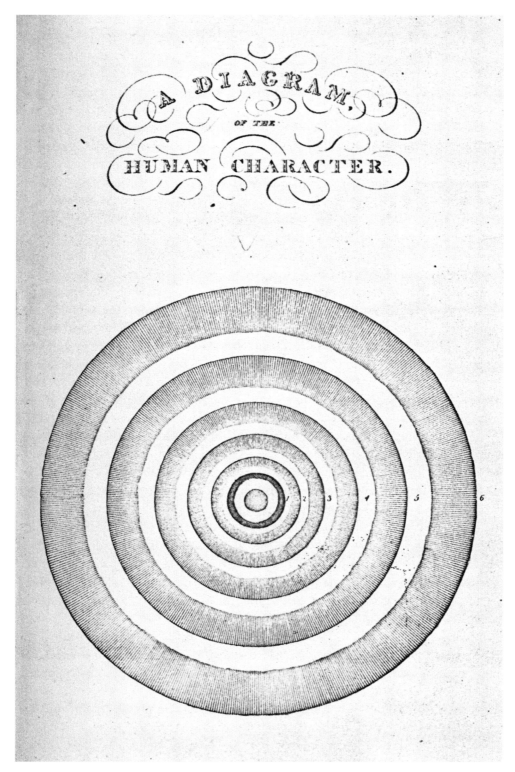

FIGURE 2.20. Circular diagram showing the social determinants of individual character. The innermost ring represents the influence of childhood circumstances, including parents; the second ring represents the influence of schooling; the third, religion; the fourth, class; and so on. From *A Diagram Illustrative of the Formation of the Human Character Suggested by Mr. Owen's Development of a New View of Society*, 1824. Courtesy University of Wisconsin–Madison Libraries.

portraying systems as hopelessly complex, diagrams suggested clear connections and possible solutions to problems in need of correction. Masquerier's diagrams of geographic division and the National Reformers' township and village plans operated similarly. By nesting individual lots within a village plan, which was nested within the township grid, which was nested within a county grid, and so on up to the scale of the planet, these diagrams suggested that individual freedoms and needs would be guaranteed within a transparent and orderly social framework. A harmonious and just society was possible. All that was required was a better *system*.

As John Bender and Michael Marrinan have pointed out, as representations, diagrams are powerful because they assume "that the world is ordered," and they offer users ways to correlate and understand that order.[100] This magical ability to conjure order out of the chaos of reality is related to diagrams' abstraction—their radical and selective reduction of information to that which can be conveyed through lines and a few shapes. Urban plans and maps are types of diagrams: they provide images of an ordered world in synoptic, telegrammatic views that allow readers to see relationships between parts, as well as between parts and the whole. As such, plans and maps are laden with potential instrumentality. By offering views of territories or systems, they influence how individuals navigate or intervene within those worlds or systems. In another context, the theorist Fredric Jameson has written about the need for "cognitive maps" of society, representations and forms of art that aid individuals in the modern world in grasping the totality (i.e., the larger global capitalist system) that conditions their individual experiences. Jameson argues that cognitive maps are critical to any sociopolitical project, since "the incapacity to map socially is as crippling to political experience as the analogous incapacity to map spatially is for urban experience."[101] And while Jameson insists that "cognitive maps" are not literal maps, literal maps (or, in this case, territorial diagrams) can sometimes perform the function of cognitive maps. The land reformers' township grid and octagonal village, when considered alongside Masquerier's system of scientific geography, Skidmore's conjectural diagrams of property distribution, and Owen's diagrams of the relationship of individual to society, offered something like a "cognitive map." The diagrams presented viewers with an abstraction of the current unjust system of society and invited them to imagine a different configuration.

Of course, the National Reformers' diagrams were still very much circumscribed by the worldviews of their creators, white working- and middle-class men in the mid-nineteenth-century United States. The very tools of geometric abstraction and synoptic diagrammatic vision that these reformers deployed to counter the existing unjust system of society were being used during the same period by European and American colonial powers, in the form of land surveys, plats, and maps, to dispossess Indigenous peoples and to conquer territory, both in the Americas and elsewhere. Many workingmen recognized the injustice of white Americans' expropriation of Indigenous lands, but their attempts to resolve the contradiction were never entirely convincing. Though the National Reformers promoted a universal right to the land and portrayed land as a common inheritance, they clung to a model of individual possession. That is, their imaginations were bound by the figure of the grid, with its logic of subdivision into individual parcels. In using the grid to represent their utopian vision, they were working with a geometry deeply entangled with settler colonialism, Enlightenment rationality, and a logic of individualism. As Jameson reminds us, all utopias are "irredeemably class-based" and bound by the limits of what is thinkable by specific individuals within a specific historical context.[102] If the National Reformers' geometric utopias reflected their status as "children of Enlightenment" and settlers wedded to land, labor, rational persuasion, and individual independence as the keys to a more just and egalitarian society, their story also demonstrates that images of utopia are never simple or static blueprints but instead are multiply determined and mutable.[103] By placing these images back into the visual-cultural worlds from which they emerged, we begin to see more clearly the manifold and contradictory ways that geometric utopian diagrams communicated to audiences. Less than five years after the land reformers began publishing their grid and village schemes, another New York–based printer would take up their example and offer his own geometric diagram for attaining personal independence.

CHAPTER 3

Cultivating the Liberal Self
Orson Fowler's Octagon House

In 1856 a couple named Isaiah and Ann Wilcox built an unusual house on a farm in Camillus, New York, a few miles west of Syracuse. Rising two stories over a basement and surmounted by an eight-sided cupola, the house was a perfect octagon in plan (Figures 3.1 and 3.2). With its rotational symmetry making it hard to tell front from back, the house must have been an odd sight, standing out conspicuously from the rectangular Italianate, Greek revival, and vernacular farmhouses nearby. Its walls, twenty-two inches thick at the base, were constructed not of conventional brick or wood but of a novel mixture of gravel, sand, and lime, covered in stucco. Stranger still was the interior plan: an arrangement of four large rooms forming an irregular Greek cross with an octagonal stair in the center and a hodgepodge of small triangular closets and trapezoidal rooms wedged in between the main spaces.

Not much is known about the Wilcoxes or why they chose to build this unconventional dwelling. Isaiah, born in Rhode Island, was fifty-one years old when the house was constructed, and Ann, born in Connecticut, was fifty-four; they had two grown children, ages twenty and seventeen.[1] The Wilcoxes moved to Camillus, a town founded on the former lands of the Onondaga nation, in 1841. Five years later Isaiah purchased the fifty-acre site on which they would later build the octagon house. Like others in the upstate New York region, an area known at the time as a hotbed of radicalism, Isaiah opposed slavery: his name is listed on a petition opposing the Fugitive Slave Law, and in an 1856 letter to his brother he recommended Frederick Douglass's *My Bondage and My Freedom*. Little evidence survives about what the Wilcoxes' neighbors thought of the eight-sided dwelling. Perhaps some in their community agreed with a writer in the *Prairie Farmer* who deemed octagonal houses "odd looking" and "not homelike in appearance."[2] Others may have admired the structure and resolved to build similar ones for themselves—a possibility underscored by the fact that several more octagons appeared in the surrounding countryside within the next decade.

95

FIGURE 3.1. Wilcox House, Camillus, New York. Photograph by author.

What we do know is that the Wilcoxes almost certainly modeled their house on a plan that appeared in Orson Fowler's 1853 book *A Home for All; or, The Gravel Wall and Octagon Mode of Building New, Cheap, Convenient, Superior and Adapted to Rich and Poor*, a revised and expanded version of a work first published in 1848. At the time, Fowler was best known as one of the United States' leading practitioners of phrenology, the science of reading an individual's character from the shape of the person's head. The floor plan of the Camillus house is very similar to one in Fowler's publication labeled "the best plan yet" (Figure 3.3), and the dwelling included many features—such as concrete walls, encircling covered porch, and cupola—that the book recommended. *A Home for All* was a minor sensation in its time. It went through at least six printings within a decade, and versions of Fowler's octagonal plans were reprinted in countless newspapers and other house manuals. In the half century after its publication, the book inspired the construction of hundreds of octagonal houses in the United States and Canada, mostly concentrated in the Northeast and Midwest but some as far west as San Francisco (Figure 3.4).[3]

A Home for All presented the octagon house as a singular innovation, part of the wave of reforms sweeping the United States in the mid-nineteenth century. "Why so little progress in architecture," Fowler decried, "when there is so much in all other

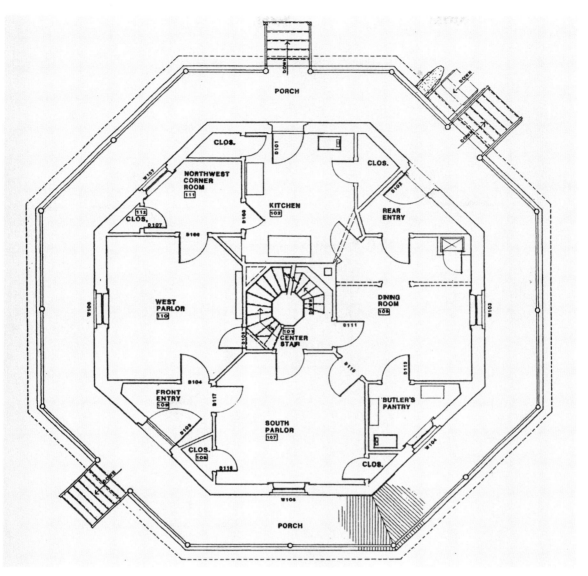

FIGURE 3.2. Plan of the Wilcox House, Camillus, New York. Courtesy Crawford & Stearns / Architects and Preservation Planners, PLLC.

matters? Why continue to build in the same SQUARE form of all past ages? Is no *radical* improvement of both the external form and internal arrangement of private residences, as well as *building material,* possible?"[4] His leading claim was that eight-sided dwellings were cheaper to build because they required less material than rectangular buildings to enclose the same amount of space. They also provided more convenient internal arrangements of rooms—so much more convenient that they would facilitate greater health and happiness in their inhabitants. Thus, Fowler predicted, prosperity and wellness would flow to builders of eight-sided homes. He directed his book especially toward working- and middle-class Americans. His goal was "to bring comfortable dwellings within reach of the poorer classes."[5]

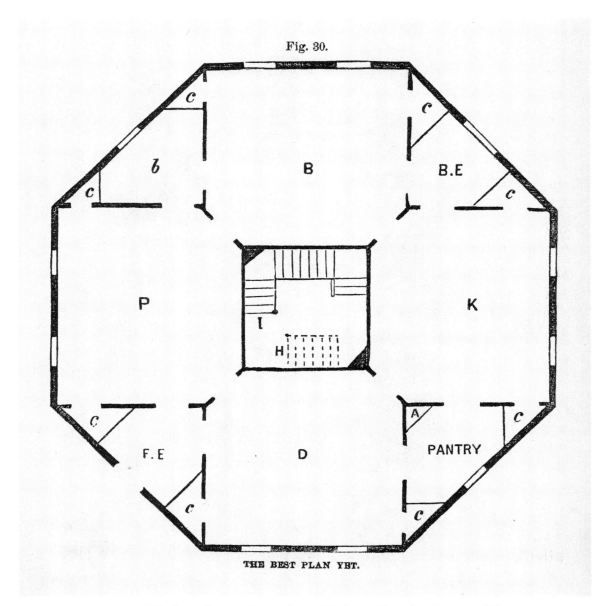

FIGURE 3.3. "The best plan yet." From Orson Fowler, *A Home for All,* 1854 edition. Courtesy Getty Research Institute / Archive.org.

The impact of *A Home for All* was widespread, immediate, and also short-lived—the mania for eight-sided houses crested and fell within about a decade.[6] By the 1880s, the phrenologist's own eight-sided dwelling had been dubbed "Fowler's Folly," and in 1897, it was razed (Figure 3.5). Since then, the subject of octagon houses has resurfaced periodically in the popular imagination, but almost always in proximity to words like "whimsy," "fad," "fancy," "anomaly," and "failure."[7] Whereas previous scholarly accounts of the octagon house have focused on narrating its story as a curiosity,

FIGURE 3.4. Nineteenth-century octagon houses. Unless otherwise noted, photographs are from the Library of Congress, Historic American Buildings Survey. *From upper left corner:* McElroy House, San Francisco; Octagon House, Custer County, Nebraska (History Nebraska); Longwood, Natchez, Mississippi (Carol M. Highsmith Archive, Library of Congress, Prints and Photographs Division); Woodruff House, Ripon, Wisconsin (photograph by author); Holmes House, Laurens, South Carolina; Pierce House, Towerville, Pennsylvania; Tucker House, Chelsea, Massachusetts; Octagon House, Mystic, Connecticut (The George F. Landegger Collection of Connecticut Photographs in Carol M. Highsmith's America, Library of Congress, Prints and Photographs Division); Robinson House, Somerville, Massachusetts (Somerville Museum); Stone House, Lena, Illinois; Octagon House, Afton, Minnesota; Russell House, Bloomfield, Iowa; Wilcox House, Camillus, New York (photograph by author); Richards House, Watertown, Wisconsin; Scott House, Wiscasset, Maine; Langworthy House, Dubuque, Iowa.

FIGURE 3.5. Orson Fowler's own octagon house, Fishkill, New York. From Orson Fowler, *A Home for All,* 1854 edition. Courtesy Getty Research Institute / Archive.org.

identifying precedents for its eight-sided form, describing it as a forerunner of architectural functionalism, or correlating Fowler's architectural proposal to his peculiar phrenological theories about the body, this chapter approaches the octagon house as an episode in the unfolding phenomenon of geometric utopianism, an artifact of the period's faith in architecture as a tool of reform, carried out through specific modes of visual rhetoric.[8] Like the land reformers described in chapter 2, Fowler believed that the redesign of the built environment could help Americans of modest backgrounds meet the challenges of an emerging capitalist society. In fact, in a lengthy footnote in *A Home for All,* he expressed his support for the land reformers' cause, citing their proposals to guarantee homesteads for all and put an end to foreclosures.[9] This is not surprising: both the octagon house and land reform emerged from the overlapping circles of reform publishing in New York City (Fowler's office was located just a few blocks from the National Reform Association's headquarters in Lower Manhattan).[10] But whereas the land reformers had proposed "land for the landless" as the remedy for the injustices of capitalism, Fowler's solution was "homes for the homeless." And whereas the land reformers had denounced the existing system of society as the cause of individual misery and sought new *social* arrangements, Fowler put the onus on *individuals*: "He who, in a country of liberty and plenty, cannot rise from the deepest poverty to comparative comfort, lacks either the wisdom to plan, or the energy to execute, his liberation from his galling yoke."[11] The land reform movement had emerged from an Enlightenment, republican, artisan political culture centered on land as the source of personal independence and societal equality; Fowler's octagon house, in contrast, was oriented to a rising liberal, capitalist society in which individual optimization was the highest goal.

Understanding the content of Fowler's reform ideas is only half the story. The most striking thing about the octagon house—what set it apart from the other domestic reform proposals of the day, and was arguably the cause of both its swift success and its relatively rapid decline—was its bold and unusual shape. This can be connected to another persistent enigma of the octagon house: How did it become so popular? How were the Wilcoxes, and hundreds of other Americans like them, persuaded to build a novel and untried kind of dwelling? This problem might appear trivial, especially considering the brief life span of the octagon house as a cultural formation, yet it opens onto broader questions: What caused select Americans in the nineteenth century to act on new reforms and beliefs, including adopting new building types and cities? Indeed, how does anyone become convinced to abandon caution and convention and try something new? In short, fads, precisely because of their ephemerality, offer an exceptional opportunity to explore the possibility and mechanisms of sudden cultural change.

Answering these questions requires investigating not just *what* Fowler asserted but also *how* he made these claims. That is, we must attend to his rhetorical techniques and particularly to his use of visual evidence. Like the land reformers, Fowler drew on the long-standing association of geometric diagrams with certainty and demonstration to argue for the facticity of his assertions. But if the workingmen were "children of Enlightenment," Fowler's closest kin was the showman and "prince of humbug" Phineas T. Barnum. Adapting techniques well honed by Barnum and tailoring them to a mass democratic, market society, Fowler addressed audiences and readers as skeptical, engaged participants, whether he was peddling phrenology or eight-sided houses. A thorough reading of the octagon house thus requires not only that we grapple with Fowler's claims about how the house would aid in self-cultivation and self-improvement but also that we explicate how his visual-rhetorical techniques convinced many people to choose a novel and unconventional form of dwelling. Fowler's octagon house constructed liberal subjects in a double sense: through its purported functional effects on its inhabitants, and through its appeal to readers who exhibited the liberal subject's characteristic traits of individualism, independent thinking, and rationality.

"Know Thyself": Phrenology and the Visual Rhetoric of Self-Improvement

Before he became a proselytizer for eight-sided houses, Orson Fowler rose to fame as one of the leading American practitioners of popular phrenology. Originating in the ideas of the Viennese physician Franz Joseph Gall at the end of the eighteenth century, phrenology in its American incarnation offered something like what popular psychology offers today: it merged a scientific theory of the mind with a program for self-understanding and self-improvement. Building on the lineaments of earlier faculty psychology, phrenology's principal tenets were, first, that the brain is the seat of the mind; second, that mental "faculties" or attributes could be associated with specific, distinct zones of the brain; and third, that the development of these faculties could affect the size and contours of the cranium.[12] Thus, character traits theoretically were legible from the shape of the head—an idea indelibly associated with the iconic diagram of a human head carved into zones corresponding with various traits (Figure 3.6). While Gall was pessimistic about the conclusions to be drawn from his investigations (he thought that the existence of innate powers meant that human nature was essentially fixed), his successors Johann Gaspar Spurzheim and George Combe transformed phrenology from a deterministic science into a progressive doctrine of individual and social improvement. Individuals might be born with certain aptitudes and tendencies, but these could be guided and shaped through education.[13] Troublingly, this capacity for progress was represented as racially determined, with white Europeans and Americans deemed implicitly capable of self-advancement while other racial groups, especially Africans, were described as immutably deficient in the higher mental capacities.[14]

Orson Fowler and his brother Lorenzo continued and Americanized what Spurzheim and Combe began, cultivating phrenology into a full-fledged credo of practical self-improvement directed primarily to white working- and middle-class individuals. Orson had become interested in phrenology while still a student at Amherst College. After graduating in 1834, he abandoned a plan to join the clergy and decided to try his hand at lecturing on the subject. Capitalizing on the national vogue for popular lectures on entertaining and useful topics, he first found success as a phrenological speaker and soon began to supplement his lecturing with writing.[15] His book *Phrenology, Proved, Illustrated, and Applied* was published in 1837 and went through sixty-two editions in the next twenty years. It was the first in a steady stream of books that Fowler wrote on a wide array of subjects throughout his life.[16] Over the next two decades, the Fowler brothers, along with their sister Charlotte and brother-in-law Samuel Wells, established a veritable media empire centered in New York City, publishing their own writings as well as those of supporters like Walt Whitman (Fowler and Wells issued the first edition of *Leaves of Grass* in 1855). The firm also put out periodicals such as the *American Phrenological Journal* (with more than twenty thousand subscribers by 1848) and the *Water-Cure Journal*.[17] In addition, the family company spread the gospel of phrenology through lecture tours and a museum, the Phrenological Cabinet, where busts of the famous and infamous were exhibited and consultations and head readings were dispensed (Figure 3.7). The Phrenological Cabinet was reported to rival P. T. Barnum's American Museum (located just a block away) in popularity. In the 1850s the family added a patent office to their operations.

Recent scholarship has illuminated phrenology's sizable influence on nineteenth-century American culture and society, especially in the realms of education and the arts.[18] Historians have also noted phrenology's affiliations with radical reform; its popularity among working-class communities in France, Great Britain, and the United States; and its status as a counterdiscourse opposed to more academic or

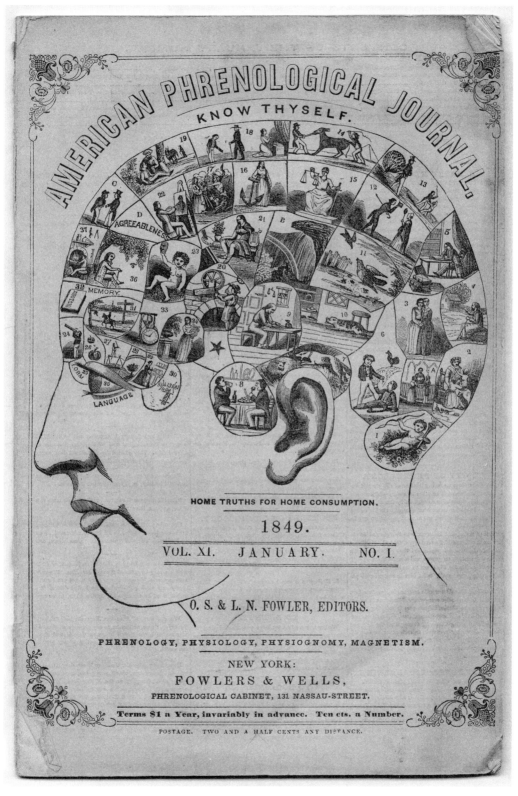

FIGURE 3.6. Title page of the *American Phrenological Journal,* January 1849. Courtesy Amherst College Archives and Special Collections.

THE PHRENOLOGICAL MUSEUM OF FOWLER & WELLS, NO. 308 BROADWAY.—EXAMINING ROOM.—(See Page 211.)

FIGURE 3.7. The Fowlers' Phrenological Museum and Cabinet at 308 Broadway, New York City. From *New York Illustrated News,* February 18, 1860. Courtesy American Antiquarian Society.

establishment-endorsed psychologies.[19] Overall, however, scholars have tended to be critical of phrenology's ideology and politics. Roger Cooter, for example, has argued that in England it was promoted by middle-class reformers to inculcate normative, bourgeois values among the working class.[20] And literary scholars such as Christopher Castiglia and Russ Castronovo have associated Fowlerian phrenology in particular with the nineteenth-century "interiorization" of U.S. political life— that is, the growing preoccupation with self-scrutiny and self-management of individual appetites and desires at the expense of public association and democratic engagement.[21]

While I am indebted to these interpretations, my focus here is on *why* phrenology appealed to so many mid-nineteenth-century Americans. Specifically, I am interested in the way phrenologists presented claims about how human psychological attributes could be managed to improve individuals' lives, and how these claims were advanced through specific visual and rhetorical techniques. As we shall see, Fowler applied tactics of persuasion honed in his phrenological practice to his marketing of the octagon house.

How to explain the popularity of phrenology in the nineteenth-century United States? First, in an age obsessed with self-betterment, "self-culture," and self-made men, the Fowlers promised to reveal to Americans their own proclivities and inborn tendencies so that they could direct their self-improving energies and maximize their chances of success.[22] The motto of the family's phrenological journal was the Delphic maxim "Know thyself" (Figure 3.6). Phrenology contributed to a burgeoning genre of health literature and conduct and advice manuals that addressed the large numbers of young men and women migrating from rural areas to America's industrial cities, offering an early version of what today would be called "self-help."[23] Fowler's publishing company fed the popular appetite for books answering questions about topics like whom to marry, what occupation to pursue, and how to rise from poverty to riches. As part of its extensive catalog of works, the firm published books on phrenology, water cures, mesmerism, physiology, cholera, vegetarian cooking, digestion, hygiene, marriage, pregnancy and childbirth, love and parenthood, education, and memory, as well a series of pocket manuals that included the titles *How to Write, How to Talk, How to Behave,* and *How to Do Business.*

Fowler's subspecialty as a phrenologist was amativeness, the faculty governing sexuality, marriage, and reproduction. His voluminous writings on these subjects are an illustration of Michel Foucault's argument that the nineteenth century, despite its reputation for prudery, witnessed a veritable discursive explosion on the subject of sex.[24] Fowler described sexuality as "the grand motor wheel of everything human": the origin of life and of innate character traits, and therefore a determinant of future conduct.[25] In his books, he dispensed advice on how to find a compatible mate, as well as the best means for controlling "improper" sexual impulses such as masturbation and homosexuality and cultivating heteronormative sexual attraction. As Brian Connolly has observed, Fowler's sexual theories centered on two related preoccupations: the cultivation of the bourgeois family as the site of proper sexual training and the healthy reproduction of white Anglo-Saxon Americans during an era of rising immigration and nativism.[26] Americans of Anglo-Saxon stock had an obligation to reproduce, Fowler warned, or else those of "foreign origin" would soon "outnumber the descendants of the Puritans."[27] Like good health, proper reproduction was thus not only a matter of self-interest but also a racial-nationalist obligation.[28]

Second, phrenology gained popularity because, in addition to promising self-knowledge, it purported to reveal the truth about other people at a time when society was becoming more anonymous and depersonalized. During the middle decades of the nineteenth century, rapid urbanization, increasing mobility, and an expanding market economy brought strangers into novel and, for many, uncomfortable proximity. The specter of "confidence men" and "painted women"—symbols of urban deceit and hypocrisy—loomed large in the middle-class imagination. In this environment, people sought guidance and assurance in choosing spouses, employees, and business partners.[29] Scott Sandage has argued that in the 1840s, phrenology, daguerreotypy, and credit reporting constituted a triad of new "sciences of the self" dedicated to observing, evaluating, and recording individuals' "real" characters.[30] Both phrenology and daguerreotypy (the first widespread photographic technology, introduced in 1839 and initially used primarily for human portraiture) claimed to make the interiority of human beings legible on the surface.[31] That Fowler and Wells shared an address after 1854 with a daguerreotypy supplier is perhaps no coincidence.

Third, like photography, phrenology purported to offer a truer, more objective window onto the world. Appealing to the era's prevalent scientism, the Fowlers emphasized phrenology's status as a "comprehensive," "profound," and "true science."[32] As they wrote in *The Illustrated Self-Instructor in Phrenology and Physiology,* phrenology "puts the finger of SCIENTIFIC CERTAINTY upon every mental faculty . . . and thereby reduces mental study to that same *tangible* basis of *proportion* in which all science consists; leaving nothing dark or doubtful."[33] In a time of rapid cultural and social change, phrenology promised to dispel uncertainty and offer precise, reliable diagnoses and prescriptions for individual conduct.

Fourth, phrenology billed itself as a science, but it could equally well be described as a form of rhetoric, concerned more with persuasion than with finding the "truth" of the brain's operations. This rhetoric, like phrenology itself, was highly dependent on visual representation and practice. After all, phrenology was premised on the ability to discern deep insights about individuals from cursory evaluations of the outward forms of their heads. Its pedagogy, as Jan Goldstein observes, was "simple, swift, and graphic."[34] Eschewing a depth model of psychological knowledge, phrenology instead emphasized superficiality, visibility, accessibility, and ease of learning and transmission. American phrenologists' reliance on visual persuasion can be seen in the abundance of visual materials deployed by the Fowlers and others. This reliance on clear graphic communication is nowhere more evident than with the iconic phrenological head, which rendered inherently hard-to-see phenomena such as personality traits immediately visible to the eye. Notably, the Fowlers revised Gall's relatively sedate and scientific-appearing version of the cranial diagram, which featured a skull, discreet numbers, and a textual legend; their more vivid version showcased a head adorned with dozens of illustrated vignettes (Figures 3.8 and 3.6).[35] The new version made phrenology's insights even more graphically appealing and quickly available. Beyond this famous head, phrenological publications were often copiously illustrated with engravings of famous men and women, frequently juxtaposed in pairs to show contrasting endowments of particular faculties. In this way, the Fowlers trained readers to see and interpret visual evidence in order to form their own judgments. Another important visual document was the phrenological chart that the Fowlers gave clients as part of their head readings (Figure 3.9). This chart delineated individuals' propensities and aptitudes, and was annotated with handwritten numerical values and occasionally additional notes. Phrenological charts reflected the nineteenth-century American fascination with information printed in statistical tables and data lists, part of the broader general appetite for scientific and useful information.[36] The charts not only made phrenological knowledge of self and others easily comprehensible, but their design also lent phrenology the trappings of objectivity and scientificity. Numbers gave the charts an aura of precision, even though they represented subjective, relative ratings rather than actual measurements. Made to look technical and authoritative, and sometimes decorated with borders and other graphic elements mimicking the style of official certificates, the eye-catching charts, as Fenneke Sysling points out, "were more a matter of rhetoric" than objective science.[37]

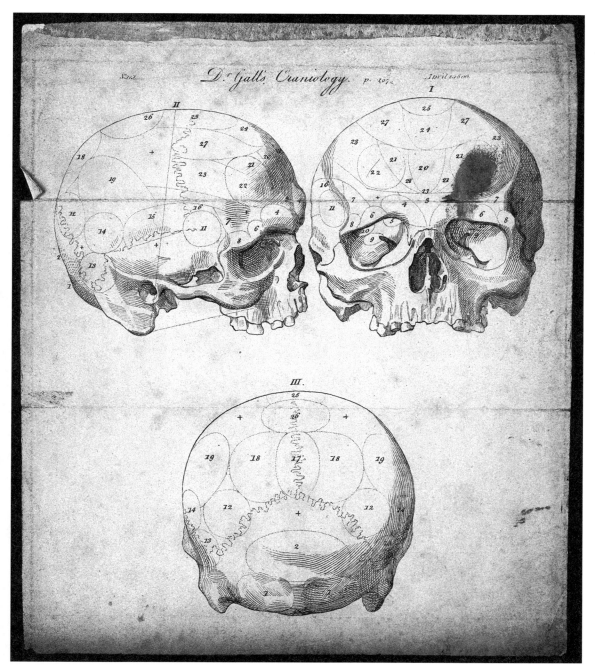

FIGURE 3.8. Three perspectives of a skull labeled according to Gall's system of phrenology. Engraving, 1806. Courtesy Wellcome Collection.

Yet perhaps the most important factor in the popularity of Fowlerian phrenology was the way the brothers managed to merge an aesthetic of objectivity with the techniques of popular visual entertainment. The Fowlers made it their mission to *show* Americans exactly how phrenology could be made useful in daily life, by appealing to

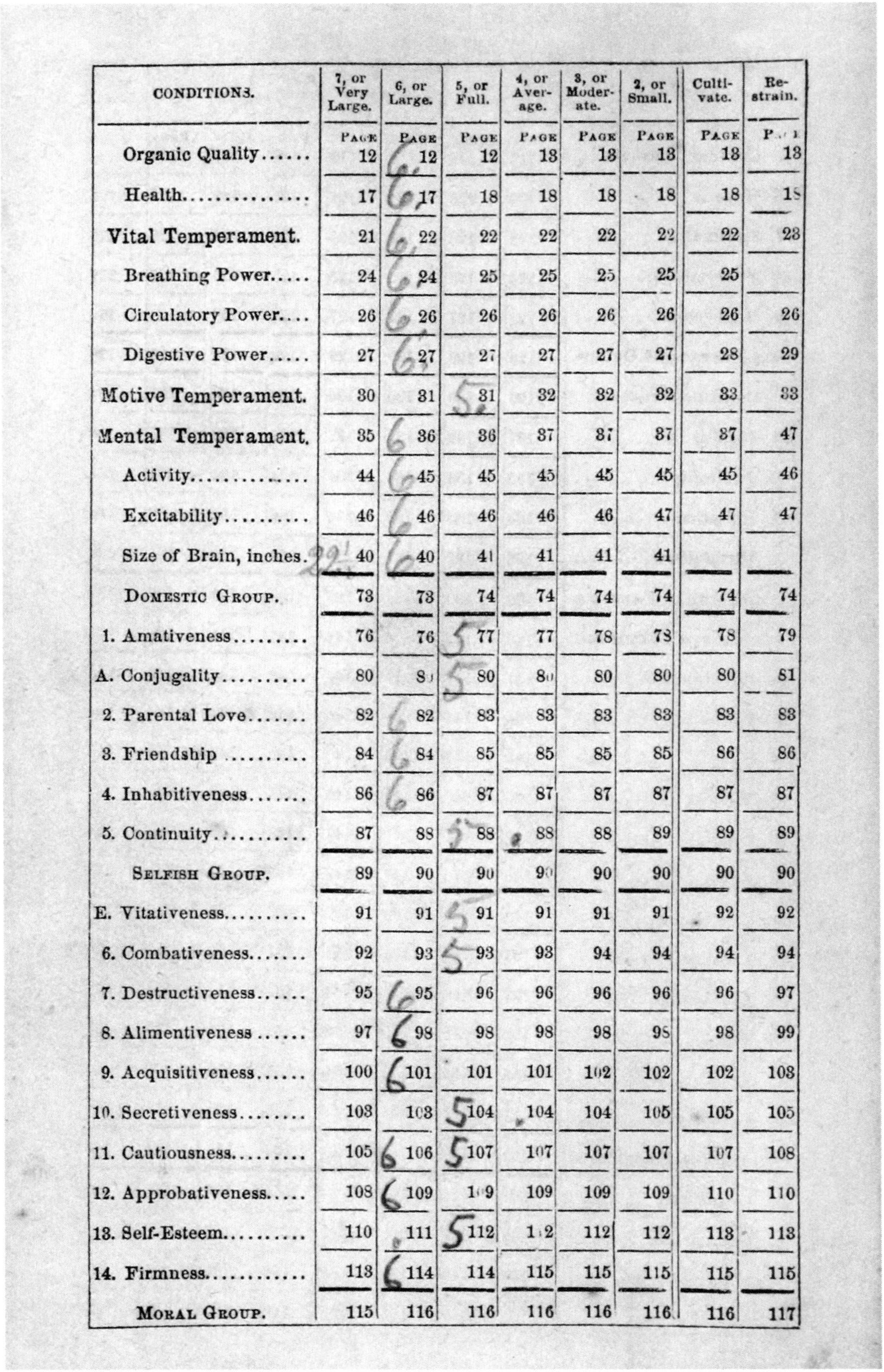

CONDITIONS.	7, or Very Large.	6, or Large.	5, or Full.	4, or Average.	3, or Moderate.	2, or Small.	Cultivate.	Restrain.
	PAGE	PAGE	PAGE	PAGE	PAGE	PAGE	PAGE	P. I
Organic Quality......	12	12	12	13	13	13	18	13
Health...............	17	17	18	18	18	18	18	18
Vital Temperament.	21	22	22	22	22	22	22	23
Breathing Power.....	24	24	25	25	25	25	25	
Circulatory Power....	26	26	26	26	26	26	26	26
Digestive Power.....	27	27	27	27	27	27	28	29
Motive Temperament.	30	31	31	32	32	32	33	33
Mental Temperament.	35	36	36	37	37	37	37	47
Activity.............	44	45	45	45	45	45	45	46
Excitability.........	46	46	46	46	46	47	47	47
Size of Brain, inches.	40	40	41	41	41	41		
DOMESTIC GROUP.	73	73	74	74	74	74	74	74
1. Amativeness........	76	76	77	77	78	78	78	79
A. Conjugality.........	80	80	80	80	80	80	80	81
2. Parental Love......	82	82	83	83	83	83	83	83
3. Friendship	84	84	85	85	85	85	86	86
4. Inhabitiveness.......	86	86	87	87	87	87	87	87
5. Continuity.........	87	88	88	88	88	89	89	89
SELFISH GROUP.	89	90	90	90	90	90	90	90
E. Vitativeness.........	91	91	91	91	91	91	92	92
6. Combativeness.......	92	93	93	93	94	94	94	94
7. Destructiveness......	95	95	96	96	96	96	96	97
8. Alimentiveness	97	98	98	98	98	98	98	99
9. Acquisitiveness......	100	101	101	101	102	102	102	103
10. Secretiveness........	103	103	104	104	104	105	105	105
11. Cautiousness.........	105	106	107	107	107	107	107	108
12. Approbativeness.....	108	109	109	109	109	109	110	110
13. Self-Esteem.........	110	111	112	112	112	112	113	113
14. Firmness............	113	114	114	115	115	115	115	115
MORAL GROUP.	115	116	116	116	116	116	116	117

FIGURE 3.9. A phrenological chart with annotations from a reading. From O. S. Fowler and L. N. Fowler, *The Illustrated Self-Instructor in Phrenology and Physiology*, 1859. Courtesy U.S. National Library of Medicine / Archive.org.

nineteenth-century audiences' desire to see for themselves. As Neil Harris and James Cook have insightfully argued, an era of rapid scientific discovery and technological invention had generated a general mood of both credulity and skepticism. In the age of the telegraph and the railroad, nothing seemed impossible, yet every claim required proof.[38] And at a time when illustrated newspapers, museums, lithography, and daguerreotypy were making images more accessible than ever before, the best proof was the kind that could be seen with one's own eyes, either witnessed in person or absorbed through printed materials. Harris has described the rise in the nineteenth-century United States of what he calls an "operational aesthetic," exemplified in visual exhibits that exposed their processes of operation, that were empirically testable, and that invited audiences to debate the veracity of what they had seen. The proliferation of statistical tables, how-to manuals, diagrams of machinery, sea novels, and lyceum lectures all reflected the rise of an operational aesthetic in which it was believed "any problem could be expressed clearly, concisely, and comprehensively enough for the ordinary man to resolve it." The operational aesthetic was fueled by a democratic impulse, visible in the increasingly popular practice of pitting laypeople's capacities for observation and judgment against the knowledge of traditional experts. In the popular literature, experts began to be ridiculed as pedantic and foolish; readers were invited to trust their own eyes, experience, and common sense.[39]

No American of the nineteenth century purveyed the new performative, democratic, operational sensibility more skillfully than P. T. Barnum. Through exhibits such as the "Feejee mermaid" (in actuality a monkey torso and fish tail sewn together), the showman revealed his awareness that part of the amusement lay in the act of eye-witnessing, and in the resulting argument and controversy over what one had seen. A whiff of fraud (often planted by Barnum himself) only increased ticket sales (Figures 3.10 and 3.11).[40] Borrowing from Barnum's playbook, the Fowlers also engaged in performative tests that took advantage of the era's fascination with optical verification. They thought earlier advocates of phrenology had focused too much on theory, neglecting pragmatic usefulness and the need for visible proof. If people were to be won over to the science, they argued, it would not be through *"reasoning* upon the subject, as by *practical application of its principles."*

> What do the common people, or even scientifick men, care about the *arguments* adduced in support of any new subject or science? Before they will believe in it, or even *listen* to it, they must see its truth *practically demonstrated.* Indeed, the world will *never* believe, either in any new mechanical invention or improvement, or in any proposed discovery, however reasonable or useful it may be, until they see it fully and fairly tested by actual *experiment.*[41]

In order to demonstrate the truth of phrenology to Americans practically, the Fowlers staged "epistemological contests" between themselves and audience members that granted the observers a significant and active role in determining what to believe.[42] In an 1836 handbill, the brothers promised to prove their claims irrefutably and to "meet opposition publicly, and on *any ground*—either by fair argument, or by application of the principles of the science to the heads and skulls of animals, or *to the*

FIGURE 3.10. Barnum invited reporters to examine the "Feejee mermaid" in order to drum up interest in the specimen in advance of its public display. Illustration from P. T. Barnum, *The Life of P. T. Barnum,* 1855.

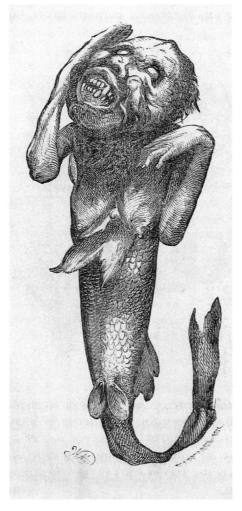

FIGURE 3.11. The "mermaid" was composed of a monkey torso and fish tail sewn together. Illustration from P. T. Barnum, *The Life of P. T. Barnum,* 1855.

heads of individuals selected by the audience—either with or without *their eyes covered*—and let phrenology stand or fall by this test."[43] As the Fowler team traveled the country performing cranial readings, communities would try to confound the visiting "professors" by putting forward decoy subjects, such as clergymen disguised in loud colors. In other instances, the brothers would engage in double-blindfold tests in which one sibling was taken away while the other, blindfolded, read the character of a subject by feeling the person's head. Then the first brother would return and be asked to read the same person, also blindfolded.[44] As with Barnum's planted suspicions, the inconclusiveness of these epistemological contests contributed precisely to their popularity.[45] Such public performances were trials not only for the phrenologists but also for audience members, who regarded the events as matches of wits and incredulity.

The Visual Rhetoric of the Octagon House

Fowler applied many of the strategies that he used to promote phrenology to the marketing of the octagon house. Building on the themes of his books on phrenology, memory, marriage, and self-culture, he presented the house as yet another tool for self-improvement. Fowler positioned himself as an outsider (today we might say "disrupter") to the architectural profession, and the octagon house as a more functional and practical alternative to the houses found in conventional house pattern books. Publications by professional architects and landscape designers such as Alexander Jackson Davis and Andrew Jackson Downing upheld an ideal of gentility, cultivation, and refined taste.[46] These values were exemplified in neat suburban homes embowered in trees that presented an "ordered tranquility" and expressed the character and class status of their inhabitants (Figure 3.12).[47] In contrast, Fowler played up his status as an amateur—one who deployed his common sense, reason, and outsider viewpoint to criticize professionals' so-called expertise and their inordinate focus on matters of style over practical concerns of cost, function, and inhabitation:

> Was any innovation ever made on any art that the *professors* of that art did not ridicule? Their *craft* is in danger. To admit that any one else knows more than they do, impeaches themselves. The practitioners of any art are the very poorest of all judges of proposed improvements in it. All their prejudices and pride, as well as purse, are against any outsider teaching *them* any thing. Don't let their ridicule scare you. . . . When will Old Fogies in all departments learn that man is progressive? When will man learn to trust their own common sense, instead of conservative leaders? Let them laugh on. Next summer will show them, for hundreds of houses will then be built to open their eyes, and turn them to ridicule.[48]

Fowler thus positioned himself as the advocate of ordinary men and women fighting against the wasteful stylings of experts. A concern for functionalism would be the layperson's defense against the pretensions of builders and architects, as well as the increased expenses associated with them.

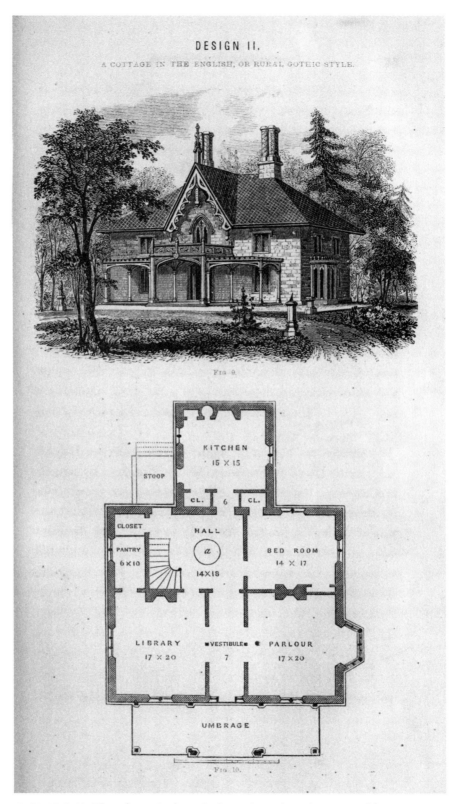

FIGURE 3.12. Plate from Andrew Jackson Downing, *Cottage Residences,* 1842. Whereas Fowler focused on the functionality of the plan, professional architectural critics like Downing were preoccupied with issues of style and taste. Courtesy UC Berkeley Libraries / Archive.org.

The phrenologist's leading rationale for the house's octagonal shape was that it enclosed space more efficiently than a square or rectangle, and so required less building material to encircle the same volume. Theoretically this would make the house less expensive to build and therefore a better choice for those with little cash. The octagon, Fowler claimed, was exactly two and a half times more efficient than a "winged house" (a house with an irregular plan), a type then being advocated by Downing and other proponents of the fashionable Gothic revival style.[49] To persuade his readers, Fowler included comparative diagrams of plans alongside calculations of the perimeters and square footages enclosed. Fowler's diagrams and calculations are striking for their rudimentary quality. They resemble the illustrations in an elementary mathematics primer geared toward very young children (Figure 3.13). A blank square takes up almost two-thirds of a page, and another diagram, showing a square with the corners cut off to form an octagon, occupies a full half page. Obviousness was precisely the point: the images were intended to appear self-evident, elementary, and irrefutably clear. Fowler extolled the immediacy of pictures over words, quoting Horace Mann on the importance of drawing: "A few strokes of the pen, or pencil, will often represent to the eye what no amount of words, however well chosen, can communicate."[50]

Another key advantage claimed for the octagonal shape was that it produced a compact plan with an efficient circulation system. The shape reduced the number of steps that inhabitants, particularly women, needed to take while completing housework or otherwise moving about the home. As Victoria Solan has shown, Fowler was one of the leading voices in the nineteenth century, along with Catharine Beecher, for positioning the house as a site for cultivating health, particularly the health of white, Anglo-Saxon women at a time of growing concern about immigration.[51] Besides allowing housewives to streamline their movements, another feature of the house that Fowler asserted would improve the health of the inhabitants was the dome room at the apex of the structure, which would make an ideal play area for children, gymnastics room for women and girls, or dancing room. He claimed that the provision of such spaces was a matter of life and death, especially for delicate women. "How many hopeless invalids, now dying by inches, would such rooms in our buildings restore to life, health, and happiness! How many a child save from a premature grave!"[52] According to Fowler's theories of scientific reproduction, healthier women would also make for healthier, stronger children.[53]

Once again, Fowler furnished illustrations to underscore his point, in this case, a pair of diagrams featuring dashed lines indicating occupants' movements (Figure 3.14). One diagram showed the circuitous paths that a person would have to take in a conventional house. The other demonstrated the comparatively shorter, more direct paths connecting the dining, kitchen, sitting room, and parlor spaces in an eight-sided house. Fowler explained that "the difference, especially to a weakly woman, between going from room to room by a few direct steps, and by those long and crooked roads, as illustrated by those tracks or dotted lines in the two houses, is very great—MORE THAN DOUBLE—in the square, compared with the octagon house." Fowler did not, however, suggest that housewives lessen their overall load; rather, the octagon would permit housekeepers to do "TWICE THE WORK."[54]

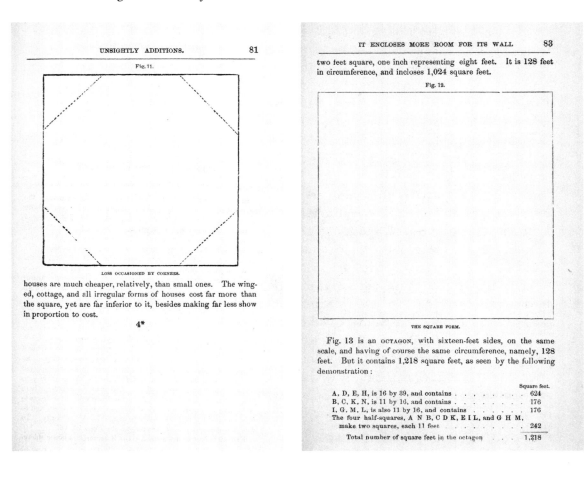

Fowler's pathway diagrams anticipated the circulation and flow diagrams that architects began to draw in the 1870s as well as the reformer Christine Frederick's diagrams of improved kitchen circulation, which appeared in her 1913 book *The New Housekeeping* and in turn inspired modernist architects in the 1920s (Figure 3.15).[55] Like Frederick, whose diagrams were influenced by the ideology of scientific management, Fowler used his proto–flow diagrams as evidence, to convey how the octagon house would promote efficiency and combat fatigue in its inhabitants. In light of the subsequent history of such diagrams, Fowler has sometimes been described as a prophet of architectural functionalism, along with the mid-nineteenth-century American sculptor Horatio Greenough, who similarly urged his fellow Americans to eschew "ill-arranged, ill-lighted, and stifled rooms" dressed up in Greek facades and instead begin with function "as the nucleus, and work outward."[56] I would like to use this connection with later modernist diagrams to make a slightly different point, however. Paul Emmons has observed that Frederick's drawings offered a "narcotic of facticity" even as they promulgated a new aesthetic of efficiency and cleanliness.[57] Something similar can be said about Fowler: the diagrams did not just illustrate efficiency, they also manifested an *aesthetic* of efficiency, one that borrowed the graphic

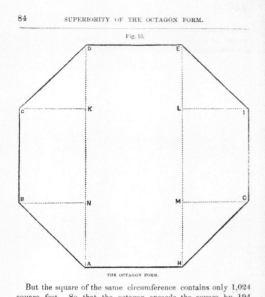

FIGURE 3.13. Diagrams purporting to demonstrate that an octagon encloses space more efficiently than a square. From Orson Fowler, *A Home for All*, 1854 edition. Courtesy Getty Research Institute / Archive.org.

techniques of mathematical primers and technical drawings to create an image of objectivity and proof.

Indeed, although Fowler couched his advocacy for the octagon primarily in functional terms, he also linked these to an aesthetic case for the house. Not only was the eight-sided house cheaper and more convenient, he suggested, but it was also more beautiful than the traditional rectangular house with wings. In the revised 1853 edition of *A Home for All*, Fowler further developed his argument regarding the importance of form to beauty. Echoing the classical and picturesque architectural precepts that had guided Jefferson's turn to octagons, Fowler wrote: "Some forms are constitutionally more beautiful than others. Of these the spherical is more beautiful than the angular, and the smooth and undulating than the rough and projecting." The octagon more closely approximated the sphere than did the winged house—ergo, it was more beautiful. These aesthetic principles, Fowler argued, relied on "an immutable law of Nature."[58]

What is interesting is not only the way that Fowler seemed to adopt the terms of contemporary debates over aesthetics but also how he urged readers to confirm his assertions with their own eyes:

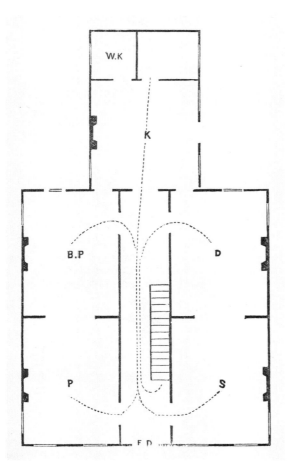
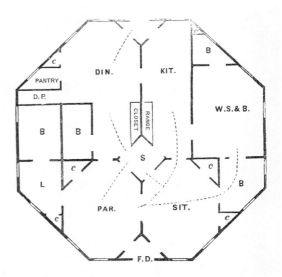

FIGURE 3.14. Diagrams purporting to demonstrate the greater efficiency of circulation in an octagon house over a "winged" house. From Orson Fowler, *A Home for All*, 1854 edition. Courtesy Getty Research Institute / Archive.org.

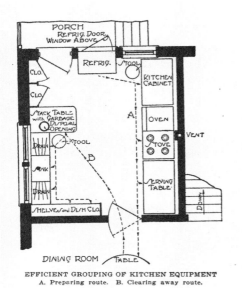
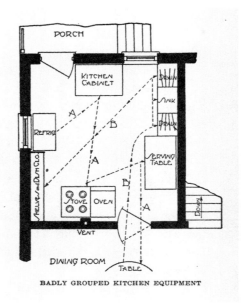

FIGURE 3.15. Comparison of badly and properly arranged kitchens. From Christine Frederick, *Household Engineering*, 1919.

> Look at these two figures, the octagon and the winged, or even the square, and say which strikes you as the most noble looking and truly beautiful. The octagon solid, massive, compact, and spherical; the winged full of outs and ins, all long and no wide . . . the octagon beautifully proportioned every way, the winged out of all proportion . . . in short, the octagon perfectly beautiful and the winged a violation of every principle of taste and beauty. . . . You have only to look at our ground plan of the three figures to see which is incomparably superior to both the others.[59]

Here Fowler used the imperative voice to instruct his readers to "look" and to form their own judgments. This was a democratizing gesture that rendered aesthetics into a matter for any ordinary person to judge.

Rituals of Visual Verification

In Fowler's handling, diagrams and pictures became part of a ritual of verification, a Barnumesque stratagem of inviting viewers to become skeptical and engaged subjects. In *A Home for All,* Fowler channeled the rhetoric of the showman by challenging disbelievers to perform their own reckonings: "If such doubt my figuring, they will find their own to agree substantially with these results, for arithmetic cannot lie."[60] Several readers took Fowler up on this challenge. The May 1854 issue of the *American Phrenological Journal,* for example, included a letter from Thomas W. Ritchie, a reader in Canada, asking for more details about Fowler's construction method. Ritchie wrote that he had done his own figuring and concluded that the octagon was in fact even more superior to the square house than Fowler contended: "I have laid down several octagons with the scale and dividers, and find that an octagonal figure contains nearly *one-fourth* more than a square of the same outer surface." (Fowler had correctly estimated the octagon to contain one-fifth more space than a square.) The phrenologist's published response is odd but telling. He explained that he had been conservative in his calculations and that the errors had to do with the printing process: "Its cause was, that the stereotyping process slightly *contracts,* and I made my calculations from plate proofs. Hence all the figures will be found a trifle *less* than the size ascribed to them."[61] Fowler's rather absurd explanation—that he had calculated the building's area and perimeter from a stereotype plate image—reminds us that the octagon house was above all an artifact of print, composed of ink and paper as much as brick and mortar.

Readers' letters in several serial publications give evidence of the eagerness with which middle-class Americans took up the role of active, critical testers of the octagon house idea. In 1858, the *Country Gentleman,* for example, published a series of articles and letters initiated by S. H. Mann of Beloit, Wisconsin. Mann identified himself as "not a mechanic, but . . . a progressive" with a "deep interest in whatever is designed to promote the happiness of man." He had read Fowler's book but found fault with its plans and submitted his own improved version (Figure 3.16). Mann favored rooms that were more rectangular and without cutoff corners, and he preferred to separate the kitchen from the rest of the house with a hallway, to prevent the passage of heat,

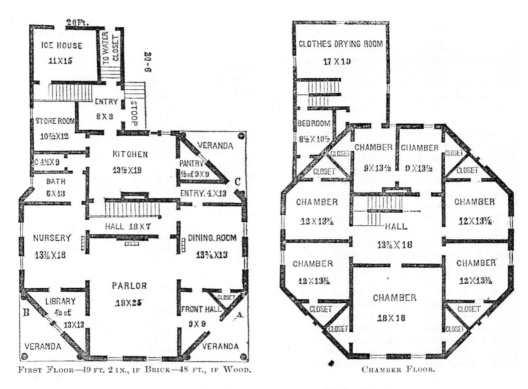

FIGURE 3.16. Octagon house plans by S. H. Mann. Published in the *Country Gentleman*, January 7, 1858.

smells, and flies. Other readers responded in turn, offering their own opinions and suggestions, and the debate was carried on through at least nine subsequent issues.[62] Another example of an individual taking inspiration from and improving on Fowler's invention can be found in a notice for a hexagonal house that would purportedly supersede the octagonal buildings of the previous decade, published in an 1870 issue of *Southern Home*. This turned out to be a design patented by Harriet Morrison Irwin (Figure 3.17). The article, in citing the many benefits of the hexagonal house over a rectangular one, mimicked Fowler's arguments for the octagonal house (it would be less expensive, more spacious, and more beautiful) but additionally pointed out that hexagonal rooms would "fit into each other without loss of space."[63]

In addition to offering feedback on the layout of the octagon house, readers addressed Fowler's claims about its material efficiency. In the original edition of *A Home for All*, he advocated employing a "board wall" system made of solid wood planks laid on top of each other. Acknowledging that timber was becoming increasingly scarce in the northeastern United States owing to deforestation, Fowler suggested that scrap and knotty woods be used and also that builders consider planting trees to replenish the nation's supply.[64] In the 1853 edition, he presented a new technology that he called the "gravel wall"—essentially concrete composed of lime, stone, and gravel, which he called "Nature's own building material."[65] Fireproof, decay resistant, and made from materials readily at hand, the gravel wall was four times cheaper than

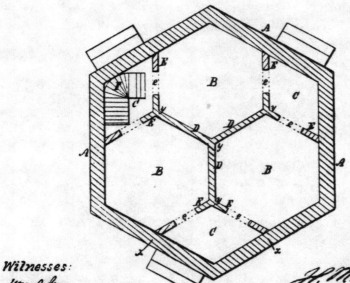

FIGURE 3.17. Harriet Irwin, patent for hexagonal house, 1869.

FIGURE 3.18. Joseph Goodrich's hexagonal hotel in Milton, Wisconsin. Photograph by Alexander C. Guth. Library of Congress, Historic American Buildings Survey.

wood by Fowler's calculation, making it even more possible for those with virtually no financial means to build a house.[66] Fowler had discovered the technique while on a phrenological tour in Wisconsin, where he had come across a hexagonal gravel-wall building erected by an innkeeper named Joseph Goodrich (Figure 3.18).[67] Goodrich apparently also understood well the operational aesthetic. As a demonstration of the strength of his invention, he invited Fowler to strike the walls of his hotel with a sledgehammer for six cents per blow.[68] Fowler was converted and by 1850 was erecting his own grand octagon house using the system.

The introduction of the gravel wall exposed a flaw in Fowler's logic, however, as George Barrett, an astute reader and a mill owner in Spring Valley, Ohio, pointed out. Whereas Fowler had originally advocated the octagon form as a way to minimize building expenses by reducing the amount of wood needed, the comparatively inexpensive gravel-wall system obviated this need for economy. Barrett thus adopted the idea of the new material but dispensed with Fowler's recommended shape and built his own conventional-plan house, "at times tremulous and wavering" in the face of neighbors' scornful skepticism about his use of concrete. Pleased by the result, he wrote his own book promoting the material.[69]

Perhaps the most dramatic narrative of personal verification was that of a reader named J. S. Thornton of Pawtucket, Rhode Island. After reading *A Home for All,*

Thornton retained some doubts about the viability of Fowler's ideas. He resolved to visit the phrenologist's house in Fishkill, New York, "believing that if I could *see them,* I could settle the matter at once." Thornton described the feeling of revelation upon seeing Fowler's house, including the cognitive effort required "to take in the *newness* of the idea, and the *vastness* of the pile." His thoughts "became truant and unmanageable—disowned their *affinity*—flew *off* in wild *incoherency.*" After collecting himself, Thornton approached the building and "gave a tap here, to test its hardness, and a thump there, to see how easily its parts might be disconnected." Having confirmed the concrete octagon's solidity with his own senses, he returned home and resolved to build a concrete house, which in turn inspired its own round of visual verification. His neighbors all "expressed a desire to *see it done,* but none *to do it.*" A "great cloud of witnesses" watched over the enterprise. Upon the structure's completion, Thornton recounted, a gentleman from a neighboring town visited to settle his own nagging doubts about concrete. Within a half hour, Thornton was able to reassure the man by taking him on a tour of recently erected concrete houses.[70] The rhetoric of the octagon house thus traveled through several relays, all linked through narratives of visual experience and performative self-verification. A printed geometric diagram and calculations were seen and then augmented by firsthand witnessing of a constructed building. The narration of this experience was then disseminated in print, generating its own round of visual verification experiences. In this way, an untested idea not only gained adherents but also generated its own culture and feedback loop of visual proof.

Not everyone was convinced of the octagon house's merits, however. The genteel editors of *The Horticulturalist,* after printing a mostly positive review of an octagon house in 1850, by 1856 were savaging the house's "pitiful narrow passages, the multiplicity of corners (each of which, as every mechanic knows, increases the expense), the skew angles," all of which produced a "hot, crowded, and eccentric house." The editors summed up the objections to the octagon house as three: "1. The poor architectural appearance. 2. The inconvenience of the 'conveniences.' 3. That the superior cheapness of this description of house is not so great as it has been made out to be."[71] Such negative reviews must have turned some Americans away from the octagon house. Yet, following Barnum's insight that public skepticism and controversy could serve to attract attention, the published debates about the strengths and shortcomings of the octagon may also have fueled the desire of others to see, and to decide, for themselves.

The Circulation of the Octagon House

As hinted by the above analysis, the brief and sudden popularity of the octagon house was made possible not only by Fowler's specific rhetorical techniques, which engaged readers as active, skeptical witnesses, but also by the multiple media through which the image of the octagon house circulated, initially in printed publications and eventually in built, architectural incarnations. The history of modern fads suggests that

FIGURE 3.19. Design for a small octagonal cottage. From Charles Dwyer, *The Economic Cottage Builder,* 1856. Courtesy Winterthur Library, Printed Book and Periodical Collection.

ideas gain influence not because they are good but because they are transmitted across multiple discursive communities, the more widely the better. This is no less true of the octagon house, which moved rapidly through the mid-nineteenth century's culture of reprinting, in which permissive copyright regulations enabled the frequent reproduction of articles and images across multiple publications and diverse media communities.[72]

To start, Fowler deployed his family's significant media operation to promote *A Home for All.* Both the 1848 and 1853 editions of the book were repeatedly reviewed, puffed, and debated in the pages of the *American Phrenological Journal,* and advertisements for the book were placed in other books published by Fowler and Wells.[73] The importance of the Fowlers' media operation as a medium of dissemination has been suggested by Rebecca McCarley, who found in her study of midwestern octagon houses that they tended to spring up in areas where subscribers and agents of the *American Phrenological Journal* lived, as well as in locations Fowler visited during his lecture tours in the 1850s.[74] While the initial publication of *A Home for All* received some notice, reprinting accelerated rapidly after the release of the revised edition. Stories about octagon houses, with or without reference to Fowler, began cropping up in publications ranging from middle-class parlor magazines to evangelical publications to regional farm journals, in titles as diverse as *Godey's Lady's Book, United States Magazine and Democratic Review, Christian Parlor Magazine, The Horticulturalist,* and

FIGURE 3.20. Oriental villa. From Samuel Sloan, *Sloan's Homestead Architecture,* 1861. Courtesy American Antiquarian Society.

Genesee Farmer.[75] Octagon houses were also reproduced in cottage and house manuals, such as John Bullock's *The American Cottage Builder* (1854), Zephaniah Baker's *The Cottage Builder's Manual* (1856), Charles Dwyer's *The Economic Cottage Builder* (1856), Daniel Jacques's *The House* (1859), and Samuel Sloan's *Homestead Architecture* (1861).

The diversity of these publications shows the house's chameleonic quality as it moved through different communities of readers. In one context, such as Dwyer's pattern book, the octagon house could be described as a modest dwelling type, ideal for "men of small means" and costing approximately $300 to $500 to frame (Figure 3.19). In another, like Sloan's *Homestead Architecture,* it was rendered as a fantastical Orientalist villa, estimated to cost around $40,000 (Figure 3.20). (Fowler had listed

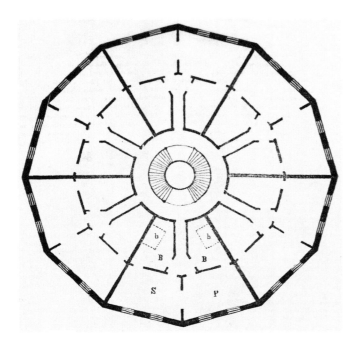

FIGURE 3.21. Plan of a twelve-sided associative dwelling inspired by Fowler. Published in the Fourierist journal *The Harbinger*, November 11, 1848. Courtesy American Antiquarian Society.

the cost of a modest octagon with twelve-foot, six-inch sides at $1,100.)[76] A writer in the general-audience publication *Holden's Dollar Magazine* could ambivalently praise the first edition of *A Home for All* as "novel as well as excellent," containing aphorisms that were "sensible, but peculiar," while agricultural journals addressing farmers presented the octagon house as a pragmatic and novel plan offering good ventilation, well-lit spaces, and a convenient arrangement of rooms.[77] The political valences of the octagon house also changed depending on the writer and the platform, and the design of the building itself was sometimes adapted accordingly. An 1848 issue of the Fourierist newspaper *The Harbinger* included a proposal for a twelve-sided "associative dwelling" and named Fowler's octagon house as inspiration.[78] The writer imagined a two-story, 7,500-square-foot structure with a central circular space covered by a retractable glass roof (Figure 3.21).[79] While some socialists embraced the octagon house, other reviewers regarded it as a sign of shifting tides in the world of reform, away from more ambitious, communitarian utopian enterprises and toward more individualistic solutions. In a lengthy review of *A Home for All* published in the *Literary Union*, the author favorably contrasted the practicality and modesty of the octagon house idea with the misguided efforts of socialist reformers who "dream dreams of dazzling brilliancy" yet "never waken to realize that they are only dreams." The writer argued that the octagon house was a "plan of reform tangible to all and practical *for each individual alone.*"[80] For the *Literary Union* reviewer at least, Fowler's house represented a path of pragmatic and individually based improvement that compared favorably to socialism, land reform, and other ambitious systemic reform efforts. Here was a change that individual Americans could make on their own, without the need for collective action.

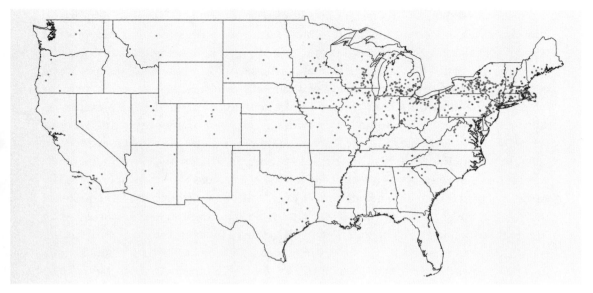

FIGURE 3.22. Map of octagon houses built in the nineteenth century. Drawing by author.

Conspicuous Individualism

Who were the readers of Fowler's octagon house books and of the other publications in which the octagon circulated? What compelled so many to follow Fowler's instructions and build their own eight-sided dwellings? The historical evidence indicates that the majority of octagon houses were erected neither by radical reformers nor by the working-class men that Fowler had taken care to address, but instead by prosperous farmers, artisans, merchants, and professionals from New England and New York. The prototypical octagon house builder resembled the enterprising character delineated by Ralph Waldo Emerson in "Self-Reliance": the man "from New Hampshire or Vermont, who in turn tries all the professions, who *teams it, farms it, peddles,* keeps a school, preaches, edits a newspaper, goes to Congress, buys a township, and so forth, in successive years."[81] The hotbeds of octagon house building were lands just behind the "frontier"—upstate New York, western Massachusetts, Michigan, Wisconsin, and Ohio—lands settled by whites and seized or stolen from Indians just a generation or two earlier (or, in some cases, still unceded), though octagons could also be found in the South and as far west as California (Figure 3.22). It is no accident that the traits idealized by Emerson and Fowler are also those associated with settler colonizers—characteristics such as independence of mind, self-sufficiency, resourcefulness, and industry.[82]

While some of the men who built octagons were exceptionally eccentric, most builders were rather ordinary, like the Wilcox family in Camillus. Timothy Younglove, a prosperous grape farmer in Hammondsport, New York, offers another case in point. In 1859 Younglove built a large, two-story octagon house, twenty feet on each side, with eighteen-inch-thick concrete walls, finished with a cupola. Although aware of the reforms of the day (his letters mention temperance, abolitionism, Millerism, and phrenology), he does not seem to have been especially radical. A supporter of the Democratic Party, Younglove voted against granting suffrage to freed African Americans in 1846.[83] He was a practical man who served as an officer of the local wine company and as town superintendent of common schools. He was a former surveyor who, in a friend's words, was "versed in mathematics [and knew] the pleasure resulting there from."[84] While no direct evidence survives of his precise motivations for building an eight-sided house, fifteen years earlier he had helped construct an octagonal schoolhouse in his community—a reminder that, while the octagon house was seen as a novelty, it was not entirely *ex novo,* the ground having been prepared by earlier polygonal vernacular structures.[85] John S. Moffat was another early adopter of the octagon house. Born just north of Ithaca, New York, in 1814, Moffat worked as an itinerant schoolteacher in upstate New York for several years. Unhappy with his unsettled state, he moved with his family to Hudson, Wisconsin, in 1854, where he took up a position as a clerk in the U.S. Land Office for the Chippewa District. Moffat's job was to help facilitate settler acquisition of land recently ceded through treaty by the Ojibwe (Chippewa) nation. One year after moving to Hudson, he built an eight-sided house (Figure 3.23).[86] An article in the *Hudson North Star* in June 1855 announced, "The first building on O. S. Fowler's octagon plan, ever constructed in the North-West, is now being built in this village by John S. Moffat, Esq." The writer cited Moffat's rationales for building the octagon house as precisely the ones put forward by Fowler: that it would enclose more space than a rectangular house as well as provide a more convenient arrangement of rooms. The rooms in an octagon house are "so much more contiguous, so much better placed as regards each other, so much better graduated as regards size, some larger, others smaller, and especially so many closets, which renders a house so convenient, that it really captivates the women, and promotes every family end."[87]

As this article hints, men like Moffat and Younglove were likely drawn to the octagon plan in part because they believed Fowler's claims for the house's economy and convenience. These were pragmatic men, interested in science and mathematics, who saw the octagon house as part and parcel of the kinds of technological advancements they were witnessing around them. They were persuaded to adopt an untested, novel plan because they believed it was cheaper and more functional than traditional alternatives. Their willingness to buck convention and try the new ostensibly bespeaks a reformist outlook and independence of mind praised by Emerson and Fowler. In *A Home for All,* the phrenologist had invited such men to reject the advice of experts like Downing and instead trust their own eyes, judge for themselves, and follow their own pragmatic reason rather than social convention. As J. S. Thornton, the Rhode Island octagon house builder, explained in a letter to the *American Phrenological Journal:*

> It requires a man of pluck to take a new enterprise like this upon his shoulders, and swim against the current of custom and popular opinion. He must feel, not only that "what has been done, can be done" again, but that things may and should be done which have never been done before. He must have a lively con-

FIGURE 3.23. John Moffat House, Hudson, Wisconsin, 1855. Courtesy Wisconsin Historical Society, WHS-5671.

sciousness of his manhood, of his individuality, and his accountability. He must breathe deep and strong, think large thoughts, and give them utterance for the good of his kind, though some old conservative hardhead crack at his presumption. He must allow himself to be inspired by the thought that he is making an effort to raise his mark in the world still higher for humanity.[88]

Thus, according to Thornton, octagon houses were signs of their builders' independence, their ability to go against conventional wisdom in the pursuit of larger social improvement.

The notion that the shape of the house could manifest its owner's character echoed Fowler's phrenological theories, specifically the idea that outward forms could reveal inner attributes. In *A Home for All,* Fowler argued that houses were expressions of human beings' faculties of "Constructiveness" and "Inhabitiveness."

Constructiveness, located near the temple, encompassed an instinct and talent for making, dexterity in the use of tools, and a disposition to tinkering and building machinery, while Inhabitiveness, located at the back of the skull, led human beings to seek and crave a home, "an abiding-place, which shall be the centre of most of the joys of life."[89] These faculties followed the paradox characteristic of American phrenology in general: they were innate and determinative of future behavior and yet could be cultivated. Fowler argued that houses reflected their makers' characters: "As a general rule, a fancy man will build a fancy house; a practical man, a convenient house; . . . a weak man, an ill-arranged house."[90] In a more absurd twist on this principle, he suggested that "men with the eagle form of nose and physiognomy" would "build on high ground, where they can have a commanding prospect." More seriously and problematically, he identified a deterministic scale of racial types correlated to building capacities, beginning with the lowest "orang-outang" and the "Bosjowan" (builders of the "lowest class of human architecture") and proceeding up through the "Hottentot, Carib, Indian, Malay, and Caucasian, [who] build houses better, and still better, the higher the order of their mentality."[91]

Ultimately, the doctrine of progress prevailed in Fowler's book. Constructiveness was an inherently progressive faculty. Human beings' instinct for building led them to strive constantly for advancement: "Year after year should add one comfort and improvement after another to our homes, till the earth becomes literally studded with paradises, full of life and happiness."[92] Fowler claimed that anyone could build an octagon house and thus enhance their life situation. Building and owning a home was not just a confirmation of a person's character; like Fowler's phrenological prescriptions, it could help the individual advance in an age that idealized striving and "self-made" men.

Although Fowler presented the octagon house as a tool for self-advancement, at least some of his readers seem to have treated it as an expression or evidence of their success. The octagon's formal conspicuousness lent itself to what the sociologist Thorstein Veblen would later call "conspicuous consumption," whereby wealthy or prominent men used their homes and other purchases to establish an "invidious distinction" between themselves and others. Grand, "high-style" octagon houses constitute a significant subset of mid-nineteenth-century examples.[93] Fowler's own four-story house with a cupola was the first prominent example, one that achieved wide circulation in the form of William Howland's frequently reprinted perspective engraving, featured in the 1853 edition of A Home for All (Figure 3.5). Two midwestern governors also erected grand octagons: Leonard Farwell of Wisconsin built a 9,000-square-foot, three-story house with a cupola, twenty-five feet on each side, in 1852–54.[94] John Wood, who had served briefly as governor of Illinois, followed suit, erecting a luxurious eight-sided house veneered in marble in 1864. John Richards, a Massachusetts-born lawyer and mill owner, built a large brick-and-limestone octagonal house in Watertown, Wisconsin, in 1854. At four stories tall and with twenty-two-foot sides, the house featured several elements recommended by Fowler, including encircling porches, a central staircase, a cupola, a cistern with running water, a dumbwaiter, and a ventilation system.[95] Perhaps the most flamboyant octagon house

FIGURE 3.24. Samuel Sloan, Longwood, Natchez, Mississippi, built circa 1860. Courtesy Library of Congress, Historic American Buildings Survey.

was built by the cotton planter and slave owner Haller Nutt in Natchez, Mississippi. Designed by Samuel Sloan, Nutt's Orientalist villa, Longwood, featured brick walls with elaborate white wooden ornament and a large onion dome. Begun in 1860, construction of the 30,000-square-foot house was interrupted by the Civil War, and it was never finished (Figure 3.24).

Octagon houses were well suited to establishing an owner's individuality or distinctiveness, whether defined by progressive-mindedness or affluence. Their shapes were inherently conspicuous, standing out from their neighbors and calling attention to themselves. Like the visual practices attached to phrenology itself, or Fowler's geometric diagrams, the houses offered an immediate graphic legibility. A reviewer in The Horticulturalist compared eight-sided houses to enlarged versions of the "little wooden parallelopipeds used in teaching children solid geometry, dropped into the middle of any sweet, natural landscape."[96] The magazine explained the negative aspect of this conspicuousness, pointing to the house's "ungraceful general outline," "abrupt perpendicularity," and formal incongruousness with the landscape. A review of Fowler's Fishkill mansion described its appearance in more positive terms as "noble, massive, grand, and imposing," but similarly emphasized its pronounced visual difference. Its siting on a hilltop rendered it "the observed of all observers."[97]

As these quotations indicate, the house itself could become an effective form of visual rhetoric, a way of communicating messages about the owner and the owner's values. Although Fowler had criticized Downing and others for emphasizing the exterior styling of a house as a vehicle for expressing genteel character, the eschewal of polite cultural aesthetics in favor of a more ostensibly functional, distinctively shaped, neoteric architecture was its own visual statement. The octagon house communicated through form rather than through ornament. Functionalism could be just as rhetorical as the conventional architectural styles.

By the end of the 1850s, octagon houses, along with their cousins hexagonal and circular houses, were increasingly identified in the popular imagination with owners who were different, even eccentric. Rather than writing off this association of octagons with eccentricity as yet another sign of their historical marginality, it is worth inquiring whether octagon houses instead revealed in extreme form precisely the character traits prized by modern liberal capitalist society: independence of mind, skeptical rationality, and a drive to compete and to stand out, as well as a tolerance for differing opinions and lifestyles. Daniel Jacques, in presenting readers with a perspective and plan of Enoch Robinson's round house in Somerville, Massachusetts, editorialized: "There are queer people in the world—a great many of them—and it is not strange that there are also queer houses. Now, as our little book is made for everybody, it is but just that queer people and their houses should be represented in it."[98] (And this was in a book published by Fowler and Wells.) The *Prairie Farmer* opined that the octagonal or circular house would not, "on the whole, suit the eye of most people. . . . There is something about it, perhaps, induced by association, which has an outrie [*sic*] look. . . . We are aware, however, that tastes differ, and there are people who will be odd, and who look natural only when they look odd. Such will be suited with an odd looking dwelling, and we would not interfere with their privilege."[99] Sereno Edwards Todd similarly wrote in his house pattern book of 1868: "Eccentric people only, fancy that an octagon dwelling is their 'beau ideal' of a dwelling-house. If a person desires something that is more odd than convenient, let him build a rotunda, or a dwelling with eight sides."[100]

These critics conveyed their judgment in a spirit of tolerance. Octagons were strange, but they suited some individuals, who should be allowed to indulge their fancies. In mid-nineteenth-century America, during a time Emerson called the "age of the first person singular," some even counted eccentricity as a virtue. Philosophers such as Emerson and Henry David Thoreau, after all, were making intellectual arguments for self-reliance and nonconformism.[101] After he published *Walden* in 1854, Thoreau was widely labeled an "eccentric" for his renunciation of social norms.[102] In his 1859 essay "On Liberty," John Stuart Mill also defended eccentricity as a pillar of liberal society—a mark of freedom of thought and a necessary stimulant for progress:

> In this age the mere example of non-conformity, the mere refusal to bend the knee to custom, is itself a service. Precisely because the tyranny of opinion is such as to make eccentricity a reproach, it is desirable, in order to break through that tyranny, that people should be eccentric. Eccentricity has always abounded when and where strength of character has abounded; and the amount of eccen-

tricity in a society has generally been proportional to the amount of genius, mental vigor, and moral courage which it contained.[103]

Eccentricity and liberalism went hand in hand. Here we see the multiple valences of "liberalism," an ideology that upheld individual freedom (as long as that freedom did not impinge on others), individual rights, and a free market, and also entailed a belief in progress and the amelioration of social inequities. In contrast to tradition-bound conservatism, liberalism encompassed a willingness to entertain new ideas, since progress could be achieved only through an openness to unorthodox views.[104] At the core of liberalism was the individual, a term that itself, as Raymond Williams later observed, could be divided into two distinct senses: on the one hand, the sense of the primacy of each person as a constituent and independent element of society; and on the other, the romantic sense of the uniqueness and personality of each person.[105] In the nineteenth-century United States, individualism manifested itself in the pervasive middle-class concern for self-construction and self-improvement, as well as in a sense of democratic agency. Every person (or at least every white man) was understood to have a right to self-definition and judgment.

Fowler's brand of phrenology and his octagon house advanced these multiple senses of both liberalism and individualism. Like others preaching self-reliance and self-culture in the nineteenth-century United States, Fowler promoted the idea that each person's unique combination of traits and faculties could be cultivated as part of a process of self-construction. On a rhetorical level, too, Fowler advocated trusting in one's own reasoning and experience, believing one's own eyes, rather than blindly following convention or custom. His octagon house, a figment of visual rhetoric thoroughly steeped in an operational aesthetic, was directed toward, and helped conjure, this pragmatic, striving (and presumably white and male) individual. But whereas Thoreau and Emerson advocated a philosophical form of independent thought and self-culture because they believed that it could elevate society as a whole to a higher ethical and spiritual state, Fowler's stated goals were more earthbound: to enable people to maximize their own lot through owning a house, attaining health, and developing a sense of possessive individualism. His octagon house was a resolutely liberal utopia, one that marked a turn away from republican and socialist utopian imaginings and toward an individualist definition of self-maximization and self-realization as the ultimate goals. In elevating the goal of each individual owning his own home, he affirmed the Jeffersonian ideal, upheld by the land reformers, of property ownership as the means to independence, thus implicitly tying his house to one of the key tenets motivating settler colonialism. Yet, as we have seen, the octagon house also had an ideological flexibility as well as visual potency that derived from its curious merging of iconicity and facticity. In 1854, these qualities would be seized upon by an English-born reformer who would launch an improbable utopian enterprise: an eight-sided vegetarian colony that he imagined would contribute to overcoming the most entrenched obstacle to freedom in America, the institution of slavery.

CHAPTER 4

Picturing Sociality without Socialism
The Kansas Vegetarian Octagon Colony

In the spring of 1855, the Fowlers and Wells publishing company began printing notices of a new enterprise in its reform journals: an octagonal vegetarian colony to be established in the recently organized Kansas Territory. At the time, Kansas was a key battleground in two related but distinct conflicts: the national struggle over the expansion of slavery and the ongoing expropriation of Indigenous land and removal of Indigenous people. Yet the founder of the octagonal colony, English immigrant and journalist Henry S. Clubb (1827–1921), painted a rose-colored picture of the territory. In the pages of the *Water-Cure Journal,* he announced the formation of a joint-stock company to build a permanent home for vegetarians. Out west, he predicted, renouncers of flesh-eating would find "rich soil, salubrious and healthful climate, pure water." He extolled the benefits of collective settlement, which would prevent members from feeling "solitary and alone in their Vegetarian practice" and from sinking into "flesh-eating habits." Lastly, he announced that the colony would adopt a novel urban form: "an octagon plan of settlement," inspired by Orson Fowler's eight-sided house.[1] Wood-engraved diagrammatic plans of the octagon city were published separately in a foldout broadsheet, showing a town with a central park and eight radiating avenues dividing wedge-shaped farm lots, as well as a central building taken directly from Fowler's *A Home for All* (Figure 4.1).[2]

Perhaps the most extraordinary fact about this vegetarian octagon colony scheme is that more than seventy families signed on to the plan, with the first band of settlers heading out in March 1856.[3] The colony was an almost immediate failure. Beset by mosquitoes, malaria, and disorganization, some of the would-be colonists left before the first winter, while others divorced themselves from the colony but remained in Kansas. Within a year, as one historian chronicled, "hardly a trace of the settlement remained" except for a nearby stream known to this day as Vegetarian Creek.[4]

Subsequently, the story of the Kansas Vegetarian Settlement Company has been

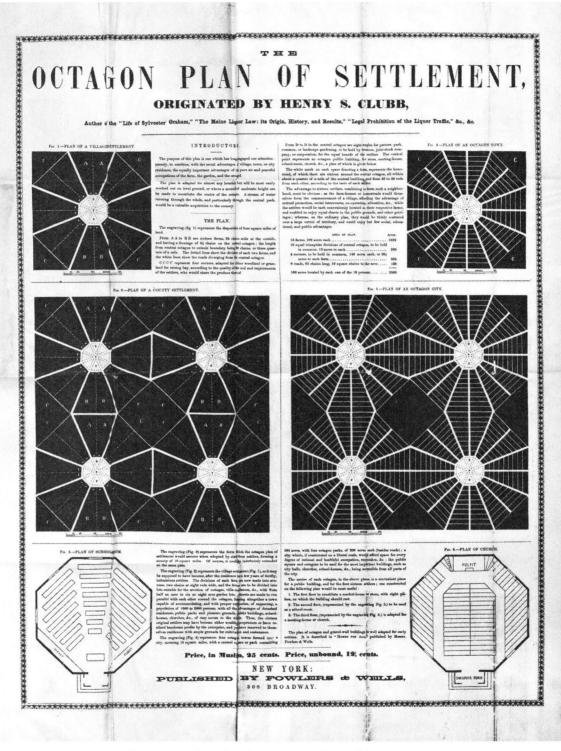

FIGURE 4.1. *The Octagon Plan of Settlement,* bound broadsheet, 1855. 56 × 43 cm. Courtesy Newberry Library.

regarded by most historians as a footnote to a footnote—a quixotic, tragicomic episode in the narratives of Fowler's octagon, "Bleeding Kansas," and vegetarianism.[5] The enterprise's apparently eclectic mixture of dietary reform, real estate speculation, and unconventional urban planning, sprinkled with a dash of antislavery conviction, appears to be an extreme example of the romantic reform movements that swept the United States from the 1830s through the 1850s.[6] In an 1844 essay, "New England Reformers," Ralph Waldo Emerson gently mocked the vast array of "projects for the salvation of the world" circulating around him: "One apostle thought all men should go to farming, and another that no man should buy or sell, that the use of money was the cardinal evil; another that the mischief was in our diet, that we eat and drink damnation." Although he admired the spirit of experimentation and the "restless, prying, conscientious criticism" that these movements embodied, Emerson was ultimately skeptical of most of these reform efforts, arguing that individuals should focus on self-reform as the necessary precursor to societal transformation.[7]

Like Fowler's octagon house, Clubb's vegetarian colony emerged during a transitional period within nineteenth-century reform, when many women and men who had been engaged in abolition, socialism, or labor activism in the 1830s and early 1840s were turning in new directions, often toward more individually or inwardly focused pursuits, including phrenology, spiritualism, magnetism, and water cures.[8] By the late 1850s, most of these reform energies would be eclipsed and subsumed into the antislavery cause, as the nation hurtled toward civil war. If Fowler's octagon house reflected an emerging liberal individualist creed of health, thrift, and self-advancement that would become hegemonic after the war, then Clubb's plan for a collective octagon could be regarded as a late bid for creating a community of radicals, but one that adopted a much weaker form of association than the communitarian and utopian projects of the 1830s and early 1840s. The vegetarian society attempted to reconcile an ethos of individualism with a diminished form of collectivity, proposing something akin to a sociality without socialism.[9] Whereas men like Owen and Fourier had conceived of communities housed in grand palaces in which labor, housing, education, and (in some cases) property were communalized, Clubb's city was careful to preserve individual ownership of land and advertised itself to prospective settlers as a means of getting in on the booming speculation in western lands. Vegetarian ideology reflected this tension between individualistic and social motives. Many midcentury vegetarians saw the reform of diet and bodies as connected to the larger transformation of the world; for example, they believed that flesh-eating contributed to the violence and aggression underlying slavery. Yet this focus on individual behaviors and lifestyles could also appear inadequate to the enormous conflicts and problems afflicting American society. This incongruity of means and ends, individualism and large-scale societal change, vegetarianism and slavery, is vividly symbolized by the juxtaposition of Clubb's colony with events happening nearby in Kansas. For at nearly the same moment that the members of the Octagon Settlement Company were attempting to establish their vegetarian paradise, the U.S. government was orchestrating the removal of Indigenous people, including the Kanza, Osage, Potawatomi, Kickapoo,

Delaware, and Cherokee Indians, from their reservations in eastern Kansas. And less than one hundred miles away from Clubb's settlement, John Brown (later of Harpers Ferry fame) was leading a small band of abolitionist fighters in what became known as the Pottawatomie massacre, in which five pro-slavery settlers were killed, one of a series of violent incidents leading to the eruption of war. Against the backdrop of Indigenous decimation and escalating sectional conflict, Clubb's harmonious vegetarian haven, a place where he hoped "birds shall fill the air with melody without fear or trembling," could not but appear naively fanciful.[10]

These contradictions manifested themselves in the visual representation of the vegetarian colony, especially as contrasted with the imagery employed by contemporary antislavery advocates. At the same moment that Clubb was publishing stark geometric plan diagrams of his octagon city, emphasizing its benefits as a place of "mutual protection, social intercourse, [and] co-operation," illustrations of bloody confrontations between pro- and antislavery forces were also appearing in print. The juxtaposition of these two kinds of pictures—one abstractly representing harmony, the other vividly depicting armed conflict—offers an opportunity to consider the position of geometric utopianism within the wider context of mid-nineteenth-century visual-political culture. If Clubb's octagon plan drew on the resonances of Enlightenment order, reason, and self-evidence to project a utopian community of like-minded individuals, antislavery images appealed to the passions and sentiment by visualizing personal violation and violence. Whereas one painted a portrait of a future ideal city, the other claimed to provide "eyewitness" testimony of present wrongs in order to incite immediate action. With their origins in the older aesthetics of artisan radicalism, geometric utopian images could appear abstruse and theoretical, removed from the passionate on-the-ground agonism of the conflict over slavery.

Henry Clubb and Transatlantic Vegetarian Radicalism

Clubb's career offers a revealing glimpse of the origins of the transatlantic vegetarian movement, which lay in the confluence of late eighteenth-century English Swedenborgianism, romanticism, health reform, and urban, working-class radical movements.[11] Movement vegetarianism began in England as a physiological and spiritual reform centered on the belief that abstention from eating meat could improve health and that eschewing the violence and impurity of industrial butchery and meat consumption could enable the cultivation of a higher spirituality. The idea of linking flesh-eating to bloodshed, cruelty, and "base" impulses led English and, later, American vegetarians to connect dietary reform to causes like abolition, pacifism, women's rights, and the progress and reform of society generally. The rise of vegetarianism can also be understood as an oppositional reaction to urbanization, industrialization, and capitalism. As more people moved from the farm to the city, some grew wary of commercial and industrial food production and romanticized a more "natural" way of life, close to the earth. The best-known American proponent of vegetarianism, Sylvester Graham, preached that a vegetarian diet provided an antidote to the overstimulation, "impure air," and "unwholesome employments" of city life; he also critiqued commercially produced bread, which he associated with industrial capitalism, and asserted the superiority of homemade, whole-grain bread (Graham crackers are named after him).[12] Graham linked a meatless diet to a regulated body and a higher level of intelligence and morality. The Boston educational reformer Bronson Alcott, influenced by English transcendentalist interlocutors, similarly stressed vegetarianism as a path of personal purification and edification.

As this brief sketch of nineteenth-century Anglo-American vegetarianism hints, one of the tensions in historical interpretations of the movement concerns the extent to which it was focused on individual reform versus broader social reform. Adam Shprintzen argues that the movement shifted from a more radical political orientation before the Civil War to a more consumerist and individualistic ethos by the end of the century. Other scholars, following in Emerson's footsteps, have treated vegetarianism as one of a variety of eclectic "romantic reforms" taken up by Americans in the mid-nineteenth century. As such, it can be easily swept into the critiques leveled by historians against romantic reform: for example, that it was too focused on individual perfectibility, ignoring systemic and institutional changes.[13] Yet such critiques often ignore the nuanced ways in which reformers of the time saw self-reconstruction as a necessary precondition to societal transformation—an idea that writers on the politics of vegetarianism have addressed recently.[14]

Clubb's biography was interwoven with this larger history. Born in 1827 in Colchester, Essex, he was the youngest of nine children in a Swedenborgian family.[15] In his teens, he was converted to vegetarianism through the proselytizing of William G. Ward, a commercial traveler and family friend who described "the horrors and cruelties of the slaughter house and the dangers of eating the flesh of animals killed there, under various degrees of suffering and disease."[16] At fifteen, Clubb joined the Concordium at Ham Common, Richmond, Surrey (about ten miles outside London), an experimental community and alternative school founded by the mystic and reformer James Pierrepont Greaves (1777–1842).[17] Greaves, a disciple of the Swiss pedagogue Johann Heinrich Pestalozzi, named the school at the Concordium Alcott House, after Bronson Alcott. In an 1842 essay titled "English Reformers," Emerson called Greaves a "very remarkable person" who "has connected himself with almost every effort for human emancipation."[18] Like many of the American transcendentalists whom he admired, Greaves believed that individual reform of the inner person was a necessary first step to achieve social transformation. While supportive of experiments with association and communalism, the group at Ham Common insisted that such associations must be based on cultivating individuals' spiritual state, their connection to the universal spirit and conformance to love as a governing law.[19] Greaves and his followers therefore saw Alcott House as "a preparatory practical school" where spiritual training would ready individuals "for the community, the phalanstery, the republic, and the universal commonwealth."[20]

Members of the community at Ham Common practiced strict vegetarianism and teetotalism, observing an ascetic daily regimen. They woke at dawn, bathed in cold water, worked for an hour in the garden, and then ate a breakfast of oatmeal, porridge, bread, fruit, and water. After breakfast, they engaged in instruction or schooling. Lunch was followed by two hours of individual education and instruction and two hours of work for the community. After a simple dinner, members dedicated an hour to social communion.[21] Like other early vegetarians in England, Greaves and his followers saw diet and spirituality as linked. Flesh-eating, a practice associated with violence and killing, forced men to remain mired in lower, animal existence. In contrast, a vegetarian meal, "being simple, leaves the intellect clear, and the energies renewed for the various mental and physical employments which will follow."[22] Clubb echoed these views many years later in a 1903 pamphlet titled *Thirty-Nine Reasons Why I Am a Vegetarian,* in which he cited the spiritual benefits as the foremost reason to abstain from eating meat: "I believe that human life is destined to become a divine life. That man is created for a higher condition than that of a carnivorous or an omnivorous animal." Man had the choice: he could either "sink himself to a level with the lower animals or by cultivating intelligently his higher faculties . . . enjoy the rapture of the spiritual and celestial life."[23]

Although the philosophy of the Concordium stressed human beings' inner, spiritual development, it also held that such development was best carried out in the company of others rather than in isolation. "Singly, the aspiring mind finds itself weak and inefficient," therefore the Concordium would offer an "associated residence of human beings in concert." In "social union," the prospectus for the community explained, "an accelerated progress is obtained."[24] This strategy of withdrawing from the world while remaining in community was a common one within reform movements on both sides of the Atlantic in the 1830s and 1840s, as evidenced in the numerous Fourierist, Saint-Simonian, Owenite, and sectarian communities that sprang up during these decades. Emerson cast a critical eye on the mania for association in the United States, writing skeptically of the false "magic" that communards saw in the power of fraternity: "I have failed, and you have failed, but perhaps together we shall not fail."[25] He stood strongly in the camp of individualism, yet his words testify to the extraordinary interest among transatlantic radicals in association and combination as the means by which individual actions could bring about large-scale societal change. If transcendentalism and socialism represented two antipodal reform ideologies at midcentury—the former emphasizing individual conscience and the latter stressing collective solutions for systemic social problems—then vegetarianism sought to mediate between the two perspectives. Vegetarians believed that participation in meat slaughter and consumption contributed to violent urges; abolishing these practices would help regulate and elevate the general standard of morality. But vegetarian transcendentalists such as Bronson Alcott also argued that personal practices such as abstention from meat, sugar, and cotton offered a way to protest the plantation economy, a connection also articulated by Henry David Thoreau. Practiced collectively, individual dietary habits could thus have larger reverberations. The reform of individual bodies could lead to the creation of a more peaceful and harmonious society at large.

Like the Fowlers' Phrenological Depot in New York, the Concordium was a gathering point for international reformers and utopians in the 1840s. Ham Common was located in the rural outskirts of London, and thus within the penumbra of metropolitan reform activity. Robert Owen visited on three occasions, and several of the Concordium's members were former Owenites.[26] Alcott visited in 1842 and was so impressed that he brought two key Concordium members back with him to Massachusetts to establish his own short-lived vegetarian colony, Fruitlands.[27] The technological utopian John A. Etzler stayed at the Concordium for a period in 1843–44, around the same time that Clubb was in residence.[28]

Clubb spent about a year at the Concordium, during which he taught shorthand, learned the craft of printing, and assisted with the publication of the community's periodical, *The New Age, and Concordium Gazette*. After leaving the community, he worked as a shorthand teacher and reporter and started a society dedicated to Pitman phonography. Advocates of shorthand believed that the adoption of a simpler, more natural system of writing would widen access to literacy and thereby accelerate the reform of society.[29] Clubb also continued to write about vegetarianism for movement journals like the *Truth Tester* and *Vegetarian Advocate*. His articles eventually drew the attention of James Simpson, the president of the Vegetarian Society, who hired Clubb as his secretary and as editor of the society's journal, the *Vegetarian Messenger*. This combination of interests—in writing reform, printing, and journalism—was shared by many geometric utopians, reflecting their attention to modes of communication, visual rhetoric, and persuasion as crucial elements in social transformation.

Through Simpson, Clubb joined the Bible-Christian Church, a Swedenborgian-influenced sect that practiced temperance and vegetarianism. The church was a key conduit in the transatlantic circulation of vegetarian ideology. All of these encounters put Clubb at the heart of the early English vegetarian movement, centered in Manchester, England. One of the principal aims of the vegetarian organizations and their related publications was to counter popular perceptions of their eccentricity and marginality. Vegetarian societies in England and the United States thus organized and cultivated community through dinners and conventions.[30] One dinner organized by the Vegetarian Society, attended by Clubb and held in Manchester in 1849, was described in the *Vegetarian Advocate* as a "festival of a very brilliant character." A detailed report of the affair was published alongside a diagram showing the ceremonial arrangement of seats and the placement of foods on the banquet table. The dinner included molded barley, beetroot, savory and mushroom pies, molded sago, and assorted custards. The attendees offered toasts while imbibing water, "a beverage which never does harm."[31] An image of a similar 1851 dinner published in the *Illustrated London News* depicts a refined, lively gathering (Figure 4.2), departing from the mainstream characterization of vegetarians as emaciated, misanthropic cranks. Such events drew on the tradition of "radical conviviality" associated with working-class rituals centered on toasting and dining (traceable to the 1790s), which James Epstein has identified with the construction of a politicized

FIGURE 4.2. The Vegetarian Society banquet at Freemason's Tavern, London, 1851. From *Illustrated London News,* August 16, 1851. Courtesy University of Michigan Libraries / Hathitrust.

plebeian public sphere.[32] If the mystical sect at Ham Common offered Clubb one early model of sociality, then the urban vegetarian communities of Manchester and (later) London offered another.

In the late 1840s, Clubb also became involved with another radical movement: Chartist land reform, a working-class cause with ties to the American workingmen's land reform efforts.[33] Vegetarianism and land reform overlapped in that both were agrarian-oriented methods for empowering nineteenth-century individuals to overcome the ills of modern urban, industrial life. In 1848 Clubb was the local secretary for both the Vegetarian Society and the National Land Company, an organization founded by Chartist leader Feargus O'Connor to resettle urban workers onto small farms.[34] Chartism had begun in 1838 as a working-class movement for universal suffrage and more democratic political representation before turning in the 1840s toward a more conservative idea of "self-help" based on land reform, in some ways paralleling the arc of the American workingmen's movement, as described in chapter 2.[35] Following the model of the English "friendly society," O'Connor advocated pooling contributions from workers to purchase land, subdivide it, and then rent allotments to individual shareholders.[36] He formed the Chartist Co-operative Land Company in 1845, and by the following year established the first Chartist estate at Herringsgate, soon renamed O'Connorville (Figure 4.3).[37]

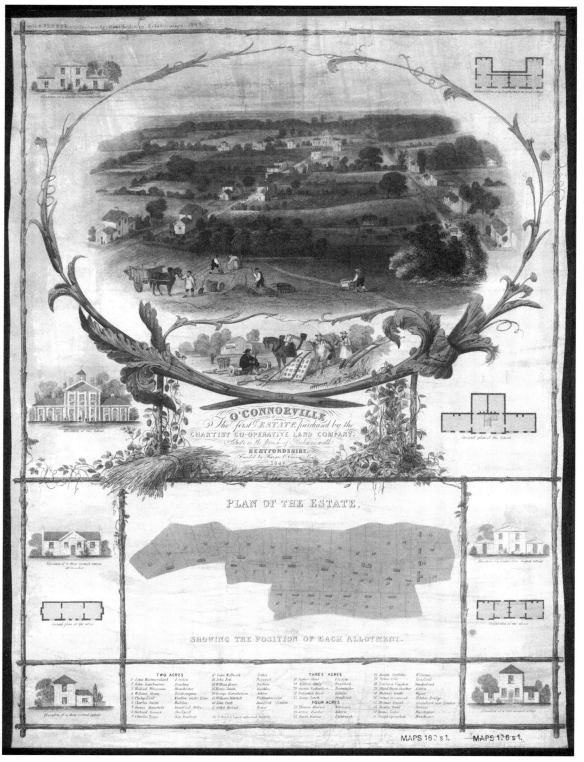

FIGURE 4.3. O'Connorville (1847), a land settlement founded by the Chartist Co-operative Land Company in Hertfordshire, England. Copyright British Library Board, Cartographic Items Maps 162.s.1.

142 *Picturing Sociality without Socialism*

The English land reformers adopted positions similar to those of their contemporary American counterparts. Rural land would be a safety valve to siphon off excess workers from cities, enabling wages to rise.[38] Land allotments would enable workers to attain political and economic independence, as well as control over their own time and resources. In contrast to the American workingmen, who advocated for plot sizes of 160 acres, the Chartists believed that 2 acres, intensively cultivated, would be sufficient to support a family—a reflection of the very different conditions of land and population on either side of the Atlantic.[39] The Chartists' land reform schemes sometimes veered into the morally paternalistic and conservative. In 1850–51, for example, Clubb was involved in the Fox Hill Bank Temperance Garden, an allotment scheme founded by Simpson that linked land reform to temperance and vegetarianism. Workers were given small gardens to cultivate as a type of useful, "uplifting" pursuit.[40] In a series of public lectures in 1849, Clubb argued that "the surest way for the working-classes to secure their independence, health, and elevation in society, was to depend upon their own resources, and make the best possible use of what they already possessed." Calculating that the average worker could save £50 annually by converting to a vegetarian diet, Clubb concluded that the worker, not the factory owner, was responsible for the "want and misery of his family and dependents." In terms that are strikingly similar to the message of self-uplift being promoted by Orson Fowler in his octagon house book, published just a year earlier, Clubb wrote: "If you wish to improve the condition of yourselves and families, look not to your master, or to the government, but look to yourselves."[41] Such schemes yoked vegetarianism to the cultivation of capitalist virtues such as thrift and self-discipline, moderating its potentially radical critique.

By the time Clubb emigrated from England to the United States in 1853, he was twenty-six years old and already a veteran of several radical movements. The existence of a transatlantic reform network allowed him to quickly find a community of sympathetic minds in Philadelphia and later New York City.[42] One of his first stops was at the Fourth Annual Meeting and Festival of the American Vegetarian Society at the American outpost of the Bible-Christian Church in Philadelphia.[43] Shortly thereafter, Clubb was hired as a journalist for the *New York Tribune,* edited by Horace Greeley, one of the major advocates of land reform in the United States. Clubb also worked as a writer and editor for Fowlers and Wells, authoring two books on temperance and editing a volume by Sylvester Graham, as well as the firm's *Illustrated Vegetarian Almanac of 1855.* In contrast to the spiritually oriented vegetarian philosophy that Clubb had absorbed in England, Graham's rationale for dietary reform centered on health—specifically, the notion that physical debility could be caused by an overstimulated physiological system.

Bleeding Kansas

Shortly after his arrival in the United States, Clubb became caught up in the most heated political debate of the day: the issue of whether slavery should be extended into the West. Vegetarians on both sides of the Atlantic associated the consumption of meat with violence, greed, and cruelty, which, in turn, they linked to phenomena such as slavery, capital punishment, war, and the subjugation of women. This led many vegetarians to ally with movements for abolition, pacifism, and women's rights. While working as a congressional reporter for the Democratic newspaper the *Washington Union,* Clubb watched the debates over the Kansas–Nebraska Act with active interest.[44] Signed into law by President Franklin Pierce in 1854, the act essentially opened a vast new swath of Indian land to white settlement. It also brought to a head a decade of tensions between southerners and northerners over the extension of slavery into new territories and states. The act superseded the Missouri Compromise of 1820, which had prohibited slavery in new states north of 36°30' north latitude, except for Missouri. The new law instead divided Nebraska (which should have been free under the old statute) into two territories and enacted a policy of "popular" or "squatter sovereignty," allowing settlers in those areas to vote on whether to allow slavery within their borders. Widely regarded as a concession to slave states, the 1854 act provoked massive outrage among northerners and antislavery advocates, eventually leading to the formation of a new political party, the Republican Party, and providing an important impetus in the agitation leading to the Civil War.[45] The fight over Bleeding Kansas marked an important turning point in white northerners' attitudes toward antislavery. If earlier radical abolitionists like William Lloyd Garrison had emphasized moral suasion and railed against the inherent evil and injustice of slavery, by the late 1840s the arguments of more moderate white antislavery advocates centered increasingly on the idea of "free soil"—that is, stopping the expansion of the southern "Slave Power" into the western territories. Only when antislavery intersected with white northerners' concerns over future access to western lands and which economic-cultural system ("free labor" or slave) should prevail did it gain widespread traction among whites.[46]

The Kansas–Nebraska Act set off a race between pro- and antislavery groups to populate the newly delineated territories. Pro-slavery settlers and "border ruffians" flooded Kansas from neighboring Missouri to found the cities of Leavenworth and Atchison (Figure 4.4). Not to be outmaneuvered, antislavery groups created the New England Emigrant Aid Company, the Connecticut Kansas Colony (also known as the Beecher Bible and Rifle Colony), the Union Emigrant Aid Company, and the Worcester County Kansas League. These groups established Lawrence, Osawatomie, and Topeka (Figure 4.5).[47] The self-proclaimed aim of the New England Emigrant Aid Company was "to dot Kansas with New England settlements" so that "no matter how heterogeneous the great living mass which flows into the Territory may be, it will all eventually be moulded into a symmetrical form."[48] As this quotation suggests, many "free state" settlers were motivated by a desire to claim the western territories for themselves and people like themselves—that is, whites—rather than by abolitionist conviction. In fact, a large majority of "free-staters" voted to exclude not only slavery but Black people from the territory at their convention in October 1855.[49]

Traditional accounts of Bleeding Kansas often overlook the fact that it was not just an important scene in the run-up to civil war but also an arena of white settler colonialism and Indigenous dispossession.[50] The land that free- and slave-state

FIGURE 4.4. "A Peace Convention at Fort Scott Kansas." Illustration of a confrontation between pro- and antislavery factions in 1858. From Albert D. Richardson, *Beyond the Mississippi,* 1869.

proponents were fighting over was Indian Territory. As Paul W. Gates points out, at the time that Kansas was opened up to settlement, "there was not within it an acre of land that was available for sale," since the federal government had not yet negotiated the necessary cessions from Indigenous title holders.[51] Beginning in the 1820s, the United States, as part of the policy of Indian removal from the eastern and Great Lakes states, had relocated several Native nations, including the Delaware, the Shawnee, the Kickapoo, and the Potawatomi, to the region, promising them "permanent residences" there (Figure 4.6).

Within a generation, squatters and speculators were illegally encroaching on Indian lands and pressuring the federal government to validate their claims retroactively. The United States eventually obliged by creating a homestead policy and path to statehood for Kansas and Nebraska, while forcing Indians residing in those areas to sign new treaties ceding their lands and then move into Oklahoma and beyond. As Jeffrey Ostler has observed, during the entire period of Bleeding Kansas, fifty-six deaths motivated by the conflict over slavery were officially recorded, while in 1855 alone, four hundred members of the Kanza nation perished from smallpox. These latter deaths, and similar ones suffered by other Indigenous peoples, were casualties of Indian removal and the hardships created by displacement and dispossession.[52] With the Kansas–Nebraska Act the U.S. government thus reneged on two promises: it

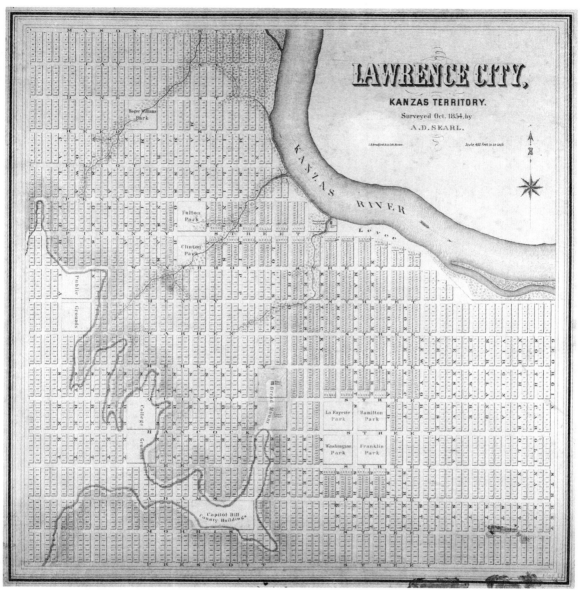

FIGURE 4.5. Plat of Lawrence, 1854. L. H. Bradford & Co. Courtesy Kansas State Historical Society.

violated its earlier commitment to keep slavery out of the West, and it failed to honor the territorial sovereignty it had previously granted to Native Americans.

The government's primary motivation for defaulting on these earlier agreements was the need to satisfy the "insatiable land-hunger" of white settlers.[53] Whether pro- or antislavery, most of the one hundred thousand people who migrated to Kansas from 1854 through 1860 did so for reasons that had less to do with political conviction than with a desire to claim a homestead or profit from a boom in western land values. Even

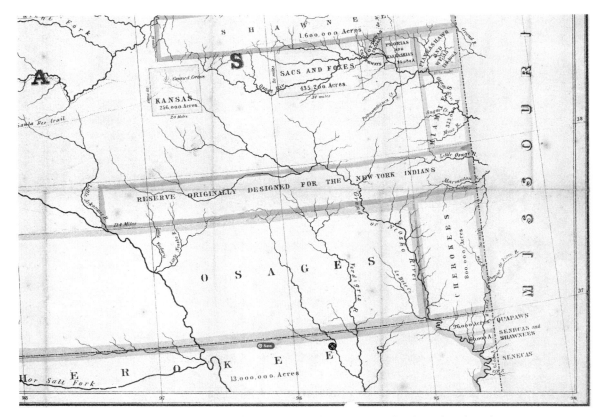

FIGURE 4.6. Detail of a map of Nebraska and Kansas Territories, showing the location of Indian reserves in southeastern Kansas according to the treaties of 1854. Created by Seth Eastman and published by Lippincott, Grambo & Company. Courtesy Beinecke Rare Book and Manuscript Library, Yale University.

the northern emigrants were motivated by speculation in land. As David Reynolds writes, "The leaders of the [eastern emigrant aid societies], such as Eli Thayer of Worcester and Amos Lawrence of Boston, were businessmen trying to turn a profit in Kansas." They "opposed slavery not on moral grounds but because they wanted to foster laissez-faire capitalism in the Territory."[54]

The passage of the Kansas–Nebraska Act contributed to a massive boom and speculative rush in western land. Some speculators sought opportunities to stake homestead claims, but lots in still-unbuilt towns offered quicker and larger returns. In the three years after the passage of the act, hundreds of towns were founded, or at least advertised, as part of an urban real estate bonanza. The writer and Union spy Albert D. Richardson, who visited Kansas in 1857, recalled the feverish atmosphere: "Nearly all transactions were cash, and money was plentiful, though commanding from three to five per cent a month. Shares often doubled in price in two or three weeks. Servant girls speculated in town lots. From enormous buff envelopes men would take scores of certificates elegantly printed in colors, representing property in various towns, and propose to sell thousands of dollars worth, certain to quadruple in value within a few months!"[55] So frenetic was the pace of city founding that, according to Richardson, some jokingly "proposed an act of congress reserving some land for farming purposes before the whole Territory should be divided into city lots."[56]

A Vegetarian Antislavery Colony

Amid these two fevers—sectional conflict and speculative urbanization—Henry Clubb began to organize his vegetarian colony in 1855.[57] The first notice of the Vegetarian Kansas Emigration Company (also referred to as the Vegetarian Settlement Company) was printed in *The Illustrated Vegetarian Almanac for 1855*. The first line of the announcement made an oblique reference to the debates between slave- and free-state settlers, addressing itself to "Vegetarians who are desirous of promoting freedom in Kansas by going to live there."[58] Yet most subsequent advertisements and articles about the colony downplayed references to "freedom," focusing instead on the spiritual, physical, and financial benefits that the community would provide to members.[59] The main concern of the company was aiding vegetarians to create a community of the like-minded, where dissidents from society's dietary norms could live according to their convictions. Its founders sought to secure for vegetarians "at least ONE TRACT OF LAND on this fair earth free from the stain of habitual bloodshed; where they can adopt the most complete physiological principles, uninterrupted by the established customs of society; where they can enjoy the beauties and bounties of Nature without violating her laws."[60] Embedded in this passage are two ideas common to many early nineteenth-century utopian communities, whether sectarian or secular: the idea of secession from dominant social mores and the notion of being able to live by a different set of principles.

From the beginning, the Vegetarian Settlement Company's promotional materials repeatedly trumpeted the benefits of community and proximity, signaling its founder's urban orientation. Clubb wanted to create a town that would grow, rather than simply provide settlers with rural homesteads. The primary aim of the colony was to gather together those who "would perhaps settle at remote distances from each other, and feeling themselves solitary and alone in their Vegetarian practice, might sink into flesh-eating habits."[61] For a reform movement that was based on personal conviction and practice, closeness to other believers was crucial for both emotional and practical support, especially since vegetarians were often mocked in mainstream society.[62] An article in the *Chicago Daily Tribune* poked fun at the members of the Kansas vegetarian colony and their meager "diet of turnips and other garden sass."[63] A sense of ostracism from the mainstream had helped to motivate the founding of Grahamite vegetarian boardinghouses in several cities as early as the 1830s. The need for association was even stronger on the frontier, where isolation on large homesteads was a common complaint. An 1856 prospectus for the Octagon Settlement Company stated the importance of sociality in even broader terms: "In isolation men become indifferent to the refinements of civilized society, and sometimes sink into barbarism; but living in proximity in this way, will cause emulation to excel in the arts of domestic and social life, and in the elevating influences of mental and moral cultivation."[64]

Promotional materials for the company linked this desideratum for sociality with the physical features of Clubb's eight-sided plan. An article titled "The Octagon Style of Settlement" in the *American Phrenological Journal* pointed out that "on the ordinary plan of settlement, on square farms, settlers become isolated, and sometimes their nearest neighbors live at a distance of some twenty or thirty miles, rendering border life unfavorable to cultivation and refinement."[65] In contrast, the geometry of the octagon plan would facilitate sociality, even in the community's earliest stage of development. For example, the farm plots would be arrayed radially around a central park rather than mimic the rectangularity of the land ordinance grid.[66] With each house sited at the narrower, central end of its lot, families would be within walking distance (an eighth of a mile) of their nearest neighbors. Each home would also be within a quarter mile of an octagonal central public building, intended to house a market, school, and meetinghouse or church. The colony's prospectus specified that the central building would be a space for frequent assemblies, featuring discussions of "agriculture, physiological, mechanical, and other sciences, politics, theology, and morals." The schoolhouse would provide educational advantages to children, and its "peculiarly healthy" location within a large park would guarantee plenty of playground space and "pure air around the building." The community would also include a hydropathic establishment, a scientific institute, and a "Museum of Curiosities and Mechanic Arts." Through this vibrant communal intellectual life, the "greatest amount of intelligence will be kept active, and the dulness and monotony, often incident to country life, avoided."[67] The prospectus thus betrayed the metropolitan bias of its author, demonstrating the broader historical point that, as David Hamer and John Reps have argued, settlement of the West was as much an urban process as a rural one.[68] One can speculate that Clubb anticipated re-creating in Kansas some of the lively atmosphere of the vegetarian banquets and meetings he had attended in Manchester, London, New York, and Philadelphia. In the octagon city, settlers could live on their farms *and* enjoy the pleasures of urbanity—Eden and Babylon would be combined. Specifically addressing "dwellers in cities," Clubb offered that his octagon plan would enable urbanites to engage in "pursuits of agriculture, horticulture and gardening" in a way that was "compatible with refinement, and education, and social intercourse."[69]

The touted advantages of urban community were more than social and intellectual; they were also economic. Clubb's characterization of the pecuniary benefits of the colony betrayed a careful, but contradictory, balance of socialism and individualist capitalism. In an early notice for the colony, Clubb hinted at the influence of some radical economic ideas, stating, for example, that the "concerted action" of vegetarians would enable a "system of direct dealing" between producers and consumers, "without the enormous profits of speculators and retailers coming between these respective parties."[70] In this language we can hear echoes of the early labor radicals' critique of middlemen in the market economy, a critique that was also central to Josiah Warren's ideas on equitable commerce (described in the next chapter). Moreover, as with the National Reform Association's octagon village plan, a measure of equality was built into Clubb's scheme. A relative leveling of land values would be achieved through the progressive sizing of lots, so that those closer to the center would be smaller.[71] Egalitarian aims could also be detected in the vegetarian plan's generous apportionment of shared lands. In addition to the large central park devoted to pasture, commons, or landscape gardens, the corners "left over" from the octagon's inscription within the square boundaries of the land ordinance grid lines were to be held in common and used as woodland or grassland for hay. (These are labeled C in Figures 4.1 and I.1.) Four octagon villages would be established in a grouping within a large square of sixteen square miles, in the center of which an agricultural college would be located. Adding together the central park, corner woodlands, and public roads, no less than one-third of the total acreage of the colony would be held in common, a remarkably high figure.[72]

Yet promotional materials for the octagon settlement made clear that this was no socialist Owenite or Fourierist community—a reflection of the general disillusionment with communitarianism by the mid-1850s. The prospectus for the Octagon Settlement Company took pains to stress its individual rather than collective ownership structure: "Every shareholder possesses, in his own right and title, the land included in his or her lots corresponding to his or her shares." Cooperation would not be allowed to interfere with the principle of individual reward for individual effort: "Every member will reap the full reward of his or her own industry, and will not be subjected to loss by the indolence or indifference of other members, the cooperative principle being adopted so far as to *promote,* and not to supersede, individual enterprise."[73] Like many emigration companies, the octagon colony was organized as a joint-stock company in which subscribers pooled capital by buying shares.[74] The collective funds would go toward purchasing provisions and setting up mills, streets, and a school. Members of the octagon colony were required to pay a $1 entrance fee, plus purchase 20–240 shares for $5 each, with each share entitling the member to a city lot averaging an acre.[75] Shares could be paid in either money or labor, and payment could be made in installments. This was no philanthropic enterprise but a "generous business cooperation of capital and labor."[76]

Although the joint-stock company structure was not uncommon among nineteenth-century communitarian settlements (several American Fourierist phalanxes were organized in this way), in the Kansas vegetarian colony the structure's essentially capitalist logic was foregrounded.[77] The colony's publicity materials stressed the pecuniary advantages to individual settlers, promising that "the prospects of forming a city of considerable wealth and importance are very good" and that "every shareholder may reasonably anticipate a handsome return for capital and labor invested."[78] The organizers pledged that those whose labor exceeded the value owed on their shares would be paid interest for their effective "loans" to the company, "in the same way as capitalists."[79] They also predicted that, given the colony's "favorable" location, "there is no doubt but shares will rise rapidly in price" and might even double after

January.[80] This was not irrational exuberance. As Albert Richardson observed in 1867, at the height of the speculative bubble, prices for urban lots in Kansas were doubling in a matter of weeks: "Any thing was marketable. Shares in interior towns of one or two shanties, sold readily for a hundred dollars."[81] Even as the prospectus appealed directly to the "capitalist" in each prospective settler, it also pledged to secure members "against the impositions of speculators" by ensuring that the company's provisions would be "sold at prices agreed upon by the members, or subject to their control."[82] Thus, the vegetarian colony paradoxically promised its members both the advantages of and protection from capitalism. Such assurances were a symptom of the scheme's attempt to reconcile opposing values. It promoted urbanity within rural environs and offered the spiritual benefits of social intercourse as well as individual material gain.

Picturing the Future

The contradictions inherent in Clubb's project were papered over by the simplicity of the colony's visual image, the plan diagram, which was prominently featured in publicity materials. No other eastern emigration company seems to have created a similarly graphic icon. The circulars of the New England Emigrant Aid Company, Worcester County Kanzas League, and New York State Kansas Aid Society were dry, unillustrated documents, though the American Settlement Company did feature decorative title fonts in its text-only advertisement (Figure 4.7). And although some towns were represented in lithographed plans, these were different from the octagonal plan. Nearly all other town plats featured standard rectangular grids punctuated with public parks, colleges, or rivers (Figure 4.5). In contrast, the vegetarian octagon colony did not just take a novel form; it prominently featured a bold, eye-catching plan in its publicity materials.

Given Clubb's Chartist background and the close affiliations between Chartism and American land reform, the plan for the colony was likely influenced at least in part by the National Reformers' octagonal "republican village plan" of a decade earlier, discussed in chapter 2. Clubb, however, went further in transforming the shape into a marketing feature. Whereas the National Reformers never referred explicitly to their plan's shape, Clubb pointedly called his design "the octagon plan of settlement," taking advantage of its association with Fowler's "invention" of the octagon mode of building, with its valences of novelty and ingenuity. The publicity materials for the colony treated the octagonal figure as a logo, an instantly recognizable image that gave the enterprise a distinct identity.

Clubb consistently rendered the plan in white lines on a black ground—the inverse of the land reformers' drawing—accentuating its striking cobweb-like geometry and transforming the hub-and-spoke organization into a visual icon. David Hamer has observed that, in the 1850s, city boosters throughout the West began aspirationally describing various towns as "hubs," centers from which influence and control flowed out into the surrounding countryside. Such "central cities" and "Centervilles" were often depicted in atlases as the origins of magnetic fields or as hubs with spokes radiating

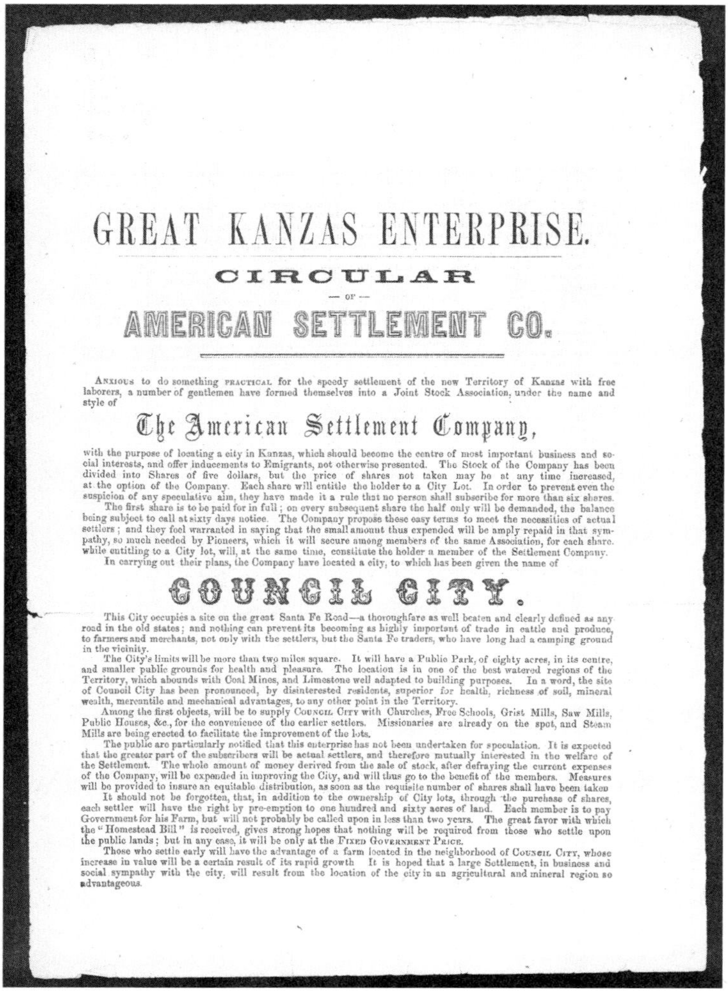

GREAT KANZAS ENTERPRISE.

CIRCULAR

— OF —

AMERICAN SETTLEMENT CO.

ANXIOUS to do something PRACTICAL for the speedy settlement of the new Territory of Kanzas with free laborers, a number of gentlemen have formed themselves into a Joint Stock Association, under the name and style of

The American Settlement Company,

with the purpose of locating a city in Kanzas, which should become the centre of most important business and social interests, and offer inducements to Emigrants, not otherwise presented. The Stock of the Company has been divided into Shares of five dollars, but the price of shares not taken may be at any time increased, at the option of the Company. Each share will entitle the holder to a City Lot. In order to prevent even the suspicion of any speculative aim, they have made it a rule that no person shall subscribe for more than six shares.

The first share is to be paid for in full; on every subsequent share the half only will be demanded, the balance being subject to call at sixty days notice. The Company propose these easy terms to meet the necessities of actual settlers; and they feel warranted in saying that the small amount thus expended will be amply repaid in that sympathy, so much needed by Pioneers, which it will secure among members of the same Association, for each share, while entitling to a City lot, will, at the same time, constitute the holder a member of the Settlement Company.

In carrying out their plans, the Company have located a city, to which has been given the name of

COUNCIL CITY.

This City occupies a site on the great Santa Fe Road—a thoroughfare as well beaten and clearly defined as any road in the old states; and nothing can prevent its becoming as highly important of trade in cattle and produce, to farmers and merchants, not only with the settlers, but the Santa Fe traders, who have long had a camping ground in the vicinity.

The City's limits will be more than two miles square. It will have a Public Park, of eighty acres, in its centre, and smaller public grounds for health and pleasure. The location is in one of the best watered regions of the Territory, which abounds with Coal Mines, and Limestone well adapted to building purposes. In a word, the site of Council City has been pronounced, by disinterested residents, superior for health, richness of soil, mineral wealth, mercantile and mechanical advantages, to any other point in the Territory.

Among the first objects, will be to supply COUNCIL CITY with Churches, Free Schools, Grist Mills, Saw Mills, Public Houses, &c., for the convenience of the earlier settlers. Missionaries are already on the spot, and Steam Mills are being erected to facilitate the improvement of the lots.

The public are particularly notified that this enterprise has not been undertaken for speculation. It is expected that the greater part of the subscribers will be actual settlers, and therefore mutually interested in the welfare of the Settlement. The whole amount of money derived from the sale of stock, after defraying the current expenses of the Company, will be expended in improving the City, and will thus go to the benefit of the members. Measures will be provided to insure an equitable distribution, as soon as the requisite number of shares shall have been taken

It should not be forgotten, that, in addition to the ownership of City lots, through the purchase of shares, each settler will have the right by pre-emption to one hundred and sixty acres of land. Each member is to pay Government for his Farm, but will not probably be called upon in less than two years. The great favor with which the "Homestead Bill" is received, gives strong hopes that nothing will be required from those who settle upon the public lands; but in any case, it will be only at the FIXED GOVERNMENT PRICE.

Those who settle early will have the advantage of a farm located in the neighborhood of COUNCIL CITY, whose increase in value will be a certain result of its rapid growth It is hoped that a large Settlement, in business and social sympathy with the city, will result from the location of the city in an agricultural and mineral region so advantageous.

FIGURE 4.7. Circular of the American Settlement Company, 1855. Kansas State Historical Society.

outward.[83] In the same vein, Clubb's graphic cobweb lent his city the appearance of an especially magnetic centrifugal force.

Clubb's investment in the plan is reflected in the care with which he printed it, especially as compared with the land reformers' much rougher village drawing. Fowler and Wells issued a large broadsheet version of the plan, titled *The Octagon Plan of Settlement*; the twenty-two-by-seventeen-inch folded sheet could be purchased bound in muslin hardcovers for twenty-five cents, or unbound for twelve and a half cents (Figure 4.1). This document is notable for its large size and for its striking white-on-black illustrations of the colony. The most distinct feature of this broadsheet, aside from the bold geometry of the plan, was Clubb's attention to the graphic depiction of the settlement's future development over time. Hamer has described western town plats as "essentially maps of the future."[84] While many if not most western city plats projected plans for imaginary grand metropolises far different from the reality on the ground, Clubb's was unusual in presenting four stages or versions of his plan side by side, from a "village settlement" to a "county settlement" to an "octagon town" and eventually an "octagon city." In taking this approach, Clubb was drawing on an ideology repeated by many nineteenth-century commentators who saw the settlement of the frontier as an evolutionary process beginning with the displacement of Indigenous populations by white pioneers and culminating in the rise of cities. J. M. Peck, author of an 1836 guidebook for emigrants, for example, described a pattern of three waves of settlers rolling one after the other, beginning with the itinerant pioneer who ventured into the wilderness, supplanted by the agricultural settler who cleared roads and built mills and schoolhouses, followed by the "men of capital and enterprise" who transformed the small village into a "spacious town or city."[85] Yet by the time easterners arrived in Kansas in large numbers in the 1850s, this sequential model was being overturned, with cities being planted as readily as homesteads and agriculturalists arriving along with merchants and artisans.[86]

Also notable about Clubb's diagrams was what they did not represent. Unlike some contemporary prospective town plans or earlier utopian ones (such as Owen's perspectival images of New Harmony), they were relentlessly abstract, with no indication of topography, vegetation, or landscaping. For all the invocations of social intercourse and cooperation in the company's written descriptions, the publicity materials included no illustrations of people. Hewing to diagrammatic representation ensured that the octagon city remained on the plane of the ideal, an abstract plan uncompromised by material realities. This extreme visual spareness, marked by an eschewal of figurative or realistic representation, meant that readers had to fill in the gaps, to project in their own minds how life might actually unfold in the octagon city.

Representation versus Reality: The Failure of the Octagon City

Predictably, events on the ground were precisely the opposite of the orderly, harmonious vision projected by the black-and-white drawings. The first meeting of the Octagon Settlement Company was held on May 16, 1855, at Russell Trall's Hydropathic School at 15 Laight Street, New York. Clubb's official title was secretary; Charles H. De Wolfe, a "gentleman" from Philadelphia, served as president. That summer, the company sent a water cure physician named Dr. John McLauren to Kansas to find a location. He selected a site forty miles west of Fort Scott, along the banks of the Neosho River, in unceded Osage territory.[87] In the time-honored practice of town site boosters, the company subsequently "puffed" this location in all of the colony's promotional materials. It was said to feature an abundance of waterpower, timber, coal, limestone and sandstone, pure-water springs, and fine, rolling prairie. Some parts of the land had been known "on rare occasion to produce *two full crops of corn* within the year." In a more poetic vein, the scenery was described as "very beautiful," with "the surface undulating like the waves of the ocean subsiding after a storm."[88]

Around August 1855, the leaders of the Vegetarian Kansas Emigration Company decided to broaden their reach by establishing a second colony, committed to temperance but without the vegetarian requirement. This was to be located across the river from the vegetarian colony; its official name was the Octagon Settlement Company.[89] By 1856, a prospectus listed more than sixty members of the Vegetarian Company and fourteen of the temperance Octagon Company, including eighteen farmers, four physicians, three teachers, two mechanics, a lecturer, two single women, and three widows. They hailed from states as far apart as Georgia and Wisconsin as well as from Canada. Members were advised that the first party would depart St. Louis by steamer on April 2, 1856.[90]

In early promotional literature, Clubb warned readers against expecting too much: "Care and caution is necessarily taken to avoid raising the expectations of those desiring to embark in such an enterprise, in order to prevent disappointment."[91] After arriving in Kansas, he seems to have abandoned such circumspection. In a May 1856 article in *Life Illustrated,* Clubb reported that the first group of settlers had arrived and the first octagon settlement had been surveyed, with avenues 120 feet wide and a central park embracing "several beautiful hills or knolls on the southwest side" of a prairie. A total of eight octagon settlements were in the process of being surveyed. Glossing over the colony's occupation of Osage lands, he reported that the Indians had visited and had "behaved in a very friendly manner." While Clubb acknowledged that residents were "enduring some of the inconveniences common to the commencement of all settlements," he assured readers that "a great majority" had expressed themselves "well pleased with the location, and all agree that it must be one of the best that Kanzas can furnish." He projected that they would "soon all be comfortably housed on sites where there is an almost perpetual breeze." Clubb concluded on a happy note: "The sound of the axes is heard echoing through the woods, and the merry voices of women and children are filling the air with gladness."[92]

Such descriptions were a far cry from reality on the ground. One community member, Miriam Davis Colt, would later recount that upon her group's arrival at the octagon city in May, "not a house [was] to be seen." The promised mills had not been built. What had been described in brochures as a powerful river, sure to support a thriving light industry, was barely a creek. "Can any one imagine our disappointment," she wrote. Instead, the new settlers found families living in tents, "some of cloth and green bark just peeled from the trees . . . stuck up on the damp ground, without floors or fires." Clubb himself was living in a "cabin made of an old Indian wigwam and tenting."[93] Colt reported that the octagon city had been surveyed, but, the land being wetter than expected, most of the earlier settlers had repaired to higher ground a mile away. A "center octagon" had been built—a log cabin, sixteen by sixteen feet, without doors or windows—and served as an initial shelter for arriving colonists.[94] Another settler, Watson Stewart, recorded his impression: "After spending one day in conversation with Mr. Clubb, our Secretary, and other members of the Company on the ground, we became convinced that the company would prove a failure."[95] Stewart left the colony and settled independently nearby. Colt's family headed back east after a few months of wrestling with fever, theft, rattlesnakes, and other calamities, but her husband and young son died before they could complete the return journey. Most of the other early settlers departed just as quickly.

The reasons for the vegetarian colony's demise were common to many failed speculative towns and utopian settlements, from Brook Farm to Fruitlands. Often such communities were founded by urban intellectuals who romanticized agrarian life and the return to Eden but had little practical experience with farming. About Clubb, Stewart wrote: "He was wholly unacquainted with Western life; he was an Englishman, about thirty years of age, with a wife but no children; had been connected with the *New York Tribune,* I think, as a reporter, and knew nothing outside of office work." Stewart came to a similar assessment of his fellow colonists: "They were mostly from the far East; mechanics, professional men, and men from offices and stores in the cities, and altogether unable to adjust themselves to frontier life."[96]

Another factor contributing to the colony's rapid downfall was the loose commitment of its members to the project and to the cause of vegetarianism. As numerous historians of communitarianism have observed, sectarian colonies bound by faith or by a charismatic leader tend to outlast secular ones because they are connected by tighter ideological sinews.[97] The members of the Kansas octagon colony had been attracted to it for a variety of reasons, ranging from profit to health, a fact reflected in the range of appeals within the community's own promotional materials. Some had been touched by reform fervor and were subscribers to Fowler and Wells publications like *Life Illustrated* and the *Water-Cure Journal.*[98] Colt, for example, wrote that having converted to vegetarianism for health reasons, she and her husband looked forward to living among "people whose tastes and habits will coincide with our own."[99] She believed that going as part of a company would allow the family to escape the hardships confronting those going singly: "It will be better for ourselves pecuniarily, and better in the future for our children."[100] Stewart was a stonecutter from Indiana, born in 1827 to a New Light, temperance, and antislavery family; his father was an advocate of Thomsonian medicine, including "vegetable remedies, cold and hot baths, etc." But his motives for joining the Kansas colony were also individualistic: he had established himself successfully in the business of gravestone engraving, yet, like many, he viewed true independence as lying in a homestead, and he "cherished a hope of sometime removing to the country and engaging in farming."[101] In mixing a predilection, if not quite a radical conviction, for vegetarianism with ideas about the mutual economic benefits to be gained by joining the company, Colt's and Stewart's profiles illustrate a quality that made the octagon vegetarian community different from the Ham Concordium. The Kansas colonists were not a tight-knit group of believers committed to a shared ascetic regimen or spiritual mission, operating under the sway of a charismatic father figure, but were instead a loose affinity-based assemblage. Clubb had founded the company on the assumption that community could be generated out of commonality, facilitated by a centralized urban plan that would provide the proximity and physical infrastructure for social exchange. Since the octagon plan was never realized, its community-producing capacities were never tested.

Representation and Reality

The failure of the octagon settlement cannot be attributed solely to its unique plan or its reform principles. Countless speculative towns in Kansas never made it beyond paper, or else rapidly disappeared, during the land boom and subsequent Panic of 1857. Many easterners, and not just idealistic vegetarian abolitionists, traveled west with unrealistic expectations and romanticized notions about agrarian life based on textual or visual representations. A recurring trope in the imagery and literature of western settlement was the distance between representation and reality, between towns "on paper" and their execution on the ground. Nearly every settlement company or speculative town projected an image of a city that was far different from reality. Albert Richardson recounted in 1867:

> On paper, *all* these towns were magnificent. Their superbly lithographed maps adorned the walls of every place of resort. The stranger studying one of these, fancied the New Babylon surpassed only by its namesake of old. Its great parks, opera-houses, churches, universities, railway depots and steamboat landings made New York and St. Louis insignificant in comparison.[102]

Richardson satirized the chasm between projection and actuality in a pair of drawings of the city of "New Babylon," as depicted in "fancy" and in "fact" (Figure 4.8). In the first, the town is represented in a plat that includes intersecting railroad lines, steamboat landing, gridded streets, a university, a grammar school, churches, a female seminary, and a large park. In the second drawing, the "reality" of the town is represented by a vignette showing a single log cabin, labeled "saloon," alongside a tepee, scattered rocks, and a pair of men idling.

As Richardson wrote, most of these would-be Kansan metropolises, depicted so grandly in large lithographs, in reality consisted of "one or two rough cabins, with perhaps a tent and an Indian canoe on the river in front of the 'levee.'"[103] Richardson's rendering of the city of New Babylon was itself a riff on a pair of illustrations of an American city called "Eden" described by Charles Dickens in *Martin Chuzzlewit* (1842–44). In the Dickens images, one scene shows two well-dressed men looking at a map of a city on the wall of a surveyor's office. Visible on the map are labels like "market," "pump," "wharf," and "botanical garden." The next image depicts the city "as it appeared in fact": a backwoods scene featuring two rudely built log cabins, one with a sign for "Chuzzlewit & Co., Architects and Surveyors," and the other with a sign reading "Bank" and "National Credit Office" (Figure 4.9). Near the first cabin, a man wields an axe, as if to chop off a tree limb, perhaps to prove his claim, while another sits despondently with head in hands. Notably, in both the Richardson and Dickens images, the unreal, puffed representation is associated with a city plat larded with amenities, whereas "reality" is rendered in a figurative vignette—a visual stand-in for the "eyewitness" account. What Richardson and Dickens were both satirizing was how a technical form of representation, the surveyor's plat, had been co-opted by city boosters to lend a sense of plausibility to their fabrications. Ironically, these

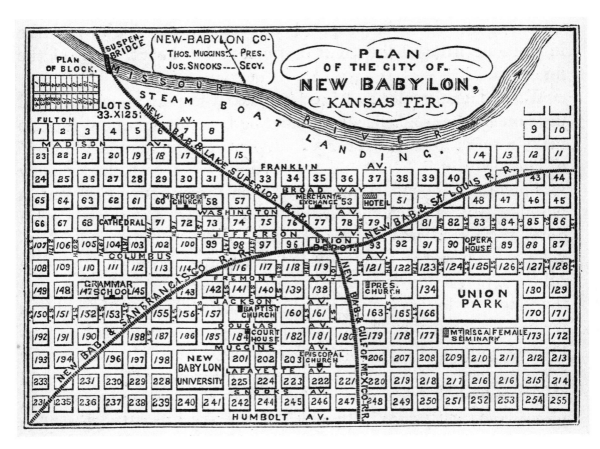

FIGURE 4.8. Hypothetical Kansas city of New Babylon "on paper" and "in fact." From Albert D. Richardson, *Beyond the Mississippi,* 1869.

FIGURE 4.9. A fictional western American city called Eden, as depicted in the land office and in actuality. From Charles Dickens, *Martin Chuzzlewit,* 1842–44.

contortions were enabled by the very abstraction of the plan: it was easy, after all, to draw geometric figures on a piece of paper. Thus, by midcentury the idea of the town plan as a fictive "representation" versus a figurally rendered "reality" had become a trope of the American West.

Colt referred to Kansas as a "fairy-land," a place swirling in false representations. In a similar vein, Richardson recorded the ingenious dissimulations by which settlers in Kansas "proved" their claims. Preemption laws required that settlers build habitable dwellings of certain dimensions to demonstrate that they were residing on the land and improving it. But sometimes, "the only building upon the claim was one whittled out with a penknife, twelve *inches* by fourteen," a circumvention vividly and comically illustrated in Richardson's book (Figure 4.10).[104] Such subterfuge was emblematic of the speculative atmosphere that had enveloped western lands. All of these schemes were based on exploiting the gap between the reality of a thing and its representation, whether that representation took the form of an engraved city plan or the description of a claimant's "house." Images contributed to a sense of unreality that seemed to reflect the general condition of the capitalist market, in which all that was solid seemed to melt into air, as Karl Marx famously put it. Yet the fever generated by the prospect of rapid financial gain was exactly the kind of "overstimulation" that vegetarianism was designed to oppose.

FIGURE 4.10. Preemption subterfuge. Illustration from Albert D. Richardson, *Beyond the Mississippi*, 1869.

The status of Clubb's octagon diagram amid such discursive conditions was ambiguous. Although its straight lines and scale seemed intended to suggest the sobriety and credibility of the engineer, its excessively formal geometry also hinted at its unreality and mere "paper" existence. Yet the plan also betrayed a desire for something beyond the dreams embodied in the typical speculative town grid. The octagon's shape, rendered in spare white lines on a black background, enticed settlers with the promise that individuality and sociality, country and city, wealth and simplicity, could be harmoniously reconciled in one form.

Images of Harmony and Discord

At nearly the same moment that Clubb was publishing his octagon city diagrams, representations of a much different sort were emanating from Kansas. In late 1855, tense images and news of violent skirmishes between free-staters and "border ruffians" from Missouri began circulating in the northern press, leading to the nickname "Bleeding Kansas." Events such as the sacking of the free-state settlement at Lawrence and the subsequent murder of five pro-slavery settlers near Pottawatomie Creek by John Brown and his followers occurred less than one hundred miles from the vegetarian colony. The proximity of these events is signaled by the fact that one young member of the Vegetarian Settlement Company, James H. Holmes, left the colony in the summer of 1856 and later joined Brown's brigade.[105]

Comparing Clubb's diagrams of the octagon city with images of Bleeding Kansas offers an opportunity to contrast two different types of visual rhetoric, and modes of politics, circulating at this moment—one utopian and the other agonistic. Whereas Clubb's diagrams projected a state of ideal sociality and harmony, the images of Bleeding Kansas portrayed a condition of violence and strife. Whereas the former offered fictional depictions of a hoped-for reality to come, the latter presented themselves as "eyewitness" accounts of "real" current events. The title page of Charles W. Briggs's *The Reign of Terror in Kanzas* (1856), for example, portrayed a white antislavery man with his hands raised, apparently being tarred and feathered by the group of armed, bearded, pro-slavery agitators surrounding him (Figure 4.11). The subtitle of the book elaborated on other aggressions suffered by northern migrants at the hands of the border ruffians: "Men have been Murdered and Scalped; Ministers of the Gospel Tarred and Feathered; Women dragged from their Homes and Violated; Printing Offices and Private Houses Burned; Citizens Robbed, &c., by Border Ruffians." Another picture published in 1856, a lithographed cartoon by John L. Magee depicting southern congressman Preston S. Brooks viciously attacking antislavery senator Charles Sumner with a cane in retaliation for an incendiary speech that Sumner had given days earlier, gained wide circulation and helped rally northerners to the cause (Figure 4.12). These images portraying white antislavery men as victims of aggression enacted by pro-slavery instigators and politicians both reflected and contributed to the increasingly aggressive tenor of the national debate.

The pictures also reflected the way that Bleeding Kansas reoriented antislavery

FIGURE 4.11. Title page of Charles W. Briggs, *The Reign of Terror in Kanzas,* 1856. Courtesy Newberry Library / Archive.org.

Picturing Sociality without Socialism   161

FIGURE 4.12. Lithograph of pro-slavery congressman Preston S. Brooks caning antislavery senator Charles Sumner, 1856. 34 × 49 cm. Courtesy Library Company of Philadelphia.

politics. As noted previously, the fight over Kansas was really a struggle between northern and southern white people (as well as railroad interests) over access to Indian land. In contrast to the older Garrisonian model of abolition, which had focused on slavery as a moral wrong and argued for the fundamental rights of the enslaved to freedom, moderate antislavery politics, as practiced by the Free Soil and Republican Parties, was concerned primarily with opposing the expansion of slavery into the West and neutralizing the threat posed by the southern "Slave Power" to the interests of northern white men. Yet the violence of the clashes that occurred in Kansas, following on the heels of the Fugitive Slave Act, convinced an increasing number of Americans—white and Black, northern and southern—that a larger conflict was unavoidable. And it led to a shift in strategy among abolitionists, particularly Black abolitionists, away from the older Garrisonian ideal of moral suasion and nonviolence, and toward greater militancy and a belief that freedom must be seized by force rather than persuasion. As Kellie Carter Jackson puts it, Kansas was the moment when "abolitionists recognized the need for more than the printing press and financial resources: . . . actual arms were required."[106]

These changes in the politics of opposition to slavery are reflected in the evolving visual imagery of the movement. Starting in the 1830s, American abolitionists had incorporated pictures into their tracts, pamphlets, almanacs, and children's literature as part of a larger strategy to generate support for their cause.[107] Perhaps the most famous piece of abolitionist visual propaganda was a medallion originally issued in the 1780s by Josiah Wedgwood depicting a shackled enslaved man with the caption "Am I not a Man and a Brother?" (Figure 4.13).[108] This representation and others like it (a version featuring an enslaved woman circulated later) used images of enslaved Black bodies to call upon white viewers' humanitarian sympathies. A related genre of abolitionist imagery graphically depicted enslaved and formerly enslaved men and women being persecuted, abused, and sometimes tortured, often based on actual reports of events (Figure I.4). Designed to elicit empathy for enslaved people among white readers, as well as outrage at the cruelty of southern slaveholders, such images have been criticized by numerous scholars for depicting African Americans primarily as passive victims rather than as sovereign subjects or active agents of liberation. In highlighting the "pain of others," these scholars argue, the images deploy pornographic tropes to appeal to the self-affirming, paternalistic, sentimental sensibilities of white reformers.[109] Other recent historians have argued that such interpretations too quickly dismiss the potential of radical empathy as a legitimate and effective impetus to political action. Further, they ignore examples of antislavery imagery in which African Americans were portrayed as active agents, inadvertently reinforcing the focus on white abolitionists and suppressing the role of Black abolitionists.[110]

While the earlier type of sensational images of enslaved people continued to be deployed into the 1850s, these now circulated alongside a different genre of antislavery image, to which the pictures of Bleeding Kansas belong. These later pictures portrayed the debate over slavery as a conflict between opposed groups of white men. They focused not on the enslaved Black person but on the injured white northerner. Matthew Fox-Amato has written of a shift in abolitionist visuality "from the centrality of idealization and imagination to the growing importance of documentary evidence."[111] He traces the rise of photographs casting white abolitionists as "martyrs" and "rebels," men who had engaged in direct action against slavery and were imprisoned or suffered violence because of it. The printed representations of Briggs's tarred and feathered antislavery man and Charles Sumner being caned are part of this subgenre of imagery. Such pictures were circulated primarily to generate sympathy and outrage among white readers on behalf of other white people. This category reached its apotheosis with the representations of John Brown following his capture and trial for leading the audacious Harpers Ferry raid. In the weeks leading up to his execution, Brown was portrayed in the mainstream press as a madman. But among abolitionists, he was eulogized and venerated. In Brown's case, however, depictions of the hero-martyr spoke meaningfully to both Black and white viewers who opposed slavery. As Jackson observes, one reason African Americans idealized Brown (who, it should be noted, was himself inspired and assisted by many Black abolitionists) was that he allowed them "to underscore their own radicalism" and to point subtly to "black violence as a threat to white supremacy" without engaging in direct violence themselves.[112] For both Black and white abolitionists, the Harpers Ferry raid was a critical

FIGURE 4.13. "Am I not a Man and a Brother?" Woodcut, sold at the Anti-Slavery Office, New York City, 1837. Courtesy Library of Congress, Rare Book and Special Collections Division.

turning point, foreshadowing the possibility that ending slavery would require taking up arms.

Even as the imagery of antislavery changed from the 1830s to the 1850s, two things remained consistent. The first was an ethos of virtual eyewitnessing, of enabling readers to experience "with their own eyes" the injustices wrought by slavery, as a powerful incentive to action. The second was the idea that images had a special capacity to affect spectators, to activate sentiments, to speak to the heart, not just the mind. Whether it was an image of a fugitive slave being hunted by snarling canines or a white northern settler being tarred and feathered by border ruffians, the visual rhetoric of antislavery was designed to provoke feelings—a combination of sympathy for the enslaved, outrage and indignation against the slaveholder, and admiration for the white abolitionist martyr—as opposed to rational or intellectual objection.

Comparing the pictures of Bleeding Kansas with the geometric diagrams of the vegetarian colony, one cannot help but be struck by the dissonance between these two kinds of images. Juxtaposed against the inflammatory documentary images, the geometric utopian plans appear cool, dispassionate, and abstract.[113] With their precise geometry, neat modularity, and relentless symmetry, the plan diagrams evoke a world of order and harmony modeled on the perfection of nature as seen in the honeycomb of the bee or a spider's web. They depict a society in which individual and collectivity are idealistically composed in symmetrical balance rather than engaged in real and impassioned conflict. They exalt association rather than agonism and appeal to an older Enlightenment aesthetic of reason rather than to the passions aroused by a sense of injustice or empathy. They orient viewers toward imagined futures rather than the pressing problems of the present. When we consider the context of Bleeding Kansas and assess Clubb's focus on the spiritual and economic well-being of the colony's presumably white settlers, his downplaying of abolition and the struggles of the enslaved in the company's literature, and his apparent obliviousness to the Indigenous people who were being dispossessed to enable his haven to spring up, the enterprise seems hopelessly myopic, if not downright hypocritical.

In critiquing the vegetarian octagon colony, however, we might be cautious about overgeneralizing its lessons. Perhaps it is not that utopian images can never inspire, or that images of violence are always more effective at rousing people to act. No less a figure than Frederick Douglass, speaking on the subject of "pictures and progress" during the depths of the Civil War a decade later, would defend the importance of taking an hour's relief from the "horrors of the battlefield" and an "age of money, merchandise, and politics, a metallic, utilitarian, dollar-worshipping age," to indulge in humankind's "dreamy, clairvoyant, poetic, intellectual, and showy side; the side of religion, music, mystery, and passion, wherein illustrations take the form of solid reality and shadows get themselves recognized as substance: the side which is better pleased with feeling than reason, with fancies than with facts, with things as they seem, than things as they are, with contemplation rather than action, with thought rather than work."[114] Clubb was not wrong to dream of a world where birdsong would fill the air, and vegetarians could come together over a simple repast and together plot a less violent and agitated world. But his images were not compelling enough to sway a society headed for the moment in a very different direction.

CHAPTER 5

Toward More Transparent Representation
The Hexagonal "Anarchist" City of Josiah Warren

In 1873 Josiah Warren, often described as the United States' first homegrown anarchist, published *Practical Applications of the Elementary Principles of "True Civilization," to the Minute Details of Every Day Life,* a pamphlet reflecting on his long career as a social reformer.[1] In his twenties, Warren had been a member of Robert Owen's New Harmony colony in Indiana. That community's rancorous collapse convinced him that all efforts at cooperation based on combining property and interests were doomed to fail. He spent the remaining forty-seven years of his life working to bring about "all the harmonic results aimed at by Communism" through means "exactly opposite to and away from Communism."[2] In *Practical Applications,* Warren recounted his experiences setting up a series of communities dedicated to creating a more "equitable commerce" while preserving the absolute "sovereignty" of the individual. Of settlements such as Utopia, Ohio, and Modern Times, New York, Warren proudly observed that residents had been able to obtain good houses with little cash simply through their own toil and exchanges of labor with neighbors, all while avoiding the dissension to be found in socialist communities.

At the end of the pamphlet, Warren included two crudely printed diagrammatic plans of a hexagonal city, accompanied by nine "points suggested for consideration in laying out towns" (Figure 5.1). The plans and their related principles could be read as a spatial analogue of Warren's individualist ideology. The six-sided layout would provide each family with a private plot of three to five acres, separated from neighbors by roads. Six houses would be clustered around a "building for public purposes" to form a small neighborhood or section. Aggregating these neighborhood units produced a field-like city devoid of any large, symbolic urban center—no city hall, no central park, no downtown. In this decentralized, cellular, low-density city, Warren predicted, all residents would be free to pursue their own ends, without interference from one another or from superseding authorities. His ideal, as he wrote

165

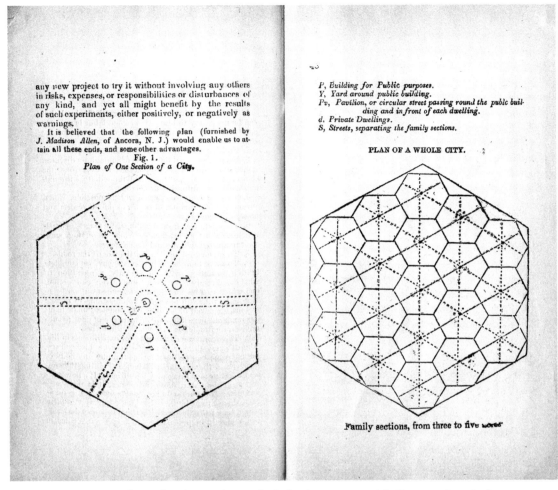

FIGURE 5.1. Plans of a city section and whole city. From Josiah Warren, *Practical Applications of the Elementary Principles of "True Civilization,"* 1873.

elsewhere, was that "each person, like a planet, can move in his own orbit without disturbing others."[3]

Given their appearance in 1873, after the cataclysm of the Civil War had extinguished much of the utopian fervor of the previous decades, the hexagonal plans are enigmatic. Not only do they have a quality of belatedness, postdating the other geometric utopias discussed in this book by a decade or more, but they are also late in the chronology of Warren's own life. Published when Warren was seventy-five and in the twilight of his reform career, the pamphlet was largely a retrospective survey of ideas and experiments. Warren was not even the creator of the hexagonal city. He credited its design to J. Madison Allen of Ancora, New Jersey, a little-known vegetarian, trance spiritualist, and spelling reformer who served a stint as principal of the Blue-Anchor Industrial Institute.[4] The institute was an educational establishment in Ancora, a spiritualist community whose organizers dreamed of building a unitary palace, model homes, a cooperative store, a hygienic institute, and a lecturers' retreat.[5] Whether Warren's inclusion of the plans for a hexagonal city in *Practical Applications* emerged from an extended collaboration between the two men or developed from a slight association is unclear. The hexagonal city was an anomaly, even an apparent contradiction, in Warren's thinking. Although he had founded several utopian communities from the 1830s onward, he had never evinced much interest in urban plans, and nowhere else had he proposed a specific physical layout for a community. The plans thus raise a thorny question: Why would someone so devoted to the individual's freedom from external constraints and to the "abolition of systems and systems making" have advocated such an apparently rigid geometric scheme?[6] In the hexagonal city we find the paradox of a formalist project endorsed by someone who railed against coercive, superimposed forms. The project thus returns to one of the central problems addressed throughout this volume: that of understanding the relationship between form and politics as more than a matter of simple functionalism and considering what other rhetorical or political work the geometric diagrams may have been performing.

Warren and Allen's hexagonal city offers an illuminating case study in geometric utopianism for several other reasons. To begin, Warren was thoroughly embedded in the world of the geometric utopians. His biography intersects with those of virtually every other major figure and project described in this book. He and Lewis Masquerier, the creator of the land reformers' octagonal republican village, were friends and interlocutors.[7] Orson Fowler, popularizer of the eight-sided house, published two of Warren's books, and octagon dwellings seemed to crop up habitually in Warren's orbit—at least two were built in Modern Times. Warren and Allen also likely knew of Henry Clubb's octagonal vegetarian colony plan. Allen credited Fowler and Wells's books on phrenology with leading him to the adoption of vegetarianism, and he came into contact with Clubb at some point.[8] And, as described in the next chapter, Warren's ideas about "equitable commerce" would inspire John Murray Spear's associates to develop their own spiritualist version of an anticapitalist temple of commercial exchange in the mid-1850s.[9] The density of these connecting threads indicates that, while geometric utopianism might not have been central to Warren's oeuvre, he was a principal figure in the cultural milieu that promoted geometric urban and architectural plans as instruments of social reform.

The most compelling reason for exploring Warren's thought and experiments, however, is that they help illuminate a mystery that pervades geometric utopianism: why so many of the creators of these schemes were also preoccupied with language reform and specifically with creating new alphabets and orthographic systems. Warren, Allen, Masquerier, and Clubb all spent considerable time on the restructuring of language and writing systems. Warren's writings make clear that his individualist social philosophy was deeply influenced by his theories of language and communication. Allen also was the author of several orthographic reform pamphlets, including *The Natural Alphabet, for the Representation, with Types or Pen, of All Languages* (1867); *The Panophonic Printing Alphabet, for the Philosophical Representation of All Languages,*

Based upon an Original and Comprehensive Classification of the Elementary Sounds (1867); *Normo-graphy: Normal, or Natural Writing, Full Style, for Beginners* (1872); and *The Pan-Norm-Alpha* (1872). Masquerier went so far as to engrave his own reformed alphabet on his tombstone (see chapter 2, including Figure 2.19). And Clubb worked for many years as a shorthand reporter, having been taught that shorthand was vitally important to social reform. Was this shared obsession simply a coincidence, a reflection of the early nineteenth-century movement in orthographic reform that encompassed developments such as Noah Webster's attempts to reform American spelling and the popularization of Isaac Pitman's shorthand? Or does some deeper connection obtain between an interest in language and the impulse to design geometric cities and houses?

As the geometric utopian who most clearly linked his social reform ideas to his theories of language, Warren offers an opportunity to explore these questions. Thus, the methodology adopted in this chapter differs from that of the previous ones. Rather than relating the hexagonal city diagrams to other kinds of visual representations or visual-rhetorical techniques, here I delve into Warren's ideas about printing, language, and money and relate these beliefs to broader histories and ideas about representation in the nineteenth century. Warren's views on the economy, politics, and reform, as well as his late turn to plan diagrams, were shaped not only by a deep current of semiotic pessimism—his conviction that verbal language was inherently ambiguous and therefore the source of political conflict—but also by semiotic utopianism—the belief that the creation of more transparent modes of communication and the lifting of the veils of mediation from language, politics, and the economy could lead to social harmony.[10]

Josiah Warren, Experimental Reformer

Born in Boston in 1798, Warren was a classic nineteenth-century polymath: an inventor, musician, printer, and social reformer.[11] By 1821, he was living in Cincinnati and had received his first patent, for a lard-burning lamp. He soon turned his attention to the arena of printing, focusing on techniques for making printing less costly and therefore more accessible to people of little means. In 1830, he announced the creation of a new kind of press that used inexpensive lead matrices stamped with types, rather than the usual copper matrices stamped with costly steel punches.[12] By 1832, he was advertising a "family printing apparatus" that could fit into the home as a piece of parlor furniture (Figure 5.2). Warren continued his innovations in the 1840s, producing one of the first continuous-sheet roller presses before turning his attention to cheaper methods of typefounding (casting type) and stereotyping (creating full-page printing plates).[13] For the former, he proposed substituting a homemade mixture of shellac, tar, and sand for the more expensive type metal. For the latter, he pioneered a formula for clay matrices onto which one could draw, hand-letter, engrave, or impress type.[14] In December 1845, he announced in the *Indiana Statesman* the arrival of what he called "universal typography"—apparently referring to his new stereotyping

The Warren Printing Machine.

The above is a representation of the new Printing Machine, (for job work,) recently made for us by the brothers of the Newark Machine-shop. It is an invention of Mr. Josiah Warren, the socialist writer, and founder of 'Modern Times,' who kindly allows us to avail ourselves of his improvement. The merits of this press consist in its simplicity and portability, making it convenient for use in families and Associations. It is well adapted to Job Printing, and with a small quantity of type, would form a capital appendage to every large business establishment. With a little instruction, merchants and others could learn to print handbills and do their own advertising; and the pleasure of this exercise in the Printer's art would equal its economy.

The operation of the Press is explained as follows: The roller extending across its bed is adjusted to a proper pressure on the type by setscrews, and then by turning the crank it is rolled back and forth over the form. A single passage of the roller is sufficient for an impression.

The cost of the Press is from $50 to $75.

FIGURE 5.2. Notice of Josiah Warren's home printing machine. From *The Circular,* April 15, 1854. Courtesy Swarthmore College Peace Collection.

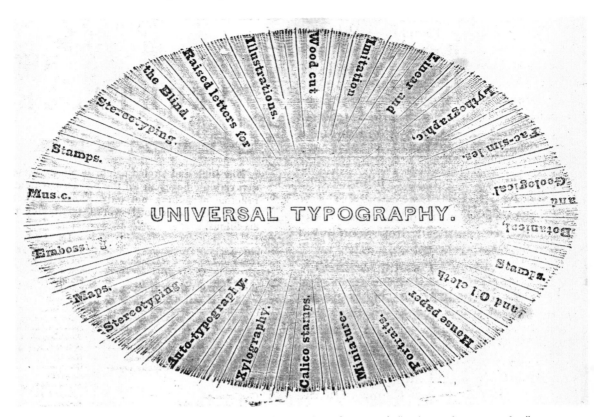

FIGURE 5.3. Illustration accompanying notice of Warren's "universal typography." From the *Indiana Statesman,* December 27, 1845. Courtesy Willard Library.

technique—and touted its flexibility, cheapness, and utility, especially for amateur and rural printers (Figure 5.3).[15]

Warren saw these efforts to reduce the costs of printing technology as integral to social reform. Printing was a form of political power: "It is well known," he wrote, "that printing is a power that governs the destinies of mankind: and therefore, those who can control the Printing Press, can control their fellow creatures."[16] Yet this extraordinary power of print was increasingly monopolized by the affluent men who controlled the major daily newspapers, particularly as mechanization raised the capital requirements for starting a press or a newspaper.[17] As Warren observed, "The means of printing are so expensive, that the great mass of the people are totally deprived of their use—while the wealthy few (by their capital or influence,) wield this mighty engine."[18] Anticipating the democratizing arguments that would be made in the next century about photocopying machines and the Internet, he claimed that his home press would enable every person to essentially be their own printer, "to send his or her thoughts abroad, without submitting to any of those neutralizing and degrading trammels and exactions imposed by party interests, sectarian feelings, or other partial influences" that characterized most printed newspapers at the time.[19] In a premonition of "open source" principles, he added that the granting of "monopoly

Toward More Transparent Representation   171

by patents" was an "absurd custom," and he invited anyone to take advantage of his invention for democratizing printing, free of charge.[20] (Warren nevertheless obtained two patents for his printing inventions, in 1835 and 1846.)

Throughout his life, Warren acted as his own printer, setting and printing pamphlets such as the one containing the hexagonal city diagrams. He used his self-made printing machine to put out his own four-page weekly newspaper, the *Peaceful Revolutionist,* beginning in 1833, casting the printing plates on the same stove where his wife cooked.[21] These publications have a homemade quality, visible in the lack of uniform size and crispness in the typography, idiosyncratic capitalization, and uneven lines. Warren defended the unpolished print quality of the newspaper, scoffing at those who would dismiss the "voice of poverty and suffering because it cannot speak with 'new type,' 'fine paper,' 'large sheet.'" His aim instead was to "show at how cheap a rate the voice of improvement can be heard."[22] Self-printing his newspaper also allowed Warren to experiment with several unconventional elements of graphic design. Using his clay stereotyping technique, he was able to mix illustrations, handwriting, and type more freely than was typical at the time. His pamphlets variously incorporated his own handwriting, hand-inscribed musical notation, facsimiles of labor notes, and the hexagonal city diagrams. Longer publications such as *Equitable Commerce* featured a system of thematic indexing: letters and numerals in the margins allowed a reader to quickly find where a given theme (e.g., "the proper, legitimate, and just reward of labor") was addressed (Figure 5.4). Warren also liberally deployed typographic variety to convey emphasis and tone. His pages are lively visual concoctions of exclamation marks, italics, sentences in all capitals, and large and small type.

Warren further applied his inventor's approach to the reform of society itself: from the 1820s to the 1870s, he undertook a series of experiments with alternative economic systems and communities, all premised on achieving the goal of equity while preserving individual rights and interests. In the mid-1820s he joined Owen's New Harmony community in Indiana, where he served as the band leader and music teacher and worked in the colony's printing office. New Harmony's rapid collapse left Warren disillusioned. While historians of the community have pointed to several factors contributing to its demise—including internal disputes over the pooling of resources, Owen's lack of direct involvement with daily operations, and a shortage of practical farmers and mechanics—Warren attributed the failure to one thing: communism.[23] People were just too different, he claimed, their interests and viewpoints too distinct, to press into a shared mold. All attempts at joint enterprise ignored the fundamental law that human beings were bound to disagree. Recounting his experience at New Harmony, Warren wrote that the community wore itself out "by incessant legislation about organizations, constitutions, laws, and regulations all to no purpose." The members had expected that their shared devotion to the cause of social reform would lead to harmony. Instead, "the more we desired and called for union, the more this diversity seemed to be developed: and instead of that harmonious co-operation we had expected, we found more antagonisms than we had been accustomed to in common life."[24] Out of this experience, Warren began to wrestle

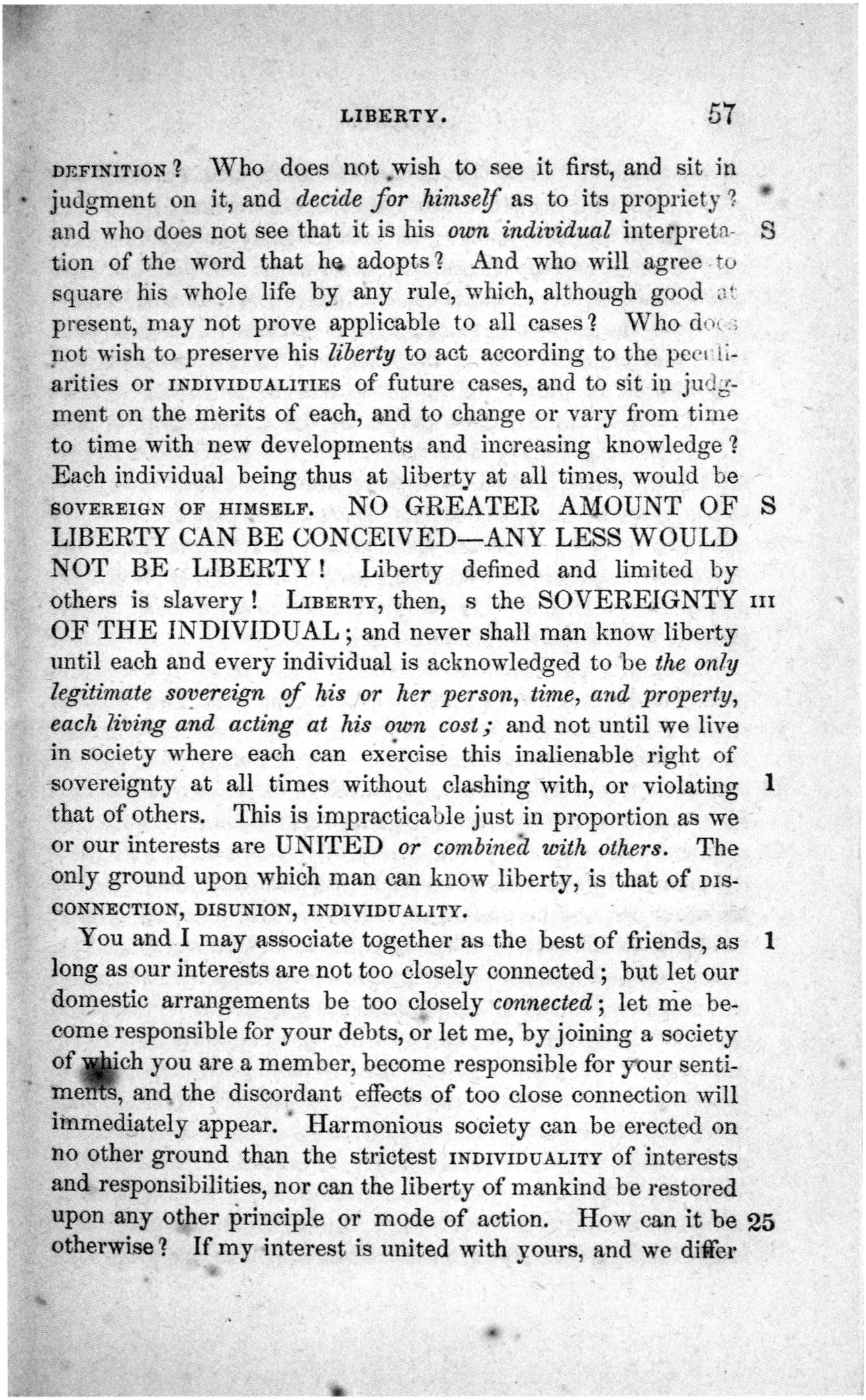

LIBERTY. 57

DEFINITION? Who does not wish to see it first, and sit in judgment on it, and *decide for himself* as to its propriety? and who does not see that it is his *own individual* interpretation of the word that he adopts? And who will agree to square his whole life by any rule, which, although good at present, may not prove applicable to all cases? Who does not wish to preserve his *liberty* to act according to the peculiarities or INDIVIDUALITIES of future cases, and to sit in judgment on the merits of each, and to change or vary from time to time with new developments and increasing knowledge? Each individual being thus at liberty at all times, would be SOVEREIGN OF HIMSELF. NO GREATER AMOUNT OF LIBERTY CAN BE CONCEIVED—ANY LESS WOULD NOT BE LIBERTY! Liberty defined and limited by others is slavery! LIBERTY, then, s the SOVEREIGNTY OF THE INDIVIDUAL; and never shall man know liberty until each and every individual is acknowledged to be *the only legitimate sovereign of his or her person, time, and property, each living and acting at his own cost;* and not until we live in society where each can exercise this inalienable right of sovereignty at all times without clashing with, or violating that of others. This is impracticable just in proportion as we or our interests are UNITED *or combined with others.* The only ground upon which man can know liberty, is that of DISCONNECTION, DISUNION, INDIVIDUALITY.

You and I may associate together as the best of friends, as long as our interests are not too closely connected; but let our domestic arrangements be too closely *connected;* let me become responsible for your debts, or let me, by joining a society of which you are a member, become responsible for your sentiments, and the discordant effects of too close connection will immediately appear. Harmonious society can be erected on no other ground than the strictest INDIVIDUALITY of interests and responsibilities, nor can the liberty of mankind be restored upon any other principle or mode of action. How can it be otherwise? If my interest is united with yours, and we differ

FIGURE 5.4. Josiah Warren used emphatic typography and a marginal indexing system to highlight his points. The letters in the margin correspond to specific themes that recur throughout the book. From Josiah Warren, *Equitable Commerce,* 1852. Courtesy Library of Congress / Archive.org.

Toward More Transparent Representation 173

with the idea that the separation of individuals, rather than union, might be the key to social harmony, eventually developing what he called the principle of "individual sovereignty." This was the idea that individual pursuits should be radically separated and that each person should have absolute control over his or her own actions, body, and circumstances. Warren defined his ideal thus:

> When one's person, his labor, his responsibilities, the soil he rests on, his food, his property, and all his interests are so *disconnected, disunited* from others, that he can control or dispose of these at all times, according to his own views and feelings, without controling or disturbing others; and when his premises are sacred to himself, and his person is not approached, nor his time and attention taken up, against his inclination, then the individual may be said to be practically SOVEREIGN OF HIMSELF.[25]

On the basis of the principle of individual sovereignty, Warren opposed most forms of combination, cooperation, incorporation, and government itself. He condemned voting and government by majority, which he said inevitably led to a minority living under laws not agreeable to them. Decrying demands for unity and "one-ness" of mind or action, Warren wrote emphatically, "WE SHOULD BE NO SUCH THING AS A BODY POLITIC! EACH MAN AND WOMAN MUST BE AN INDIVIDUAL—NO MEMBER OF ANY BODY BUT THAT OF THE HUMAN FAMILY!"[26] He did not rule out all forms of cooperation—only those that unnecessarily mingled individuals' interests. For example, he recognized the benefits of division of labor. He also approved of boardinghouses, whose communal dining rooms enabled savings of labor and expense, so long as the arrangements were entered voluntarily and preserved the freedom to withdraw at will. (A supporter of women's rights, he believed such collective dwellings had the potential to "relieve the females of the family, from the dull, mill-horse drudgery to which they otherwise are irretrievably doomed.")[27] Voluntary and unambiguous forms of mutual assistance were acceptable, as long as individuals' distinct interests remained disentangled.

Warren's position reflects a characteristic of homegrown American anarchism: its extreme individualism bordered on libertarianism, in contrast to French or Russian anarchism, which advocated cooperativism and syndicalism as avenues of non-state-based social organization.[28] Drawing on libertarian seeds in the thought of Thomas Jefferson and Thomas Paine, Warren's principle of individual sovereignty could also be seen as an extreme variant of the liberal ideology that was becoming consolidated in the nineteenth century—a worldview that defined "freedom" both positively, as in the freedom *to* pursue one's own ends, and negatively, as in freedom *from* restraint by others or by government. Warren wrote relatively little about the most glaring example of the denial of individual sovereignty during the period, chattel slavery, but he did briefly address the topic in a book written in the midst of the Civil War, in which he framed the conflict rather myopically as a dispute between two clans. (He also pointed out that the same right of self-sovereignty claimed by southerners applied to enslaved people as well.)[29] The proximity of Warren's thought to the core of liberal theory is indicated by the fact that John Stuart Mill adopted Warren's phrase "sovereignty of the individual" in one of the canonical treatises of nineteenth-century liberalism, *On Liberty* (1859).[30]

Warren was no free market liberal in the current sense, however. Although he disagreed with Owen about the means of reforming society, he concurred wholeheartedly with the utopian industrialist's goal of creating a more equitable society, free of the exploitation and suffering that a rapacious market economy had introduced. Like Owen, the urban workingmen discussed in chapter 2, and the European anarchists Pierre-Joseph Proudhon and Mikhail Bakunin, Warren was moved to propose reforms in response to the rampant inequalities and exploitations of a society being torn apart by, in his words, "the grinding power of capital."[31] Warren shared these figures' rejection of the emerging economic order, which they believed was characterized by the concentration of wealth and power in "monopolies" (especially banks), at the expense of ordinary workers.[32]

Warren developed his own distinct solution, suggesting that a more "equitable commerce" could be attained through the application of a principle he called "cost the limit of price." The source of economic oppression and inequality, he claimed, was the practice of allowing the price of a given article to be determined by the vagaries of the market rather than by the object's "real" cost, defined as the amount of labor employed in making it (that is, by its exchange value rather than its labor value). As an illustration of his principle, he cited the traveler dying of thirst who requests a glass of water from a stranger. The value of the water to the traveler is extraordinary, but its cost to the giver is nothing. On Warren's principle, the price should be free. Yet under the prevailing system of price based on market value, "the most successful speculator is he who can create the most want in the community and extort the most from it." The current system, he wrote passionately, was "the origin of *rich* and *poor!* the fatal pitfall of the working classes! the great political blunder! the deep-seated, unseen germ of the confusion, *insecurity,* and iniquity of the world!"[33] Warren's economic ideas relied on the labor theory of value developed by Adam Smith and modified by David Ricardo. In the 1820s, the idea that all value derives from labor, and that labor thus should be justly compensated, became a rallying cry among early critics of capitalism, from Owen and the "Ricardian socialists" William Thompson, John Gray, and John Francis Bray to American workingmen radicals like Thomas Skidmore.[34] Warren shared the workingmen's producerist ideology, which upheld labor as the source of legitimate wealth and condemned middlemen, speculators, capitalists, bankers, landlords, and all others who "live on the labor of others, and themselves perform none, or if any, a very disproportionate share."[35] But he reserved his fiercest critiques for those who speculated in land and buildings, men whom he saw as preying on the distress of the "landless and the houseless."[36]

To wrest the market away from parasitic intermediaries whose activities inflated or depressed prices, distorting the "true," labor-based value of goods, Warren proposed an alternative economic system based on direct, equal exchanges of "labor for labor," building on an idea first put forward by Owen.[37] In 1827, Warren introduced

Toward More Transparent Representation   175

FIGURE 5.5. Example of a labor note used in Josiah Warren's "time store" system. Courtesy Working Men's Institute Museum and Library, New Harmony, Indiana.

a type of currency system using labor notes denominated in hours of work, for example, in carpentry or sewing (Figure 5.5). He also established "time stores" where individuals could exchange these notes with others, the first of which opened in Cincinnati on May 18, 1827, at the northwest corner of Fifth and Elm Streets.[38] By his own account, this experiment was moderately successful, breaking even after two years and garnering positive responses from customers and even some neighboring storekeepers who saw the rationality of his system, despite the fact that the time store was undercutting their prices. Formulated in the 1820s, Warren's labor exchange system presumed a relatively small-scale artisanal and agricultural economy in which most people entered the market as individual producers and consumers. Thus, in proposing his labor exchanges, Warren rejected not only the shift to combination advocated by socialism but also the increasingly interconnected and abstracted relations of labor, commerce, and finance that were being ushered in by an emerging capitalist economy.[39]

Encouraged by his early successes, Warren gradually worked his way up to establishing a series of small communities where the principles of equitable commerce would be tested out: Equity, Ohio, in 1835; Utopia, Ohio, in 1847; and Modern Times, New York, in 1851.[40] One of his main goals in doing so was to develop an economic system that could meet people's essential needs, especially the need for affordable homes. Modern Times, which Warren founded with the New York reformer Stephen Pearl Andrews, was the longest lasting of these experiments, surviving about thirteen years before disbanding.[41] Warren established a time store there, along with a printshop and a "Mechanical College," a vocational school that offered instruction in printing, stereotyping, bricklaying, and carpentry.[42] By 1854, the town boasted sixty to seventy residents. Founded during the period when Fowler was publishing his own

FIGURE 5.6. Octagonal schoolhouse at Modern Times, built in 1857. Courtesy Brentwood Public Library and Brentwood Historical Society.

octagon house treatise as well as Warren's *Equitable Commerce,* Modern Times bore the unmistakable stamp of Fowler's influence. The village came to feature two octagonal structures, one a house built by carpenter William Upham Dame and the other a school built in 1857 (Figure 5.6).[43] Warren experimented with building houses out of homemade gravel-and-mortar bricks, a cost-saving measure inspired by Fowler that made it possible to erect homes with little capital. As Warren recounted, "Those who never had homes of their own before, suddenly had them."[44]

Modern Times was governed by Warren's principle of "individual sovereignty," the rule that each person should be allowed to choose his or her own mode of living so long as it did not encroach on others. But adherence to this principle ended up contributing to the community's demise. After the controversial health reformers and free love proponents Thomas Low Nichols and Mary Gove Nichols moved to town, Modern Times began attracting all manner of eccentrics, each one believing that, as Warren put it, "the salvation of the world depended on his displaying his particular hobby." Warren later recounted the arrival of these individuals with humor. Besides the free lovers, there was a man who preached and practiced nudism, a woman who dressed in men's clothing ("she cut such a hideous figure, that women shut down their windows and men averted their heads as she passed"), and another young lady who lived almost wholly on unsalted beans and "tottered about a living skeleton for about

Toward More Transparent Representation   177

a year." Warren did not approve of these practices, and he was frustrated that the popular press seized on them to undermine the community's reputation. Yet he stayed true to his principle of individual sovereignty and tolerated all. "Whoever tries what is vulgarly called 'Free Love,'" he wrote, "will find it more troublesome than a crown of thorns: and there is not much danger of its becoming contagious." Warren refused to impose his own mores on others and celebrated their right to live according to their own principles. Reflecting on the scandals surrounding Modern Times, he wrote, "There must be FREEDOM TO DIFFER before there can be peace or progress. . . . The world needs new experiences and it is suicidal to set ourselves against experiments, however absurd they may appear."[45]

The Hexagon City: Cellular Experiments

As the founder of an alternative currency, time stores, and several utopian communities in Ohio and New York, Warren approached reform as a practitioner rather than a theorist. He saw the communities as practical trials. Like later anarchists who favored "propaganda by the deed" rather than by words, Warren saw himself as engaged primarily in "experimental action" rather than verbal argumentation.[46] He was not the kind of reformer who was prone to dreaming about social palaces or speculative city plans, so the appearance of two diagrams of a hexagonal city in *Practical Details* poses something of a mystery (Figure 5.1). One diagram shows a "section of a city" with six lots radially arranged around a public building and yard. Each wedge-shaped lot contains a private dwelling and is separated from its neighbors by streets, indicated by dashed lines.[47] The second diagram depicts an entire city composed of nineteen of these neighborhood-scale hexagons tiled together to form a larger six-sided figure. The drawings are labeled with letters indexed to an adjacent legend, in the manner of a scientific illustration. The diagrams are spare, lacking in detail. The print quality is crude—the dashed lines are irregularly spaced, the inking uneven—indicating that the images were probably printed using Warren's clay stereotyping technique.

Crediting the drawings to "J. Madison Allen of Ancora, NJ," Warren presented these plans without fanfare, describing them primarily in the plainly instrumental terms that characterized much nineteenth-century reform discourse. In the accompanying text, subtitled "Points Suggested for Consideration in Laying Out Towns," Warren articulated several advantages of the hexagonal organization. These points correlate directly with Warren's ideologies of individual sovereignty and equitable commerce. The plans also resemble—and depart from in telling ways—earlier geometric utopian schemes such as the land reformers' village and township and Henry Clubb's vegetarian octagon city, suggesting that Warren and Allen may have been influenced by these earlier plans (Figures 2.2 and 4.1).

Whereas Clubb, for example, had emphasized the capacity of the octagon city to provide for individual ownership of land *and* the benefits of sociality, Warren, as we might expect, stressed the ways in which the hexagonal city would enable individual sovereignty. Because the lots in Warren and Allen's hexagonal city would be divided not just by property lines but also by roads, each lot would become a kind of island. Warren wrote that cities should be laid out to minimize "mutual disturbance" between neighbors and prevent the spread of fire and disease. Unlike the vegetarian plan, with its centralized organization intended to promote sociality and community cohesion, Warren and Allen's hexagon scheme would accentuate the isometric autonomy of the cells. When aggregated, the separate lots in his plan resulted in a nonhierarchical, centerless settlement. In the octagonal vegetarian colony, the leftover spaces could be combined to provide commons for grazing and woodlands. The anarchist scheme, in contrast, took advantage of the hexagon's capacity to tile with no leftover space to eliminate such shared spaces (Figure 5.1). In each of the roughly equal yet distinct cells, Warren imagined individuals could exercise and enact their own desired lifestyles—as long as these did not impinge on their neighbors.

At the same time, concordant with Warren's interest in economic justice, the plan promised to promote equality. Echoing the language of the workingmen land reformers, Warren suggested that by granting each household a small lot of 3 to 5 acres (much smaller than the land reformers' 160-acre or Clubb's 102-acre rural lots), the plan would ensure that each settler had all the land necessary to support a family while cutting off the power to "monopolize" the soil.[48] And as in the land reformers' and vegetarian settlements, concentrically organized neighborhood plans would provide "equal advantages of locality," such as proximity to roads, businesses, and amenities, while minimizing the distances between dwellings and stores. In Warren's plan, though, this central organization operated only at the scale of a six-house cluster. When nineteen of these urban sections were tiled together to form a "city" of more than one hundred households, the result was a town with nineteen public buildings evenly distributed over the whole hexagon, with no overriding center.

The hexagon's geometry had yet another advantage: its capacity for tiling suggested that a community could grow through repetition and self-replication. Enlargement, Warren pointed out, would not require "emigrations to remote regions." Twenty-five years earlier, Warren had written of the process of community growth in geometric terms, describing his experimental settlements as "circles" that would grow until those living at the perimeter were too far from schools and businesses. At that point, "another nucleus has to be formed. . . . Each nucleus extending its growth outward till the circles meet—obliterating all national lines, national prejudices, and national interests, and in a safe, natural, and rapidly progressive manner reorganize society."[49] This passage illustrates not only how Warren's reform imaginary was already conceived in spatial, geometric terms, long before its instantiation as an image, but also the way this self-propagating model was understood to be an instrument of a gradual, universal project of social transformation. The hexagonal plan would enable a peaceful revolution in which the new social system would initially exist side by side with the old, and then eventually expand to encompass the entire globe. Yet we should also note that Warren's model of growth offers yet another reminder of the colonizing logic that underlies utopianism.[50]

Perhaps most important, Warren saw the geometry of the plan as facilitating so-

Toward More Transparent Representation 179

cial difference, experimentation, and the dissemination of his ideas through emulation and propagation. He articulated a vision of the hexagon city as a kind of ludic machine to instigate social experimentation, an idea that anticipated in some ways the anarchist idea of the "temporary autonomous zone."[51] As he explained in the points accompanying the plans:

> The world needs free play for experiments in life. Almost every thinker has some favorite ideas to try, but only one can be tried at a time by any body of people, and there is but little chance of getting the consent of all to any thing new or untried. If a new project can find a half a dozen advocates, it is unusually fortunate: If a hundred experiments were going on at once, there might be fifty times the progress that there would be with only one. To attain this very desirable end, it should be practicable for the few advocates of any new project to try it without involving any others in risks, expenses, or responsibilities or disturbances of any kind, and yet all might benefit by the results of such experiments, either positively, or negatively as warnings.[52]

Warren saw change as occurring through a proliferation of individual, unpredetermined, ground-up efforts rather than through a concerted collective program. Implied in the juxtaposition of text and image was the idea that the hexagon city would speed the pace of progress by acting as an incubator for new ideas. At the root of Warren's individualism, then, was not a simple defense of self-interest and private property but an abiding commitment to the rights of persons to be separate, to hold their own viewpoints and to try new forms of living.

Like many American reformers in the first half of the nineteenth century, Warren operated on what the historian Arthur Bestor calls the "patent-office model of the good society," the belief that a better future could be realized through small-scale trials.[53] Under the patent-office model, social transformation would come about through the initiation of a full-scale model of the new society alongside the old one, rather than through the sudden overthrow of the status quo. The improved model would attract followers by virtue of its manifest superiority, gain imitators, spread, and gradually overcome the existing order, ushering in revolution without strife or bloodshed.

Yet there was a tension in this idea, one that has a latent corollary in the geometry of the plan. On the one hand was the notion of the hexagonal city as a cellular incubator, an array of petri dishes, all with different social experiments occurring in them. On the other hand was the concept of a model being perfected and then replicated identically across the landscape—a form of isometric repetition well suited to the geometry of the hexagon. One interpretation of the hexagon emphasized independence and difference; the other stressed expansion through repetition of the same. Warren seemed to affirm the latter viewpoint when he wrote that the plan would provide a model "in a small way, yet complete in itself" and capable of "continuously extend[ing] outwards." Future growth would "be only a repetition of what has already been done."[54] Perhaps this is less a contradiction than a double entendre embracing the two aspects of the patent-office model of social reform: invention and propagation. Warren's own reform activity encompassed both facets. He was engaged simultaneously in designing new social mechanisms and devices (labor notes and time stores) and in reproducing and disseminating the news of his innovations so that they could be adopted more widely (through his creation of new, inexpensive printing devices and techniques).

"Bewildering Labyrinths": The Corruptions of Language and Money

In his own estimation, Warren had succeeded at the first aspect of reform (invention) but had achieved only modest success in the latter (propagation), a disappointment that he linked directly to the limitations of the medium of print. He complained that "the public have learned but very little of the subject [of his labor exchange experiments], because the common, mercenary news papers could not or would not do it any justice, and it has been kept out of them as much as possible." He therefore resorted next to publishing his own books, but found that "people will not buy books on a subject that they feel no interest in, and they cannot feel an interest in that which they know nothing about." Warren concluded: "The little progress that has been made, has been mostly effected by giving away the works published to here and there one who could be induced to look at them. It is easy to see that no ordinary private resources could make very rapid or extensive progress in that way."[55]

As a reformer, Warren preferred actions to words, but he recognized that actions could have little effect if they were not transcribed into words and disseminated in print. But the problems of representation and reproduction ran deeper than simply the prosaic challenges of publicity; they touched on a core tension in Warren's philosophy. For the extreme individualist, the transmission of one's ideas to another person is always fraught.[56] Communication between two parties always threatens to entail an imposition on or coercion of one subject by the other, with attendant confusions and misunderstandings. Warren's individualist credo was undergirded by a deep skepticism about the inadequacy of verbal language and the limits of communication. In his book *Equitable Commerce,* for example, he explained that the problems with associations and governments stem from the fundamental ambiguity of words, which invariably generate hermeneutic diversity and disagreement: "A creed, a constitution, laws, articles of association, are all liable to as many different interpretations as there are parties to it . . . that which is blue to one is yellow to another and green to a third."[57] Warren tended to attribute contemporary political conflicts (including those over slavery, expansion, and capitalism) to differences in interpretation of language, rather than to the substance of any disagreements. Writing about the constitutional nullification debates in 1833, Warren framed the controversy as centering on the ambiguity of words like "union," "a thing so extremely indefinite that perhaps there are no two individuals concerned who can construe or apply it alike."[58]

In identifying the inherent ambiguity of language as an essential source of political conflict, Warren was tapping into a long tradition that extended back to Plato and Thucydides and was revived in the late eighteenth- and early nineteenth-century United

States. As scholars such as Thomas Gustafson, Michael Kramer, Kenneth Cmiel, and Sandra Gustafson have shown, many Americans during this period, drawing on the linguistic theories of John Locke and others, identified the imprecision of language as a key problem of democratic, republican politics.[59] In the debates over the passage of the U.S. Constitution, for example, Anti-Federalists accused the Federalists of using vague and abstract terms to veil their intention to erect a new despotic central government that would threaten the very liberties that Americans had recently won. Opponents of the Constitution deemed phrases such as "common defence," "general welfare," and "necessary and proper" to be hopelessly indefinite and claimed that they would lead to abusive overstepping of the blurry boundaries between the federal and state governments. The ratification of the Constitution was enabled in part by the verbal somersaults that resulted in the omission of the words "national" and "slave" from the text—contortions that would be the source of debate and rancor throughout the early nineteenth century, eventually contributing to the outbreak of civil war. On the other side were defenders of the draft Constitution such as James Madison, who asserted, in *Federalist* No. 37, that all new laws, however skillfully written, would be "more or less obscure and equivocal" until their meanings could be parsed through specific future applications and judicial decisions. Echoing Locke, Madison argued that, while writers should always strive for maximum clarity, language is an inherently "cloudy medium":

> Besides the obscurity arising from the complexity of objects, and the imperfection of the human faculties, the medium through which the conceptions of men are conveyed to each other adds a fresh embarrassment. The use of words is to express ideas. Perspicuity, therefore, requires not only that the ideas should be distinctly formed, but that they should be expressed by words distinctly and exclusively appropriate to them. But no language is so copious as to supply words and phrases for every complex idea, or so correct as not to include many equivocally denoting different ideas. Hence it must happen that . . . the definition of them may be rendered inaccurate by the inaccuracy of the terms in which it is delivered. And this unavoidable inaccuracy must be greater or less, according to the complexity and novelty of the objects defined.[60]

The idea of an inherent and troubled link between republicanism (a form of government reliant on negotiation and tacit consensus among different people) and language continued to circulate in the nineteenth century. In the 1820s, Noah Webster argued that the "popular errors proceeding from a misunderstanding of words" were "among the efficient causes of our political disorders," and this belief motivated him and other early nineteenth-century reformers to attempt to stabilize and clarify meanings through reformed spellers and dictionaries.[61] Samuel Gridley Howe, reflecting on his work in language acquisition with the deaf and blind woman Laura Bridgman, wrote in 1848:

> [The] vagueness of people's ideas about the meaning of the words they use becomes the source of misunderstanding and mischief without end. . . . What

wars and fightings among nations, what disputes and quarrels among individuals, what polemics among divines, what protocols among statesmen, what speeches and fees among lawyers, might have been saved to the world, if certain words, written down hastily, had been clearly understood by the writers and by the readers![62]

Yet the ambiguity of language was arguably essential to the existence of the republic, enabling temporary (if precarious) unity where it might not otherwise exist and helping to prevent various factions and interests from descending into a Babel-like confusion. In *Democracy in America,* Alexis de Tocqueville observed that a "natural taste for abstract terms" prevailed among citizens of a democratic republic, as manifested in the omnipresence in the United States of vague notions such as "equality." He saw both positive and negative effects emanating from the imprecision of language, which "widens the scope of thought and clouds it."[63]

Warren was fundamentally antipathetic to such linguistic ambiguity. He saw the opacity of words as the source of government's evils, as exemplified in empty political rhetoric. In an 1830 essay in the *Free Enquirer,* he complained about the senseless verbal rhetoric that defined American elections: "The routine of words in praise of our party and in abuse of the others are generally the same, or vary so little." His proposed satirical solution to the problem involved two machines that would replace newspapers, pundits, and party operatives, spitting out phrases like "scoundrel," "traitor to his country," "heartless demagogue," "hero," "patriot," "defender of his country," and "friend to infant manufacturers" in endless succession. This invention, he noted, would save both "the addling of so much (or so little) brains" and a great deal of paper.[64]

Warren's views on language were influenced by an obscure book titled *The Philosophy of Human Knowledge; or, A Treatise on Language,* published in 1828 by an upstate New York banker named Alexander Bryan Johnson. In 1833, Warren credited this book with helping him escape from the "bewildering labyrinths of verbal delusions called arguments and controversies."[65] Johnson's treatise was a philosophical meditation on the problem of linguistic ambiguity in the pursuit of knowledge. Drawing on a tradition of critiques of language among philosophers such as Francis Bacon, Thomas Hobbes, and Locke, Johnson argued that many grave errors in philosophy, science, and society at large could be traced to the equivocality inherent in language. Adopting a radically nominalist view of language, he posited that words have no necessary relationship to the objects or sensations they represent. The meaning of a given word changes depending on its referent: "We all know that when the name George refers to Washington it is dignified and venerated; when it refers to a vagabond reeling through our streets, it has an entirely different signification."[66] In a revised and expanded version of his book, published in 1836, the banker compared the fundamental emptiness of language to paper currency, noting that neither has any innate value:

> We employ words as though they possess, like specie, an intrinsick and natural value; rather than as though they possess, like bank notes, a merely conventional, artificial, and representative value. . . . Some banks, when you present

their notes for redemption, will pay you in other bank notes; but we must not confound such a payment with an actual liquidation in specie. We shall possess, in the new notes, nothing but the representative of specie. In like manner, when you seek the meaning of a word, you may obtain its conversion into other words, or into some verbal thoughts; but you must not confound such a meaning with the phenomena of nature. You will still possess in the new words, nothing but the representatives of natural existence.[67]

Johnson was not alone in seeing paper money and language as analogously vacuous forms of representation during this period of U.S. history.[68] Ralph Waldo Emerson likewise railed against the corruption of language using a metaphor that contrasted the emptiness of paper currency with the "real" value intrinsic in specie (metal currency such as gold and silver): "New imagery ceases to be created, and old words are perverted to stand for things which are not; a paper currency is employed, when there is no bullion in the vaults. In due time the fraud is manifest, and words lose all power to stimulate the understanding or the affections."[69]

Johnson's and Emerson's shared recourse to monetary metaphors to describe the inadequacy or corruption of language can be understood only in reference to the ongoing debates over the nation's currency system. Both were writing in 1836, at the height of Andrew Jackson's Bank War, when money became synonymous with instability and debates over monetary policy were often framed as struggles between a "monopoly power" of wealthy bankers and the honest toil of artisans and farmers. Before the Civil War, the United States had no federal paper currency. Confronted with a chronic shortage of specie, Americans carried out everyday market transactions using a bewildering variety of banknotes issued by hundreds of state-chartered or state-regulated banks, along with shinplasters—paper money issued by nonbank entities such as stores, named after the square patches of paper used by Revolutionary-era soldiers to cushion their shins. As historians of the nineteenth-century U.S. monetary system such as Stephen Mihm, Jeffrey Sklansky, and Joshua Greenberg have shown, the result was a chaotic environment in which farmers and workers were often paid in banknotes of dubious value that they could redeem or exchange only at a discount—a frustrating experience.[70] After Jackson dismantled the Second Bank of the United States in 1836, banknotes issued by wildcat banks (fly-by-night institutions located in remote areas where redemption would be difficult) and just plain counterfeit notes proliferated. Banknote tables and counterfeit detector publications arose to fill the need for information in an economy shifting from localized transactions to more anonymous, distant, and abstract exchanges. New state-chartered banks issued a vast quantity of low-quality money and loans that helped inflate a speculative bubble in western land and real estate. In 1837 the bubble collided with a sharp decline in global cotton prices and the suspension of specie payments by several banks, leading to an acute financial crisis that brought deep economic suffering to a wide swath of Americans. Artisans, workers, and small farmers were especially hard-hit. As Sklansky observes, the money question in the nineteenth-century United States was at its core a class-based conflict between labor and capital, "between cash-poor households and moneyed men, between producers and patricians."[71] While the majority of workers simply wanted a stable paper currency or medium in which to receive wages and carry out purchases, some adopted the more extreme position of the Loco Focos, who insisted that only "hard money" could hold inherent value and linked paper money to "monopolies" and abstract financial institutions beyond the worker's orbit. Paper money appeared to many farmers and artisans as fraudulent, valueless pieces of paper plied by bankers and designed to rob workers of the hard fruits of their labor.

The association of paper money with uncertain value informed Emerson's and Johnson's common recourse to the analogy of money with language. For Johnson, words, like banknotes, were mere representations. Echoing transcendentalist thinkers and nineteenth-century reform pedagogues, Johnson held that true knowledge came from direct sensory experience of "real" things, natural phenomena, and concrete objects.[72] Therefore words should be linked, whenever possible, to concrete things and experiences. But tethering language to experience had another important virtue for Johnson—one that would be especially relevant for Warren—namely, the obviation of "controversy and confusion." Disagreements often arose, Johnson believed, when two people used a single word to refer to slightly different entities. By avoiding the opacity of words and referring directly to phenomena, speakers were more likely to produce propositions that "command our assent."[73] Johnson compared this mode of argumentation from experience to the authority of geometric axioms. "Why are things which are equal to the same, equal to one another?" Trying to prove such a statement definitively through words alone would be impossible, but the problem could be solved by referring to concrete objects, such as two sticks of equal height. "The necessity is not verbal, nor logical, nor dependent on common consent. It is precisely what you will discover by the experiment."[74] In Johnson's phrasing one can detect the political implications of his epistemological speculations. Concrete, visible phenomena capable of "commanding assent" would enable a way around the more arduous process of negotiating "common consent" through verbal persuasion. That is, reasoning from sensible facts could alleviate not just scientific controversies but perhaps also political ones by securing universal agreement rather than potentially unstable consensus reliant on artfully ambiguous verbal constructions.

Warren's experiments with labor notes and time stores were likewise intended to redress the linked problems of monetary instability and community disagreement. Like the Loco Focos, Warren railed against the semiotic volatility of money, which "represents robbery, banking, gambling, swindling, counterfeiting, etc., as much as it represents property; it has a *value* that varies with every individual that uses it." His solution was to try to come up with forms of representation that would be more transparent. Against this instability in values, he argued that a circulating medium should have just one purpose: "that of *standing in the place of the thing represented,* as a miniature represents a person."[75] Compared with the variable and phantom quality of money, Warren believed his labor notes were "stand-ins" for things that were real and concrete: "bone and muscle, the manual powers, the talents, and resources, the property, and property-producing powers of the *whole people*—the soundest of all foundations."[76] He designed both the notes and the time store system to retain this quality of transparency. Extant examples reveal that the notes, which Warren printed himself, bore many of the visual conventions of existing banknotes, including a long, rectangular shape, pictorial vignettes in the center and at the ends, and denominations notated within elliptical shapes in the upper and bottom left corners (Figure 5.5).[77] But Warren's labor notes were also distinguishable from conventional notes in their details. They lacked the precise steel engraving, fine geometrical lathework, images of classical architecture, and prominent institutional names that banks at the time typically used to project a sense of stability and authority.[78] Instead, the labor notes were more like promissory notes, preprinted with blank spaces to be filled in with the name of the giver and recipient at the time of exchange. They promised the bearer a specific number of hours of a specific kind of labor to be performed by the giver (two hours of sign painting or three hours of carpentry, for example), which could alternatively be redeemed in a set amount of corn if preferred. (Warren explained that corn served the purpose well because it was relatively imperishable, "too bulky [to] be stolen or secretly embezzled," and—unlike scarce commodities such as gold and silver—almost as universally held as labor itself: "Everybody who has land, can raise it.")[79] Later versions of the notes included the phrase "Not transferable," indicating that, unlike typical banknotes, which became more abstract and specious in value the farther away they circulated from their originating institutions, the labor notes were intended, at least initially, to be exchanged within a local economy.

Equally important, Warren believed his system of equitable commerce preserved individual sovereignty. Unlike the workingmen's campaign for a homestead policy, labor notes and time stores did not rely on legislation, which had to be campaigned for and passed through governmental bodies—political processes reliant on words and therefore conducive to misunderstanding and conflict. Participation in labor-for-labor exchanges was entirely voluntary, and every individual could be "supreme judge of the price of her or his labor—No committees, no votes of majorities nor any other a r t i f i c i a l or delegated power has anything to do with it."[80] People would adopt the labor exchange system because it worked, allowing individuals to acquire food and clothing, and to obtain homes at fair costs. Here, Warren hoped, was a noncompulsory, nonpolitical path to social reform: a peaceful revolution.

A More Transparent Representation

The theory behind Warren's labor exchange system was that it would establish a clear, unequivocal relationship between the labor notes and the labor hours they signified—that is, between representation and represented. Warren applied a similar principle in his work on orthographic and notational reform, striving to create written representations that would be more transparent. Like many geometric utopians, including Allen, the creator of the hexagonal city plan, Warren was avidly interested in the reform of spelling, writing, and notational systems. These men were not alone. They represent only one episode in a long history of European and English language reform efforts intended to counter the supposed corruptions and confusions of language. Forays into what Sophia Rosenfeld has called "semiotic utopianism" include seventeenth-century efforts to find a universal, philosophical language and eighteenth-century French philosophes' attempts to recover a more natural language of sign and gesture that could counter the perceived "abuse of words."[81] By the nineteenth century, some of these language reform schemes in the Anglo-American context were fixated on correcting the irregularity and cumbersomeness of English spelling by creating systems in which signs more closely and consistently resembled the sounds of words.[82] As Lisa Gitelman recounts, the English reformer Isaac Pitman's shorthand system, first developed in the 1830s, was also known as "phonography" or "sound-writing," and was based on the idea that transcribing spoken language into symbols would yield a more "natural" form of writing.[83] Pitman claimed that his shorthand system would facilitate literacy and speed the pace of social reform. By enabling thoughts to be transcribed seven times faster, the system would allow one person to accomplish the work of three hundred years in a lifetime, and writing could finally "keep pace with invention."[84] Additionally, a more transparent system of writing would enable more effective communication between people, leading to greater understanding and social harmony. Allen predicted that his "pan-norm-alpha" (a universal "natural" alphabet applicable to all languages) would be a "stepping-stone to a Universal Language and . . . universal peace, intelligence, virtue and happiness" (Figure 5.7).[85] Warren affirmed these ideas when he wrote in *Equitable Commerce* that phonography would soon "work a total revolution in literature and book education." In fact, he connected the representational logic of shorthand, based on "individualizing the elements of speech and the signs which represent them," to his own principle of individuality. By "giving to every *Individual* element an *Individual* sign or representative," clarity in writing could be achieved and confusion avoided.[86]

Warren's own efforts in notational reform were concentrated in the area of music. His goal was to make the reading and playing of musical notation available to all. In the 1830s and 1840s, he published a new system of musical transcription aimed, like Pitman's shorthand, toward more transparent correlation between sign and sound, between form and content. Warren claimed his method would signify the elements of sound "exactly in the *notes themselves.*"[87] For example, he proposed that the volume of a note be represented by its size, with a "swelling" of volume indicated by a corresponding swelling in the shape of the note (Figures 5.8 and 5.9). By a similar logic, the relative length of the stem of the note would represent its length in time. With his musical notation system, Warren aspired to create a form of writing in which the signs indicated some essential attribute of the signified (the duration or volume of musical notes, for example) through visual resemblance. Drawing on the linguist Charles Sanders Peirce's triadic definition of icon, index, and symbol, we might say that Warren tried to make his musical notations more like "icons," signifiers that

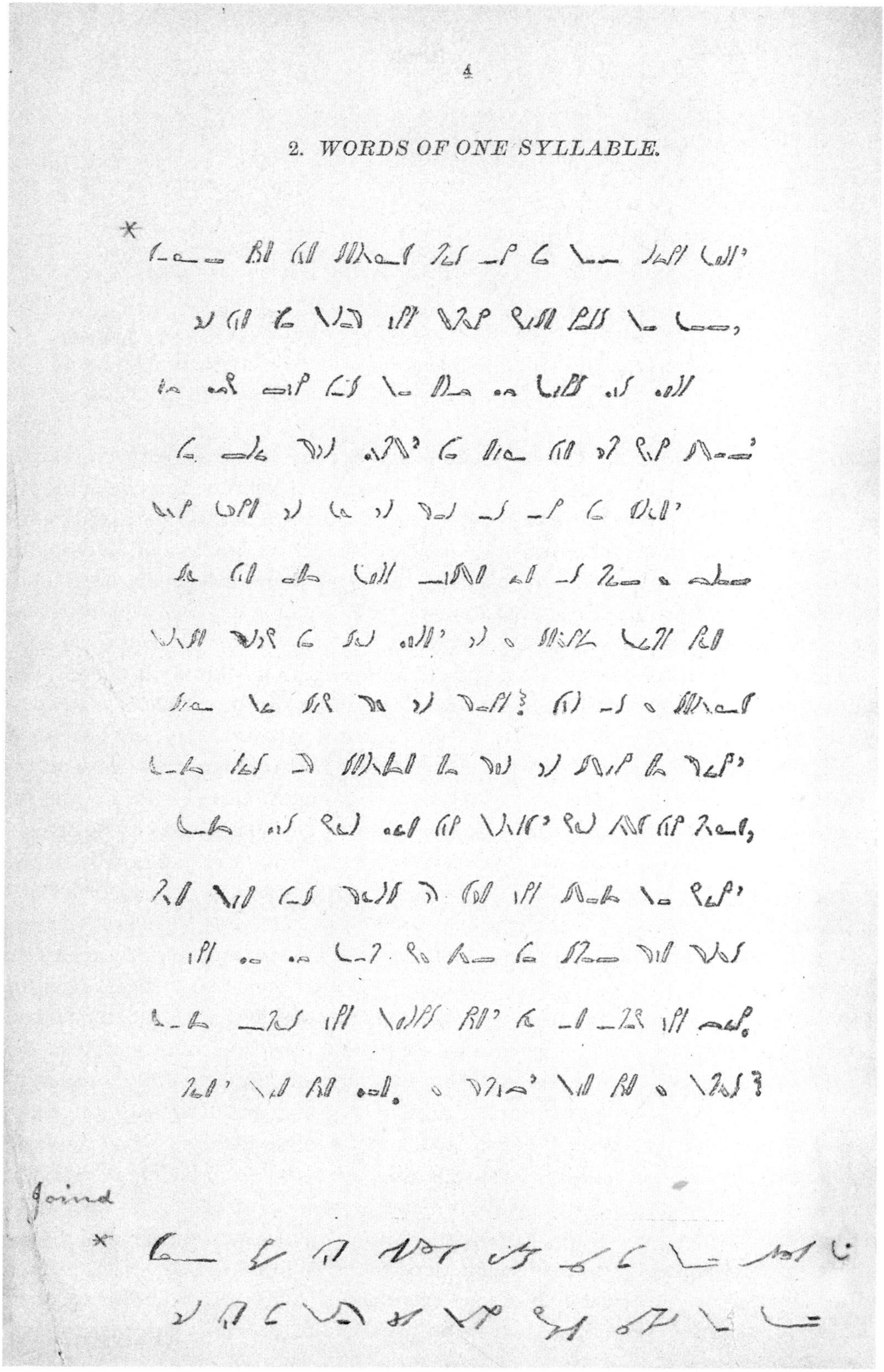
4
2. WORDS OF ONE SYLLABLE.

FIGURE 5.7. Words written in J. Madison Allen's "pan-norm-alpha," or universal alphabet. From James Madison Allen, *Normo-graphy,* 1872. Courtesy New York Public Library.

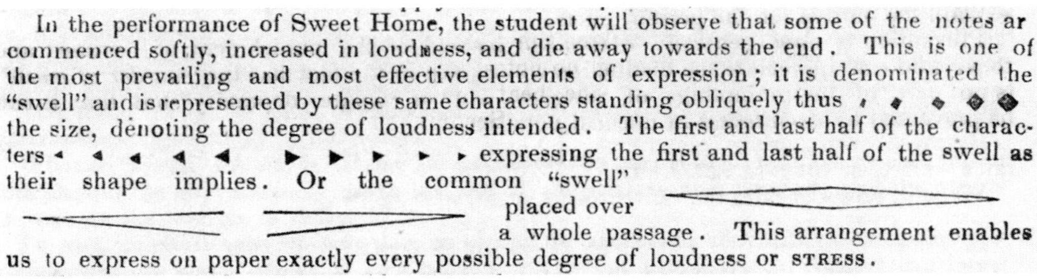

188 *Toward More Transparent Representation*

In the performance of Sweet Home, the student will observe that some of the notes are commenced softly, increased in loudness, and die away towards the end. This is one of the most prevailing and effective elements of expression; it is denominated the "swell" and is represented by these same characters standing obliquely thus ◂ ◂ ◂ ◆ ◆ the size, denoting the degree of loudness intended. The first and last half of the characters ◂ ◂ ◂ ◂ ◂ ▸ ▸ ▸ ▸ ▸ expressing the first and last half of the swell as their shape implies. Or the common "swell" placed over a whole passage. This arrangement enables us to express on paper exactly every possible degree of loudness or STRESS.

FIGURE 5.8. Illustration from Josiah Warren, *Written Music Remodeled, and Invested with the Simplicity of an Exact Science,* 1860, showing how in Warren's reformed notation the forms of notes would reflect the musical effects, in this case a swelling of volume.

have a physical resemblance to the signified, rather than symbols—signifiers with no physical resemblance, whose connection to the signified relies on convention.[88] Warren believed that his new musical notation, by creating a more mimetic and therefore immediate relationship between sign and musical effect, would make it easier to learn to read music, rendering the pleasures of music more universally accessible. Whereas before, music had been used to subjugate the masses, now it could be deployed to emancipate and elevate the people.[89]

Warren's efforts to create new systems of representation, whether in the form of labor notes or musical notations, contained an inherent paradox. Warren wanted to make language clearer so as to foster greater access and agreement, even as he argued that differences in interpretation were inevitable. One way to account for this contradiction is to understand that he saw words and images as different kinds of representations. Whereas images were iconic (in the Peircean sense), resembling the objects they represented, words had only arbitrary relationships to their signifieds. Thus, Warren could compare the veracity of images favorably to the variability in the value of paper money, writing, "[A] picture that would represent at one time a man, at another a monkey, and then a gourd, would be just as legitimate and fit for a portrait, as a common money is fit for a circulating medium."[90] His comment about the absurdity of a picture that could simultaneously represent a man, a monkey, and a gourd relied on a commonly held assumption that pictures were more transparent than words, owing to their iconic nature. As W. J. T. Mitchell has pointed out, the belief that images are more "natural" than words and provide more unmediated and accurate representations has long been a staple of Western culture. "The image is the sign that pretends not to be a sign, masquerading as (or for the believer, actually achieving) natural immediacy and presence. The word is its 'other,' the artificial, arbitrary production of human will that disrupts natural presence by introducing unnatural elements . . . the alienating intervention of symbolic mediation."[91] Warren likewise believed that words were subject to changeable and diverse interpretations, but pictures (and writing that resembled pictures) were clear, their meanings certain, and thus implicitly capable of producing consensus.

MUSIC. [*New words.*]

A ROUND FOR THREE VOICES.

When the first voice arrives at 2, the second begins at 1 and the third voice follows in the same manner.

Thou lend'st to mirth a soft'ning part,
Thou bring'st relief to the aching heart,
    Thou mak'st a heaven without art.

Thou'rt welcome when dear friends have met,
With strangers, still more welcome yet,
    Thou'rt welcome till life's sun is set.

Thy magic power makes cold hearts warm,
Makes strangers friends and friends more firm,
    O greatest power that's free from harm!

Thy discords turn to harmony,(*third voice Fine.*)
Even so do ours when touched by thee,(*second voice Fine.*)
    O haste thy range o'er land and sea!

THE STARVING WORKMEN. [*New words.*]

A ROUND FOR THREE VOICES.

FIGURE 5.9. Page from Josiah Warren, *Written Music Remodeled, and Invested with the Simplicity of an Exact Science,* 1860, illustrating Warren's reformed notation. At the bottom is a song titled "The Starving Workmen, a Round for Three Voices."

Machine Drawings, Drawings as Machines

Explicating Warren's theories of language helps us understand his and perhaps other geometric utopians' turn to diagrams. As discussed in earlier chapters, diagrams were a form of drawing associated early on with geometry and with proof. And as we saw with Johnson's references to geometric axioms, geometry continued to be linked in the nineteenth century to the idea of sure demonstration or proof. Warren voiced this idea, too, in writing that his cost principle was as true, "uncompromising, and as exclusive of all errors" as a principle of arithmetic or geometry.[92] By the nineteenth century, diagrams were increasingly associated with technical drawings, including drawings of machines. Whereas the 1828 version of *Webster's American Dictionary of the English Language* defined the diagram as "In geometry, a figure, draught or scheme delineated for the purpose of demonstrating the properties of any figure, as a square, triangle, circle, &c. Anciently, a musical scale," by 1886, in *Webster's Complete Dictionary of the English Language,* this definition was augmented to include "Any illustrative outline, figure, or drawing" and a cross-reference to "*indicator diagram (steam-engines)*."

Warren would have had an intimate familiarity with diagrams of machines from his work as an inventor. He submitted drawings with his patent applications for a printing press in 1835 (Figure 5.10) and a new kind of stereotyping composition in 1846.[93] The hexagon city plans shared in the conventions of technical drawing: they were two-dimensional orthographic projections, focusing on contour rather than surface, with no shadows or indications of texture, color, or material. The information communicated was diagrammatic, limited to shape, relative size, and the organization of parts to whole. Technical drawing manuals of the time distinguished between working drawings (orthographic projections like plans and elevations) and more "ornamental views" (like perspectival pictures). Whereas the latter were intended primarily for popular audiences, pictures of the first type constituted a medium through which, as one 1870 manual writer observed, "the thoughts of a designer can be most clearly conveyed to a workman, who can thence construct the objects represented."[94] That is, working drawings were not just depictions *of* machines but were in a sense machines themselves, instruments that helped bring about a transmutation from thought to reality. And they acquired this transitive power through their communicative transparency—their ability to convey the thoughts of the designer to the workman, with minimal loss or mistranslation (at least in theory).

For Warren, a plan diagram might have seemed an especially appropriate medium to convey a program of social reform because it was a working drawing, something intended to facilitate the execution of an idea or design. The medium of a technical drawing may also have made sense to Warren because he conceived of society itself as a kind of machine and of the process of reform as akin to inventive tinkering. Metaphors of machinery permeated his political writing. In *Equitable Commerce,* for instance, he wrote, "Society is a complicated machine, which will not work rightly in the absence of some of its necessary parts."[95] Elsewhere he asserted that the key issue in fixing society, as in fixing machinery, lay in solving the problem of friction

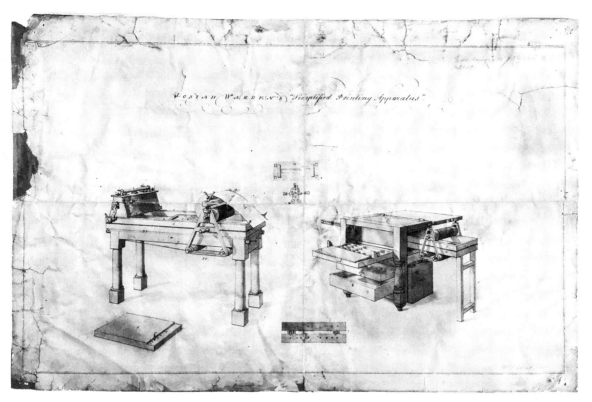

FIGURE 5.10. Josiah Warren's drawings of an improved printing press, submitted for patent in 1835. Courtesy Working Men's Institute Museum and Library, New Harmony, Indiana.

between parts—that is, disagreements and conflicts. "*Joint Stock necessarily involves joint management*; . . . joint management, in such new and complicated movements is impossible. That we cannot construct any *verbal organization* that will not wear itself out by its own friction."[96] The solution for social friction was a new system that would separate individuals and free them from the doomed effort to negotiate differences through words. Warren often compared the social reformer to a machinist, a tinkerer:

> The organization of society is artificial—an invention, a contrivance; and the most ingenious person would be likely to succeed best in this, for the same reason that he would succeed best in the invention of any machine, combining a number of elements, for the accomplishment of any certain object; but, to succeed well in either, he must understand well the objects to be accomplished; . . . the principles involved, and he must be able to trace any defect to the proper cause—not alter a wheel when it is a lever that is in fault, nor *apply more power to force it forward,* when the wheels are out of gear; *but look into the causes, trace the connection of one part with another, till he comes to the fault, and* **THERE IS THE POINT TO APPLY THE REMEDY.**[97]

Toward More Transparent Representation

This passage is striking for the way it describes society as a contrivance—something made by human beings and therefore capable of being fixed by them—in contrast to the organic metaphors for society that would become popular by the second half of the century. If Warren's hexagonal city plans bore some resemblance to his patent drawings, it might be because he saw his role of social reformer as similar to that of a machinist who diagnoses a problem and tests various solutions through trial and error before arriving at a fix.

The Rhetoric of the Diagram

Although much remains unknown about the hexagon city plans, an understanding of Warren's ideas about the relationship between political and pictorial representation grants us a more complex view into why he might have chosen to include the diagrams in his final book. Their seemingly straightforward, unadorned quality resonated with his larger philosophy of politics and representation. Starting with a critique of verbal ambiguity as the source of political conflict, Warren pursued clearer modes of communication that could yield more universal agreement, even as he simultaneously and paradoxically insisted that no such consensus was possible. More transparent forms of communication—whether a diagrammatic musical notation, a more direct form of economic exchange, or a plan drawing that would enact equality and individual sovereignty—would be "machinelike"; that is, they would perform their functions without speaking. In this way they could communicate clearly without passing through layers of mediation and hermeneutic ambiguity.

Throughout his life, Warren professed a suspicion, even an apprehension, of words as a medium not only for attaining community agreement but also for propagating his reform ideas. Writing was an endeavor fraught with peril, so he preferred to speak through his actions and experiments, through his time stores and communities. In *Equitable Commerce,* he wrote:

> I have many times sat down to perform the task now before me; but when I contemplated the overwhelming magnitude of the subject—the bewildering complication of its different parts—the liability to err, to make wrong impressions through the inherent ambiguity of language, and the impossibility of conveying new ideas by old words, I have shrunk with fear and trembling from the task, have laid down my pen in despair, and returned to the silent, but safe, though tardy, language of experimental action. This speaks unequivocally to those who see and study it.[98]

Anxious about the misunderstandings produced by words, Warren wanted the success of his concrete experiments to demonstrate to his fellow Americans the benefits of his ideas and to inspire replication and further experimentation. Yet even "action" and "demonstration" were occasionally accompanied by flourishes of rhetoric that revealed them to be less transparent than Warren believed. Like his contemporaries Orson Fowler and P. T. Barnum, Warren understood the need to prove his arguments to a skeptical public and even seemed at moments to relish the performative aspect of demonstration. In his books, for example, he vowed to approach his reform proposals as trials and to stand by the results of his experiments. He promised that if schemes such as the time store failed, revealing some "unforeseen radical defect," then he would "let all systematic reforms entirely alone."[99] Warren may not have fully embraced the role of writer, but he was not completely averse to the rhetorical techniques of the showman.

Warren disavowed political argument, but in the end he could not do without it. Persuasion, appeal, and advocacy were necessary if he wanted his ideas to be enacted. Warren knew this well. He fretted when his experiments did not receive adequate coverage in mainstream newspapers, and he invented home printing machines to bring the power of publishing to ordinary people. This is why, in addition to his work launching time stores and communities, he wrote and published a cornucopia of pamphlets, tracts, books, and even his own newspaper. In these printed artifacts, Warren deployed plain speech, exclamation marks, and myriad typographic innovations to try to convey his points as clearly as possible. In the hexagonal city diagrams, as in all of his books and manifestoes, and even his experiments with labor notes, time stores, and communities, Warren strove to offer an unequivocal form of representation—a nonrhetorical form of rhetoric—in order to carry out a politics without ambiguity or political strife. He and his fellow geometric utopians turned to the artifice of geometric diagrams and the ostensibly transparent translational agency of machine drawings to present their ideas. Yet the labor notes, the time stores, and the geometric diagrams were not enough to bring about Warren's hoped-for "peaceful revolution." There would be no way around disagreement and struggle, no circumventing the democratic agonism that is a requirement of all significant social transformation.

CHAPTER 6

Models, Machines, and Manifestations
The Spiritualists' Circular Utopias

MACHINE:

1. An artificial work, simple or complicated, that serves to apply or regulate moving power, or to produce motion, so as to save time or force.
2. An engine; an instrument of force.
3. Supernatural agency in a poem, or a superhuman being introduced into a poem to perform some exploit.

     —Noah Webster, *An American Dictionary of the English Language* (1841)

In the mid-1850s, word of another set of geometric utopias began circulating, this time emanating from a group of spiritualists based in Boston and western New York. In breathless tones, Simon Crosby Hewitt (1816–1860), an associate of the medium John Murray Spear (1804–1887), announced that a "new order of society" based on co-operation rather than individualism was dawning and would require a corresponding new architecture. Intelligences in the spirit world were poised to introduce "an entirely new, more beautiful, and in every way, more perfect system of architecture, than the world has yet known."[1] The new mode of building would simultaneously reflect human beings' attainment of a finer spiritual condition and exert a salutary influence on inhabitants, helping speed progress toward a society characterized by "a divine organization, a true socialism." More specifically, the new architecture would be round in form and modeled on the human figure, avoiding sharp angles that might "pain the eye" and "disturb the body." Filled with pleasant odors and soothing colors, the buildings would be constructed of a novel material, a "cement or mineral paste, capable of being moulded into any form, becoming speedily hard as granite, and available at small expense."[2] The group produced plans for a circular city, a series of

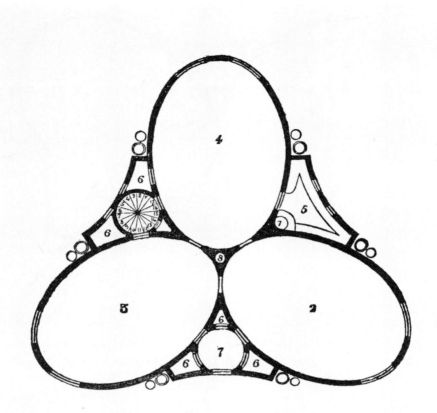

FIGURE 6.1. Nine-room home of harmony. From Simon Crosby Hewitt, "Architecture of the Future—Designs for Homes of Harmony, Transmitted from the Spirit World," in *Robert Owen's Millennial Gazette,* July 1, 1856. Courtesy Kahle / Austin Foundation / Archive.org.

elliptical "homes of harmony" (Figures 6.1–6.3), and a circular structure to house an institution of "equitable commerce" (Figure 6.4). Spear and his colleagues published diagrammatic plans of these designs in pamphlets, journals, and a book, constructed a physical model that they exhibited at spiritualist meetings, and even attempted a full-scale prototype.

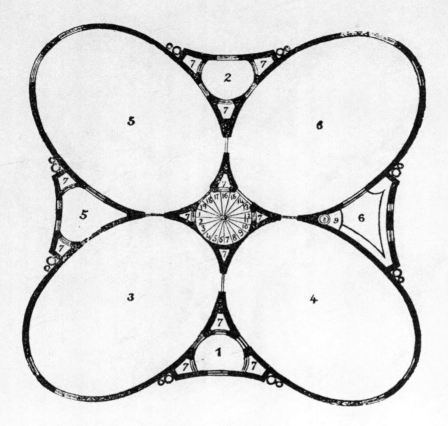

FIGURE 6.2. Fourteen-room home of harmony. From Simon Crosby Hewitt, "Architecture of the Future—Designs for Homes of Harmony, Transmitted from the Spirit World," in *Robert Owen's Millennial Gazette,* July 1, 1856. Courtesy Kahle / Austin Foundation / Archive.org.

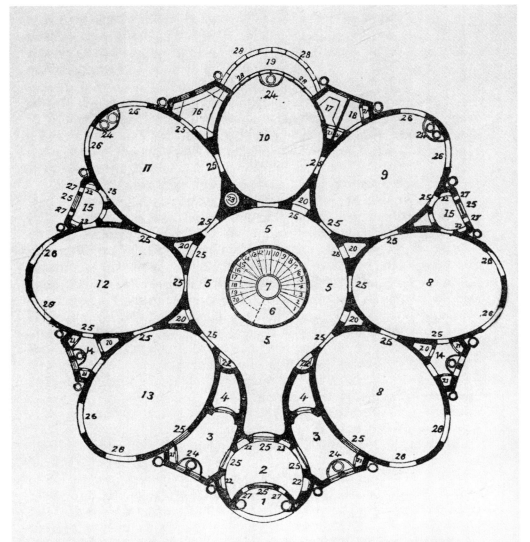

HOME OF HARMONY.—GROUND PLAN OF FIRST STORY.

1. Niche Entrance.
2. Entrance Hall.
3. Reception Rooms.
4. Wardrobes.
5. Inner Hall.
6. Spiral Stairs.
7. Opening for Light.
8. Drawing Rooms.
9. Music and Amusement Rooms.
10. Breakfast Room.
11. Kitchen.
12. Dining Room.
13. Family Parlour.
14. Ladies Dressing Rooms.
15. Side Entrances.
16. Pantry.
17. China Closet.
18. Musical Cabinet.
19. Conservatory.
20. Closets.
21. Cupboards.
22. Niches.
23. Chimney.
24. Toilets and Patent Wash Bowls.
25. Doors.
26. Windows.
27. Side Lights.
28. Iron and Glass.

FIGURE 6.3. Large home of harmony. From Simon Crosby Hewitt, "Architecture of the Future—Designs for Homes of Harmony, Transmitted from the Spirit World," in *Robert Owen's Millennial Gazette,* July 1, 1856. Courtesy Kahle / Austin Foundation / Archive.org.

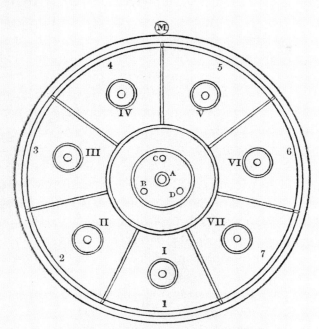

PLAN OF A COMMERCIAL STRUCTURE.

A. Position of Leading Mind. B. Purchaser. C. Receiver. D. Transmitter. I to VII. Heads of Departments. M. Outside Messenger. 1. Department of Nutriments. 2. Garments. 3. Fuels, Lumber, etc. 4. Implements. 5. Furnishings. 6. Books, Papers, etc. 7. Remedials.

FIGURE 6.4. Plan of a commercial structure imparted by the spirits. From A. E. Newton, ed., *The Educator*, 1857. Courtesy Huntington Library.

The new heavenly architecture was just one of the many inventions that the spirits imparted to Spear and his circle throughout the 1850s, all intended to bring about a more harmonious, refined, and elevated world. These visions included an electric ship modeled on a duck, an interplanetary communication network, and a machine that would tap into the "electrical life-currents of the universe" to generate unlimited energy. The sources of these rapturous ideas were intelligences in the higher life desiring to "lay deep and comprehensive schemes of social amelioration for earth's inhabitants."[3] In the spiritualists' telling, these quasi-magical buildings and devices would sweep away the contradictions and conundrums of nineteenth-century American society and usher in a new world. In the new social order, human beings would live in more tranquil homes, engage in fairer forms of economic exchange, move about freely, and communicate with ease; social relations in general would be characterized by "Equality, Justice, and Social Harmony."[4]

These visions of utopian buildings and machines could easily be cast as the eccentric figments of fevered nineteenth-century imaginations. Even fellow spiritualists expressed skepticism. Emma Hardinge, a believer and author of a sympathetic early history of the movement, wrote that Spear and his followers were "far too much bent upon the starry idealities of a spiritual existence to realize the obstacles of a material one, and too much concerned in the possibilities of the future to perceive the impossibilities of the present."[5] In spite of these accusations of ethereal idealism and impracticality, however, Spear and company's myriad preoccupations—communication with the dead, telegraphic networks, perpetual motion machines, improved houses, noncapitalist forms of commerce—were not so improbable or peripheral as they might seem. A wealth of scholarship over the past four decades has demonstrated that nineteenth-century spiritualism was no fringe movement. Embraced by a significant number of Americans (as much as a third of the population, by one estimate), spiritualism emerged from the encounter of liberal Protestantism with some of the signal technological developments of modernity.[6] It was, as John Lardas Modern argues, a "religion born of the secular age."[7] Spiritualism responded to the contradictions of a world in which technological and social progress seemed limitless yet existing society remained imperfect and intractably conflicted over slavery, territorial expansion, and the conditions of industrial labor.

The spiritualists' turn to geometric utopias presents a distinct variation on the themes of visual rhetoric and politics that are central to this book. In putting forward new building types and machines, the members of Spear's circle were following the familiar pattern of nineteenth-century American utopians, seeking a path to "peaceful revolution" through the creation of small-scale, replicable models. And like those other reformers, they deployed the tools of print media to advance their vision and attract followers. However, in contrast to the land reformers, phrenologists, vegetarian abolitionists, and anarchists, whose grids and octagons were steeped in visual associations with rationality, mathematical proof, and functionalism, the spiritualists tended to place equal if not greater emphasis on atmosphere and sensation. In describing their geometric architecture and their broader program of social reform, they frequently evoked the sensorial dimensions of a nonexploitative society, relying on the force of what we might call "enchantment." As explicated by scholars such as Jane Bennett and David Morgan, modern enchantment encompasses the feeling of pleasurable wonder that one experiences in the face of particular images or objects. In Bennett's theorization, enchantment is an emotional state that can direct individuals to adopt a more generous and ethical disposition toward the world.[8] In Morgan's account, it is a mechanism by which individuals negotiate their own agency or lack of agency in the world, since enchantment rests on the affective power that other people or objects have over us. Enchantment also evokes the possibility of magic, the capacity for bringing about metamorphosis or change.[9] Building on these ideas, I argue that the spiritualists' geometric utopias deployed enchantment as a means to mobilize believers in efforts to carry out societal reform. Presented as divine epiphany rather than human invention, their ideal world seemed not only wondrous but also preordained. Justified by revelation rather than rational argument, the spiritualist utopia would attract followers through ambience and aesthetics. If spiritualism, at its core, was premised on the possibility of direct communication between the living and the dead, then its geometric architecture and broader reform vision sought to produce a similarly direct transmission. A better world would not be ushered in primarily through cumbersome verbal arguments or legislation but through noncoercive influxes, uncanny visions, and magnetic forces, which buildings could help channel. In a sense, the spiritualists were offering a unique answer to some fundamental questions regarding persuasion and sociopolitical transformation in modern democratic societies: How do people come to agreement? And once in agreement, how do they act in concert to effect change?[10] The spiritualists' response was that a new society could not simply be reasoned and demonstrated. It must be vividly felt, imagined, and desired.

Spiritualism: A Religion for a Secular Age

The larger movement that gave rise to the spiritualists' architectural visions began in New York State in the 1840s. At its simplest, spiritualism entailed a belief in the possibility of communication with the dead, typically through the intercession of a medium. Following a well-publicized series of "spirit rappings" received by two sisters, Kate and Margaret Fox, outside Rochester in 1848, the movement rapidly gained popularity in the United States and later Britain. From the 1850s onward, mediums and trance speakers, the majority of them women, became ubiquitous in the northeastern United States.[11] Spiritualist practice was highly decentralized, occurring primarily in the parlors of private homes rather than in churches or public meeting places. Typically, a small number of individuals gathered in a "circle" at which a medium received and transcribed messages from the spirit world, sometimes facilitated by a planchette (a small heart-shaped piece of wood attached to a pencil) or other apparatus. Spiritualism appealed to Americans for diverse reasons, among them the promise of communing with departed loved ones, the enjoyment offered by the mysterious spectacle of young women performing in a trance state, and the opportunity to partake in an ostensibly secular, empirical form of faith.

As the historian of religion Catherine Albanese has argued, the upswelling of nineteenth-century spiritualism can be counted as one chapter in a long and diverse tradition of American metaphysical belief, beginning in the colonial period, that drew on Renaissance mysticism and hermeticism, intermingled with African and Native spiritual practices, eventually giving rise to the New Age movement and Eastern mysticism in the twentieth century. Spiritualism exhibited several characteristic features of metaphysicalism: an emphasis on the mind, intuition, clairvoyance, telepathy, altered states of attention, and visionary manifestations; a belief in an essential correspondence between the macrocosm and the microcosm, between the spirit world and the earthly realm; an interest in invisible energies or fluids flowing through the universe; and, finally, a faith in the possibility of personal and social healing through magic rituals and mental will.[12]

The immediate antecedents of American spiritualism can be found in Shakerism, mesmerism, Swedenborgianism, and liberal Protestantism. Spiritualist belief in the possibility of communication between the living and the dead, for example, was preceded by the "Era of Manifestations" in several Shaker communities. From the 1830s through the 1850s, myriad human "instruments" received ecstatic visions and prophecies from the spirit world, resulting in what the Shaker leader F. W. Evans termed "sensuous facts and physical demonstrations"—fervent dances, midnight rituals, speaking in tongues, and gift drawings, including mandala-like diagrams of heavenly cities that the spirits permitted certain human instruments to visit (Figure 6.5).[13] Several Shakers would go on to become spiritualists by the 1850s. Another important influence on Anglo-American spiritualism was Emanuel Swedenborg, the Swedish scientist and Christian mystic who published his oneiric visions of a universe organized into spheres, comprising three heavens and three hells, across which "influxes" of a diffuse divine energy flowed. Swedenborgian ideas impressed transcendentalists like Ralph Waldo Emerson, as well as Andrew Jackson Davis, the "Poughkeepsie Seer" who blended Swedenborgianism with Fourierism in his own philosophy of "harmonialism."[14] Mesmerism was another stimulus. Invented by the German doctor Franz Mesmer and first popularized in France, mesmerism merged with phrenology in the United States to become phrenomagnetism, a practice premised on channeling the flows of energy ("animal magnetism") emanating from human minds to help heal the self and even society. Mesmerism and its offshoots supplied a Newtonian language of gravitational and energetic flows to those seeking to explain the possibility of unseen transmissions between minds. Finally, spiritualism had immediate roots in liberal Christianity, especially denominations such as Universalism and Unitarianism, which had moved away from a Calvinist emphasis on original sin and predestination and toward the ideas of a benevolent loving God, universal salvation, and human selves capable of constant progress and improvement. Universalists believed that the progress of the human soul continued after death, an idea that made them especially receptive to the possibility of communications from the world beyond this one. This helps to explain why a number of prominent Universalist ministers, Spear among them, made the transition to spiritualism by the 1850s.[15]

Spiritualists saw their beliefs as more rational and scientific than those of traditional Christianity and hence better suited to the modern age of machines and inventions. Their preoccupation with invisible flows of energy took inspiration in particular from new technologies of media and communication. Samuel Morse's telegraph, with its seemingly magical capacity to transmit messages over long distances, became an omnipresent figure in spiritualist literature, memorialized in the title of the movement newspaper *The Spiritual Telegraph*.[16] The telegraph was more than a metaphor. Drawing on phrenomagnetic theories, the spiritualists believed that electrical energy was a kind of universal fluid that literally passed through and between people, and between the worlds of the living and the dead, and that could be channeled.[17] This literality is reinforced by an illustration that appeared in Davis's 1853 book *The Present Age and Inner Life* (Figure 6.6), depicting the connection between spirits and a séance circle as a cable. Davis described séances as akin to charging a "spirit battery" and

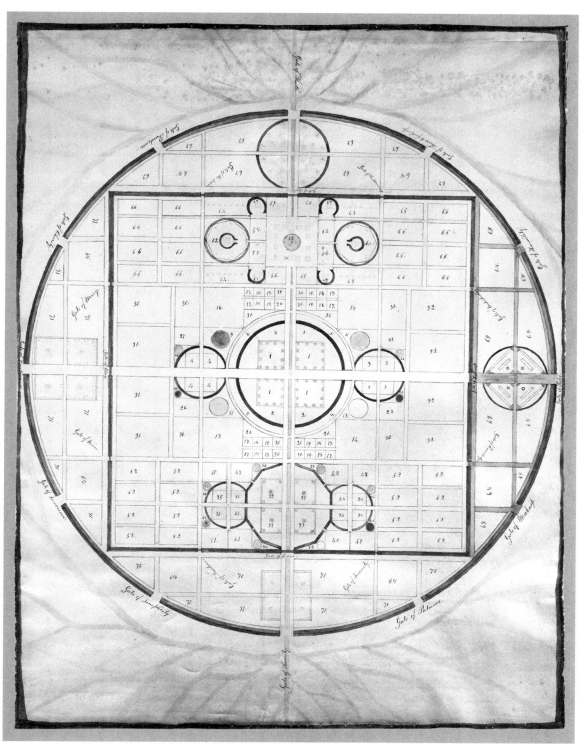

FIGURE 6.5. Map of the Holy City by Shaker seer Polly Ann (Jane) Reed, 1843. Philadelphia Museum of Art: Gift of Mr. and Mrs. Julius Zieget, 1963, 1963-160-5.

FIGURE 6.6. Illustration of "telegraphic correspondence" between a spirit circle in the heavens and a "mundane party" in the earthly realm. From Andrew Jackson Davis, *The Present Age and Inner Life,* 1853. Courtesy Yale Library / Archive.org.

FIGURE 6.7. Charging a "spirit battery." From Andrew Jackson Davis, *The Present Age and Inner Life,* 1853. Courtesy Yale Library / Archive.org.

recommended specific arrangements as conducive to the flow of messages. Males and females, embodying positive and negative principles, respectively, should be seated in alternating places and hold a magnetized rope connected to zinc and copper plates and terminating in a pail of water (Figure 6.7). Davis's instructions combined the precision of engineers' specifications with the haziness characteristic of metaphysical speculation: "These plates should be *dodecahedral,* or cut with *twelve* angles or sides, because, by means of the points, the volume of terrestrial electricity is greatly augmented . . . which the circle requires for a *rudimental aura* (or atmosphere) through which spirits can approach and act upon material bodies."[18] In the spiritualist cosmology, the universe was full of electrical, magnetic, and gravitational forces that practitioners could tap into, just as scientists and inventors had done. The careful choreography of bodies and apparatus around a table—or, as we shall soon see, through architecture—could help channel these signals and flows.

Committed empiricists, the spiritualists were preoccupied with the problem of proof. To allay skeptics, they repeatedly sought to produce material manifestations of the universe's invisible forces using an array of devices, including "cameras, magnets, metal cables, speaking trumpets, clocks, scales, pressure gauges, radiometers, planchettes, [and] ouija boards," to register, gauge, and make visible signs from the unseen spirit world.[19] The scientist Robert Hare, for example, developed a special device called a "spiritoscope" to authenticate spiritual phenomena and in the process was converted from skeptic to believer (Figure 6.8). In the 1860s, spirit photographers claimed to capture ghostly presences through the lens of the camera, that imagined organ of truth.[20] As with P. T. Barnum's wonders, the tinge of the hoax that attended spirit photographs and other forms of proof only served to magnify spiritualism's audience. Spirit photographs, automatic writing, trance performances, and even

FIGURE 6.8. The spiritoscope, a device to verify spirit manifestations, invented by Robert Hare. From Robert Hare, *Experimental Investigations of the Spirit Manifestations*, 1855. Courtesy Library of Congress / Archive.org.

architectural diagrams and models were all symptoms of spiritualism's propensity for concrete demonstrations, as well as its affinity with the culture of visual spectacle.

With their orientation toward rationality, empiricism, technology, free thought, and progress, spiritualists not surprisingly were also ardent believers in social reform and the possibility of creating a more perfect society. As historians such as Ann Braude and Mark Lause have pointed out, spiritualists were actively involved in the era's major radical and reform movements, including women's rights, abolition, free love, health reform, associationism, and land reform.[21] Two of the Fox sisters' earliest supporters were the prominent Quaker abolitionists Isaac Post and Amy Post. Davis promoted Fourierist ideas in formulating his own theory of harmonialism—the idea that bringing the world and its inhabitants into accord with the laws of love and association would result in the attainment of a higher, more peaceful state. And spiritualists were prominent members of several utopian communities, including Hopedale and Modern Times, and even founded a few of their own, such as Harmonia (where Sojourner Truth would settle). Other scholars have taken a dimmer view of spiritualism's political commitments. Bret Carroll and Russ Castronovo have called attention to the quietistic, even authoritarian undertones beneath spiritualism's apparent progressivism, evident in its emphasis on republican order, individualism, and passive interiority or withdrawal.[22] Christine Ferguson has identified a strong current of racial determinism and eugenicist ideas within spiritualist writing.[23] And Albanese has observed that spiritualist approaches to reform lacked intellectual "ballast" and were often unmoored from any concrete plan of realization. If progress was inevitable, a simple matter of the earthly world coming into accord with the laws of nature and the dictates of the spiritual realm, then political argument and struggle would seem to be obviated.[24] Why bother with mundane campaigns or agitation when transmissions and influxes from the spirit world would magically guide the world on the path to reform?

From Politics to Metaphysics: John Murray Spear

The tensions between activism and accommodation, revolution and revelation, that afflicted spiritualism as a whole were also apparent in the biographies of leaders such as Spear. Like many others, Spear arrived at spiritualism following an earlier period of radical political activity. Born in Boston in 1804, he began his career as a Universalist minister and an active abolitionist, pacifist, and advocate for prisoners' rights.[25] Recruited by William Lloyd Garrison as a traveling abolitionist lecturer at a time when the cause was unpopular even in the North, Spear was severely beaten by a hostile mob in Portland, Maine, on December 24, 1844.[26] Shortly after this incident, he resigned his ministry and devoted himself full-time to reform, focusing on the issues of prisoners' rights and abolition of the death penalty. With his brother Charles he established a newspaper, *The Hangman,* later renamed *The Prisoner's Friend.* He also cofounded the Massachusetts Society for the Abolition of Capital Punishment and engaged in direct assistance to prisoners, helping with bail payments, legal representation, and support for newly released inmates. During the 1840s, Spear's political style was radical, strident, and confrontational. Outraged by ministers who defended capital punishment, for instance, he sent a petition to the Massachusetts state legislature proposing that such clergymen be required to act as hangmen.[27]

Spear's approach to reform took a metaphysical turn in 1847 after he read Davis's book *Divine Revelations,* and he received his first direct communications from the spirit world in 1852.[28] Henceforth he would learn of desirable new reforms from an association of spirits who explicated various "wise schemes" for a new and better era.[29] This "Association of Beneficents"—whose members included Benjamin Rush, John Howard, Benjamin Franklin, and Thomas Jefferson—was one of seven such "departments" in Spear's version of the spirit world: the others were the Electricizers, Elementizers, Educationizers, Governmentizers, Healthfulizers, and Agriculturalizers. Each was responsible for reforming a particular area of society, including religion, education, architecture, government, fashion, and diet. All of these were overseen by the General Assembly. Spear published a visualization of the order of the spiritual world, which took the form of a diagram featuring a central circle with spokes connecting to satellite circles (Figure 6.9). The spirits employed Spear as their earthly agent for communicating the structure of their society and instructed him on how to implement mirror institutions on earth. The overarching motif of these plans was "harmony," a

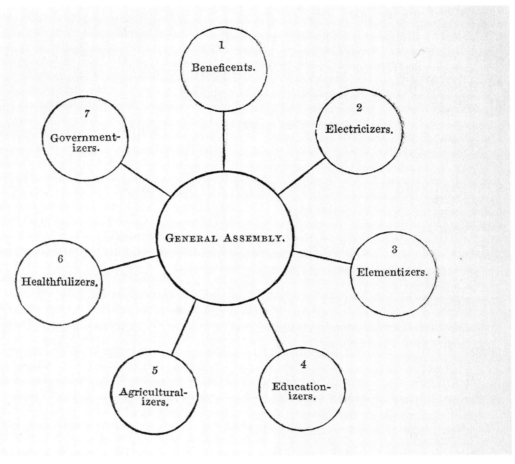

FIGURE 6.9. Diagram of the organization of the spirit world, as envisioned by John Murray Spear. From A. E. Newton, ed., *The Educator,* 1857. Courtesy Library of Congress / Archive.org.

concept that was paradoxically both vague and pragmatic. As the spirits explained: "We come to harmonize things apparently discordant, and out of discords to bring concords. We come to instruct the uninstructed of things supereminently practical. . . . We come to promulgate a more critical knowledge of Nature's laws. We come to raise the low to conditions eminently high."[30]

Spear's turn away from radical political agitation and toward a model of social advocacy based on divine revelation is a biographical narrative shared by many of his associates. Hewitt, for example, came to spiritualism after working as a lecturer for the ten-hour workday movement with the New England Workingmen's Association.[31] John Orvis and John Allen were also involved in the workingmen's movement and were part of the Brook Farm experiment in the mid-1840s before turning their attentions to reforms emanating from the spirit world.[32] Following their conversions, all these men shifted to an ostensibly more passive, nonconfrontational style of reform premised on bringing "harmony" to a conflicted and troubled world. While the spirits affirmed many of the positions that Spear and his friends had formerly advocated—including an end to competitive commerce, slavery, and war—they proposed a different path to accomplish these aims. No longer would these men intentionally face down hostile audiences, hoping to convert them through a mixture of agonistic oratory, reason, and suasion. Reform would occur instead through the "influx" of revelation from the spirits to earth. Spear and his associates' visions reflected several common elements of spiritualist rhetoric, including an emphasis on the inward, spiritual origins of reform over material conditions. The spirits opined that the present-day inhabitants of earth were too focused on external matters. Insisting that "the external is but the elaboration of the internal," the spirits instead emphasized the need to cultivate the divinity within each individual.[33] Another marker of the spiritualists' gentler approach to reform was the pervasiveness in their writing of organic images of wholeness, harmony, individuals' rapport with the cosmos, and the frictionless reconciliation of opposites, especially individuality and sociality. The spirits deemed the latter the "grand problem of the times."[34] Social reconciliation and even perfection would come about as each individual followed his or her inner divinity, becoming more spiritualized and governed by the gravitational pull of the laws of social cohesion.

Dei Ex Machina

It would be a mistake, however, to regard the spiritualists' shift to more ethereal approaches to social transformation as a straightforward slide into quiescence. The spirits themselves proclaimed, to the contrary, that their intention was "to inspire the inactive to high states of activity."[35] One key to unraveling the paradox of the spiritualists' apparent simultaneous passivity and activity is the machine. The answers presented by the spirits for resolving the principal problems of society were frequently literal dei ex machina. Machines, after all, by definition, were instruments that "produce[d] motion, so as to save time or force"; the word "machine" could also refer to a literary device, "a superhuman being introduced into a poem to perform some exploit."[36]

Spear and his colleagues received several visions for potentially revolutionary devices from the department of Electricizers, headed by Ben Franklin. The invention for which they gained the most notoriety was the "Electric Motor" (sometimes referred to as the "Electrical Motor"), a device that promised to revolutionize transportation, production, and communication by drawing its energy not from the conventional sources of steam or water but from the "electric life-currents of the universe." As the spirits announced through Spear in 1853: "Unto your Earth a child is born. Its name shall be called the ELECTRICAL MOTOR. It is the offspring of *mind*,—of the union of mind with matter impregnated by invisible elements. It is to *move* the moral, scientific, philosophical, and religious worlds."[37] The Electric Motor would fuel ships "with greater power and more economy than steam," enable "nations [to] communicate with each other without the aid of wires or submarine cables," and allow the planets to "hold mental communication."[38]

Instructions for the machine's construction were transmitted from the spirits to Spear, who was described as merely the passive conduit of the information, being "quite destitute of either inventive genius, scientific knowledge in either of the departments involved, or even ordinary mechanical abilities."[39] Such disavowals of prior knowledge were a common trope in spiritualism, a way of bolstering divine rather than human origins of mediums' visions. Over the course of ten months, Spear and his associates put aside their own doubts and dutifully followed the spirits' direction in building a model of the motor at High Rock Tower in Lynn, Massachusetts (Figure 6.10).[40] A detailed description of the apparatus was published in *The Educator*, a volume collecting Spear's visions; the passage suggests that the machine resembled an orrery, a type of mechanical model of the solar system illustrating the motions of the planets that was popularized during the eighteenth century. Built on a circular wooden table three feet in diameter, the Electric Motor consisted of "metallic bars, plates, wires, magnets, insulating substances, peculiar chemical compounds," arranged "in accordance with the relations of positive and negative, or masculine and feminine."[41] Each element of the machine corresponded functionally to a body part. A series of suspended zinc and copper plates constituted the "brain" of the machine, while metallic conductors or "attractors" pointing upward corresponded to human hairs, the body's aerial collectors of atmospheric energy, including the energy that carries memories.

In spring 1854, the Electric Motor underwent a series of trials involving circles of individuals sitting around the table in the manner of a séance while the machine was charged with a static generator. According to Alonzo E. Newton, in the culminating tests, Spear encased himself in the apparatus and entered a trance condition for more than an hour. A witness described seeing "'a stream of light,' a sort of umbilicum, emanating (from the encased person) to and enveloping the mechanism."[42] The spirits next indicated that someone of even "finer" stuff was required to act as the human medium. Since the bodies and minds of females, as a class, were considered to be in a purer condition than those of males, Sarah Newton, Alonzo's wife, was recruited. What happened then is unclear, though a few observers intimated that Sarah experienced childbirth-like symptoms.[43] Alonzo later wrote, "*Something* had been imparted. . . . A slight pulsatory action became perceptible in the extremities."[44] In the spiritualist newspaper *The New Era*, Hewitt announced momentously, "The Thing Moves!"[45]

The machine's operations had explicitly erotic overtones: "The wires connecting the [male and female elements] represent sexual interminglings. . . . This mechanism is no longer destitute of activity. Slight and joyous motion exists, which will increase as the matrixal processes pass to their completion."[46] Given the insinuation of sexual impropriety and the machine's failure to produce more than a few vibrations, the annunciation of the Electric Motor caused both controversy and consternation in spiritualist circles.[47] Many questioned its purpose and also the means used to activate it. Newton claimed hyperbolically that it was "subjected to a merciless storm of public ridicule and contemptuous criticism, compared with which the flagellations

FIGURE 6.10. High Rock Tower, Lynn, Massachusetts, scene of a spiritual congress witnessed by Andrew Jackson Davis, as well as the birth of Spear's Electric Motor. From Andrew Jackson Davis, *The Present Age and Inner Life*, 1853. Courtesy Yale Library / Archive.org.

and stake-burnings of ancient martyrs might have been coveted."[48] The apparatus was moved to Randolph, New York, where it was destroyed by locals in August 1854.[49]

The Electric Motor was preposterous and fantastical, yet it was also not simply the mad delusion of isolated zealots. Around the same time that Spear and his colleagues constructed the Electric Motor, a medium named Jonathan Koons in Athens, Ohio, also built a "Spiritual Machine," an illustration of which was published in *Scientific American* in 1855 (Figure 6.11).[50] According to John Buescher, Spear sent some of his associates to visit the Ohio apparatus in 1854.[51] Koons's Spiritual Machine was designed to allow otherworldly beings to manifest their presence through sound. Fitted with drums and bells, the device was paired with a violin, a harmonica, a tambourine, and a trumpet that were played by "invisible hands" during public performances. Like Spear's motor, Koons's machine was built on top of a table and included copper and tin plates and zinc-wrapped copper wires for collecting and conducting electric currents. In the absence of any extant pictorial illustration of Spear's Electric Motor, the published drawing of Koons's device hints at what the former may have looked like. Along with Davis's séance circle, these mechanisms to capture and transmit electromagnetic and spiritual energies reflect spiritualists' understanding of the world as a space saturated with unseen but dense possibilities of interconnection and networking.

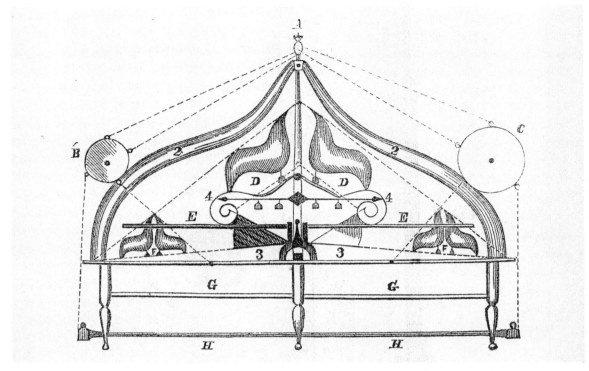

FIGURE 6.11. Jonathan Koons, Spiritual Machine. Published in *Scientific American*, February 3, 1855. Courtesy American Antiquarian Society.

Unlike Koons's machine, Spear's Electric Motor was meant to do more than reveal the presence of spirits: its aim was to realize the utopian possibilities opened by the age of steam. As Andreas Malm has observed, mid-nineteenth-century authors routinely described James Watt's steam engine as a utopian, almost magical, invention. "Showered in mystical allegories and analogies," the engine was "virtually deified," celebrated for having "accomplished more than any other machine for the promotion of the comfort, convenience, and well-being of mankind."[52] Though the steam engine relied on coal as its "prime mover," it was often described as an automatic, self-fueling, living entity, an object possessing powers of enchantment. Malm argues that the fetishization of the steam engine ideologically served to obscure the human labor the invention was intended to replace. While many early nineteenth-century workers and critics of industrialization saw the new machines as antagonistic to the interests of labor, some utopians hoped that the new power-generating devices could be turned to opposite ends. As Davis, the Poughkeepsie seer, argued in a text describing Spear's Electric Motor, the problem was not the machines themselves but that control over machines was concentrated in the hands of capital.[53] Properly directed, he asserted, machines could liberate human beings from toil and material constraint and facilitate the movement of people and goods farther and faster.

In seeking a perpetual (today we might say "renewable") source of power, Spear was reviving a tradition of fascination with devices capable of mimicking or replacing human labor that extended back to medieval and Renaissance engineers' experiments with automata and perpetual motion machines powered by water, wind, and wheels.[54] By the early nineteenth century, the search for "a new motive power" had been revived by techno-utopians such as the German American engineer John A. Etzler, who proposed designs for machines capable of harnessing the wind, tides, and solar power to generate unlimited energy and bring about a paradise on earth (Figure 6.12).[55] In 1852, Darius Davison announced in *Scientific American* that he was awaiting patent approval for an invention, a "new motive power" relying on a novel combination of heat, steam, gas, and a vacuum "that could help power ocean and river vessels, locomotives, factories, agricultural machines, irrigation systems, and more."[56] Like all grand quests, the pursuit of new sources of power inspired a few outright humbugs. In 1812, an inventor named Charles Redheffer exhibited a much-discussed perpetual motion machine in Philadelphia that turned out to be attached via a cord hidden in the wall to a hand crank on the floor above, powered by a human operative.[57] Spear's Electric Motor thus channeled the nineteenth-century utopian imagination about machines' potential to reform the world, while also flirting with the spectacular, entertaining, and phantasmagoric dimensions of the era's technological fascination.

For the spiritualists, the new sources of power were potentially utopian, not only for their promise to yield greater efficiency, speed, and capacity of production and transportation but, more important, for their capacity to generate new social relations and encounters. New machines, the spiritualists believed, could be used to induce social connection rather than competition. Davis argued, for example, that if the new motors could be applied to power "aerial cars" moving through the sky between countries, they would help bring about "a universal brotherhood of acquaintance." "Persons once estranged, when brought in contact, face to face, feel the throbbings of a new friendship."[58] Machine would morph into medium, facilitating global exchange, connection, and eventually social harmony.

The Electric Motor episode thus reveals not only the spiritualists' general fascination with new technologies but also, ultimately, their preoccupation with the possibility of an ideal form of social connection and exchange.[59] In his analysis of the intersections between spiritualism and telegraphy, John Durham Peters argues that spiritualists pursued a particular model of intersubjective communication: the dream of speaking like angels, of exchanging ideas without misunderstanding or loss. "Ghosts and angels haunt modern media," Peters writes, because of "their common ability to spirit voice, image, and word across vast distances without death or decay."[60] The possibility of transparent communication was critical to the spiritualists' model of social reform. Such lossless transmission could enable cooperation and social harmony, overcoming what the spiritualists saw as the key problem of the times: the solipsism of individualism, which led to disagreement. Josiah Warren had confronted the same conundrum, but his solution was to separate people to avoid disunity. For the spiritualists, transparent communication would solve the vexing political problem of

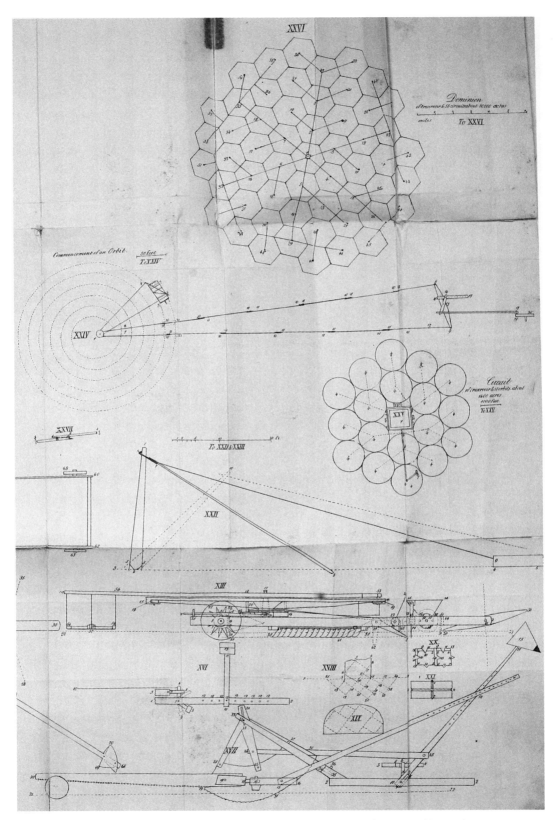

FIGURE 6.12. "Mechanical system to perform the labors of man and beast by inanimate powers, that cost nothing, for producing and preparing the substances of life." From John A. Etzler, *The New World*, 1840.

how to achieve consensus around a specific vision of a future society. Just as mediums channeled transmissions between angels and human beings, telegraphic networks and new motive powers would facilitate understanding, agreement, and friendship among peoples on earth.

Modelizing the New World

An understanding of the significance of communication helps to illuminate another key dimension of Spear and his fellow spiritualists' turn to new machines and architecture: the paramount importance of *models.* Supplementing human mediums, models were another kind of "medium"; they could serve as vehicles for transmitting the inventions of the spirit world to the mortal one. The words "model" and "modelize" recur throughout the group's writings. In *The Educator,* Newton claimed that the Electric Motor would "modelize, or illustrate to the eye, the grand principle of universal and perpetual Motion, as it exists in Nature."[61] That is, the Electric Motor was *modeled on* nature and its forces and was also a *model for* a new kind of engine. It was both derivative and projective, at once a reflection of the universe's laws and a projection of something new. The concept of the model expressed the spiritualists' understanding of the world as governed by hidden correlations and order, as well as their philosophy of social change, especially their beliefs about how divine invention could yield earthly reform.

As defined in the 1841 edition of Webster's *American Dictionary of the English Language,* "model" had seven distinct but overlapping meanings. A model could be a "copy; representation; something made in imitation of real life," such as an "anatomical model of the body." It was also a "pattern of something to be made," including a "form in miniature of something to be made on a larger scale; as, the model of a building." Finally, it connoted an ideal, "a thing to be imitated"; for instance, "Washington, as a model of prudence, integrity and patriotism." Spear's references to models encompass all of these definitions—imitation, prototype, and ideal. Many of the innovations imparted by the spirits were to be "modeled on" existing objects or organisms. For example, the spirits directed the community to build an electric ship based on the model of a duck and a sewing machine on the model of a human arm. (The group worked on the electric ship for almost five years, with the help of a Maine shipbuilder named David Densmore. Intended to be made of iron, lined with salt, and driven by electricity generated from the "personal magnetisms" of sensitive mediums, it would move through the water "with lightning speed, and supersede all other sea-going craft.")[62] This kind of analogical thinking reflected the spiritualists' belief in a grand cosmic harmony encompassing all things. Like other adherents of esoteric religions and probably drawing immediately from Swedenborgianism, the spiritualists saw correspondences everywhere: the human body was round, like a seed or the sun; the Electric Motor was like a body.[63] The preoccupation with correspondences was critical to the spiritualists' ideas about social reform, for it allowed them to connect new contrivances with familiar phenomena. In the spiritualist cosmology, no invention was *ex novo.* Anything new could be tied through analogy or precedent to some previously existing entity, whether in the mortal world or the heavenly one.

For the spiritualists, models based on correspondence did not just manifest a harmonious universe governed by a divine order; they had a practical and communicative function as well. Inventions like the Electric Motor, the electric ship, and the sewing machine were *modeled on* the universe's motions, ducks, and human arms, but they were themselves also regarded as exemplary *models for* replication and dissemination. Concrete models offered an antidote to excessive abstraction and the unimaginability of the new. The spirits instructed Spear that the human mind requires "something tangible; something which can be pictured to the vision, as a guide, or a copy to be imitated. . . . In all important enterprises it is desirable to have thus before the mind a model or embodiment of the thought."[64]

Here we can glimpse the rhetorical dimension of the spiritualists' models. Like the other concrete manifestations incorporated into spiritualist practice—spirit drawings, photographs, rappings—the spiritualists' models offered tangible phenomena to skeptical nineteenth-century audiences. Successfully realized models provided proof of concept, which in turn helped to persuade potential followers. Spear's spirits claimed that a "*model* of a better social state must be constructed,—*a miniature world,* which, on inspection, will meet the approval of sincere and earnest inquirers. . . . The first great work is *to construct a model,*—to show man that that which the mind is capable of conceiving *can be brought forth.*"[65] The visibility of the model was critical to its rhetorical value, demonstrating that even the most fantastic of proposals was workable. But more than feasibility, the model's ability to tether the existing to something yet to be realized was central to its capacity for producing enchantment or wonder. Morgan observes that images are ideal vehicles of enchantment because they can perform a kind of magic trick or metamorphosis: the bending of "the rules of conventional appearance to portray an alternative world."[66] The same could be said of the spiritualists' models. For those inclined to believe, they provided visible evidence of the possibility of transformation, linking the familiar, existing world of objects to the utopian world to come.

Circular Cities, Harmonial Homes

The models produced by the spiritualists encompassed not only machines but also eventually new communities and buildings. In 1853, the spirits instructed Spear and his colleagues that the time was ripe for a band of "courageous persons" to inaugurate a "model society."[67] Under the direction of the invisible teachers, the group established a model colony in Kiantone, a small town in western New York, which they variously called "Harmonia," "The Domain," "The Home Domain," and "Homeville."[68] The site of a mineral spring whose healing properties had been discovered by some clairvoyants a year earlier, Kiantone was determined to have "peculiarly favorable electrical emanations, producing a specially salubrious and spiritualizing atmosphere."[69] Like other nineteenth-century communitarians, Spear's group regarded this colony as a

Models, Machines, and Manifestations   **217**

replicable model, a prototype that, once realized, would "kindle other fires in different sections of this earth" and ultimately lead to a larger social transformation.[70]

Shortly after Kiantone's founding, Hewitt published a series of articles in *The New Era* expounding on a vision for a new "circular city." Existing buildings and cities were "fragmentary and angular," qualities that he linked to the prevailing ethos of "individual selfishness." As society became more organic, then, it would adopt a more circular form. Adapted from nature, the circle was "more economical of space, etc., of very much greater utility in arrangement, and vastly more beautiful in appearance" than the angular form.[71] A subsequent article offered a detailed description of the city. It would have four sections, each one centered on an oblong square containing a grand "unitary mansion." Each of the domed, five-story unitary mansions would contain a central kitchen, laundry, dining halls, reception rooms, and public parlors. These amenities would serve the residents of the mansion as well as families living in sixty-three adjacent "Cottage Homes," thus relieving members of the community of "most of the disagreeable household work." Planted with trees and compactly arranged to encourage pedestrianism, the "Circular City," Hewitt suggested, could just as well be called the "Forest City."[72]

In other publications, Hewitt elaborated on these ideas, focusing on the scale of the home. Around 1853 he began to receive instructions from the spirit world for a new kind of dwelling, a "home of harmony," to be modeled on the human body.[73] He published several diagrammatic plans of these houses in *Robert Owen's Millennial Gazette* in 1856 (Figures 6.1–6.3).[74] The three plans, which ranged in size, were all characterized by a parti of oval rooms arranged radially around a central point or core. The smallest version consisted of a three-story structure with three rooms on the ground floor devoted to a parlor, kitchen, and dining area. The largest was a grand building of unspecified height, intended for an association or cooperative organization. The ground floor of this last structure featured seven large oval rooms—two drawing rooms, a music and amusement space, a breakfast area, kitchen, dining room, and family parlor—as well as a series of smaller chambers intended as reception areas, ladies' dressing rooms, musical cabinet, and conservatory. One can speculate that this plan was a reworking of the "unitary mansion" concept that Hewitt had published two years earlier. Spear's followers apparently built several small prototypes of these structures at Kiantone. Oliver Chase, who grew up near the village, recalled in 1904 that "ten or twelve cottages, square, round and octagon, were built, these were divided into rooms, painted the colors of the rainbow."[75] The structures were said to be domed and ranged in diameter from ten to thirty feet. The available evidence suggests they were far more rudimentary than the elaborate schemes published by Hewitt (Figure 6.13).

Following the pattern of relying on analogical models, the spirits explained via Hewitt that the harmonial home should be modeled on the body; specifically, its circular form should mirror the "charming rotundity" of the human body.[76] The spirits directed Hewitt to examine a human skeleton as a model for the building. Unable to procure a complete skeleton, he was forced to join one together from parts. At night

FIGURE 6.13. The last oval house at Kiantone. From Ernest Miller, "Utopian Communities in Warren County, Pennsylvania," *Western Pennsylvania Historical Magazine* 49, no. 4, 1966. Courtesy Detre Library and Archives.

he would place a chart he had made under his pillow, and in the morning he would be aroused by revelations, including "electrical flashes" of circular and oval rooms.[77] In adopting the body–building analogy, Hewitt (and his spirits) was reviving a classical architectural trope going back to Vitruvius and merging it with theories circulating in the mid-nineteenth-century American literature of health and physiology. The idea of the human body as a kind of "house" was a popular theme in books by writers such as William Andrus Alcott (Figure 6.14).[78] Orson Fowler, too, had compared the body to a house, emphasizing especially the idea of the kitchen as a stomach. Passages from Hewitt's descriptions track so closely with Fowler's that there is little doubt of the phrenologist's influence.[79] Yet whereas Fowler had been concerned primarily with the functional ways in which the house could affect human bodies (providing healthy air through ventilation, spaces for exercise, and compact organization to save labor), Hewitt cast his body–building analogies in more symbolic-analogical terms. Of the harmonial home's tripartite arrangement, he explained that the lower apartments corresponded to the abdominals and therefore contained a kitchen. The central floor housed the vital and respiratory organs: the dining room was the stomach, the worship room the heart, the mother's private room the liver. Above these, the cupola cor-

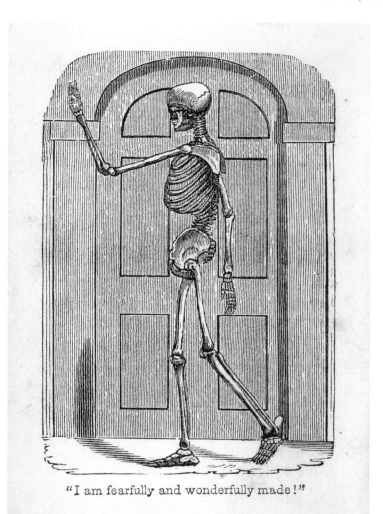

FIGURE 6.14. Illustration of analogy between house and body. From William Andrus Alcott, *The House I Live In*, 1839. Courtesy University of California Libraries / Archive.org.

responded to the brain and was where reading, writing, and thinking would occur. Windows were like eyes; the door was the mouth. A vertical, circular, hollow shaft, corresponding to the spinal cord, nerves, and blood vessels, provided communication among the stories, via "sliding apparatus, spiral staircases, bell-wires, speaking-tubes, water-pipes."[80] Elsewhere, Davis described such body–building analogies as constituting a new architectural theory of "correspondential edificialism."[81]

Hewitt followed the convention of spiritualist mediumship in stressing that he had no previous education and "knew nothing of architecture, or even of geometry, from books." He insisted that the design of the houses had been guided by "invisible educators."[82] Yet the architecture transmitted by the spirits undoubtedly had earthly referents. Hewitt was almost certainly familiar with Fowler's octagon house book, and he may also have seen a house manual by Zephaniah Baker, a Universalist minister and spiritualist residing in Worcester, published in the same year Hewitt announced

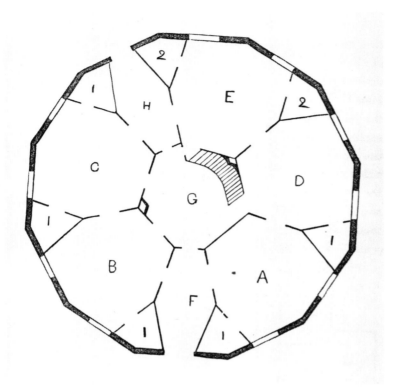

FIGURE 6.15. Twelve-sided house from Zephaniah Baker, *The Cottage Builder's Manual*, 1856. Courtesy University of Illinois Urbana–Champaign / Archive.org.

his homes of harmony. Baker's book, itself indebted to Fowler, presented several circular, octagonal, and twelve-sided plans, one of which bears a close resemblance to the largest of Hewitt's homes of harmony in its use of radially arranged rooms within a dodecagonal envelope (Figure 6.15).[83] Not far away, in Somerville, Massachusetts, Enoch Robinson constructed a circular house in 1856 or earlier (Figures 6.16 and 6.17). More distantly, Hewitt may also have known of precedents such as Jefferson's plan of the first floor of the University of Virginia Rotunda (Figure 6.18), which was said to have been influenced by the ground-floor plan of the Désert de Retz (Figure 6.19).[84]

In denying any knowledge of these architectural precedents—indeed, any knowledge of architecture whatsoever—Hewitt was reinforcing the divine inspiration of the homes of harmony. As Morgan has argued, this kind of displacement or obscuring of authorship is a technique of enchantment. It performs the trick of making "things that human beings make return to them as something *not* humanly produced." Agency is thereby transferred from human beings to the objects themselves, which appear more "autonomous and alive."[85] By emphasizing the heavenly origin of his architecture and his status as a mere instrument for manifesting these revelations from the spirit world, Hewitt invested what would otherwise appear as simply another set of model house plans with an uncanny aspect. The houses were familiar yet strange, recognizable yet otherworldly. As with Shaker gift drawings, the diagrams of spiritual houses were saturated with an aura of prophecy and thus demanded heightened

FIGURE 6.16. Robinson House, Somerville, Massachusetts, built circa 1855. Courtesy Somerville Museum.

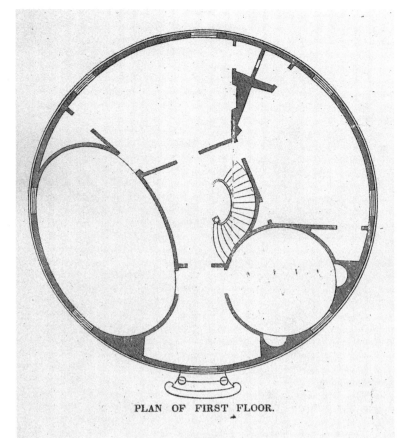

PLAN OF FIRST FLOOR.

FIGURE 6.17. Plans of the Robinson House, Somerville, Massachusetts, built circa 1855. Courtesy Somerville Public Library.

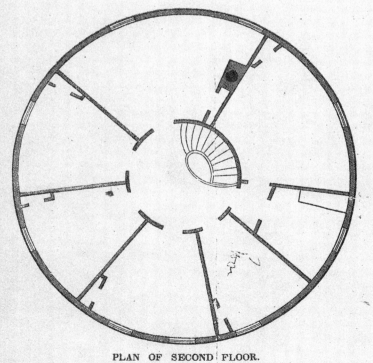

PLAN OF SECOND FLOOR.

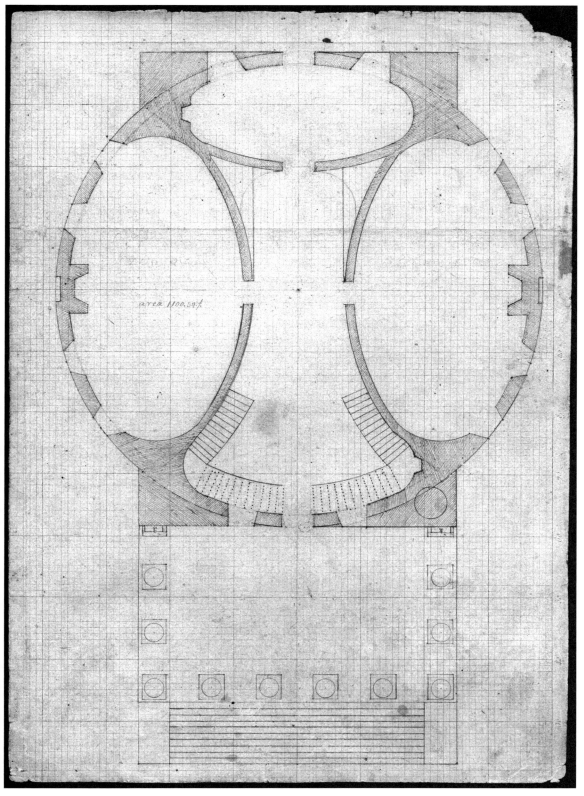

FIGURE 6.18. Thomas Jefferson, University of Virginia Rotunda, first floor plan, 1826. Thomas Jefferson Papers, Albert and Shirley Small Special Collections Library, N-330r.

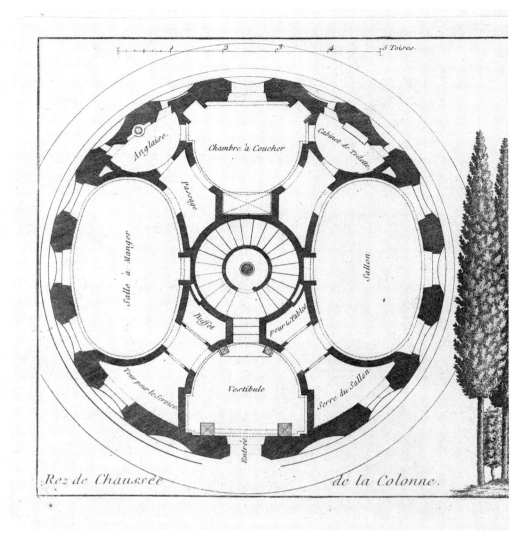

FIGURE 6.19. François Racine de Monville, Désert de Retz, plan. From Georges-Louis Le Rouge, *Détail des nouveaux jardins à la mode,* volume 13, 1785. Courtesy Getty Research Institute / Archive.org.

attention from viewers. The homes' aura of enchantment invited readers to approach them in a mood of reverence and mindfulness.

An Aesthetic of Circularity

The sententious quality of the homes was accentuated by their circular geometry. The form of the houses reflected a general aesthetic of circularity that suffused spiritualist practice and cosmology. Understanding the polyvalent significance of the circle is critical to explicating the spiritualists' theory of societal reform. In addition to its correspondences to the human body, the rounded shape of the homes of harmony had multiple resonances. For one thing, the spiritualists subscribed to a tradition extending back to classicism in which circles were identified with the elemental geometry of nature, visible in the human body, seeds, and other "natural" objects.[86] Circles signified an ordered universe with a single center and clear hierarchy, and circular diagrams were prominent in the visual language of Newtonian and Copernican science. These diagrams influenced esoteric and Neoplatonic visual representations, which in turn shaped the visual imagination of Swedenborg and his American descendants Davis and Spear (Figure 6.20).[87] The visual influence of early modern astronomy can be seen, for example, in Spear's diagrams of the organizational structure of the heavens and of a new spiritualized social order that took the form of nested circles or circles arranged in hub-and-spoke compositions (Figures 6.9 and 6.21). These diagrams are notable for their simplicity and abstraction. Printed in black and white, and composed of nothing but circles, straight lines, and textual labels, the diagrams are strikingly reticent, especially when compared with the sometimes florid textual descriptions that accompanied them.

The spiritualist diagrams had other, less obvious referents as well. Perhaps not coincidentally, at around the same time, large enterprises such as railroad companies also began to use circular organizational diagrams (Figure 6.22). The historian Alfred Chandler has cited such diagrams as evidence of how modern management structures emerged in the middle of the nineteenth century to deal with the growing scale and complexity of business. According to Chandler, as the U.S. economy shifted from a system in which agriculturalists and commercialists exchanged goods in local country stores to one in which layers of jobbers, importers, factors, brokers, bankers, agents, and other middlemen increasingly directed the flow of goods across the nation and even the globe, Adam Smith's "invisible hand" (a term that itself evokes angelic agency) came to be seen as inadequate to the tasks of coordination. Beginning in the 1840s, railroad companies led the way in enacting a "managerial revolution" by developing methods and systems to coordinate geographically dispersed operations.[88] In the case of both the spiritualists' and railroad organizations' charts, circular diagrams offered a way to cognitively organize an increasingly complex world, to make palpable a hidden networked order, and to suggest the harmonious coordination of parts.

The spiritualists were drawn to circles not only for their connotation of order but also for their aesthetic and atmospheric qualities. The term "circle" was used to designate the primary unit of spiritualist practice, the séance gathering, which typically occurred in the environment of the private home. Circles thus carried associations of intimacy, tranquility, and domesticity. In focusing on the site of the house as a primary object of transformation, the spiritualists were affirming popular midnineteenth-century ideas about the home as a refuge from the chaos and discord of the capitalist market.

The tranquility of the domestic circle was no mere metaphor. Hewitt, Spear, Davis, and other spiritualists also advanced a set of particular psychophysical ideas about how circular spaces could help transform human subjects, which would in turn lead

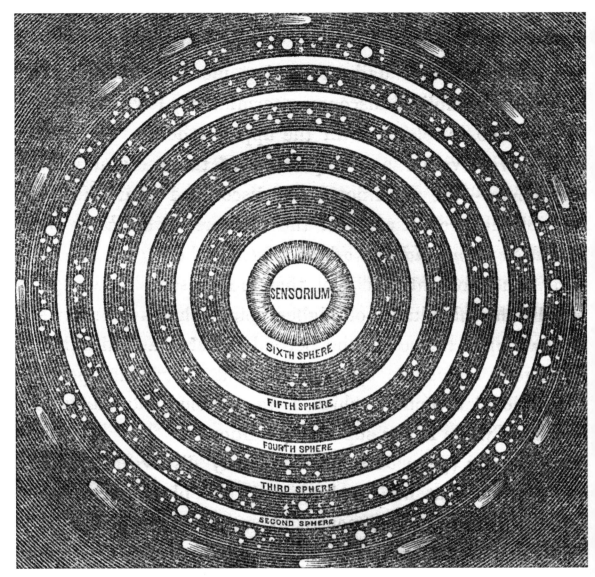

FIGURE 6.20. Diagram of the spiritual spheres. From Andrew Jackson Davis, *The Magic Staff: An Autobiography*, 1857. Courtesy University of California Libraries.

to broader social transformation. These ideas blended nineteenth-century functionalist physiology with eighteenth-century sensationalism.[89] If Fowler had argued that the layout of octagonal houses would literally preserve the physical and psychic health of mothers by saving them steps and providing them with quiet spaces, then the spiritualists extended this logic to a physiologically based psychology of sensation. The angles of ordinary buildings, they asserted, "not only disturb the body, unfavorably affecting the elements, but will also pain the eye. *Angular* persons do not notice this; but the more spiritual, the more perfectly or roundly unfolded, are affected somewhat as if pierced by sharp pins."[90] For his homes of harmony, however, Hewitt chose oval

Models, Machines, and Manifestations 227

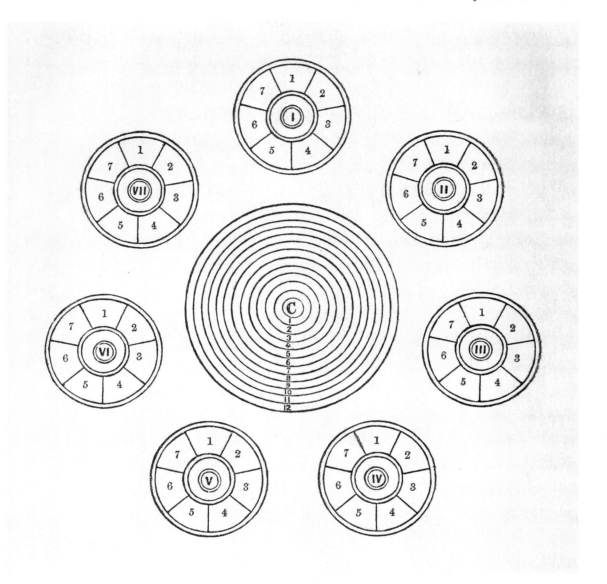

FIGURE 6.21. Diagram of the church and her offspring, as envisioned by John Murray Spear. From A. E. Newton, ed., *The Educator,* 1857. Courtesy Library of Congress / Archive.org.

rather than perfectly circular rooms. He believed that "a perfectly *round* structure" lacked "elegance": "It produces a monotonous effect, which wearies the mind. But the *oval* is more agreeable. The eye is pleased with its graceful sweep; and not unfrequently greater beauty and economy can be secured by its adoption."[91] Exposure to such beautiful forms would, in turn, exert an elevating influence on the beholder.

To provide a comfortable atmosphere for refined souls, each house should have a "holy of holies," a quiet space, sheltered from disturbance, "where spiritual beings may congregate at will, write out their thoughts, if they choose, or impress them on

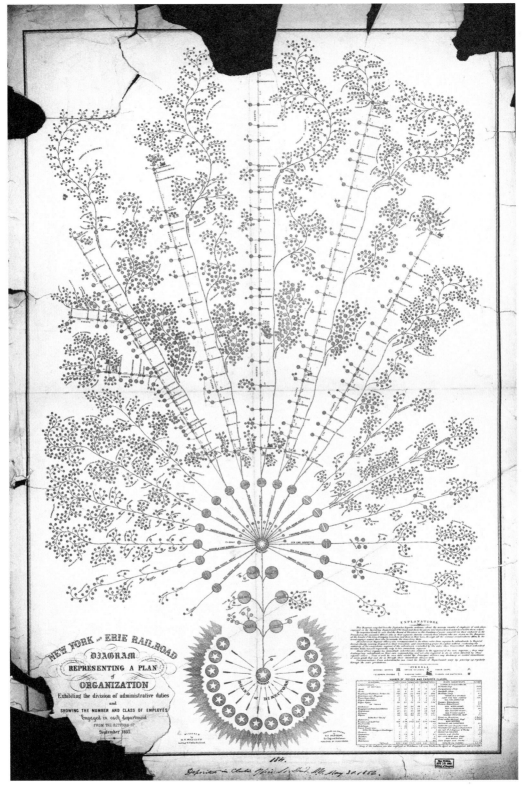

FIGURE 6.22. Organizational diagram of the New York Erie Railroad, 1855. Note the diagram of the board of directors at the bottom. Library of Congress, Geography and Map Division.

the mind." The holy of holies should contain an altar, sacred tablets, a font of pure water, divine statuary, and other spiritual objects "adapted to bring out and intensify the diviner, nobler faculties of the human soul." This sanctified space was imagined as "secluded from the noise and bustle of life" and from the external world, where "all things are astir." The holy of holies also embodied the individualistic orientation of spiritualist practice, in terms that echo transcendentalist belief. In this space, "I would be alone; I would be my own priest, and worship God in my own way, without an intermediate."[92]

The concern for providing a space of quiet, individual privacy—a retreat within the retreat of the home—also reflected the Kiantone spiritualists' particular beliefs about women and reproduction, beliefs that can be related to a troubling pattern in mid-nineteenth-century radical reform thought. Like other spiritualists, Spear's circle was generally supportive of women's rights and of women's greater economic and sexual autonomy, including what was then called "free love," which essentially entailed the right to choose one's mate (or mates). (Spear himself became embroiled in a "free love" scandal when he began an extramarital relationship with a women's rights advocate named Caroline Hinckley.) Yet they also relied on essentialist notions of women as more elevated, finer souls, as receptive vessels, and as mothers, an idea that fed the spiritualist emphasis on careful reproduction as a mechanism for social reform. Echoing Fowler, and perhaps directly influenced by him, Spear devoted special attention to the effects of the domestic environment on pregnant women and mothers. The mother required "an apartment which she can call her own," where she could "retire from the world." This private space was needed for gestational health, he suggested: "She should not be interrupted or startled by any occurrence in the building; because the slightest incident sometimes disarranges all the earlier processes, and miscarriage results."[93] Like Fowler, the Kiantonists believed that the sense impressions a mother received during pregnancy would be transmitted to her fetus.[94]

The spiritualists' preoccupation with sexual generation and what they termed "wombology" reflected their belief that reproduction was one path of societal transformation. Spear argued, for example, that one advantage of a separate, self-selected colony was that it would allow for a small group to engage in more careful mating and the gestation of "truly harmonious, intelligent, and advanced minds." In the future society, an astrologer, "a person properly instructed in the subject of *interblendings,* of harmonious combinations, could teach individuals how to select suitable partners." Spear's astrologer essentially took on the role that Fowler had assigned the phrenologist: advising individuals on their own character, the proper paths for their self-improvement, and how to find appropriate mates. Careful reproduction would have larger social repercussions: "The astrologer could combine persons with reference to their individual horoscopes; and thus gradually, but with scientific precision, could a social framework be constructed, taking the place of villages, towns, and states."[95] In the 1860s, the utopian John Humphrey Noyes would develop the idea of scientific procreation into a system he called "stirpiculture" at his colony in Oneida, New York.[96] By promoting self-cultivation and strategic mating as the paths for the model's dissemination, the spiritualists were thus subscribing to an idea that was circulating

230 Models, Machines, and Manifestations

widely among nineteenth-century reformers: that a better society could not only be designed or engineered; it could be "bred."[97]

Angels in the Market: A Circular Institution of Equitable Exchange

The guiding principle behind the spiritualists' domestic architecture was that circular geometry could create a space that would help calm minds and cultivate refined souls, leading to the elevation of society. Similar ideas informed the spiritualists' proposal for an institution of "equitable commerce." In 1855, a group calling themselves the New England Association of Philanthropic Commercialists (led by Spear's colleague Orvis) published a thirty-six-page pamphlet titled *Equitable Commerce: A Proposal for the Abolition of Trade, by the Substitution of Equitable Exchange, with Full Plans and Details, in a Series of Papers Communicated from the Spirit-Life.*[98] In it, the group outlined a vision for replacing the current market system, which they deemed mere "trade," with a new system of equitable commerce. Whereas the existing capitalist system produced individual aggrandizement of the few to the detriment of the many, the latter would elevate commercial transactions into exchanges based on love and cooperation that would benefit all classes of society. Equitable commerce would be a "magic wand wherewith not only to strike down Trade and its oppressions, but also to initiate a Divine Social Order."[99]

While presented as a vision imparted from the spirits, here again revelation drew on earthly sources recently circulating in Boston and New York—in this case the ideas of the proto-anarchist Josiah Warren. By the mid-1850s, Spear and Orvis had come into contact with Warren and Stephen Pearl Andrews, cofounders of the utopian colony Modern Times on Long Island, New York, and vocal critics of the predatory nature of the capitalist market.[100] As discussed in chapter 5, Warren was a former Owenite who wrote several pamphlets on the subject of equitable commerce and, beginning in the late 1820s, experimented with alternative market systems that pegged the cost of goods to the amount of labor required to make them, while prohibiting disproportionate profits and speculation. To advance his ideas, he devised a system of labor notes and established several time stores and colonies to test the principles on which they were based. Andrews and Warren, perhaps not coincidentally, were believers in spiritualism but did not generally address it in their publications on equitable commerce.[101]

The circle around Spear borrowed the term "equitable commerce" from Warren but departed from his program in several respects. Warren's proposal for new mechanisms to exchange labor reflected his fundamental producerism, his belief in labor as the only legitimate source of value. In contrast, the spiritualists were concerned less with giving labor its due than with creating a highly choreographed and aestheticized marketplace governed by a vague yet powerful "love principle." And whereas Warren, an ever-pragmatic inventor, created plans that were practical and immediately implementable, the spiritualists' scheme was atmospheric and idealistic.

Once again, the spiritualists' central concern was with expediting communication and fostering more harmonious relations between subjects. The spiritualist pamphlet *Equitable Commerce* posited that market transactions were fundamentally social relationships, consisting of acts of interaction and exchange. "Commerce is finally, intercommunication; is simply giving; simply receiving." Individuals could not provide all their own needs in isolation, contrary to the fantasy of self-sufficiency promulgated in Henry David Thoreau's book *Walden,* published in Boston just a year earlier. In isolation, the spirits opined, the human "would shrivel, grow down into his individual self, would not associate, would rarely expand." The spirits pointed out that commerce enabled individuals to obtain goods from different parts of the world (and even other planets) as well as encouraging the exchange of ideas. Rather than being based on profit, economic exchanges between individuals should be rooted in friendship and philanthropy. Equitable commerce "exchanges goods, at simple cost. It does not undertake to sponge any person . . . but exchanges intrinsic values."[102] Expelling greed and profit from market transactions, the spiritualists believed, would restore commerce to its pure form as a social interchange between individuals—a "communion" between souls.[103]

In order to establish commerce as communion, the spiritualists recognized that a range of agents and intermediaries, or "mediums" in a sense, would be required. One of the hallmarks of a market economy is that transactions are carried out by strangers across great distances rather than between acquaintances in a single limited community. In such a market, transparency of information and communication are essential to produce trust. To facilitate fair exchanges, the spiritualists introduced an array of new market roles, human agents who would be directed in their work by the spirits. A "grand organizer," a "leading, harmonious, quiet, cultivated mind," would oversee the activities of the three principal actors in each commercial transaction: purchaser, receiver, and transmitter. (A woman was an ideal receiver and transmitter, the spirits observed, because of her innate "ability to judge of garments . . . her nice discriminating taste enabling her to select the choicest foods.") In addition, a general inspector would carry out oversight, and branch agents would make careful records of each transaction; these records were "to be always open" for the inspection of an auditor. A network of traveling and local agents assigned to regions in the western United States, the West Indies, the British provinces, and Liverpool would maintain a "thorough knowledge of the condition of markets, of products, of seasons" and would transfer information about market prices to the Leading Mind.[104] Here the spiritualists were undoubtedly inspired by the ability of the recently introduced telegraph to communicate messages across great distances instantaneously; they anticipated the moment, three years later, when Samuel Morse's invention would enable commodity prices to be transmitted from New York to Chicago via wire.[105]

Elsewhere, the spiritualists suggested that supernatural intervention in the marketplace could help prevent fraud—again, by facilitating transparency in information. An essay attributed to Charles Fourier titled "Angels in the Market!," published by Hewitt in the feminist magazine *The Una* in 1855, described a market in which guardian angels would warn buyers when they were about to be cheated—for example, when they were about to be sold ersatz Madeira or poorly dyed cloth. "People would know by the angels the real value and defects of every article exposed for sale." The article predicted that this spiritual intervention in commercial affairs would lead to the creation of great exchanges in which goods would be sold from afar for fair prices, sweeping away the current market system. The description of this angelic market makes it sound eerily like Amazon.com: "Deception and bargaining would then be out of the question, the rows of shopkeepers who garnish our streets would be useless, and must return to productive labor; sales being prompt and easy, orders would be sent from a distance, saving the purchaser the expense of time and money."[106]

The new equitable commerce would be the antipode to the emerging capitalist market, which was rife with deception, predation, uncertainty, speculation, and complicated relations of interdependence among companies. In *Equitable Commerce,* the spiritualists specified that all transactions were to be carried out in specie, which "has within itself an intrinsic value," unlike paper money, which "fluctuates, is uncertain." Credit would be banned in order to prevent a repetition of the cascading failures that had occurred during the Panic of 1837: "When one large concern breaks down, smaller concerns also go down." Above all, the new equitable commerce would be smooth, orderly, and free of the tensions and complicated relations of interdependence afflicting the mid-nineteenth-century capitalist market: "With comparatively little friction, and without loss, all things would move harmoniously, commercially onward."[107]

To conjure this frictionless commerce, a new spatial environment would be required. The spirits specified that equitable exchange should occur in a temple-like edifice. Like the spiritualist city and homes of harmony, this building was to be circular, in conformity with nature's law of centrality. Unlike the plans of the harmonial homes, however, the plan of the commercial building is notably abstract and schematic. Composed entirely of nested circles and a few lines and resembling Spear's diagrams of the heavenly spheres, it is more an organizational diagram than an architectural plan (Figure 6.4).

The sparsity of information in the visual representation stands in stark contrast to the wealth of imaginative and hallucinatory detail contained in the pamphlet's text, which describes a numinous sensorial environment. An ambience of tranquility should be maintained in the central space at all times. In the center would be an elevated chamber occupied by the Leading Mind. Purchaser, receiver, and transmitter would stand just below, on a raised platform in the center of the structure, surrounded by a circular band subdivided into seven wedge-shaped departments: nutriments, garments, fuels and lumbers, implements, furnishings, books and papers, and remedials. Circumscribing these departments would be a narrow ring, or "whispering gallery," to be used by messengers tasked with silently transmitting "intelligence from branch to branch" and from the departments to the Leading Mind. A system of springs would allow goods to appear instantaneously as soon as they were called for.

The new commercial exchanges were imagined as rarefied aesthetic experiences. In time, the spirits promised, special garments suited to active life in the commercial structure would be introduced, "rendering the employees interesting persons to look upon—attraction, beauty aiding commerce." Odors "agreeable in economic methods" would be released.[108] Attending to sight, smell, touch, and sound, the spirits demonstrated that equitable commerce was not just a matter of accounting and information but also one of aesthetics and atmosphere.

The spiritualists' conjuring of this magical marketplace may seem utterly unmoored from reality. However, enchantment and capitalism are not necessarily opposed. As Walter Benjamin reminds us, capitalism in the mid-nineteenth century had at least two faces. On the one hand was the rapacious and chaotic environment that the spiritualists and others sought to remedy. On the other was the market's wondrous, phantasmagoric aspect, visible in the emergence of numerous "palaces" and "temples" of commerce at midcentury, many featuring soaring circular domes. The 1853 Crystal Palace in New York, which was modeled on the Great Exhibition building in London, featured a central iron-and-glass dome one hundred feet in diameter that was illuminated by gas lamps, becoming a glowing orb at night. The young Samuel Clemens described it as a "perfect fairy palace—beautiful beyond description."[109] Nathaniel Hawthorne similarly evoked the oneiric quality of commercial architecture in an 1843 short story titled "The Hall of Fantasy," which is set in a fantastical building that is described as a cross between a bourse, or public exchange, and the Alhambra. Featuring a lofty dome and white marble pavement and filled with a "many-colored radiance" and a "visionary atmosphere," the Hall of Fantasy is a place where, in Hawthorne's telling, the earth's inhabitants can converse with "those of the moon."[110]

Poised between fiction and fact, revelation and reality, the spiritualists' institution of equitable commerce may also be considered a utopian variation on a building type that was rising to prominence during the middle decades of the nineteenth century: the merchants' or commodity exchange. This was a site where a city's businessmen could gather at appointed times to exchange commercial information and carry out transactions.[111] After having gathered previously in coffeehouses and libraries, by the 1820s American merchants began organizing to build specialized facilities. The first New York Merchants' Exchange building was constructed in 1827, destroyed by fire in 1835, and rebuilt by 1842. Featuring a domed circular room, the reconstructed edifice was reported to be "one of the most splendid specimens of architecture in the country" (Figure 6.23).[112] Cincinnati established a merchants' exchange in 1843 and was followed by Milwaukee, St. Louis, and Buffalo. In 1848 Chicago established its Board of Trade, which quickly became the nation's premier site of commodity futures trading.[113]

The American exchanges built on earlier European precedents. In the eighteenth century, several architecturally innovative exchange buildings were erected in Europe. Departing from the traditional open-air quadrangle, several of these featured circular plans and domed rotundas, often modeled on the Roman Pantheon.

FIGURE 6.23. Interior of the Merchants' Exchange, New York City, designed by Alexander Jackson Davis, 1827. From James Dakin and Theodore Fay, *Views in New-York and Its Environs,* 1831. Courtesy Columbia Universities / Archive.org.

The new exchanges included Thomas Cooley's Dublin exchange (1769–79); Nicolas Le Camus de Mézières's corn market, the Halle au Blé (1763–67, domed in 1783 and 1813); and Robert Taylor's Bank of England brokers' exchange with a circular rotunda (1765–68, renovated by John Soane in 1795) (Figures 6.24 and 6.25).[114] That rotunda spaces seemed to suit the frenetic pace of financial trading is no accident. As Daniel Abramson has argued about Taylor's Bank of England, "Its rounded form uniquely maximized visibility and intensified opportunities for contact among the professional brokers and jobbers," allowing market actors to move "fluidly and continuously" in search of optimal prices. For this reason, "the Rotunda's circular form seemed a symbolic reflection of modern capitalism's infinite potential."[115]

With their cavernous interiors, domes, oculi, and glancing light effects, it is not surprising that these temples of commerce could be imagined as spiritual, even magical, environments. They were spaces of exploitation and deception but also of utopian fantasy and desire. Marx and later Benjamin saw the phantasmagorical qualities of the world of commodities as an aspect of capitalism's obfuscations, its capacity to veil through commodity fetishism the exploitative social relations that subtended the system.[116] In contrast, the spiritualists seized on the dreamlike elements of capitalist culture to reimagine commercial transactions as a ritualized choreography of movement, information, and sensation. Their goal was to articulate a vision of commerce as not just a bare economic exchange premised on self-interest but an intersubjective relationship rooted in social affection.

FIGURE 6.24. Rotunda of the Bank of England, designed by Robert Taylor. From John Preston Neale, *Beauties of England and Wales,* 1816.

FIGURE 6.25. Nicolas Le Camus de Mézières, Halle au Blé, 1763–67. From L. T. Ventouillac, *Paris and Its Environs,* 1829–31.

"Mind Will Be Attracted to Mind"

The spiritualists' equitable exchange was intended to be a space of tranquility and comity. But how would this serene order be maintained? What would prevent it from devolving into the chaos and disorder of the existing market? The answer was the Leading Mind. The spirits stipulated that "one single mind, and only one, must govern absolutely the whole enterprise." The political connotations of this arrangement were explicit: "Divine monarchy is just," the spirits explained. "He must rule without votes."[117] In a review of *Equitable Commerce* published in *The Liberator,* the abolitionist William Lloyd Garrison pointed to a "suspicious autocracy" in the idea of a grand, Leading Mind, comparing the system to the czardom in Russia.[118] This absolutist arrangement was reflected in the commercial institution's tranquil yet controlling architecture, with its panopticon-like organization. Just as in Jeremy Bentham's design for a centralized, circular prison where a superintendent supervises subordinates who in turn oversee an array of prisoners (Figure I.3), so, too, the design of the institution of equitable commerce would enable the Leading Mind to stand at the nucleus, elevated above the purchaser, receiver, and transmitter, and take in all operations of the market "at a glance."[119] But more than the power of visual surveillance, the authority of the Leading Mind would derive from her or his magnetism and embodiment of the gravitational laws of nature, or what Spear's friend Orvis rather hazily called the "Love principle."[120] Charismatic authority would obviate the disagreement and distrust that characterized the existing market. "Mind will be attracted to his mind; they will learn his business capacity; become acquainted with his purity of life; his devotion to principles; his desire to elevate, and unfold humanity."[121] The Leading Mind would thereby inspire followers with confidence to commence labors toward a future society. Like Thomas Hobbes's sovereign, who ends the war of all against all by getting the mass of subjects to defer to her or his single authority, the spiritualists' Leading Mind offered, with an occult spin, a seemingly quick path to harmony. Personal magnetism and authority rather than deliberation or debate would be the means for achieving consensus.

The emphasis placed on a central charismatic figure can be related to spiritualism's belief in electromagnetism as a real and powerful force, an idea shared with earlier movements such as mesmerism and phrenomagnetism. Spear's spirits, for example, spoke of "the ability of a strong mind to affect other minds, as a powerful magnet affects and controls those which are weaker."[122] As historians of mesmerism and its offshoots have pointed out, one of the titillating aspects of this family of practices was the specter of ceding control to another, of falling under the sway of external influences (Figure 6.26). Succumbing to the spell of a magnetist or hypnotist (or an otherworldly spirit, for that matter) was a form of enchantment. As David Morgan writes, "To be enchanted means to lose control at the hands of a device or feeling or experience that places one in the service of another."[123] As the spiritualists' evocation of "divine monarchy" demonstrates, such enchantment or influence was also an eminently political matter. It posed an alternative to the chaotic agonism and endless conflicts inherent to democracy. Alison Winter has observed of Victorian mesmerism's preoccupation with the physiology of influence that what was at stake was the very nature of intersubjective influence or persuasion in a modern liberal society: How do people come to agreement? How do they act in concert?[124] Translated to the arena of social reform, we can begin to see how spiritualism's reliance on enchantment addresses urgent questions for reform movements: How are ideas for alternative social systems born? How do they spread, and how do they come to influence others or have force in the world? What motivates people to commence efforts to realize a better world, to cross the threshold from belief to action? Could the "attraction of mind to mind" facilitate the process of social coordination and collective action?

Embedded within spiritualist practice and rhetoric were several competing answers to these questions. The Kiantone spiritualists' homes of harmony and institution of equitable commerce, along with their Electric Motor and other fantastical inventions, were astonishingly naive panaceas. These dei ex machina can be read as manifestations of a utopian impulse to leapfrog democratic deliberation and political struggle in favor of more undemanding, and tenuous, avenues to transformation. In stipulating that the public would be swayed by devotion to a Leading Mind or a "Love element," in attributing their proposals to divine revelation, and in

238 Models, Machines, and Manifestations

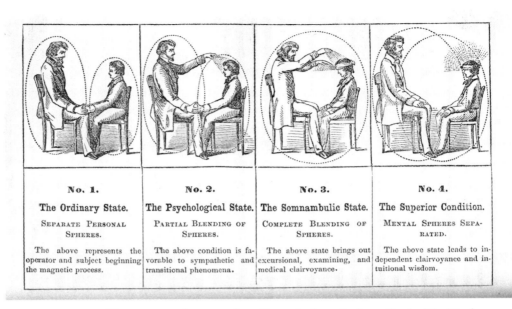

FIGURE 6.26. The process of mesmerism. From Andrew Jackson Davis, *The Magic Staff: An Autobiography*, 1857. Courtesy University of California Libraries.

legitimating their models through reference to nature's laws or to existing analogues, the spiritualists seemed to be resorting to metaphysics as a way of circumventing politics. These stratagems offered methods for convincing others without having to engage in lengthy arguments or arduous processes of debate, persuasion, and consensus building. Similarly, the spiritualists' architectural proposals bypassed logical or functional justifications by evoking the atmosphere of a nonpredatory commerce and harmonious society, supplanting substance with aesthetics. The spiritualists created diagrams and diagrammatic architectures that graphically conjured a more orderly world while providing little in the way of practical details or a concrete path to realizing that world. And at moments, they espoused visions of change that substituted biology for politics, relying on the guided reproduction of superior beings.

Yet, with the exception of their descent into proto-eugenicism, many of these seemingly far-fetched or vacuous avenues of persuasion arguably were still forms of political rhetoric. That is, they were attempts to convert audiences to a different viewpoint, an alternative ethics, or a radically transformed vision of the world, as well as bids to bring people to agreement about a course of action. It was a rhetoric that appealed not merely to logic and reason but equally to the registers of affect, aesthetics, faith, and interpersonal magnetism—in short, to enchantment. As Bennett and others have argued, enchantment (which encompasses both a sense of wonder and a feeling of being under the spell of another) can be a perilous element of politics when it takes the form of contagious suggestion, self-indulgent aestheticism, or an uncritical following of charismatic and authoritarian leaders. Yet enchantment, Bennett observes, can also be a constructive, critical, and even necessary facet of ethical and political life. It fills a void in political theory, pushing us to think not only about conscious ideology but also about the subconscious, somatic dimensions of human volition and agency, what she calls an "ethical energetics."[125]

Spear and his colleagues recognized that mobilizing people toward a radically different vision of society required more than rational persuasion. As their invisible guides imparted, "There are minds so constituted that to them *faith* or *feeling* (that is, spiritual intuition or instinct) is a higher guide than *reason*."[126] This is what the spiritualists' revelations about gravitation, magnetism, and telegraphy had taught them: other, perhaps more powerful, forces operated in the world. Paradoxically, passivity—a state of receptiveness to external influence—provided the impetus for spurts of implausible activity, leading Spear and his followers to undertake endeavors unjustifiable by conventional logic: the construction of fantastical energy-generating machines, harmonial homes, and ethereal temples of commerce. As the writers of the *Equitable Commerce* pamphlet explained:

> The cold, merely intellectual mind turns away with scorn when speech is made of *missions*—doubts whether persons are ever commissioned, or instructed, or impressed to go hither and thither; but strike out missions, and what would the inhabitants of this planet be? The true missionary feels a mighty internal impulse. He *must* go, and woe be unto him if he disregards that internal voice which speaks from his inmosts.[127]

As with other religious epiphanies, the supernatural provided a uniquely forceful catalyst to action.

Thoughts Stirred into Action

Angels could transmit messages and visions to human receptacles. They could guide the way. But lacking corporeality, they could not physically build new machines, homes, or markets. To bring the new world into existence required human hands and bodies. Ultimately Spear and his colleagues' announcements of new machines and architecture were calls to earthly, mortal action. As the group explained in *Equitable Commerce,* their goal was "to show that the hour of practical labors has come; and to call upon those who have been awaiting that hour, to enter upon sturdy, self-denying, but sublime co-operative efforts, to establish the reign of integral justice on this planet." Though they differed in their methods, their aims were not so far from those that animated other geometric utopian manifestoes. The spiritualists recognized that telepathic messages and magnetic mediums were not sufficient for reaching new eyes and ears. A physical medium was required to disseminate the vision of a new, harmonious society. Printed words, drawings, and models offered the necessary vehicles of communication. This is why they took the time to transcribe their spiritual visions into pamphlets and periodical articles, to illustrate their words with diagrams,

240   *Models, Machines, and Manifestations*

and to build models of their fantastical machines and dwellings. As they wrote in the closing pages of *Equitable Commerce*: "Before . . . much can be accomplished, these papers must be presented to the public mind." To prevent their ideas from being "lost sight of" or "only reach[ing] a very few persons," they had to disseminate them in printed form. The spirits proposed the printing of some five hundred or one thousand copies of the *Equitable Commerce* pamphlet and conceived a strategy for spreading the ideas it contained: "There should be messengers employed, whose mission it should be, to seize on the strong points, presented in these much condensed documents and amplify the same and present them verbally, to such persons, such assemblies, as from time to time, can be easily and naturally reached."[128] These were precisely the techniques of colportage and lecturing that evangelicals had developed earlier in the century and that Spear and Hewitt had utilized as proselytizers for the antislavery and workingmen's movements.

Imagining how their messages would be received, the spiritualists hoped that the published visions would have a catalyzing effect on members of the public. Models must be presented, "that thought may be stirred, and may ripen into action." Alonzo Newton posited that the transcribed trance visions would serve as "a suggester, an incentive, a stimulant to thought" that would cultivate readers' own "inquiring and truth-discerning powers."[129] Recipients of the pamphlets could "peruse them at their leisure; judge of their value, their reasonableness, their practicability." The spiritualists hoped that after reading about equitable commerce, "some few choice and able persons will become interested in this branch of philanthropic effort— will generously proffer their personal services; and peradventure, their capital, to start, and for a season (until labors become systematized) carry forward, this enterprize."[130] Associations would form, an office would open, and capital would be invested. Indeed, the work had already begun. On July 31, 1855, a group gathered in Boston had founded the New England Association of Philanthropic Commercialists, adopted a constitution and bylaws, and selected officers.[131]

In projecting and describing the ways in which their visions might be disseminated, so that they could in turn catalyze readers to act, the spiritualists around Spear showed that they cannot be written off as simply deluded visionaries, inattentive to political praxis. While enthralled by the possibility of angelic exchanges, they were— like other mid-nineteenth-century geometric utopians and social reformers—also deeply engaged in the activity of earthly communication. What separates these geometric utopians from the others explored in this book, however, is their enthusiastic embrace of the atmospheric and aesthetic aspects of geometric architecture, their attention to the persuasive possibilities of mood, modulation, and magnetism. While these tendencies could lead to fair accusations of vagueness, evasiveness, and self-indulgent fantasy, they also opened the way to important and overlooked dimensions of political culture: the power of more-than-rational modes of persuasion, the question of how to communicate a sense of the interconnectedness of peoples and worlds, the potential political usefulness of phantasmagoric images, and an understanding of how faith can compel action. The spiritualist geometric utopians demonstrated how enchantment can mobilize followers to undertake even the most implausible reform efforts. Propelled by internal voices and by the sympathetic vibrations generated in circles of believers, the Kiantone spiritualists not only imagined but, what is perhaps more remarkable, took tangible steps to construct worlds that they hoped would transcend the disjointed present.

EPILOGUE

The Afterlife of Geometric Utopianism

Geometric utopianism, along with the communitarian energies that propelled it, dwindled during the consuming cataclysm of the Civil War but did not die out entirely. Enthusiasm for formally distinct architectural and urban plans was rekindled at the end of the nineteenth century, when the rise of large-scale industrial capitalism catalyzed both a new surge of labor radicalism and a wave of efforts toward a wholesale reimagining of society. Galvanized by publications such as Edward Bellamy's novel *Looking Backward* (1888), utopians at the end of the century tended to favor large-scale, centralized, technologically driven solutions, a marked contrast to the earlier geometric utopians' focus on creating small experimental models that could spread.[1] Thus, while the geometric forms of Gilded Age ideal cities were sometimes similar to those of midcentury utopian colonies, their ideologies were often quite different. A case in point is King Camp Gillette's 1894 design for a hexagonally gridded metropolis (Figure E.1), which superficially resembled Josiah Warren's anarchist city in plan but was intended to house a vast, monolithic business-cum-government overseeing a mechanized system of production and distribution—a far cry from Warren's decentralized, anarchist settlements. Likewise, the hexagonal city grids proposed by urban planners such as the American architect Charles R. Lamb and Austrian engineer Rudolf Müller were motivated more by concerns for efficiency of movement, or sometimes by an aesthetic desire to break the monotony of the grid, than by radical social ideals (Figures E.2 and E.3).[2]

Perhaps the most faithful descendant of the midcentury American geometric utopians was a plan that few think of as very radical or utopian today: Ebenezer Howard's garden city, introduced in his 1898 book *To-morrow: A Peaceful Path to Real Reform*.[3] In this slender volume, frequently described as one of the most influential tracts in modern town planning, Howard posited a network of small, self-sufficient "garden cities" surrounded by rural land as an antidote to overcrowded, unhealthy metropolises like London. Significantly for our purposes, he illustrated his book with seven color plates, including four plans depicting a circular city. These would become some of the most

243

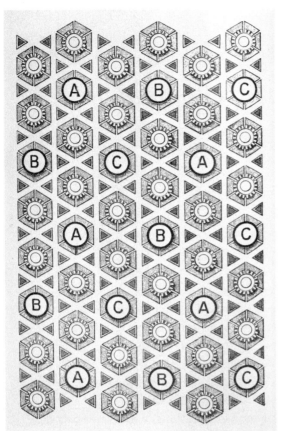

FIGURE E.1. Hexagonal metropolis plan and apartment building. From King Camp Gillette, *The Human Drift,* 1894. Courtesy Sutro Library, California State Library.

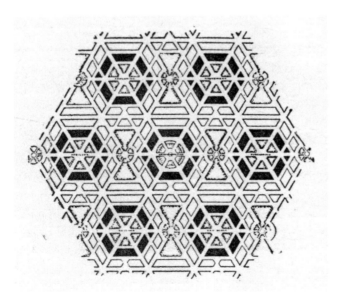

FIGURE E.2. Hexagonal city plan by Charles R. Lamb, 1904. From H. Inigo Triggs, *Town Planning, Past, Present, and Possible,* 1909. Courtesy University of California Libraries.

FIGURE E.3. Hexagonal city plan by Rudolf Müller, 1908. From H. Inigo Triggs, *Town Planning, Past, Present, and Possible*, 1909. Courtesy University of California Libraries.

iconic images of urban design history. Today, the garden city concept is often reductively seen as the anodyne antiurban vision that launched a thousand new towns, suburbs, and greenbelts around the world. When Howard's book was first published, however, it represented a radical proposal for social reform, animated by ideologies and intentions similar to those that had influenced American geometric utopians such as Warren, Lewis Masquerier, and Henry Clubb.[4] Like them, Howard saw his cities as experiments in the reorganization of land as a means of achieving a more equitable, cooperative society—experiments whose success would lead to replication. Also like them, he chose the medium of the geometric plan diagram to convey his ideas. A brief excursus on the garden city diagrams thus offers an opportunity to critically reflect on the legacy of geometric utopianism, as well as on the promises and pitfalls of utopian plans as media of sociopolitical transformation.

A Latter-Day Geometric Utopian

While it may seem strange to leap over the pond in search of the legacy of American geometric utopianism, Howard's biography reveals his many affinities to the U.S.-based reformers at the core of this book.[5] He was steeped in the same transatlantic

246   *Epilogue*

radical tradition that had shaped them and that they helped to shape. Born in London in 1850, Howard lived for a period in the United States while in his twenties. He tried his hand at homesteading in Nebraska before moving to Chicago (which was nicknamed "the Garden City"—a fact that historians point to as a potential source of inspiration), where he worked as a shorthand stenographer for several years. Like the earlier American reformers, Howard was not a professional architect or urban planner (a vocation that did not yet exist) but a chronic reformer, tinkerer, and inventor. His interests encompassed revolutionizing not only cities but also language, printing machines, and typewriters. As a teenager he taught himself Pitman shorthand, and later in life he became fluent in Esperanto. He also devised and patented a typewriter with variable spacing and an improved shorthand machine (Figure E.4).[6] Similar to Warren and John Murray Spear, Howard was interested in media and mediums. He was a lifelong spiritualist, having converted after reporting on the American medium Cora Richmond, whom he later described as "the most eloquent extempore speaker I have ever heard."[7] As readers of the preceding chapters will appreciate, these ostensibly disconnected facts of Howard's early life are more meaningful than they might at first appear. Not only do they comprise the many genealogical threads connecting him to the earlier American geometric utopians, but they also illuminate three of the main elements of the garden city plan: a focus on land organization as the key to social reform, a preoccupation with the media used to transmit new information and ideas, and a predilection for circular geometries.

At its origins, Howard's garden city was not just an urban planning proposal to reconcile city and country or to ameliorate the industrial city by integrating elements of nature, as is often depicted today. Rather, it was a bid to redress the inequities of urban, industrial capitalism and to redistribute social wealth by establishing a new cooperative model of landownership.[8] The goal of the garden city scheme was to attain "work for the workless, land for the landless," words that echoed the slogans of the National Reform Association a half century before.[9] Like others in the British radical, liberal, and socialist circles in which he traveled, Howard was preoccupied with what was known as the "Land Question." Inspired by Henry George's book *Progress and Poverty,* late nineteenth-century British land reformers such as Alfred Russell Wallace traced the problems of low wages and high rents paid by urban workers to the private ownership of land and to land speculation. Within British radical circles, one proposed solution that began to gain popularity was the nationalization of land.[10] Simultaneously, the 1880s saw a growing interest among British reformers in the establishment of "home colonies" and communitarianism as avenues for reform, a revival of strategies that had been developed by Robert Owen and the geometric utopians in the 1830s and 1840s.[11]

Howard synthesized many of these directions. In *To-morrow,* he argued that building a town on cheap rural land would lead to a rise in land values, and that this increase in value should benefit the community as a whole rather than the landlord. He devised a scheme in which residents' rents would contribute to a sinking fund used to pay off initial investors, eventually yielding collective ownership of the land.

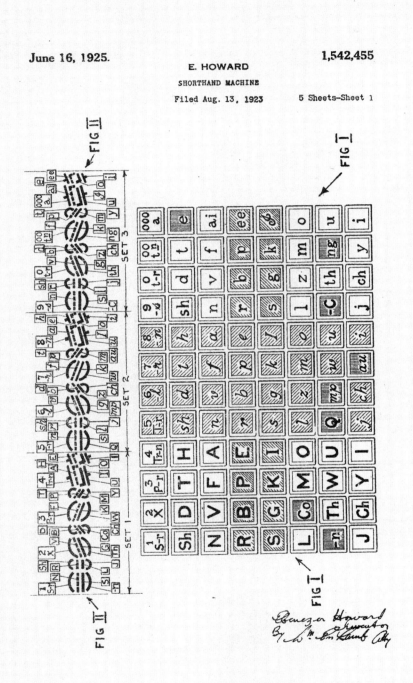

FIGURE E.4. Ebenezer Howard, patent for a shorthand machine, 1925. Courtesy National Archives at Kansas City.

FIGURE E.5. Diagram showing how rents would eventually lead to collective ownership and the funding of an old-age pension in the garden city. From Ebenezer Howard, *To-morrow: A Peaceful Path to Real Reform,* 1898. Courtesy Getty Research Institute / Archive.org.

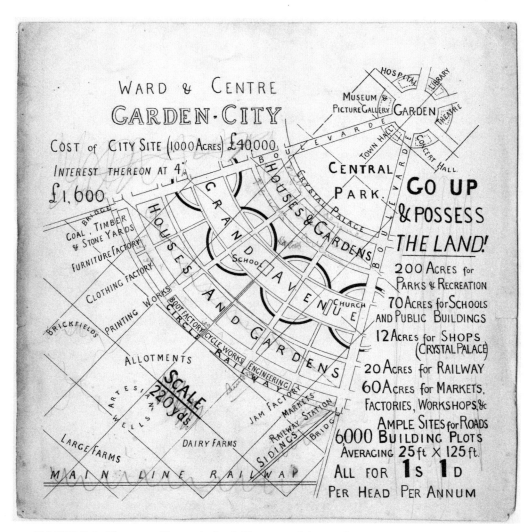

FIGURE E.6. Ebenezer Howard, draft diagram of the garden city. The slogan "Go up & possess the land!" was removed from the published version. Hertfordshire Archives and Local Studies.

Thereafter, residents' rents would go to social benefits such as an old-age pension fund. All of this would be accomplished not by the state but through voluntary, cooperative action. This put Howard at odds with contemporary Fabian socialists and Marxists, who were advocating state socialism, and more in line with an older tradition of communitarianism, as well as with contemporary proponents of decentralized cooperation such as Peter Kropotkin. Howard explained this economic scheme in a set of circular diagrams in his book (Figure E.5). Further evidence of the radical reform intentions of his project can be seen in an unpublished draft of his "Ward and Centre" diagram, on the margins of which he penciled the words "Go up & possess the land!" (Figure E.6). The omission of this provocative slogan in the published versions

250   *Epilogue*

demonstrates how Howard tempered the sharper edges of his advocacy to make his book more appealing and less threatening to a broad public.

Rhetorical Geometry

Just as the more radical edges of Howard's ideas have often been forgotten (and were suppressed at times by the author himself), so, too, his circular diagrams paradoxically are often overlooked despite their wide circulation. Historians have tended to downplay the importance of the garden city's geometry, pointing to Howard's insistence that the diagrams were meant to illustrate "broad principles" and not to be "strictly carried out in the form thus presented."[12] As is well known, the first built garden city, Letchworth, bears little formal resemblance to Howard's circular diagrams, its designers, Raymond Unwin and Barry Parker, having instead adopted the idiom of a medieval English village populated with Arts and Crafts–style buildings. As a result, the circularity of Howard's diagrams is often painted as incidental or nonessential—an impractical aspect of the project that was quickly abandoned, one of many compromises required for the city's realization in built form. Yet if the discussion in this book has shown one thing, it is that the form and representation of such urban plans *does* matter, though perhaps not in the way that architectural and urban historians are accustomed to looking for. That is, the significance of the circle is not merely as a proposal for urban form but also as an artifact of visual rhetoric—an instrument to communicate an idea for social transformation and to mobilize audiences to act on behalf of that idea.

The circle appears to have been an idée fixe for Howard, as the octagon was for Thomas Jefferson. The seven color plates in *To-morrow,* drawn by Howard with a compass and ruler, all feature circular geometries. Four of the drawings are urban-territorial plans, two are infographics showing financial and administrative schema, and one is best described as a rhetorical diagram. In the plans, the garden city is always represented in the shape of a circle, and its organizing principle is insistently circular. At its nucleus is a public park with key public buildings, including a town hall, library, theater, museum, concert hall, and hospital (Figure E.7). This central circle is surrounded by a series of rings: moving from the nucleus outward, these contain a "Crystal Palace" (composed of commercial establishments), residences and gardens, and factories and workshops. Large boulevards radiating from the center, as well as an encircling railway line, connect the city to a network of other garden cities. A diagram titled "Group of Slumless, Smokeless Cities" shows the idea expanded to a regional scale: it depicts a central circular city surrounded by six smaller, symmetrically arrayed circular garden cities, separated by belts of rural land dotted with reservoirs, cemeteries, and charitable institutions (Figure E.8). Unencumbered by topography or existing conditions, the perfectly geometrical cities float in an imaginary, idealized space. Rendered in pale colors with neat yet amateurishly set typography and overlays of delicate dashed and solid lines evoking cartographic graticules,

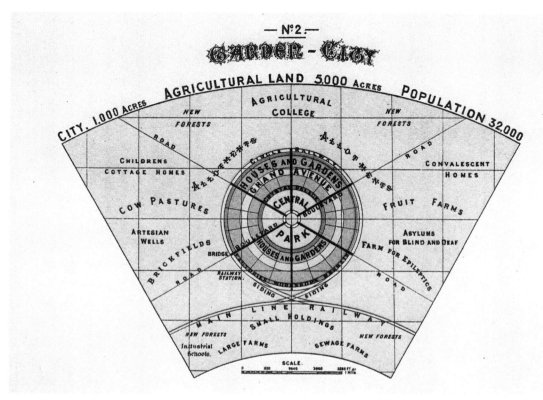

FIGURE E.7. Diagram of the garden city. From Ebenezer Howard, *To-morrow: A Peaceful Path to Real Reform,* 1898. Courtesy Getty Research Institute / Archive.org.

the plan diagrams resemble medieval rota or cosmographic diagrams as much as they do plans of existing cities.

Scholars have suggested numerous precedents that may have influenced the geometry of Howard's city, from the earlier "cobweb" cities devised by land nationalization proponents to James Silk Buckingham's 1849 plan for a model town named Victoria (square in shape but featuring a similar radial and concentric street pattern).[13] Howard mentioned Gideon Jasper Ouseley's plan of Heptapolis, published as part of a mystical, esoteric Christian text titled *Palingenesia; or, The Earth's New Birth* (1884), but he also claimed to have seen it only after conceiving of his own plan.[14] Howard's plan also bears a striking resemblance to Robert Pemberton's 1854 plan for Happy Colony; whether Howard knew of Pemberton's scheme is unclear.[15] The architectural historian Paul Emmons offers perhaps the most intriguing account, arguing that Howard's formal visual language was influenced by his spiritualist beliefs. Emmons points out the resemblances between the garden city diagrams and the circular diagrams of the government of the spirit world received by Spear, as well as other esoteric drawings that Howard may have known.[16] But as with most accounts of artistic genesis, the origins of Howard's formal language may be multiple and overdetermined.

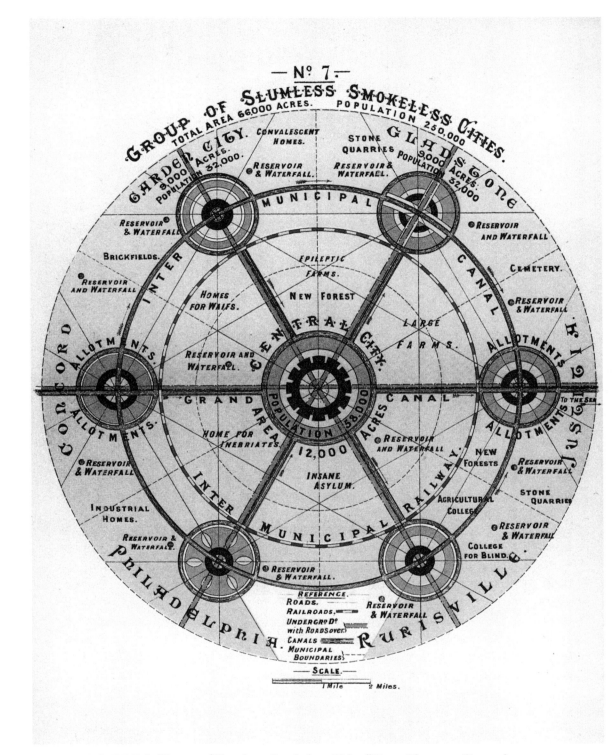

FIGURE E.8. "Group of Slumless, Smokeless Cities." From Ebenezer Howard, *To-morrow: A Peaceful Path to Real Reform,* 1898. Courtesy Getty Research Institute / Archive.org.

If we turn from the question of where the geometry came from to what it was intended to do—that is, from the questions that have traditionally preoccupied art and architectural history to those posed by visual culture studies—we have considerably more evidence. Howard's own testimony, along with that of readers of his day, points to the idea that, like the earlier American geometric reformers, he created the diagrams to arrest readers' attention and to win converts, supporters, and investors. Howard remarked in 1905 that, while he "thought the circular design might . . . be worth trying, he meant it in his book merely as a symbolic diagram. In a word, its function was accomplished when it *laid hold upon the public's interest.*" The journalist to whom Howard made this comment affirmed that the purpose of the diagrams was to "draw notice" to the project and to offer a "tangible illustration in enforcing theory." "[The City's] symmetry and simplicity, its apparent perfection of plan, attracted many ordinarily impatient of serious study. 'Why was not this thought of long ago?' was asked on all sides."[17] Thus, the purpose of the diagrams' geometric form was less to prescribe an urban plan than to produce a particular effect on readers—to make Howard's proposal appear transparent and direct, and his garden city self-evidently desirable, especially to those who would not typically give much thought to urban reform.

Rereading *To-morrow,* one finds that it is as much a work of persuasion as it is an urban design proposal. Only a small portion of the book is devoted to describing the physical design of the city. Instead, the bulk of the text and images presents a multipronged moral and financial argument for why the garden city is needed and why it will work. Nowhere is the communicative, rhetorical nature of Howard's use of illustrations clearer than in the plate titled "The Three Magnets," which encapsulates the argument of the book in an extended visual metaphor-cum-ideogram (Figure E.9). Three pink magnets with blue tips, representing the town, the country, and the hybrid "town-country," are arranged centripetally, with a block of iron filings in the center symbolizing "The People," under which is printed "Where will they go?" The type is laid out in arcs, reinforcing the underlying circular structure of the image. The text describes the "positive" and "negative" poles of each environment. The town's attractions include social opportunity, places of amusement, high wages, employment opportunities, and "palatial edifices," while its defects include high rents and prices, foul air, slums, and the exclusion of nature. In contrast, the country entices with the beauty of nature, low rents, abundant water, and sunshine but suffers from social isolation and a lack of amusement and jobs. Stanley Buder observes that the argument adopts a dialectical structure typical of nineteenth-century reform rhetoric. Thesis and antithesis are resolved in a synthesis represented by the third magnet, the town-country, which combines the best of both worlds: low rents with high wages, bright homes and gardens with an absence of smoke and slums, urban conveniences as well as natural amusements, freedom with cooperation.[18]

As a self-consciously rhetorical image, this diagram has an unsubtle, even corny, quality. The benefits and deficits of city and country are succinctly named, the answer made to seem self-evident, if predetermined. Yet what is most interesting about the

254   *Epilogue*

image is the way it represents its own rhetoricality through the metaphor of the magnet. The magnet places the reader, to whom the text is directed, in the center, in the position of "The People" who must choose among the options, ostensibly through the rational weighing of pros and cons. However, the astute reader might observe that objects moved by magnetism do not act through reasoned deliberation or will; they are pushed and pulled by forces beyond their own agency. The significance of the magnet metaphor would not have been lost on Howard, an avowed spiritualist.[19] As noted in chapter 6, magnetism (or "animal magnetism")—along with the associated arts of hypnotism, mesmerism, trance, and electrical conduction—was a practice central to nineteenth-century spiritualism. During séances, adherents often deployed magnets or other devices designed to transmit messages from the spirit world to human ears and eyes. A trance speaker or medium was understood to attract crowds through an almost gravitational charisma: "They *adhere* to him, just as filings are attracted and adhere to a magnet."[20] Occasionally, as in the case of Spear and his followers, individuals could even be propelled by these hidden powers to undertake improbable acts of healing, mechanical invention, and social experimentation. "Magnetism" thus stood for a range of indefinite spiritual, natural, and affective forces capable of moving things, bodies, and minds.

In "The Three Magnets," it is not only unseen physical and spiritual forces or rational considerations of pros and cons that can persuade people. The diagram itself has a magnetic power due to its visual features. Its circular organization focuses a spotlight on "The People" (including the reader) and their momentous decision, pulling us into a quasi-democratic drama. This power of the diagram is a critical part of the appeal of geometric utopias more broadly. For, like the earlier American images of octagonal cities and gridded republican villages, what the garden city diagrams manifest is faith in the capacity of images to provoke people to belief or action. Howard, like the earlier geometric utopians, believed that his circular diagrams could help persuade readers and compel them to join his cause. One writer in 1904 described the power of the garden city diagrams in a passage that is worth quoting at length:

> Long ago we pointed out the weak spots of the "Garden City," but we recognise that it has drawn public attention towards the question of decentralisation in a manner that could not have been accomplished by penny plain propaganda. To form an association of 2,500 members and to raise £100,000 in this way could not be done by pure practical reasoning. There must be an appeal to the passions and the tastes of the public, such as is made by the pictorial advertiser of condensed food or patent medicine. It is the method of the pill "boomer" that has made "Garden City." What if it be true that those pretty pea green and salmon pink diagrams in "Garden Cities of To-morrow," are like the Last Rose of Summer, faded and gone, and that the "magnificent boulevards" are but the ruins of a visionary Pompeii? They have served their purpose in directing public opinion. The author of that little book has done good public work, even if there is not a single practical detail in its pages. His purpose is to tickle our tastes, and stir up our emotions. He is, in fact—and we mean it as a sincere

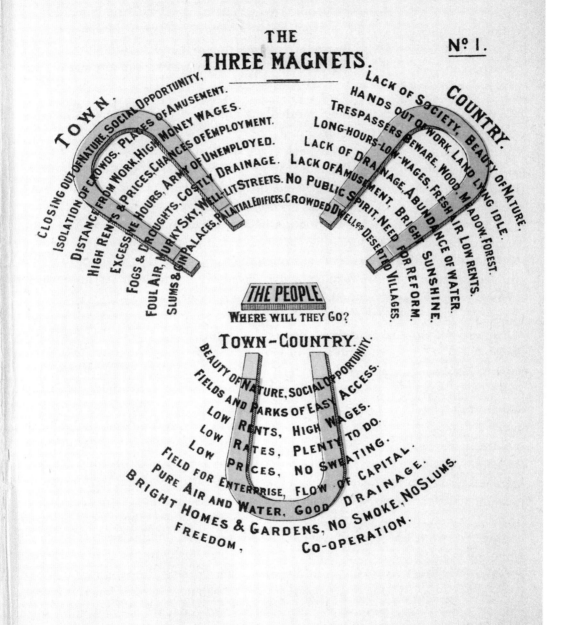

FIGURE E.9. "The Three Magnets." From Ebenezer Howard, *To-morrow: A Peaceful Path to Real Reform,* 1898. Courtesy Getty Research Institute / Archive.org.

256   *Epilogue*

> compliment—the Sunny Jim of industrial decentralisation. When our friends
> the elixir of life mongers address the crowd, they do not argue with us; they
> set before our eyes a bright coloured poster, with a bit of nursery rhyme, and
> perhaps a simple appeal to eat coagulated chestnuts and live for ever. And we
> do it. So, when Mr. Howard is inspired to preach industrial redistribution, he
> does not compile statistics, and deduce arguments therefrom, but he shows
> us those charming diagrams, and those sweet impossible ideals of communal
> ownership, and we join an association. The very name of Garden City steals
> away our hearts.[21]

The reviewer incisively if underhandedly highlighted the multiple valences of
Howard's use of diagrams—their simultaneous effectiveness and potential decep-
tiveness. The illustrations' "pretty pea green and salmon" colors appealed to the
public's "passions and tastes," not just their capacity for "pure practical reasoning."
But in calling upon the seduction of visual images, the diagrams also placed Howard
treacherously close to the techniques of commercial advertisers and snake-oil sales-
men. Beneath the reviewer's distinction between "pure practical reasoning" and
"bright coloured posters" lurks the old suspicion of graven images and a belief in
the tendency of pictures to deceive through their appeal to supposedly subrational
emotions. Such concerns were magnified in the late nineteenth century, an age when
cheap mass print was flooding the modern industrial world with pictures whose very
quantity suggested their meaninglessness as well as their immense appeal.[22]

Yet to place Howard entirely in the world of Sunny Jim, a jaunty character introduced as part of a cereal campaign in 1901, is also not quite accurate. The garden
city images are better understood instead as straddling two eras: an earlier world of
artisan printing and an emerging universe of color printing, commercial advertising,
and photography. This is what gives the diagrams their "archaic charm" or "forward-
backward looking character."[23] Borrowing from Raymond Williams, we might say
that the images combine aspects of the residual and the emergent. On the one hand,
the garden city diagrams' circular geometries hark back to an older Enlightenment-
inflected visual world of geometric and mechanical diagrams that were presumed
to be didactic, explanatory, and transparent. This was the visual sensibility that informed the diagrams of the mid-nineteenth-century geometric utopias, which were
engraved in wood and printed (sometimes on self-fabricated presses) in black and
white. By evoking mathematical and technical diagrams, both the earlier and later
geometric utopias carried an air of objectivity and "proof," dressing in the garb of
rationality and order what otherwise might have been dismissed as fanciful, unreal-
istically radical social proposals. The simplicity and geometry of the diagrams also
helped them serve as memorable visual icons, attracting readers with their graphically striking forms. On the other hand, Howard's diagrams deployed new tools, such
as chromolithography, to generate charming graphic images that could vie for attention amid an emerging universe of advertisements targeting viewers' emotions and
desires. In bridging these two worlds, the garden city diagrams combined an affect

Epilogue   257

of reason and rhetoric, sobriety and seduction. This amalgamation helps explain the images' immense appeal.

To be sure, we must be careful not to ascribe too much power to the garden city diagrams. It would be an exaggeration to attribute the impressive proliferation of Howard's ideas to the images alone. The diagrams were a critical piece of a highly organized publicity campaign mounted by Howard and his allies. Historians have pointed to this concerted propaganda effort in their endeavors to explain how a humble stenographer's manifesto for a new kind of quasi-anarchist, cooperative community achieved such unlikely global influence.[24] When *To-morrow* was first published, the garden city concept—like the American geometric schemes—was dismissed as utopian, a cause for "cranks" and "faddists."[25] But over several years, Howard and other proponents of the garden city gave lantern-slide lectures, mounted exhibitions and conferences, and formed an association to publicize their ideas and to raise funds for a first test. Howard himself was a skilled speaker and tireless promoter. Of course, also critical was the support that the garden city idea eventually received from several wealthy and well-connected men. As is well known, this patronage came at the cost of a serious dilution of Howard's social aims, as "visionaries gave way to pragmatists and enthusiasts yielded to professionals."[26] But rather than simply accept the conventional account that the garden city's success stemmed from the watering down of Howard's radical vision, we might draw another lesson: that propagandizing, organizing, and, yes, displaying a knack for creating memorable and eye-catching diagrams of a new future can sometimes be effective.

Image Politics

Focusing on the role of geometric utopian plans as rhetorical images rather than simply urban proposals offers a way to counter an age-old critique of utopian plans: that they are evasive distractions from a more properly revolutionary politics. According to a school of thought that can be traced to Karl Marx and Friedrich Engels, the production of fanciful pictures of utopia was a bourgeois diversion from "real" revolutionary struggles, which were to be carried out by workers, the colonized, and the dispossessed.[27] Such criticisms continue to be echoed today. Those who paint pictures of an ideal future are often accused of avoiding the thornier and more difficult question of how to get from *A* to *Z*. Even thinkers sympathetic to utopianism argue that it is counterproductive to create images of the future. The critic Russell Jacoby, for example, calls for an "iconoclastic" utopianism that avoids the pitfalls of the "blueprint" utopias of the past, with their attempts to paint concrete pictures of the future.[28] Others, such as David Harvey, urge a shift away from visions of a perfect state or spatial form and toward an engagement with open-ended processes. "Emancipatory politics," Harvey notes, "calls for a living Utopianism of process as opposed to the dead Utopianism of spatialized urban form."[29]

As this book suggests, oppositions between utopian plans and revolutionary process, between form and politics, may miss an important point: seemingly "perfect" geometric plans need not be static visions or antithetical to political praxis but in fact can be integral to it. When we understand pictures as forms of rhetoric, we can begin to recognize how images of transformed worlds might help carry out the work of persuasion and motivation that is essential to politics; we glimpse how images can shift imaginaries. Of importance here, however, is recognizing the particular qualities of the geometric utopias. Although their mathematically ideal shapes seem to exclude the messiness of politics, their abstraction in fact makes them well suited to being deployed as political-rhetorical media. Beyond their associations with rationality and objectivity, diagrams possess an apparent clarity, an Apollonian quality that makes them effective vehicles of communication. Because they are abstract and omit details, they lend themselves well to revealing systems and relationships and to offering a picture of the whole, a cognitive map of existing social structures.[30] At the same time, the abstraction of diagrams makes them necessarily incomplete and open-ended. Diagrams explain and clarify, but they also leave room for misuse, misappropriation, and catalyzation of the imagination in ways both anticipated and unanticipated. Thus, the true power of diagrams of utopia may lie not in their embodiment of closure, as many critics have asserted, but in their incompleteness—their capacity for provocation rather than prescription.

Unsettling Utopias

Yet the nineteenth-century geometric utopias can justly be considered evasions of politics in another sense. As I discuss in the preceding chapters, many utopias of this period depended on the logics, and sometimes the literal practice, of settler colonialism.[31] In turning toward the creation of a new kind of city on "underutilized" rural land as a solution for metropolitan problems, Howard was not only influenced by earlier theorists of British colonialism; he was also reprising the strategy of American utopians who had looked to western land (land occupied for millennia by Indigenous people) as a putative terra nullius upon which to test alternative social and physical arrangements.[32] All of the utopians were engaging in what Lorenzo Veracini identifies as a fundamental settler colonial strategy of displacement: attempting to resolve the upheavals of modernity, capitalism, and class by starting anew elsewhere. Veracini cites both Howard's garden city and the nineteenth-century American workingmen's campaign for free homesteads as two examples among a litany of instances in which settlers responded to the threats of conflict and revolution by leaving the metropole to form new communities. From the English colonization of the Americas to twentieth-century suburban flight and the creation of intentional communities, what ties these responses together, Veracini writes, is the impulse to "change the world by changing worlds." Settlers, including those motivated by liberal or progressive intentions, choose to "establish political orders elsewhere" rather than fight in place to overturn the existing political order.[33]

The links between nineteenth-century geometric utopianism and settler colonialism are deep and intrinsic. It is not just that the American utopians projected their visions onto land stolen from Indigenous peoples. For most nineteenth-century Americans, including the majority of the geometric utopians, the definitions of "equality" and "freedom" were tethered fundamentally to individual landownership and possession of a homestead and its corollary, a home. The utopians' dreams of more egalitarian townships, individual-strengthening homes, nonpredatory forms of commerce, and more harmonious social relations thus rested on Indigenous dispossession and the erasure of Native systems of land tenure. This orientation to land as the source of freedom and equality is also inextricable from the reformers' choice to use geometric diagrams—representations of the reorganization of land and space—to articulate their utopian visions.

Utopia Today

Given this history, is it time to abandon attempts to sketch ideal urban plans? Are diagrams of utopia inherently colonialist because they represent designs for the organization and distribution of space and territory? Or are other diagrams possible? Might utopian diagrams still play a role in effecting sociopolitical transformation, a role that takes advantage of the diagram's inherent open-endedness? A comprehensive answer to these questions is beyond the scope of this book. But I would like to offer a provisional response by citing a diagram I have never seen. In the conclusion to his book *Our History Is the Future,* Nick Estes describes the protest encampments at the Standing Rock Reservation that sprang up to oppose the Dakota Access Pipeline in 2016. He recounts how, on arrival, newcomers were given a hand-drawn map of the site. It included roads named for historical Indigenous leaders and noted the locations of the Indigenous nations assembled at the site, as well as the places where free food and medical care were distributed. At once descriptive and projective, the map offered a visual record of a different kind of community, "a brief vision of what a future premised on Indigenous justice would look like," and an "abolition geography" rooted in relationality, solidarity, and "making kin" between Indigenous and non-Indigenous people and land.[34] Although Estes does not include a reproduction of the site map in his book, one can imagine that it probably did not feature an abstract geometric order conceived in advance of the community's emergence but instead reflected a provisional organization that materialized in the process of its formation. The map documented an incipient society, one in which horizontal and reciprocal relationships, rather than assignment of individual property or position, took precedence. At the same time, it prefigured, or laid out principles for, a world yet to come. Estes's evocation of a map describing a radically different configuration of relations between people and land offers a tantalizing possibility: perhaps we can imagine new kinds of world-depicting and world-making images that embody principles different from the ones described in this book. Exploring the history of these earlier figures thus illuminates the conditions and limits of our own contemporary imaginations. But it also reminds us that images might still be capable of awakening, persuading, and inciting people to work toward those alternate worlds.

ACKNOWLEDGMENTS

This book has taken a long time to come to fruition and accumulated many debts along its peripatetic path. First thanks go to my advisers and teachers at Columbia University. The distant origins of this project are in a paper written for a doctoral seminar taught by Reinhold Martin, whose combination of critical rigor and utopian hopefulness has profoundly shaped my own worldview. I have benefited enormously from Gwendolyn Wright's razor intellect, mentorship, and gentle but uncompromising insistence on clarity of thought and expression. Mabel Wilson, Mary McLeod, Barry Bergdoll, and Joan Ockman have been consistently generous interlocutors, as well as models of rigorous and committed scholarship. Bernard Tschumi was one of my best teachers, despite my never taking a class with him. My stints at Columbia yielded an embarrassment of riches in terms of lifelong teachers and friends—too many to name here.

The process of writing a dissertation and then a book can be solitary and challenging. I could not have done it without Daniel Barber and Dara Orenstein, essential friends, inspired historians, and critical sounding boards who read numerous drafts and dispensed timely encouragement and enthusiasm. While a graduate student at Columbia and beyond, I benefited from the intellectual stimulation, support, and good humor of Patricio del Real, María González Pendás, Helen Gyger, Jolie Kerns, Diana Martinez, Albert Narath, Ginger Nolan, Christine Olson, Joshua Uhl, and Carolyn Yerkes. At the McNeil Center for Early American Studies, Brian Connolly, Dawn Peterson, and Elena Schneider provided historical and theoretical provocations and fellowship in the best sense. Several other friends assisted in the process of writing by reading chapters and drafts at various points, including Monica Ferrell, Kitty Chiu, Victoria Cain, and Michael Osman. I am grateful for their magnanimity of time and thought. Special thanks go to the extraordinary women in my academic writing group, who offered inestimable support, unflagging encouragement, and good tough criticism over almost a decade: Kim Anno, Nicole Archer, Paula Birnbaum, Alla Efimova, Tirza Latimer, Jordana Moore Saggese, Rachel Schreiber, and Jenny Shaw. At the California College of the Arts (CCA), I have had the great pleasure of learning from, and teaching and conspiring with, the brilliant architectural historians and theorists David Gissen and James Graham, as well as a host of other amazing colleagues, including Neeraj Bhatia, Thom Faulders, Lisa Findley, Nataly Gattegno, Jason Johnson, Janette Kim, Andrew Kudless, William Littmann, Mia Liu, Adam Marcus, Brian Price, Neal Schwartz, Catherine Veikos, the late Sandra Vivanco, and many others. I have also benefited from the support of several deans who have valued and given prominence to history and theory: sincere thanks go to Ila Berman, Jonathan Massey, and Keith Krumwiede.

This project could not have been completed without generous support from the McNeil Center for Early American Studies, Monticello Library, Graham Foundation, Whiting Foundation, Massachusetts Historical Society, MacDowell Colony, Huntington Library, and American Antiquarian Society. Fellowships from these organizations enabled travel to archives, the luxury of focusing on the project for sustained periods, and opportunities to share my work with other scholars who offered helpful references and pushed my thinking.

Several individuals, institutions, and organizations provided me with forums to present portions of this material and test out its ideas. These include Michael Osman at the University of California, Los Angeles, Dan Richter at the McNeil Center, Jonathan Massey at Syracuse University, Shannon Starkey at the University of San Diego, Pier Vittorio Aureli at the Architectural Association, art history graduate students at Yale University, CCA's Visual and Critical Studies Program, the San Francisco Art Institute, the Robert H. Smith Center for International Jefferson Studies, the University of Cambridge, C19: The Society of Nineteenth-Century Americanists, the Buell Center for the Study of American Architecture, and the Preservation Association of Central New York. María González Pendás and Whitney Laemmli, Joseph L. Clarke, Barry Katz, and Nader Vossoughian organized conferences and panels where I was fortunate to present portions of my research. Sincere thanks go to Shirley Samuels, Anne Hultzsch, and Mari Hvattum, who facilitated conference panels that grew into edited volumes in which early pieces of what became this book appeared.

A project as tentacular and inquisitive as this one could not have been completed without the assistance of countless archivists, librarians, and historians at national, state, and local historical societies. These include the staff at the American Antiquarian Society, Boston Public Library, Columbia University Libraries, Cornell University Library, Duke University Library, Huntington Library, Indiana State Library, Kansas Historical Society, Massachusetts Historical Society, Monticello Library, National Archives, New York Public Library, Queens Library, Springfield–Greene County Library, St. Croix Valley Historical Society, Ripon Historical Society, Steuben County Historical Society, Sutro Library, Syracuse University Library, University of Michigan Libraries, University of Virginia Libraries, University of Wisconsin–Oshkosh Polk Library, Wisconsin Historical Society, Worcester Historical Museum, Working Men's Institute Museum and Library, Vedder Research Library, and Yaphank Historical Society. Leonard Paul Wood and Jack and Amelia Steinbring kindly talked with me or provided access to personal and family archival materials related to their families' octagon houses.

Several scholars generously responded to my cold-call inquiries and shared notes, references, and in some cases unpublished manuscripts. They include Jamie Bronstein, Eric Foner, James Gregory, Mark Lause, Martin Perdue, Crispin Sartwell, and Shawn Wilbur. Robert Kline and Ellen Puerzer, compilers of an invaluable book and an online inventory of octagon houses, offered helpful advice.

Numerous talented and resourceful research assistants contributed their efforts to this project over the years. Amanda Simons and Lina Kudinar deserve special thanks for their painstaking and dogged work securing image scans and permissions. I am grateful for assistance from Clare Hacko, Fangying Zhu, Melody Villavicencio, Navya Sharad, and Laura Ferris. Chris Davey, editor extraordinaire, helped smooth the writing and offered essential encouragement in the manuscript's later stages.

At the University of Minnesota Press, Pieter Martin, Anne Carter, and Ana Bichanich have been wonderful to work with. Pieter especially has been a patient and wise shepherd of this project. Judy Selhorst was a wonderfully meticulous copy editor, and Fred Kameny provided expert indexing. I am grateful to the two anonymous readers who gave insightful feedback and helped me to recognize the manuscript's strengths, as well as ways it could be improved.

My deepest gratitude goes to my families, including my parents, John and Jane Cheng; my sister, Katherine Chan, and her family, Winston, Claire, Max, and Willa; and the Snyders—Diane, Jeremy, and Alyssa. Jennifer Ching is practically family, a sister in all ways except biology. I couldn't ask for a better partner than Brett Snyder, whose creativity, wit, and endless patience make everyday life a pleasure. I defended my prospectus about a month before giving birth to my first child, Xia; my second, Kai, was born halfway through the dissertation. The kids grew up with this book. As every academic who is a parent can understand, it was often heartbreaking to separate myself from them to research and write, and also heartbreaking when I couldn't work as much as I wanted to. But in the end, I could not have completed this project without the love, curiosity, humor, and joy they brought.

NOTES

INTRODUCTION

1. Clubb, *Illustrated Vegetarian Almanac,* 24.

2. For historical overviews of early nineteenth-century reform, see Mintz, *Moralists and Modernizers*; Guarneri, *Utopian Alternative*; Pitzer, *America's Communal Utopias*; Walters, *American Reformers*; Thomas, "Romantic Reform in America"; Bestor, *Backwoods Utopias*; Bestor, "Patent-Office Models." Two older surveys are also useful: Nordhoff, *Communistic Societies*; Noyes, *History of American Socialisms.*

3. Walters, *American Reformers,* 40; Bestor, "Patent-Office Models," 505.

4. Ralph Waldo Emerson to Thomas Carlyle, October 30, 1840, in Carlyle and Emerson, *Correspondence,* 308.

5. O'Sullivan, "Introduction," 30.

6. Hayden, *Seven American Utopias.*

7. Rowe, "Architecture of Utopia," 210.

8. On the historiography of American reform, including critiques, see Mintz, *Moralists and Modernizers,* introduction. For a recent critical perspective, see Gura, *Man's Better Angels.*

9. More specified that the residents of Utopia would embark on colonization as their numbers grew. Fredric Jameson observes that More's Utopia is "the prototype of the settler colony, and the forerunner of modern imperialism." Jameson, *Archaeologies of the Future,* 205.

10. Lyman Tower Sargent has argued that there is an element of utopianism motivating nearly all settler colonization; conversely, utopia for settlers consistently spells dystopia for Indigenous peoples. Sargent, "Colonial and Postcolonial Utopias." On the relationship between utopia and settler colonialism, see also Veracini, *World Turned Inside Out*; Arneil, *Domestic Colonies*; Puthoff, "'To Make Discoveries'"; Hardy, "Unsettling Hope."

11. Rowe, "Architecture of Utopia." For a historical overview of architectural attitudes toward utopia, see Coleman, "Problematic of Architecture and Utopia."

12. Picon, "Notes on Utopia," 95.

13. The word "form" has a complex array of meanings within architecture and philosophy, connoting, on the one hand, shape, and, on the other hand, an idealist essence. I use it mostly in the first sense. For a helpful historical dissection of form, see the essay titled "Form" in Forty, *Words and Buildings.*

14. Engels, "Socialism"; Marx and Engels, "Manifesto of the Communist Party," 497–99.

15. Rowe and Koetter, *Collage City.*

16. Hayden, *Seven American Utopias,* 349. See also the related critique in Coleman, "Problematic of Architecture and Utopia." Carla Yanni adopts a similar position about nineteenth-century asylums in *Architecture of Madness,* 146.

17. On the influence of environmental determinism (not to be confused with contemporary movements for sustainability or ecology) on institutional reform architecture in the nineteenth century, see Markus, *Buildings and Power*; Yanni, *Architecture of Madness*; Wallenstein, *Biopolitics.* On the impact of theories of "environmentalism" on English urban reformers, see

Buder, *Visionaries and Planners*. For a historiographic perspective, see Haskell, *Objectivity Is Not Neutrality,* chaps. 11–12. Finally, see Adrian Forty's account of the rise of environmental determinism in his essay "Function," in *Words and Buildings,* 174–95. Pointing out that the terms "environmental determinism" and "functionalism" are twentieth-century labels for nineteenth-century ideologies, Forty claims that the idea that buildings can act mechanically on individuals' behavior did not emerge until the twentieth century. Before that, any behavioral effects were credited "to the regimen[s] operated in them, not to the buildings themselves" (192). I disagree with Forty: plenty of nineteenth-century reformers linked the physical form of buildings to what happened inside them, such that this distinction is, as Forty himself admits, a fine one.

18. See Evans, "Bentham's Panopticon"; Evans, *Fabrication of Virtue*; Foucault, *Discipline and Punish*.

19. While architects today tend to avoid functionalist arguments about architecture's capacity to produce specific and predictable effects on its inhabitants, a number of recent theorists in other fields, following Henri Lefebvre's argument that space can be productive and not a mere container, have continued to emphasize the influence of the arrangement of space on bodies. See, for example, Ahmed, *Queer Phenomenology*; Levine, *Forms*. One way of reconciling these positions is to recognize that while space and architecture certainly do have concrete, formative, and sometimes burdensome effects on the bodies that inhabit them, these effects are often not the kinds of one-to-one outcomes projected by earlier proponents of architectural functionalism.

20. Here my thinking has been shaped by Benedict Anderson's argument about the important role of mass print, museum displays, maps, and other media in the construction of "imagined communities" (specifically, nations) in the nineteenth century. Anderson, *Imagined Communities*. I have also been influenced by Michael Warner's theorization of counterpublics as a critical modification of the Habermasian concept of the public sphere in which bourgeois reason reigns. Warner argues that subaltern counterpublics set themselves consciously in opposition to the dominant culture and use the circulatory media of print and performance to elevate dissenting affects and styles of existence, to call forth like-minded communities, and to thereby gain a form of public agency. Warner, *Publics and Counterpublics*.

21. On architecture's engagements with print culture during the eighteenth and nineteenth centuries, see Wittman, *Architecture, Print Culture and the Public Sphere*; Hvattum and Hultzsch, *Printed and the Built*.

22. My argument here thus goes beyond the familiar point that even unbuilt or "paper" architecture can have value because it manifests provocative and original ideas—a point that emphasizes the vision of the *creator*. Rather, my contention is that printed architectural images are important because they circulate and influence *readers*.

23. Henkin, *City Reading*.

24. On the expansion of print in the early nineteenth-century United States, see Zboray and Zboray, *Oxford History of Popular Print Culture*; Gross and Kelley, *History of the Book,* vol. 2; Casper et al., *History of the Book,* vol. 3; Starr, *Creation of the Media*. For an account of developments in England that also contains insights for the U.S. context, see Anderson, *Printed Image*.

25. Lippert, *Consuming Identities,* 15.

26. The literature on nineteenth-century photography is too vast to summarize here. On the significance of the mass reproduction of images, see Walter Benjamin's classic essay "The Work of Art in the Age of Its Technological Reproducibility."

27. For a representative sampling of the sizable scholarship on nineteenth-century visual culture, see Schwartz and Przyblyski, *Nineteenth-Century Visual Culture Reader*.

28. Wood engraving was invented by the Englishman Thomas Bewick in the 1790s. He found that engraving on the end grain of hardwood enabled the printing of higher-quality images than were possible with traditional woodcuts. This method also provided a way for images to be inexpensively integrated with text.

29. Leonard, *Power of the Press*, 99.

30. For comparison, see the analysis of working-class visual culture in England during this period in Anderson, *Printed Image*, 175.

31. Nord, *Faith in Reading*; Morgan, *Protestants and Pictures*; Goddu, "Reform."

32. Nord, *Faith in Reading*, 84.

33. Quoted in Morgan, *Protestants and Pictures*, 51.

34. Morgan, *Protestants and Pictures*, 51, 72; Morgan, *Lure of Images*, chap. 1.

35. Goddu, *Selling Antislavery*; Cutter, *Illustrated Slave*; Clytus, "'Keep It before the People.'"

36. Wood, *Blind Memory*, 97–99. I discuss antislavery imagery at greater length in chapter 4. The phrase "scene of subjection" is from Hartman, *Scenes of Subjection*. For a recent reading of antislavery visual rhetoric that challenges the view that antislavery imagery was exploitative, see Cutter, *Illustrated Slave*.

37. Clytus, "'Keep It before the People.'"

38. Quoted in Clytus, "'Keep It before the People,'" 290.

39. Laurent Baridon and Antoine Picon have pointed out that published illustrations of Fourier's phalanstery did not circulate widely in the nineteenth century. Baridon speculates that Fourier may have been hesitant to provide a definitive representation of the *phalanstère*, for fear of creating disappointment when its material realization failed to match the image. As Picon observes, the images that did exist were restrained and lacking in detail. While I would argue that published depictions of the phalanstery, including those printed by Victor Considerant in *Destinée sociale* (1832), were relatively detailed compared with the telegraphic images of the American geometric utopias, my overall thesis, that utopians strategically chose more diagrammatic forms of visual representation, concurs with Picon's. Baridon, "Fourierist Phalanstère," 372; Picon, "Notes on Utopia," 95–96.

40. Michael Charlton, quoted in Cutter, *Illustrated Slave*, 16. I am using "visual rhetoric" to refer to images and associated practices, but the term is also frequently used to reference a subdiscipline that applies the methodologies of rhetorical analysis to images. For useful introductions to visual rhetoric studies, see Hill and Helmers, *Defining Visual Rhetorics*; Olson et al., *Visual Rhetoric*.

41. Peirce, "Logic as Semiotic," 102–13, 115.

42. Bender and Marrinan, *Culture of Diagram*. For an overview of the scholarship on diagrams in the history of science, see Bigg, "Diagrams." Unlike Bender and Marrinan's study, most of the book-length works on the history of diagrams are compilations of examples interspersed with narration. See the classic works of Tufte, including *Visual Display of Quantitative Information*; *Envisioning Information*; and *Visual Explanations*. Similar compendiums, mostly oriented toward fans of graphic and information design, have proliferated in recent years. One text that treats a particular subgenre of diagram in greater scholarly depth is Rosenberg and Grafton, *Cartographies of Time*. There is also a burgeoning field of diagram studies among German-language scholars. For a sampling, see Schneider et al., *Diagrammatik-Reader*.

43. On the rise of an ocularcentric epistemology in modernity, see Jay, *Downcast Eyes*, chaps. 1–2. On popular visual pedagogy in eighteenth-century Europe, see Stafford, *Artful Science*. The persistence of ocularcentrism in nineteenth-century American popular culture challenges Stafford's assertion that visual education was eclipsed by an emphasis on literary and (unillustrated) print culture by the end of the eighteenth century.

268   *Notes to Introduction*

44. Harris, *Humbug*, 62.

45. Johnson, "On the Utility of Visible Illustrations," 67–68.

46. Hamilton, "*Federalist* No. 31," 189.

47. Stevens, *Grammar of the Machine*, chaps. 2, 5, and 6. On the splitting of mid-nineteenth-century geometric pedagogy into two branches (one oriented toward citizen-subjects and the other toward technologists and engineers), see Martin, *Knowledge Worlds*, chap. 2.

48. Gilmartin, "Popular Radicalism," 552. Gilmartin links this discussion to the passage on the "Image, Phantom, or Representative of the Commonwealth" in Locke's *Two Treatises of Government*.

49. Jameson describes the function of cognitive mapping, a concept that appears in several of his essays, as allegorizing relationships of the individual to the social totality that are by definition not representable: "to enable a situational representation on the part of the individual subject to that vaster and properly unrepresentable totality which is the ensemble of society's structures as a whole." Jameson, *Postmodernism*, 51. Jameson's concept of cognitive mapping was influenced by his reading of the urban theorist Kevin Lynch's *The Image of the City*. Elsewhere, he has suggested that literary utopias can function as such cognitive maps by making visible social contradictions in dramatic or aesthetic forms and doing so in ways that can grip the imagination and speak to larger social groups. See Jameson, *Archaeologies of the Future*, 13. My thinking has also been influenced by Toscano and Kinkle, *Cartographies of the Absolute*.

50. Susan Buck-Morss traces the history of attempts to represent the capitalist economy visually in "Envisioning Capital." She echoes Jameson's call for contemporary theories that rise to the "challenge of envisioning the social whole" (466).

51. The French philosopher Auguste Comte coined the word *sociologie* in 1839, and it was translated into English in 1843. Bestor, "Evolution of the Socialist Vocabulary," 285. In 1877, the geometric utopian Lewis Masquerier, whose work is addressed in chapter 2, wrote a book titled *Sociology; or, The Reconstruction of Society, Government, and Property, upon the Principles of the Equality, the Perpetuity, and the Individuality of the Private Ownership of Life, Person, Government, Homestead, and the Whole Product of Labor* [. . .]. He and another geometric utopian, Josiah Warren, are included among the forerunners of American sociology discussed in Bernard and Bernard, *Origins of American Sociology*.

52. Bender and Marrinan, *Culture of Diagram*, 23–24.

53. McLuhan, *Understanding Media*, 24–25.

54. Deleuze, *Foucault*, 35, 44.

55. Picon similarly argues that the "blurriness" of representations of nineteenth-century French and English utopias—their combination of precision and imprecision, abstraction and certainty—allowed them to remain "undisciplined, heterogeneous, unpredictable." See Picon, "Notes on Utopia," 101.

56. Johnson, "On the Utility of Visible Illustrations," 75.

57. "Our Present Prospects," *Working Man's Advocate*, May 18, 1844, 1, emphasis added.

58. Dunbar-Ortiz, *Indigenous Peoples' History*; Dahl, *Empire of the People*.

59. On the transformation of the U.S. economy in the nineteenth century, see Clark, *Social Change in America*; Sellers, *Market Revolution*; Larson, *Market Revolution in America*. On the global cotton industry, see Beckert, *Empire of Cotton*.

60. Several decades of debate among historians over the comparative influence of republicanism and liberalism have yielded a general conclusion that both ideologies played critical roles in the early republic, with republicanism waning and liberalism gaining the upper hand by the early nineteenth century, although republican rhetoric persisted, especially in the labor

movement, as I discuss in chapter 2. For an overview of the historiography of republican ideology, see Rodgers, "Republicanism."

61. Brownson, "Laboring Classes," 311.

62. O'Sullivan, "Introduction," 27. Thoreau cited and transformed this axiom into his own formulation in his 1849 essay "Civil Disobedience": "That government is best which governs not at all."

63. Blau, "Introduction," xxii.

64. Larson, *Market Revolution in America,* 147.

65. Sandage, *Born Losers,* 25–26.

66. Davis, *Ante-bellum Reform,* 9.

67. Calhoun, *Roots of Radicalism.*

68. Bestor offers a useful genealogy of terms related to reform and socialism in the nineteenth century in "Evolution of the Socialist Vocabulary."

69. See Walters, *American Reformers,* esp. afterword.

70. Martin, "Critical of What?"; Martin, *Utopia's Ghost,* chap. 7; Scott, *Architecture or Techno-utopia.*

71. On artisans, see Laurie, *Artisans into Workers*; Wilentz, *Chants Democratic.*

72. On women in nineteenth-century American communities, see Kolmerten, *Women in Utopia.*

73. Nineteenth-century Black utopias remain understudied. See Pease and Pease, *Black Utopia*; Nembhard, *Collective Courage,* chap. 1. On Black literary utopias, see Zamalin, *Black Utopia*; Foster, "Nancy Prince's Utopias." Carl Guarneri recounts a perverse episode involving a group of Fourierists in Louisiana who proposed an "emancipation" scheme in which Black enslaved people could earn their freedom by working to build a model phalanx for white people to inhabit. Guarneri, *Utopian Alternative,* 262–65.

74. After the Civil War, Davis transferred his land to a formerly enslaved man named Benjamin Montgomery, who continued to manage the site. Montgomery's son Isaiah lost the plantation in the late 1870s during a cotton depression and period of white revanchism, but he went on to found Mound Bayou, Mississippi, a community of formerly enslaved people. On the history of Davis Bend and Mound Bayou, see Hermann, *Pursuit of a Dream*; Rosen, *From New Lanark to Mound Bayou.*

75. I am referring here to Ernst Bloch's theory of utopia as a kind of wishing that includes prosaic daydreams of a better life, as evidenced in fairy tales, popular novels, advertisements, and other banal cultural forms. Bloch, *Principle of Hope.*

76. Hartman, *Scenes of Subjection,* 13. Cedric Robinson argues that one of the distinguishing features of Black radicalism is the lack of a "promise of a certain future." "Unlike Marxism [where] victory is inevitable eventually, in Black radicalism it is not. . . . It is about a kind of resistance that does not promise triumph or victory at the end, only liberation. No nice package at the end, only that you would be free." Robinson and Robinson, preface to Johnson and Lubin, *Futures of Black Radicalism,* 7.

77. Du Bois, *Black Reconstruction,* 494–96.

78. Buck-Morss, "Aesthetics and Anaesthetics," 8.

79. Walters, *American Reformers,* xiii.

80. Williams, *Marxism and Literature,* 122.

81. Williams, *Marxism and Literature,* 123.

82. Williams, *Keywords,* 2.

83. This turn was briefly dubbed the "new new" political history. See Waldstreicher et al., "Introduction"; Formisano, "Concept of Political Culture." For a philosophical take on the

270 Notes to Introduction

necessity of thinking about politics in terms of aesthetics, see Sartwell, *Political Aesthetics*. See also Levine's argument for political formalism in *Forms*.

84. This position has been most famously articulated by Karl Popper. For example, see Popper, "Aestheticism, Perfectionism, Utopianism." Rowe adopts Popper's position in his critique of utopian architecture. See Rowe, "Architecture of Utopia."

85. Castoriadis, *Imaginary Institution of Society*, 117–49.

1. ANTINOMIES OF AMERICAN UTOPIA

1. Johnson, *River of Dark Dreams*, 34.

2. Jefferson used the phrase "empire for liberty" on several occasions. See, for example, Thomas Jefferson to James Madison, April 27, 1809, in *Papers of Thomas Jefferson*. Musing on the possibility of U.S. territorial expansion to the south and north, he wrote: "We should have such an empire for liberty. . . . I am persuaded no constitution was ever before so well calculated as ours for extensive empire & self government."

3. On the history of the survey system, see Pattison, *Beginnings*; Berkhofer, "Jefferson, the Ordinance of 1784"; Johnson, *Order upon the Land*; Linklater, *Measuring America*; Hubbard, *American Boundaries*.

4. McCoy, *Elusive Republic*. Walter Johnson draws a slightly different contrast, describing Jefferson's vision as growth through reproduction of white households rather than intensification and densification. Johnson, *River of Dark Dreams*, 4.

5. On "decimalization," see Pattison, *Beginnings*, 46; Linklater, *Measuring America*. Also see Thomas Jefferson to Francis Hopkinson, May 3, 1784, in *Papers of Thomas Jefferson*. Jefferson proposed setting aside traditional English units of land measurement such as "feet" and "chains" in favor of units keyed to universal astronomical and physical phenomena. States would be 2 degrees, or 120 nautical miles, tall, subdivided into 100-square-mile units that he called "hundreds," which would further be subdivided into individual lots. Although Jefferson appropriated the term "hundred" from tradition, his dimensions for it were novel because he based them on the geographical mile (calculated from the circumference of the earth) rather than on traditional English measures. Jefferson believed the word "hundred" to be Anglo-Saxon in origin; it may have originally referred to a plot of land large enough to sustain approximately one hundred households. See Thomas Jefferson to Major John Cartright, June 5, 1824, in *Thomas Jefferson: Writings*, 1490–96.

6. As many have observed, the grid's obliviousness to geographical and ecological features like watersheds and ecosystems has had lasting negative environmental repercussions. George Washington complained about the survey system's lack of relation to natural topography, as did the explorer John Wesley Powell a hundred years later. See Pattison, *Beginnings*, 89; Johnson, *Order upon the Land*, 19.

7. Nichols, *Theft Is Property!*, chap. 1.

8. Nichols, *Theft Is Property!*, 32–33. Nichols quotes the Lakota philosopher Vine Deloria on this point.

9. Quoted in Wallace, *Jefferson and the Indians*, 23–24. On the historical processes of Indian dispossession in North America, see Banner, *How the Indians Lost Their Land*; Ostler, *Surviving Genocide*; Dunbar-Ortiz, *Indigenous Peoples' History*.

10. On the survey as a tool of racial-imperial governance, see Johnson, *River of Dark Dreams*, chap. 1; Dahl, *Empire of the People*, 68. James Scott similarly describes the cadastral survey as a key technology of the utilitarian modern state, deployed to extract taxes, convert land into property, and administer populations. Scott, *Seeing like a State*, chap. 1.

11. Bhandar, *Colonial Lives of Property,* 92–93. See also Blomley, "Law, Property, and the Geography of Violence."

12. For a detailed analysis of the proposed state names, as well as the publication and circulation of the maps related to the ordinance, see Julian P. Boyd, "Editorial Note: Plan for Government of the Western Territory," in *Papers of Thomas Jefferson.*

13. Thomas Jefferson to James Monroe, July 9, 1786, in *Papers of Thomas Jefferson.*

14. On the political ramifications of the sizes and shapes of states, see Zagarri, *Politics of Size*; Hubbard, *American Boundaries,* 120–21.

15. Thomas Jefferson, "A Bill for the More General Diffusion of Knowledge" (1779), in *Thomas Jefferson: Writings,* 365–73.

16. Thomas Jefferson to Joseph C. Cabell, February 2, 1816, in *Thomas Jefferson: Writings,* 1380, emphasis added. The context is a discussion of the merits of local versus state control of public elementary schools. On wards, see also Jefferson to Cartright, June 5, 1824, 1490–96.

17. Jefferson to Cabell, February 2, 1816, 1380. On ward-republics, see also Jefferson to Cartright, June 5, 1824, 1492.

18. Jefferson to Cabell, February 2, 1816.

19. Thomas Jefferson to John Jay, August 23, 1785, in *Papers of Thomas Jefferson.*

20. Dunbar-Ortiz, *Indigenous People's History,* 55.

21. Thomas Jefferson to James Madison, October 28, 1785, in *Papers of Thomas Jefferson.*

22. See Matthews, *Radical Politics of Thomas Jefferson*; Lynd, *Intellectual Origins of American Radicalism.*

23. Thomas Jefferson to James Madison, September 6, 1789, in *Papers of Thomas Jefferson.*

24. Dahl, *Empire of the People*, esp. chaps. 2–3.

25. Matthews, *Radical Politics of Thomas Jefferson*, 82–83; Hardt, "Jefferson and Democracy," 70.

26. Johnson, *Order upon the Land,* 15.

27. Johnson, *Order upon the Land,* 146. John Brinckerhoff Jackson concurs in "Order of a Landscape," 159. D. W. Meinig makes a similar point about the slow absorption of the grid as a concept. See Meinig, *Shaping of America,* 243.

28. On early Americans' ample exposure to printed maps, see Brückner, *Geographic Revolution,* esp. 9–11, 120–30.

29. The eleventh edition of *Merriam-Webster's Collegiate Dictionary* (2003) shows 1839 as the date of the first use of "grid." The term did not appear in the 1841 or 1844 editions of Noah Webster's *American Dictionary of the English Language.* Even by 1898, the definition of "grid" in *Webster's International Dictionary of the English Language* was simply "a grating of thin parallel bars, similar to a gridiron."

30. The 1828 edition of Webster's *American Dictionary of the English Language* defined the verb "checker" as "to variegate with cross lines; to form into little squares, like a chess board, by lines or stripes of different colors."

31. Thomas Jefferson to Tenche Cox, March 8, 1793, in *Papers of Thomas Jefferson.* Jefferson might have been referring to Manasseh Cutler's map of the Ohio Company lands, issued as part of an advertisement for the company in 1787.

32. Jefferson mentioned this idea in letters to friends. See Thomas Jefferson to Benjamin Rush, September 12, 1799; Thomas Jefferson to William C. C. Claiborne, July 7 and July 17, 1804; and Thomas Jefferson to Constantin François Chasseboeuf Volney, February 8, 1805, all in *Papers of Thomas Jefferson.* On these gridded town plans, see Reps, "Thomas Jefferson's Checkerboard Towns."

33. Thomas Jefferson to David Rittenhouse, March 19, 1791, in *Papers of Thomas Jefferson*.

34. "Straight-sided and right-angled houses are the most cheap and the most convenient to live in. The effect of these plain and simple reflections was decisive." "An Act Relative to Improvements Touching the Laying Out of Streets and Roads in the City of New York, and for Other Purposes," in Bridges, *Map of the City of New York*, 24.

35. Brown, "Thomas Jefferson's Poplar Forest," 129; McLaughlin, *Jefferson and Monticello*, 254; Kennedy, "Jefferson and the Indians," 120.

36. For a summary of the historiographic debates over the transition from republican to liberal ideologies, see Rodgers, "Republicanism."

37. On the chapel, see Kimball, "Jefferson and the Public Buildings." Kimball dated this drawing to around 1770, whereas Douglas Wilson has suggested a later date, 1778, in "Dating Jefferson's Early Architectural Drawings," 56.

38. Palladio, *Architecture of A. Palladio*, 45–46.

39. Jefferson, *Notes on the State of Virginia*, 265.

40. See my longer treatment of this topic in Cheng, "Race and Architectural Geometry"; see also Wilson, "Notes on the Virginia Capitol." On the relationship between aesthetic and racial discourse in the eighteenth century, see Bindman, *Ape to Apollo*; Gikandi, *Slavery and the Culture of Taste*.

41. Locke, *Some Thoughts Concerning Education*, 181; Thomas Jefferson, "Report of the Commissioners for the University of Virginia" (1818), in *Thomas Jefferson: Writings*, 459–60. On the association of geometry with reason in early America, see McCoy, "'Old-Fashioned' Nationalism," 58.

42. Jefferson, *Notes on the State of Virginia*, 266. Jefferson's relationship with the mathematician Benjamin Banneker complicates but ultimately reinforces this fundamental picture. Jefferson initially saw Banneker as evidence of the possibility of Black intellectual equality but later revised his view, questioning whether Banneker had worked independently. On the Banneker episode and Jefferson's attitudes toward African Americans more broadly, see Jordan, *White over Black*, 449–57.

43. Bergdoll, *European Architecture*, 73–75.

44. On Morris's influence on Jefferson, see Lancaster, "Jefferson's Architectural Indebtedness."

45. Morris, *Select Architecture*, 8. Jefferson owned a copy of the first edition of Morris's book, which was published in 1755.

46. Morris, *Select Architecture*, 2.

47. On the politics of the picturesque in England, see Bermingham, *Landscape and Ideology*.

48. Sokolitz, "Picturing the Plantation"; Vlach, *Back of the Big House*, 3–4. The phrase "territorial aristocracy" is from W. G. Hoskins, cited in Vlach, *Back of the Big House*, 3.

49. In the books most often cited as Jefferson's sources (works by Morris, Becker, and Gibbs), octagons appear overwhelmingly in the context of garden pavilions or in connection to landscape views.

50. Henry Wotton, *Elements of Architecture* (1624), quoted in Neve, *City and Countrey Purchaser*, 59.

51. Bhandar, *Colonial Lives of Property*, 170. Bhandar draws on Cheryl Harris's important analysis of how whiteness historically becomes a kind of property value in "Whiteness as Property."

52. Both Dell Upton and Lucia Stanton have interpreted Monticello as fulfilling Jefferson's fantasy of surveillance. See Upton, *Architecture in the United States*, 37; Stanton, *"Those Who Labor,"* 85.

Notes to Chapter 2   273

53. On Jefferson's domestic designs for friends, see Howard, *Thomas Jefferson, Architect,* 86–114.

54. Isaac Coles to John Hartwell Cocke, February 23, 1816, in *Papers of Thomas Jefferson.*

55. Howard, *Thomas Jefferson, Architect,* 112.

56. Both quotations are reproduced in Stanton, *"Those Who Labor,"* 85.

57. Stanton, *"Those Who Labor,"* 84.

58. Upton, "White and Black Landscapes."

59. Quoted in Stanton, *"Those Who Labor,"* 129.

60. McLaughlin, *Jefferson and Monticello,* 327.

61. Thomas Jefferson to John Randolph, August 25, 1775, in *Papers of Thomas Jefferson.* On Jefferson's relation to privacy and an emerging culture of public performance, see Fliegelman, *Declaring Independence.*

62. For Jefferson's octagonal prison design, see Thomas Jefferson to James Wood, March 31, 1797; and "Enclosure I: Notes on Plan of a Prison, 31 March 1797," both in *Papers of Thomas Jefferson.* Jefferson received a copy of Bentham's *Panopticon* in 1792; see Thomas Pinckney to Thomas Jefferson, August 29, 1792, in *Papers of Thomas Jefferson.* Jefferson had earlier installed "Venetian blinds" at Monticello. The first mention of them is in his Memorandum Books of 1767; see *Papers of Thomas Jefferson.*

63. McDonald, "Poplar Forest," 116.

64. The perfect geometry of the dining room was disrupted in the built version by the awkward addition of a fireplace in one corner. Jefferson's early sketches clearly indicate that he was thinking of the form as a freestanding octagon. He decided to add two porches and two stairways after construction had begun. For a detailed account of the design and construction of the house, see Chambers, *Poplar Forest.*

65. Howard, *Thomas Jefferson, Architect,* 120; McDonald, "Poplar Forest," 117. Both McDonald and Howard suggest that Jefferson was so enamored of the abstract purity of the octagonal plan that he neglected pragmatic necessities such as the communicating stair between upper and lower stories. In 1814, six years after the main block of the house was complete, Jefferson added a 100-foot wing of service rooms.

66. On the dumbwaiters at Monticello, see Martin, "Drawing the Color Line."

67. Upton, *Architecture in the United States,* 30.

68. On Mount Vernon in visual culture, see Vlach, *Planter's Prospect,* 16. The most commonly reprinted image of Monticello before the Civil War was an engraving after a painting by George Cooke, which first appeared in the *Family Magazine* in 1837. Similar images were reprinted in the *Baltimore Monument,* October 7, 1837, 4; the *New York State Mechanic,* September 3, 1842, 120; *The Family Instructor; or, Digest of General Knowledge,* 1854, 284; and the *Saturday Evening Post,* February 15, 1862, 1. See also Bear, *Old Pictures of Monticello.*

2. THE VISUAL RHETORIC OF EQUALITY

1. Higgins, *Subdivisions of the Public Lands,* 21. Higgins suggested that the grid's chief virtue was its diagrammatic quality, which allowed it to be nearly universally apprehended. Its "greatest convenience is its extreme simplicity of description. Any person, by its monuments and markings, can readily find the tract sought for." Other contemporary expressions of the instrumental-capitalist view of the land grid in the mid-1840s can be found in guidebooks for western settlers like J. H. Colton's *Western Tourist* (1839) and J. M. Peck's *New Guide for Emigrants to the West* (1836).

2. National Reform Association, *Vote Yourself a Farm.*

3. Masquerier, *Scientific Division,* 9.

4. The National Reformers' literature occasionally cited Delaware and California as potential sites. By the 1850s a few National Reformers undertook scattered efforts at organized emigration. The Western Farm and Village Association sent a cohort to Minnesota City (now Rollingstone) in Minnesota, but I have not found evidence that it was platted according to the diagrammatic plan. On the latter, see Bronstein, *Land Reform*, 242–43; Lause, *Young America*, 113.

5. See, for example, Bronstein, *Land Reform*; Lause, *Young America*.

6. Many sources can be cited for each of these main interpretations, so I will name just a few representative ones. For a synthetic interpretation of the land ordinance grid that touches on all of these readings, see Linklater, *Measuring America*. For the imperialist interpretation, see Harley, "Maps, Knowledge, and Power"; Scott, *Seeing like a State*. For the "commodification" reading, see Reps, *Making of Urban America*, 216–17. For the grid as a figure of abstract rationalization, see Sennett, "American Cities." For the grid as symbol of democracy, see Fisher, "Democratic Social Space"; Cosgrove, "Measures of America."

7. Lewis Masquerier, "Progress of Reform and Reformers," *Young America*, September 5, 1846, 1. In this passage, Masquerier further explains that the reformers must engage in political activity, not mere sermonizing: "Moral force or exhortation alone will go unheeded, unless combined with political force."

8. Masquerier, *Scientific Division*, 10.

9. An exception is Sean Wilentz's analysis of artisans' emblems and parades, in *Chants Democratic*. On visual representations of labor and sites of labor in the nineteenth-century United States, see Schulman, *Work Sights*; Rigal, *American Manufactory*; Groseclose, *Nineteenth-Century American Art*, 85–114; Schlereth, "New York Artisan"; Dabakis, *Visualizing Labor in American Sculpture*.

10. For histories of the National Reform Association, see Bronstein, *Land Reform*; Lause, *Young America*; Griffin, "Reformers' Union." I have also relied on the following histories of the nineteenth-century American labor movement: Wilentz, *Chants Democratic*; Pessen, *Most Uncommon Jacksonians*; Laurie, *Artisans into Workers*; Greenberg, *Advocating the Man*. On the contemporaneous anti-rent movement, which was also a struggle over reforming landownership but waged by farmers in upstate New York, see Huston, *Land and Freedom*.

11. Larson, *Market Revolution in America*; Sellers, *Market Revolution*. Recent revisionist accounts of the market revolution have stressed the critical role of slavery in the development of a global capitalist economy. See Johnson, *River of Dark Dreams*; Beckert, *Empire of Cotton*.

12. While historians have long asserted that economic inequality increased in the 1840s, recent scholars have suggested the picture is less clear. See Daniel Howe's summary in *What Hath God Wrought*, 538–39; see also Clark, *Social Change in America*. For the earlier view, see Pessen, *Riches, Class, and Power*.

13. John Windt and George H. Evans, "Prospectus of the People's Rights," *Working Man's Advocate*, March 16, 1844, 1.

14. Evans had been interested in land reform since the 1830s, but it became his principal focus only after 1844.

15. Locke, *Two Treatises of Government*, 288. The idea that improving a piece of unimproved land confers ownership rights precedes Locke, but he codified it as a philosophical precept and linked it to English colonization.

16. The phrase comes from LaCroix, "Labor Theory of Empire." On the use of Locke's theories to justify England's colonization of the Americas and the expropriation of Indian land, as well as Locke's direct investment in the colonization of the Carolinas, see Arneil, *John Locke and America*.

Notes to Chapter 2   275

17. Banner, *How the Indians Lost Their Land,* 150–60; Bhandar, *Colonial Lives of Property,* chap. 1. "Precarious and transient occupancy" is from James Sullivan's *The History of Land Titles in Massachusetts* (1801), quoted in Banner, *How the Indians Lost Their Land,* 152. As Adam Yirush observes, English and later American settlers made at least three distinct claims about Indigenous land rights at different periods of time. In addition to the argument that Indians did not have a right to the land because they did not farm it, at other moments, settlers acknowledged Indigenous sovereignty and strove to purchase or negotiate transfers of land through treaties. In still other circumstances, settlers invoked their right to the land through violent conquest. Yirush, *Settlers, Liberty, and Empire,* 18.

18. Over the first half of the nineteenth century, U.S. policy on the disposal of public lands evolved from a system in which land was sold at auction in large parcels or whole townships (terms that favored wealthy proprietors and speculators) to a homestead system with minimum lot sizes reduced from 640 to 40 acres by 1832 and the possibility of purchasing with credit rather than cash. These changes made it easier for small farmers and settlers to acquire land. For a succinct overview of conflicts over federal land policies in the early nineteenth century, see Huston, "Land Conflict." See also the classic accounts by Gates, *History of Public Land Law Development*; and Robbins, *Our Landed Heritage.*

19. On the ideological origins of the workingmen's theories, see Wilentz, *Chants Democratic,* chap. 4. Jefferson, too, had flirted with agrarian ideas. In 1789, he opined to James Madison that "the earth belongs in usufruct to the living" and that "the portion occupied by any individual ceases to be his when himself ceases to be, and reverts to the society." Jefferson to Madison, September 6, 1789.

20. The Gray and Black Hawk quotations appeared in multiple issues of the *Working Man's Advocate.* The source for the versions here is *Young America,* May 10, 1845, 1. Black Hawk's words appeared in his autobiography, *Life of Ma-ka-tai-me-she-kia-kiak,* 89.

21. "Agrarianism," *Atlantic Monthly,* April 1859, 25.

22. The workingmen did not shy away from such accusations, insisting in one article, "What is agrarianism but the equal right of every man to his share of the soil, and who will dare deny the right?" "Agrarianism," *Working Man's Advocate,* March 16, 1844, 2. The National Reform Association was also known early on as the Agrarian League. For the context of the term "agrarian," see Bestor, "Evolution of the Socialist Vocabulary," 262–63; Govan, "Agrarian and Agrarianism."

23. "Agrarianism," *Atlantic Monthly,* 396.

24. Made famous by Frederick Jackson Turner, the safety valve theory has subsequently been vigorously debated. See Smith, *Virgin Land,* 201–10; Shannon, "Post Mortem on the Labor-Safety Valve Theory"; Goodrich and Davison, "Wage-Earner in the Westward Movement," I and II.

25. Thomas Jefferson, quoted in Smith, *Virgin Land,* 203.

26. Alex Gourevitch classifies the land reformers' ideology as a form of "labor republicanism" that drew on classical republican ideas about freedom and applied them to a critique of modern wage labor. Gourevitch, *From Slavery to the Cooperative Commonwealth.*

27. Devyr, *Odd Book.*

28. On the parallels and connections between the English Chartist and American land reform movements, see Bronstein, *Land Reform.*

29. *Working Man's Advocate,* September 14, 1844, 1.

30. Lorenzo Veracini reads the U.S. land reform movement as an example of a broader pattern of turning to settler colonialism as a political strategy, characterized by the impulse to alter the political order by moving elsewhere, rather than by enacting revolutionary change in

276   *Notes to Chapter 2*

situ. He calls the former strategy turning the world "inside out" as opposed to "upside down." Veracini, *World Turned Inside Out,* 100–114.

31. Lause, *Young America,* 44–45; Streeby, *American Sensations,* 182–83.

32. "The Public Lands," *Young America,* February 14, 1846, 1.

33. "Memorial to Congress," in *Young America!* pamphlet, 1845, Syracuse University Library.

34. Streeby, *American Sensations,* 182–83.

35. Lewis Masquerier, "Letter of Mr. Masquerier," *Young America,* September 29, 1849, 3.

36. For the argument that the National Reformers contributed to the rise of a free soil ideology that made white workers' freedom dependent on Indigenous dispossession, see Dahl, *Empire of the People,* esp. chaps. 4–5. Note that Dahl elides Evans's "Young America" and the pro-expansionist Democratic movement of the same name.

37. "Our Present Prospects," 1.

38. Masquerier, *Sociology,* 15, 18. Born in Paris, Kentucky, in 1802, Masquerier was a kind of workingman's Jefferson, a plebeian Enlightenment tinkerer who became a convert to Owenism and was a frequent contributor to radical newspapers on both sides of the Atlantic by the 1830s. On Masquerier, see Claeys, "Lewis Masquerier." For samples of Masquerier's early journalism before the *Working Man's Advocate,* see his letters in the New York Owenite paper the *Free Enquirer,* December 7, 1834; and in *The Crisis, and National Co-operative Traces Union Gazette,* July 5 and July 19, 1834. See also his contributions to the *Boston Investigator,* May 29 and September 18, 1835; June 17, 1836; and September 4 and December 4, 1839; as well as his writing in the *New Moral World* from 1840 on.

39. Evans, "To the Working Men."

40. Masquerier, *Sociology,* 18.

41. On the history of rural–urban synthesis as an ideal in the United States, see Machor, *Pastoral Cities.*

42. For the land reformers' debates over the proper size of the grid, see *The Radical,* June 1841; Masquerier, *Sociology,* 19; Masquerier, *Appendix to Sociology,* 5–6, 14.

43. Thomas Jefferson to James Madison, June 19, 1786, in *Papers of Thomas Jefferson.*

44. Reps, *Making of Urban America,* 484–92. For another example of an octagonal radial plan for the center of St. Mary's, Pennsylvania, possibly drawn circa 1845 by Friedrich Gärtner, see Curran, *Romanesque Revival,* 85–87.

45. On the history of circular cities, see Johnston, *Cities in the Round.*

46. As in Masquerier's plan, the core of Circleville was organized with eight streets radiating from a central open space, in the middle of which sat a courthouse. Several buildings formed a perimeter ring around the central open space. By 1837, however, many of the town's citizens felt the circular radial plan was awkward and inconvenient. Calling it a hindrance to growth and a piece of "childish sentimentalism," the town obliterated most of the circular plan by the 1850s. This would have been nearly contemporaneous with Masquerier's plan, but I have found no evidence of a connection. Reps, *Making of Urban America,* 484–90.

47. Reps, *Making of Urban America,* 490.

48. Owen, *Development of the Principles.* This illustration was notable because it departed from the typical format used for views of New Harmony: an aerial view of a rectangle set amid a natural landscape (Figure I.5). Instead, the 1841 scheme was presented in the form of a foldout plan, emphasizing the formal, concentric geometries of the landscape design.

49. Aureli, "Appropriation, Subdivision, Abstraction," 152.

50. Masquerier, *Scientific Division,* 10.

51. "Rural Republican Township," *Working Man's Advocate,* March 15, 1845, 3; Lewis Masquerier, "Declaration of Independence, of the Producing from the Non-producing Class," *Working Man's*

Advocate, September 28, 1844; Lewis Masquerier, "Mental, Chattel, and Hireling Slavery," *Boston Investigator,* January 7, 1863. On the popular opposition to "middlemen" (or merchant capitalists), see Conkin, *Prophets of Prosperity,* 9–13.

52. Masquerier, *Scientific Division,* 11.

53. For Warren's influence on Masquerier, see the latter's review of Warren's *Equitable Commerce* in *Young America,* May 13, 1848, 1.

54. *Young America!* pamphlet, 15.

55. Lewis Masquerier, "Working Men!," *Young America,* February 14, 1846, 2. Later in his life, Masquerier, perhaps inspired by Josiah Warren's proto-anarchist views, took his belief in direct sovereignty and opposition to representative rule even further, writing that all citizens should "vote direct for law by means of township divisions throughout a state, and not attempt to do it through the absurdity of a supposed or charlatanic delegate. The usurpation of sovereignty, or the power of government is violated by a viceregent, by a substitute, or a so-called representative, who only votes his own identical will for law." Masquerier, *Appendix to Sociology,* 5.

56. Masquerier, *Scientific Division,* 11.

57. Lewis Masquerier, "To Reformers, Tenants, Anti-renters, Squatters, and Slaves," *Young America,* July 12, 1845, 1. Edward Pessen has observed that most nineteenth-century labor leaders "regarded the American political system as a hoax." Pessen, *Most Uncommon Jacksonians,* 124. On the land reformers' views on electoral politics and government, see Lause, *Young America,* 41–42, 56–59.

58. Lewis Masquerier, "Mammoth Memorial to Free the Public Lands," *Young America,* July 18, 1846, 2. In this article, Masquerier signaled his acceptance of politicking as a necessary evil: "It is a most humiliating condition that the sovereign people, from whom sovereignty is said never to depart, should be compelled to petition what are called their representatives, agents, or servants. . . . But as it is the universal practice for the sovereign people to petition their servants, let us once more try if there is any virtue in it." For another instance in which Masquerier defended the need for political action, see his review of books by John Pickering and Josiah Warren in *Young America,* May 13, 1848, 1.

59. "Progress of the Cause," *Working Man's Advocate,* May 4, 1844, 1.

60. Bronstein, *Land Reform,* chap. 5.

61. *National Reform Almanac for 1849,* 48.

62. By the late 1840s, the visual cacophony engendered by advertisers' various typographic novelties led to a counterreaction. James Gordon Bennett, editor of the *New York Herald,* banned all cuts and variations in font from the newspaper in 1847. See Boorstin, *Americans,* 138–39. See also Brownlee, *Commerce of Vision,* chap. 3.

63. "Progress of the Cause," *Young America,* March 7, 1846, 3. This article reported that the *People's Tribune* (a German reform newspaper) and the *Bay State Farmer* had republished the township diagrams. In 1848, H. H. Van Amringe relayed a request from readers in Wisconsin for *Young America* to republish the picture of the National Reformers' village. "Mr. Van Amringe's Mission," *Young America,* February 26, 1848, 3.

64. Lukasik, *Discerning Characters.*

65. Lester Olson categorizes allegorical images in mastheads above pamphlets, almanacs, and magazines as examples of visual rhetoric, since they appeared repeatedly, sometimes for years. Olson, *Emblems of American Community,* 8–9.

66. Elkins, *Domain of Images,* 196–97.

67. Olson, "Benjamin Franklin's Pictorial Representations."

68. Wilentz, *Chants Democratic,* 89. On British trade unions' use of emblems, see Ravenhill-Johnson, *Art and Ideology.*

Notes to Chapter 2

69. See Benedict Anderson's analysis of how maps became logos for colonial empires, and subsequently for anticolonial movements. Anderson, *Imagined Communities,* chap. 10.

70. Gombrich, *Uses of Images,* 176.

71. The print historian Frank Weitenkampf has argued that the appeal of visual symbols in American political cartoons lay in their capacity for "direct, summary expression." A "picture of a full dinner pail" in the 1890s was "more cheering to the public than a frank discussion of economic or social conditions or the tariff." Weitenkampf, "Our Political Symbols," 372.

72. *Young America,* July 24, 1847, 2.

73. On how Europeans came to overrepresent themselves as "Man," the generic human, see Wynter, "Unsettling the Coloniality." See also Mehta, *Liberalism and Empire,* chap. 2.

74. "Address by Denatus," quoted in Brückner, *Geographic Revolution,* 99.

75. Cohen, *Science and the Founding Fathers,* 56–57.

76. Letter published in the *New York Journal,* January 7, 1788, quoted in Cohen, *Science and the Founding Fathers,* 319–20n56.

77. On Peabody's diagrams, see Rosenberg and Grafton, *Cartographies of Time,* 202–6. Peabody's *Chronological History of the United States* (1856) postdates the land reformers' grids but draws from the pedagogical grids that Polish educator Antoni Jażwiński published in the 1830s.

78. Wilentz, *Chants Democratic,* 183. For more on Skidmore, see Pessen, "Thomas Skidmore."

79. Skidmore, *Rights of Man,* 5.

80. Wilentz, *Chants Democratic,* 184.

81. Skidmore, *Rights of Man,* 97–98.

82. Skidmore, *Rights of Man,* 97–101.

83. Skidmore, *Rights of Man,* 97, emphasis added.

84. Whately, *Elements of Logic,* 217.

85. Aureli, "Appropriation, Subdivision, Abstraction," 164.

86. On popular interest in cartography during this period, see Brückner, *Social Life of Maps.*

87. Just as Jefferson and the other founders had understood a relationship between the size of the grid and politics, and just as the land reformers debated the size of the land division grid, so, too, Masquerier weighed the merits of having counties composed of nine, sixteen, or twenty-five townships. The second option would not allow for a central township, whereas the third would be too large, giving rise to political disputes. Masquerier later disavowed the county level of organization and advocated township divisions only, in the interest of removing excess layers of government administration. Masquerier, *Scientific Division,* 5.

88. Masquerier may have known of an earlier scheme by the Owenite architect Stedman Whitwell, who in 1826 proposed a system for rationalizing geographical nomenclature by transposing latitude and longitude numbers into letters. In an 1826 letter to the *New Harmony Gazette,* Whitwell complained of the "confusion, uncertainty, and error" caused by the haphazard system of township naming in the United States and proposed his new method. In Whitwell's system, 1 = *a* or *b,* 2 = *c* or *d,* and so on. New York, at 40.42° N, 74.9° W, would be Otke-Notive, London would be Lafa-Tovuta. Whitwell claimed his system would allow "the situation of any place [to] be instantly known as soon as its name only, was seen or mentioned."

89. Oregon would be Oregonagerton, whose capital would be Dedekatonopolis, and California would be renamed Kaliforkovila.

90. Masquerier, *Scientific Division,* 10.

91. Masquerier, *Reformed Alphabet*; Masquerier, *Phonotypic Spelling.* The latter is reprinted in Masquerier, *Sociology.*

92. While some of the lines in Masquerier's diagrams, such as the double lines and borders,

appear to have been set using standard printer's rules, others, particularly the internal dividing lines in the diagram of the divisions of Nebrashevil, are so irregularly placed and variable that they appear to be the product of some typesetting bricolage.

93. Harley, "Maps, Knowledge, and Power," 282. The literature on empire, mapping, and gridding is too vast to cite here, but my thinking has been shaped by Scott, *Seeing like a State,* chap. 2; Mignolo, *Darker Side of the Renaissance,* chap. 6; and Brückner, *Geographic Revolution,* chap. 7.

94. As Richard A. Grounds has pointed out, from the late eighteenth century on, the widespread practice in the United States of naming settlements, counties, and states using Indigenous terms for places or peoples affirmed white conquest and a romantic mythology about the "inevitable" disappearance of Native peoples while also functioning as a technique for disavowing the theft. Grounds, "Tallahassee, Osceola," 299. See also Lorenzo Veracini's explanation of "transfer by name confiscation" in Veracini, *Settler Colonialism,* 47. For a counterperspective that argues that Indians were active contributors to the mapping of the American West, see Bernstein, *How the West Was Drawn.*

95. Masquerier, *Scientific Division,* 12.

96. On metaphorical and other transfers between the natural and social sciences, see Cohen, *Interactions.*

97. Owen, *Robert Owen's Opening Speech,* 130.

98. Masquerier published a pamphlet version of one of Owen's texts as well as his own articles repeating the Welsh reformer's theories of society. Owen, *Outline of the Rational System.* See also Lewis Masquerier, "On the Simplicity of the Structure and Operations of the Mind," *New Moral World,* July 31, 1841.

99. Bernard and Bernard, *Origins of American Sociology,* 3. See also Goodwin, *Social Science and Utopia.*

100. Bender and Marrinan, *Culture of Diagram,* 35.

101. Jameson, "Cognitive Mapping," 353. Jameson believes that realist literature met the need for cognitive mapping in an earlier stage of capitalism; thus, his writing on cognitive mapping focuses mainly on how postmodern works of literature, art, and architecture can be interpreted to perform as cognitive maps of late capitalism. See also Toscano and Kinkle, *Cartographies of the Absolute.*

102. Jameson, *Archaeologies of the Future,* 170–72.

103. The phrase "children of Enlightenment" is from Pessen, *Most Uncommon Jacksonians,* 103.

3. CULTIVATING THE LIBERAL SELF

1. This account of the Wilcox House is drawn primarily from Crawford & Stearns, "Octagon House," and notes in the "Octagon House" file at the Onondaga Historical Association.

2. "Fowler's Octagon House," *Prairie Farmer,* February 1855, 54.

3. The exact number of houses built is unknown, and estimates vary. In her introduction to a 1973 reprint of *A Home for All,* Madeline Stern puts the figure at more than 1,000, while Rebecca Lawin McCarley has found around 560 examples; see McCarley, "Orson S. Fowler." Ellen Puerzer and Robert Kline have gathered an extensive online inventory of around 1,200 round, hexagonal, and octagonal houses, schools, and other structures, some of which predate Fowler's book; see "Inventory of Older Octagon, Hexagon, and Round Houses," accessed February 8, 2023, https://bobanna.com/octagon. See also Puerzer, *Octagon House Inventory.*

4. Fowler, *Home for All* (1853), iv.

5. Fowler, *Home for All* (1853), iii.

280 *Notes to Chapter 3*

6. Walter Creese limits the octagon building wave mainly to the years between 1850 and 1857. Creese, "Fowler and the Domestic Octagon," 89.

7. For examples of books and popular articles that treat the octagon house as a historical curiosity, see Creese, "Fowler and the Domestic Octagon"; Schmidt, *Octagon Fad*; Michael de Courcy Hinds, "Domed Octagon House: Glorious Whimsy Again," *Chicago Tribune*, August 8, 1981; Dan Kelley, "A Fad from the 1800s Survives in a Dozen Connecticut Towns," *Hartford Courant*, December 28, 1980; Sarah Booth Conroy, "The Public Fancy: An Octagonal House Dreams Are Made Of," *Washington Post*, October 10, 1976.

8. The best scholarly accounts of the octagon house are Creese, "Fowler and the Domestic Octagon"; Colbert, *Measure of Perfection*, 339–68; McCarley, "Orson S. Fowler."

9. Fowler, *Home for All* (1848), 9. In the same passage, without mentioning George Henry Evans by name, Fowler followed the land reformers' example in asserting common ownership of land, based on Lockean property theory, while sidestepping the question of Native Americans' claims to that land. "Whence did government obtain its right to sell? Of the Indian. And where he his? Echo answers, Where? I would make all unimproved lands public property, till improved by actual settlers, and then only these IMPROVEMENTS saleable."

10. *Doggett's New York City Directory*, 24–25. Fowler's office was at 131 Nassau, and the National Reform Association's base was at 56 Chatham Street. In the 1840s and 1850s, this stretch of downtown Manhattan was the center of the city's publishing world, home to at least forty newspapers and magazines, as well as numerous reform organizations.

11. Fowler, *Home for All* (1848), 10.

12. On the history of phrenology in the United States, see Davies, *Phrenology*; Stern, *Heads and Headlines*.

13. Tomlinson, *Head Masters*, chap. 3.

14. Branson, "Phrenology and the Science of Race."

15. The information in this biographical sketch is drawn from Stern, *Heads and Headlines*.

16. According to John Davies, Fowler's *Love and Parentage* and *Amativeness* sold approximately forty thousand copies each, while *Matrimony, Hereditary Descent,* and *Maternity* each sold more than fifty thousand. See Davies, *Phrenology*.

17. Stern, *Heads and Headlines*, 68. The publishing firm was initially called Fowlers and Wells, but the name was later changed to Fowler and Wells.

18. On phrenology's influence in the fine arts, see Colbert, *Measure of Perfection*. On its influence in education, see Tomlinson, *Head Masters*.

19. On phrenology's appeal to the working class in England, see Cooter, *Cultural Meaning*. On its position in France, see Goldstein, *Post-revolutionary Self*.

20. Cooter, *Cultural Meaning*, 138.

21. Castiglia, *Interior States*; Castronovo, *Necro Citizenship*. See also the critique in Gura, *Man's Better Angels*, chap. 4.

22. On "going ahead" and the spirit of striving in 1840s America, see Sandage, *Born Losers*, esp. chap. 1.

23. Sokal, "Practical Phrenology."

24. Foucault, *History of Sexuality*. On nineteenth-century American discourses of sexuality, see Helen Lefkowitz Horowitz, *Rereading Sex*.

25. Fowler, *Sexual Science*, viii.

26. Connolly, *Domestic Intimacies*, 122–65.

27. Fowler, *Sexual Science*, 275.

28. Fowler's interest in sexuality can be related to the rise in the nineteenth century of what Foucault calls "biopower"—the development of techniques aimed at maximizing the life,

health, and happiness of individuals and populations. Foucault, *History of Sexuality,* 145. See also Foucault, *"Society Must Be Defended,"* 242–49.

29. Halttunen, *Confidence Men,* 129.

30. Sandage, *Born Losers,* 112–16. Sandage further points out that the Phrenological Cabinet, numerous daguerreotype studios, and the offices of Lewis Tappan's Mercantile Agency (an early credit rating company) were all located within ten blocks of one another in Lower Manhattan. On the relationship between photography and phrenology in the production of police archives, see Sekula, "Body and the Archive."

31. As a character in Nathaniel Hawthorne's *The House of the Seven Gables* (1851) argues, "While we give [daguerreotypy] credit only for depicting the merest surface, it actually brings out the secret character with a truth that no painter would ever venture upon, even could he detect it" (52).

32. Fowler et al., *Phrenology Proved,* iv.

33. Fowler and Fowler, *Illustrated Self-Instructor,* 11.

34. Goldstein, *Post-revolutionary Self,* 273.

35. In their earlier publications the Fowlers also used another version of the phrenological head with numbers and a textual legend instead of illustrations representing different faculties.

36. Harris, *Humbug,* 87–88.

37. Sysling, "Science and Self-Assessment," 273.

38. Harris, *Humbug,* 72; Cook, *Arts of Deception.*

39. Harris, *Humbug,* 57, 74.

40. Barnum, *Life of P. T. Barnum*; Harris, *Humbug*; Cook, *Arts of Deception.*

41. Fowler and Fowler, *Phrenology Proved,* v–vi.

42. Bittel, "Testing the Truth"; Bittel, "Woman, Know Thyself." Bittel takes the phrase "epistemological contests" from Katherine Pandora. For another account that emphasizes the active role taken by consumers of phrenological literature, see Michelle Gibbons's analysis of readers' letters to the *American Phrenological Journal* in Gibbons, "'Voices from the People.'"

43. Quoted in "Miscellaneous Notices," *Phrenological Journal and Miscellany* 10, no. 51 (1837): 511.

44. Stern, *Heads and Headlines,* 18–19.

45. Bittel, "Testing the Truth," 370.

46. On the rise of house pattern books in the early nineteenth century, see Reiff, *Houses from Books*; Upton, "Pattern Books and Professionalism"; Wright, *Building the Dream,* chap. 5.

47. Sweeting, *Reading Houses*; Schuyler, *Apostle of Taste.*

48. Fowler, "Notes and Queries," 19.

49. Fowler, *Home for All* (1848), 38.

50. Fowler, *Home for All* (1848), 17.

51. Solan, "'Built for Health.'"

52. Fowler, *Home for All* (1848), 71.

53. Colbert links the octagon house to Fowler's millenarian vision of massive population growth in *Measure of Perfection,* 348–53.

54. Fowler, *Home for All* (1848), 61.

55. Emmons, "Intimate Circulations."

56. Greenough, "American Architecture," 62.

57. Emmons, "Intimate Circulations," 52–53.

58. Fowler, *Home for All* (1853), 87–88.

59. Fowler, *Home for All* (1848), 83–84.

282 *Notes to Chapter 3*

60. Fowler, *Home for All* (1848), 29.

61. Fowler, "Notes and Queries," 19. For an account by another reader who checked Fowler's calculations, see Barrett, *Poor Man's Home,* 45–46.

62. S. H. Mann, "Octagon Houses," *Country Gentleman*, January 7, 1858, 17. Subsequent responses appeared in the following issues, all in 1858: January 14, April 8, April 15, April 29, May 20, June 24, July 8, July 15, October 7.

63. Quoted in Heisner, "Harriet Morrison Irwin's Hexagonal House," 117.

64. Fowler, *Home for All* (1848), 46, 95–96.

65. Fowler, *Home for All* (1853), 19–20, 45. Subsequent writers referred to Fowler's invention as "gravel-concrete" or just "concrete." See Bullock, *American Cottage Builder,* 193–94; Dwyer, *Economic Cottage Builder,* 44, 99.

66. The gravel wall was not the least of Fowler's material innovations. In the revised edition of *A Home for All,* he also raised the possibility of using glass (a material "almost as cheap as dirt, and abundant everywhere") as a flooring and roofing material (149–51).

67. On Goodrich's hexagonal hotel in Milton, Wisconsin, see Titus, "First Concrete Building"; Weisiger et al., "Grout Buildings of Milton." Much lore surrounds this structure. Titus quotes Goodrich's granddaughter's claim that Goodrich turned to concrete because he wanted a building that would withstand being set on fire by Indians. Many accounts suggest that the hotel was used as part of the Underground Railroad. For more on Goodrich, see Creese, "Fowler and the Domestic Octagon," 92–93.

68. Fowler, *Home for All* (1853), 19–20.

69. Barrett, *Poor Man's Home,* 9, 50–51.

70. J. S. Thornton, "Gravel Wall—A Letter," *American Phrenological Journal,* May 1855, 109–10.

71. "An Octagon House," *The Horticulturalist and Journal of Rural Art and Rural Taste,* July 1856, 6.

72. McGill, *American Literature.*

73. Discussion of *A Home for All* appeared in the following issues of the *American Phrenological Journal*: April 1848, May 1848, June 1852, July 1852, August 1852, February 1854, April 1854, March 1855, May 1855, June 1855, August 1855, and March 1856.

74. McCarley, "Orson S. Fowler."

75. The first edition of *A Home for All* was reviewed in *Holden's Dollar Magazine,* May 1848, 307; *United States Magazine, and Democratic Review,* March 1849, 287; and the *Literary Union,* March 1850, 125–35. The second edition was reviewed or discussed in the *Christian Ambassador,* December 10, 1853; *The Circular,* December 20, 1853, 26; *Illustrated News,* October 29, 1853, 236–37; *The Plough, the Loom and the Anvill,* January 1854; *Evangelical Repository,* February 1, 1854, 483; *Christian Parlor Magazine,* January 1854; *New York Daily Tribune,* March 9, 1854, 7; *Godey's Lady's Book and Magazine,* October 1854, 336; *Country Gentleman,* December 28, 1854, 410; May 31, 1855, 352; August 21, 1856, 123; January 7, 1858, 17; *Christian Parlor Book,* 1855, 29; and *Prairie Farmer,* February 1855, 52. Articles on octagon houses that do not mention Fowler include Henry A. Page, "Design for an Octagon House," *The Horticulturalist,* May 1850, 516–18 (this article was referenced and debated in several subsequent issues); "Rural Architecture," *New England Farmer,* October 12, 1850, 340; *Genesee Farmer,* June 1851, 125; *Southern Cultivator,* May 1, 1852, 154–56; January 1856, 18; *Wool Grower and Stock Register,* March 1856, 84; and *Country Gentleman,* June 2, 1858; July 8, 1858; July 15, 1858; June 2, 1859. Note that these are partial lists.

76. Fowler, *Home for All* (1853), 115.

77. "Holden's Review," *Holden's Dollar Magazine,* May 1848, 307.

78. O.P.H., "Associative Dwelling," *The Harbinger,* November 11, 1848, 14. For another re-

Notes to Chapter 3   283

view that linked the octagon to association, see "A Home for All," *The Circular,* December 20, 1853, 26.

79. O.P.H., "Associative Dwelling," 14. The main advantages cited for the octagon were lower housing costs and shared heating, cooking, and washing facilities rather than the house's capacity to effect equity or to critique the current social system.

80. "Reform in House-Building," *Literary Union: A Journal of Progress,* March 1850, 135.

81. Emerson, "Self-Reliance" (1841), in *Essential Writings,* 147.

82. On the self-mythologization of the settler, see Veracini, *Settler Colonialism.* On Emerson and settler colonial ideology, see Dahl, *Empire of the People,* chap. 4.

83. Amos Gregory to Timothy Younglove, September 4, 1843; James Monroe Gillett to Timothy Younglove, February 14, 1842; Orson Rickey to Timothy Younglove, July 10, 1842; Henry B. Jones to Timothy Younglove, May 8, 1838; Timothy Meigs Younglove Diary, transcribed by Leonard Paul Wood, Younglove Family Papers, Steuben County Historical Society. Unfortunately, Younglove's diaries, which cover the years 1841 to 1892, are incomplete for 1859, the year he built the house.

84. Henry B. Jones to Timothy Younglove, April 27, 1837, Younglove Family Papers, Steuben County Historical Society.

85. For Younglove's record of involvement with the octagon school construction, see Timothy Meigs Younglove Diary, entries from 1843–44. On pre-Fowlerian vernacular octagons, see Creese, "Fowler and the Domestic Octagon"; Craig, "Temples of Learning."

86. Miller, "Octagon House at Hudson."

87. "Octagon House," *Hudson North Star,* June 20, 1855.

88. Thornton, "Gravel Wall."

89. Fowler, *Home for All* (1848), 8.

90. Fowler, *Home for All* (1848), 13.

91. Fowler, *Home for All* (1848), 12.

92. Fowler, *Home for All* (1848), 18.

93. Other notable examples include the Loren Andrus House in Washington, Michigan.

94. The house was designed by Madison architect Samuel H. Donnel.

95. Ivey, "Famous Octagon House"; John Richards House, Historic American Buildings Survey, HABS No. WI-135, Library of Congress. The Richards House is said to have influenced Keck & Keck's House of Tomorrow at the 1933–34 Century of Progress Exposition.

96. "An Octagon House," 6.

97. "Country Seat Architecture—Residence of O. S. Fowler," *Illustrated News,* October 29, 1853, 236. This article was reprinted in *Godey's Lady's Book,* October 1854.

98. Jacques, *The House,* 92.

99. "Fowler's Octagon House," 54.

100. Todd, *Todd's Country Homes,* 121.

101. For a different account of nineteenth-century individualism, see Howe, *Making the American Self.* Howe reads figures like Emerson and Thoreau, and the tradition of American individualism from the eighteenth through the nineteenth centuries, as consistently driving toward the ideal of a "balanced character" in which the passions are subsumed to reason. Howe's focus on the thinking of a few elite figures—mostly northern white men—leads him to ignore broader popular forms of individualism.

102. Abelove, "From Thoreau to Queer Politics," 17.

103. Mill, "On Liberty," 135.

104. On the multiple meanings and genealogy of liberalism, see Williams, *Keywords,* 130–32.

105. Williams, *Keywords,* 114–17.

284   *Notes to Chapter 4*

4. PICTURING SOCIALITY WITHOUT SOCIALISM

1. Clubb, "Vegetarians for Kanzas," 87.

2. The broadsheet, a copy of which is held in the Newberry Library in Chicago, is undated but was most likely published in May or June 1855. The April 1855 *Water-Cure Journal* article made no mention of it, but an advertisement for the broadsheet appeared in the July 1855 issue of the *American Phrenological Journal*.

3. Clubb launched two colonies, the first for vegetarians and a second for temperance followers. Seventy-eight households are listed in an 1856 prospectus titled *The Octagon Settlement Company*. Of these, sixty-four signed up for the vegetarian colony and fourteen for the temperance colony.

4. Hickman, "Vegetarian and Octagon Settlement Companies," 384.

5. Gregory, *Of Victorians and Vegetarians*; Stern, *Heads and Headlines*; Iacobbo and Iacobbo, *Vegetarian America*. A more robust treatment of the episode can be found in Shprintzen, *Vegetarian Crusade*.

6. Thomas, "Romantic Reform in America"; Gura, *Man's Better Angels*.

7. Emerson, "New England Reformers" (1844), in *Essential Writings*, 402–3, 404.

8. Castiglia, *Interior States*.

9. My use of the phrase "sociality without socialism" is inspired by Steven Stoll's description of joint-stock companies as "communalism without communism." Stoll, *Great Delusion*, 79.

10. Clubb, *Illustrated Vegetarian Almanac*, 24.

11. On the American vegetarian movement, see Shprintzen, *Vegetarian Crusade*; Nissenbaum, *Sex, Diet, and Debility*; Carson, *Cornflake Crusade*; Iacobbo and Iacobbo, *Vegetarian America*. On the history of English vegetarianism, see Gregory, *Of Victorians and Vegetarians*; Twigg, "Vegetarian Movement in England."

12. Graham, quoted in Shprintzen, *Vegetarian Crusade*, 26. On Graham, see Nissenbaum, *Sex, Diet, and Debility*.

13. Thomas, "Romantic Reform in America"; Gura, *Man's Better Angels*.

14. A few scholars have drawn on Michel Foucault's late writings on the care of the self to reinterpret vegetarianism as a form of self-practice or *askêsis* with political implications, particularly for an environmental ethics. See Tanke, "Care of the Self"; Taylor, "Foucault and the Ethics of Eating."

15. For Clubb's biography, see *History of the Philadelphia Bible-Christian Church*, 67–89; Fowler, "In the World of Endeavor"; Gregory, "Michigander, a Patriot and Gentleman"; Shprintzen, *Vegetarian Crusade*, 78.

16. *History of the Philadelphia Bible-Christian Church*, 69. Various accounts give the year of Clubb's conversion to vegetarianism as 1838 or "around 1840."

17. Greaves founded the community in 1838 with support from a wealthy patron, Sophia Chichester, but subsequently did not take an active role in its operations. By the time Clubb resided there, Greaves had passed away. Latham, *Search for a New Eden*; Gregory, *Of Victorians and Vegetarians*, 21–30.

18. Emerson, "English Reformers," 228–29. In the same essay, Emerson mocked the raft of reform literature that Bronson Alcott had mailed back from the Concordium: "Here are Educational Circulars, and Communist Apostles; Alists; Plans for Syncretic Associations, and Pestalozzian Societies, Self-supporting Institutions, Experimental Normal Schools, Hydropathic and Philosophical Associations, Health Unions and Phalansterian Gazettes, Paradises within the reach of all men, Appeals of Man to Woman, and Necessities of Internal Marriage illustrated by Phrenological Diagrams. These papers have many sins to answer for. There is an abundance of superficialness, of pedantry, of inflation, and of want of thought" (227).

Notes to Chapter 4   285

19. These ideas were articulated in a fourteen-part series of essays, "On Association," that ran in *The New Age, Concordium Gazette, and Temperance Advocate* from September 1, 1843, through October 1, 1844.

20. *Prospectus for the Establishment*, 5.

21. *Prospectus for the Establishment*, 7. The Concordium's published schedule emphasized frequent alternations of activities, with changes approximately every two hours. This may have been inspired by Charles Fourier's notion of work as a passional activity, best carried out in short periods with frequent changes. Greaves was interested in Fourierism, though he believed that it, like Owenism, was too focused on outward reform. Latham, *Search for a New Eden*, 117. Clubb gave a slightly different account of the schedule in Austin Feverel, "Personalities: The Concordists of Alcott House," *Surrey Comet*, March 31, 1906.

22. *Prospectus for the Establishment*, 7. Julia Twigg has linked vegetarianism to a new norm in nineteenth-century genteel culture and urban industrial society that valued alertness rather than strength. Twigg, "Vegetarian Movement in England."

23. Clubb, *Thirty-Nine Reasons*, n.p. Clubb also cited a physiological/health rationale: flesh contained "a considerable quantity of decaying material forming uric acid and ptomaine poisons that cannot be taken as food without rendering the person so using it liable to the most distressing diseases." He also cited the humanitarian argument: animals that were to be killed for food were "subject to the most cruel and heartless treatment" and "excruciating pain." Consumption of flesh, like the use of tobacco and alcohol, tended to "deaden the moral and intellectual faculties."

24. *Prospectus for the Establishment*, 3.

25. Emerson, "New England Reformers," 409. Emerson was probably thinking of Brook Farm, the experimental community begun by his friend George Ripley, which Emerson pointedly declined to join.

26. On the links between Owenites and the Concordium, see Gregory, *Of Victorians and Vegetarians*, 26–28.

27. On Alcott and Fruitlands, see Matteson, *Eden's Outcasts*; Francis, *Fruitlands*; Francis, *Transcendental Utopias*; Sears, *Bronson Alcott's Fruitlands*.

28. Etzler invented machines for applying wind and ocean power to increase agricultural outputs at vast scales and wrote several books, including *The Paradise within the Reach of All Men* (1833). He delivered a series of lectures at the Concordium, and the community published two of his books in 1844, including one outlining his scheme for an emigration colony in Venezuela. Latham, *Search for a New Eden*, 163. On Etzler, see Nydahl, introduction; Etzler, *Emigration to the Tropical World*.

29. Clubb was an enthusiastic devotee of Isaac Pitman's shorthand system. As a later biographical profile recounted, "The chief pursuit in which Mr. Clubb delighted was reporting in shorthand." *History of the Philadelphia Bible-Christian Church*, 72. I address orthographic reform in depth in chapter 5.

30. The Vegetarian Society was founded in 1847 by former members of the Concordium and followers of the Bible-Christian Church. The early history of the society was marked by tensions between the first group, London-based practitioners who advocated veganism, and the latter, who were based in Manchester and condoned the consumption of eggs and dairy products.

31. "Second Annual Meeting of the Vegetarian Society," *Vegetarian Advocate*, August 1, 1849, 147–48.

32. Epstein, "Radical Dining."

33. On the links between Chartism and American land reform, see Bronstein, *Land Reform*.

286   *Notes to Chapter 4*

Clubb and two siblings helped found a colony in 1845 near Colchester dedicated to vegetarianism, shorthand, and "mutual improvement." Gregory, *Of Victorians and Vegetarians*, 44.

34. See the Chartist newspaper *Northern Star and National Trades' Journal,* January 29, 1848; April 1, 1848; and April 8, 1848. In the January 29, 1848, issue, those interested in land reform are directed to Mr. H. S. Clubb at his "Phonographic Class Rooms" in Colchester.

35. On Chartism, see Thompson, *Chartists*; Bronstein, *Land Reform*.

36. Friendly societies had originated in the seventeenth and eighteenth centuries as organizations of people who joined resources for mutual benefit and aid—for example, providing forms of insurance.

37. From 1844 through 1848, the National Land Company purchased five estates. Settlers were selected by lottery. In 1848, a committee of Parliament ordered the company to be shut down.

38. Bronstein, *Land Reform,* 11–12.

39. O'Connor advocated cultivation by spade rather than plow. According to Bronstein, spade husbandry "came to be a symbol of contented poverty, and of hand labor against the encroachments of mechanical improvement." Bronstein, *Land Reform,* 48.

40. Details about the allotment project were serialized in a series of supplements to the *Vegetarian Messenger* beginning in the January 1851 issue. Clubb was reported as delivering an address on "the advantages of the allotment system to the working classes." "Cultivation of Land," *Vegetarian Messenger,* January 1851, 9.

41. "Vegetarian Intelligence," *Vegetarian Advocate,* October 1, 1849, 15.

42. The British and American vegetarian societies had many contacts. British vegetarian journals frequently referenced Graham, Bronson Alcott, and William Alcott. William Horsell, the publisher of the *Vegetarian Advocate* (to which Clubb was a contributor) was the British agent for Fowler and Wells. For more on the links between the U.S. and British land reform movements, see Bronstein, *Land Reform,* 5.

43. *History of the Philadelphia Bible-Christian Church,* 75.

44. Clubb was apparently fired from the pro-slavery *Union* because of his abolitionist sympathies. *History of the Philadelphia Bible-Christian Church,* 76.

45. Etcheson, *Bleeding Kansas.*

46. Sinha, *Slave's Cause,* chap. 14; Foner, *Free Soil, Free Labor*; Du Bois, *Black Reconstruction.*

47. Blackmar, *Kansas,* 586–87.

48. Quoted in Langsdorf, "S. C. Pomeroy," 233.

49. Jackson, *Force and Freedom,* 85.

50. Ostler, *Surviving Genocide,* 344–58; Gates, *Fifty Million Acres*; Miner and Unrau, *End of Indian Kansas.*

51. Gates, *Fifty Million Acres,* 1.

52. Ostler, *Surviving Genocide,* 355.

53. Gates, *Fifty Million Acres,* 1.

54. Reynolds, *John Brown,* 143.

55. Richardson, *Beyond the Mississippi,* 58.

56. Richardson, *Beyond the Mississippi,* 59.

57. Clubb had been interested in Kansas at least since 1854 and was apparently working on editing the *Kansas Emigration Almanac and Guide,* to be published by Fowlers and Wells in 1855. Henry Clubb to Edward E. Hale, September 22, 1854, New England Emigrant Aid Company Papers, Kansas Historical Society. Appended to this letter is a prospectus for the then-forthcoming *Kansas Emigration Almanac.* A similar prospectus appeared in *The Illustrated*

Vegetarian Almanac for 1855, which Clubb edited and which was published by Fowlers and Wells. Whether the Kansas almanac was ever published is unclear.

58. Clubb, *Illustrated Vegetarian Almanac,* 24.

59. One exception was the constitution of the Octagon Settlement Company, which listed as the third of the company's three objectives "To promote the enactment of good and righteous laws in that territory, to uphold freedom, and to oppose slavery and oppression in every form." *Octagon Settlement Company,* 11. It is striking that this goal came third, after forming a union of individuals committed to temperance and settling Kansas.

60. Clubb, *Illustrated Vegetarian Almanac,* 24.

61. Clubb, "Vegetarians for Kanzas," 87.

62. See Shprintzen, *Vegetarian Crusade,* 34, 52, chap. 4.

63. Quoted in Shprintzen, *Vegetarian Crusade,* 82.

64. *Octagon Settlement Company,* 5.

65. "The Octagon Style of Settlement," *American Phrenological Journal,* July 1855, 17.

66. William Penn's plan for Philadelphia included a similar layout for outlying rural areas, with farm lots arranged radially. There is no evidence Clubb knew of this precedent, however.

67. *Octagon Settlement Company,* 4, 5.

68. Hamer, *New Towns,* 97–98; Reps, *Forgotten Frontier,* 2–3.

69. "Octagon Style of Settlement," 17.

70. Clubb, "Vegetarians for Kanzas," 87.

71. The prospectus stated that the lots, "although varying in size, will probably be of equal value, owing to their proximity to the centre decreasing with their increase in size." *Octagon Settlement Company,* 6.

72. The 1856 prospectus stated that in each 2,560-acre village, 928 acres were to be held in common.

73. *Octagon Settlement Company,* 6, 7.

74. Shares of the American Settlement Company, for example, cost $5 each and entitled members to one city lot; members were limited to six shares. "Great Kanzas Enterprise," circular of the American Settlement Company, 1854, Kansas Historical Society. Some organizations, like the New England Emigrant Aid Company, did not sell land directly, leaving that task to affiliated local town companies. See New England Emigrant Aid Company circular, February 13, 1855, Kansas Historical Society.

75. *Octagon Settlement Company,* 6.

76. Clubb's sales pitch is recounted in Colt, *Went to Kansas,* 20.

77. Guarneri, *Utopian Alternative,* 139; Stoll, *Great Delusion,* 79.

78. *Octagon Settlement Company,* 4.

79. Colt, *Went to Kansas,* 18.

80. Colt, *Went to Kansas,* 19. A later circular for members projected that the price of land within a few years might be $25, $50, or even $100 per acre (21).

81. Richardson, *Beyond the Mississippi,* 59. Richardson reported that 25-foot-by-125-foot lots on Leavenworth's river landing were selling for $10,000 in 1857 (53).

82. *Octagon Settlement Company,* 4, 7.

83. Hamer, *New Towns,* 137.

84. Hamer, *New Towns,* 178.

85. Peck, *New Guide for Emigrants,* 114–15. Frederick Jackson Turner would later quote this passage in his 1893 speech "The Significance of the Frontier in American History," a revised version of which appeared in his 1920 collection *The Frontier in America History.*

288 *Notes to Chapter 4*

86. Hamer, *New Towns,* 98–99.

87. *Octagon Settlement Company,* 9. Although the wording of its prospectus suggested that the Octagon Settlement Company's claim was adjacent to rather than within Osage territory, there is much reason to doubt this self-serving description. Accounts from octagon colonists Miriam Colt and Watson Stewart make clear that the settlement was located on Osage-inhabited land. Stewart later recounted: "We also learned that we might have trouble as to our lands. It was unsurveyed, we knew, when making the settlement; but now it was understood that we were on Indian lands, from which we were liable to be removed at any time." Stewart, "Personal Memoirs," n.p. See also Colt, *Went to Kansas,* 53–54, 74–76, 92, 113–15.

88. See the articles in *Life Illustrated,* December 15, 1855, 52; and February 23, 1856, 133.

89. The second company was announced in the August 1855 issue of the *American Phrenological Journal.*

90. The plan was to travel from St. Louis to Batesville, Missouri (three hundred miles) by boat and then journey the remaining fifty miles from Batesville to the settlement by wagon. *Octagon Settlement Company,* 10.

91. Clubb, "Vegetarians for Kanzas," 87.

92. Clubb, "Octagon and Vegetarian Settlements," 29. A similarly glowing account was published in the *Kansas Herald of Freedom* on May 3, 1856.

93. Colt, *Went to Kansas,* 44–45, 54, 60.

94. Whether this building was octagonal is unclear. Colt referred to it consistently in her account as the "center octagon," but always in quotation marks.

95. Stewart, "Personal Memoirs," n.p. The original manuscript of Stewart's memoirs is held at the Kansas Historical Society.

96. Stewart, "Personal Memoirs," n.p.

97. See Kanter, *Commitment and Community;* Hayden, *Seven American Utopias.*

98. Stewart, Colt, and John Milton Hadley, another member of the company, all cited the Fowlers' magazines and books. Colt recalled attending a lecture by Orson Fowler in Jackson, Michigan, on December 27, 1856, following her return from Kansas: "I have long been anxious to hear Fowler, having read so many of his works." Colt, *Went to Kansas,* 202. On Hadley, see Gambone, "Kansas—a Vegetarian Utopia."

99. Colt claimed that she turned to vegetarianism following a sleigh accident, after which a course of medicinal treatment nearly destroyed the functions of her stomach. Since then, she had survived only by exercising "the greatest amount of self-denial" in her diet and eating only "the plainest and coarsest" fare. Colt, *Went to Kansas,* 243–44.

100. Colt, *Went to Kansas,* 2.

101. Stewart, "Personal Memoirs," n.p.

102. Richardson, *Beyond the Mississippi,* 58.

103. Richardson, *Beyond the Mississippi,* 59.

104. Richardson, *Beyond the Mississippi,* 141.

105. On Holmes, see Shprintzen, *Vegetarian Crusade,* 87; Gilpin, *John Brown,* 206n68. Shprintzen provides an interesting discussion of the tension between the vegetarians' pacificism and the increasing militancy of antislavery. Clubb himself would eventually join the Union effort during the Civil War as a quartermaster, but he refused to carry a weapon.

106. Jackson, *Force and Freedom,* 87. The preceding analysis draws from her interpretation as well.

107. During the 1830s, abolitionists and evangelical Christians were two of the key advocacy groups that took advantage of decreases in printing and postage costs to embark on massive

Notes to Chapter 5   289

campaigns to distribute printed propaganda. According to Radiclani Clytus, of the 1.1 million antislavery tracts and ephemera that the American Anti-Slavery Society tried to circulate from 1833 through 1835, more than half were illustrated. Clytus, "'Keep It before the People.'" On abolitionist visual culture, see also Chaney, *Fugitive Vision*; Cutter, *Illustrated Slave*; Fox-Amato, *Exposing Slavery*; Goddu, *Selling Antislavery*; Lapsansky, "Graphic Discord."

108. On the Wedgwood medallion, see Hamilton, "Hercules Subdued"; Guyatt, "Wedgwood Slave Medallion."

109. See, for example, Wood, *Blind Memory*; Clark, "'Sacred Rights of the Weak'"; Halttunen, "Humanitarianism and the Pornography of Pain."

110. Sinha, *Slave's Cause,* 4; Cutter, *Illustrated Slave.*

111. Fox-Amato, *Exposing Slavery,* 136.

112. Jackson, *Force and Freedom,* 133. As Jackson points out, the historiography on Brown has tended to reinforce his image as a singular white hero (or madman), downplaying the facts that he drew significant moral and financial support from Black abolitionists such as Harriet Tubman, was joined in the raid by five African Americans, and was himself inspired by Black leaders such as David Walker and Nat Turner.

113. See my discussion of Marshall McLuhan's distinction between cool and hot media in the Introduction.

114. Douglass, "Pictures and Progress," 166.

5. TOWARD MORE TRANSPARENT REPRESENTATION

1. In addition to the contents described here, the pamphlet contained a reprint of a previously published essay in which Warren responded to criticisms by the Christian socialist Adin Ballou.

2. Warren, *Practical Applications,* title page.

3. Warren, *True Civilization,* 116–17.

4. Born in 1836 in Bridgewater, Massachusetts, Allen (sometimes spelled "Allyn") lived a colorful life. In the 1860s, he was listed in spiritualist newspapers as a "trance and inspirational speaker," known to occasionally channel John Adams, while simultaneously publishing tracts on orthographic reform. See *Banner of Light,* March 24, 1866; December 15, 1866; February 1, 1868; March 28, 1868; October 3, 1868; *Spiritual Republic,* March 23, 1867. In 1881 he was arrested for polygamy, and by 1886 he was reported in the press to be living with four others in a "Harmonial Home, or free love institute" in a "state of semi-starvation for months past." *Galveston Weekly News,* April 14, 1881, 2; *Macon Telegraph,* July 15, 1886, 5. Another article from the same period reported that Allen had recently deserted a "communistic" colony he had led, the "Harmonial Order of Home School Commonwealth," and that the residents of Ancora were "howling for Allen's scalp and gore." *Fort Worth Daily Gazette,* July 20, 1886, 2. On the polygamy charge: sometime between 1881 and 1893, Allen seems to have married Theresa Deckner, a woman identified in the 1880 census as a boarder in Allen's household, although he was already married to a woman named Sarah.

5. "From John Mayhew," *Spiritual Republic,* February 16, 1867, 108.

6. The phrase "abolition of systems and system making" appears in Warren, *Practical Details,* 92.

7. See, for example, Masquerier's complimentary yet critical responses to Warren's ideas in "Progress of Reform and Reformers," 1; and "'The Workingman's Political Economy' and 'Equitable Commerce,'" *Young America,* May 13, 1848, 1.

8. See "Rev. James Madison Allen," *Food, Home and Garden* 2, no. 16 (1898): 52. *Food, Home*

290   *Notes to Chapter 5*

and Garden was a vegetarian journal edited by Clubb (though this profile was published twenty-five years after Allen's hexagonal plan). Allen also references the Fowlers and Clubb in his short book *Figs or Pigs?*, 13, 17, 34.

9. Although Warren never wrote publicly about spiritualism, his private letters suggest his interest in the phenomenon as early as 1853. See Josiah Warren to unknown correspondent (probably A. C. Cuddon), March 12, 1853; and the letters from Caroline Warren to Josiah Warren dated January 25, 1855; August 26, 1855; and July 20, 1856, all in Josiah Warren Papers, Labadie Collection, University of Michigan Library. The letter of July 20 contains a reference to the spiritualist medium S. C. Hewitt's "Homes of Harmony." In addition to the links mentioned in the text, Spear was a resident of Ancora in 1867–68 and apparently knew Allen. See "Convention of Friends of Progress at Blue Anchor, NJ," *Banner of Light,* March 16, 1867; Buescher, *Remarkable Life of John Murray Spear,* 262–64.

10. I borrow the term "semiotic utopianism" from Rosenfeld, *Revolution in Language.*

11. For Warren's biography, see Bailie, *Josiah Warren*; Martin, *Men against the State*; Warren, *Practical Anarchist.*

12. Josiah Warren, "Printing in Private Families," *Free Enquirer,* March 13, 1830, 157. The best source on Warren's printing innovations is Stern, "Every Man His Own Printer."

13. According to Warren's son, the continuous-sheet press was destroyed in 1840 by printers at the *South-Western Sentinel* who were concerned that the new machine, capable of producing forty to sixty copies per minute, would put them out of work. Stern, "Every Man His Own Printer," 14.

14. Josiah Warren, Improvement in Compositions for Stereotype-Plates, U.S. Patent 4,479, April 25, 1846.

15. Josiah Warren, "Universal Typography," *Indiana Statesman,* December 27, 1845.

16. Warren, "Printing in Private Families," 157.

17. Starr, *Creation of the Media,* 135.

18. Warren, "Printing in Private Families," 157.

19. *Free Enquirer,* March 3, 1832, 152, quoted in Stern, "Every Man His Own Printer," 12.

20. Warren, "Printing in Private Families," 157.

21. Bailie, *Josiah Warren,* 38.

22. Josiah Warren, in *Peaceful Revolutionist,* April 5, 1833, in *Practical Anarchist,* 123.

23. Although Owen and many Owenites supported community property in theory, such a communal structure was never fully implemented at New Harmony. See Harrison, *Quest for the New Moral World,* 75–76, 181–82. On Owen and New Harmony, see Harrison, *Quest for the New Moral World*; Bestor, *Backwoods Utopias.*

24. Josiah Warren, *Quarterly Letter* (1867), in *Practical Anarchist,* 186.

25. Warren, *Equitable Commerce* (1852), 61.

26. Warren, *Equitable Commerce* (1852), 53.

27. Warren, *Equitable Commerce* (1852), 67.

28. Mikhail Bakunin and Peter Kropotkin were the leading exponents of collectivist and communist variants of anarchism in Europe. In contrast, Pierre-Joseph Proudhon's mutualism occupied a territory between individualist and socialist anarchism and converged with Warren's views on several points. Though there is no evidence of direct influence in either direction, Proudhon's and Warren's biographies and beliefs overlap in striking ways. Both men were printers by trade who experimented with typography, dabbled in language reform, and proposed alternate banks based on direct exchanges between producers. For these reasons, Warren has sometime been called the "American Proudhon." For a general history of

anarchism, see Marshall, *Demanding the Impossible*. On the history of American individualist anarchism, see Martin, *Men against the State*; Schuster, *Native American Anarchism*.

29. Warren, *True Civilization*, 53.

30. In his autobiography, Mill wrote, "[A] remarkable American, Mr. Warren . . . had obtained a number of followers [at Modern Times] (whether it now exists I know not) which, though bearing a superficial resemblance to some of the projects of the Socialists, is diametrically opposite to them in principle, since it recognises no authority whatever over the individual, except to enforce equal freedom of development for all individualities. . . . I borrowed from the Warrenites the phrase, the sovereignty of the individual." Quoted in Sartwell, "Introduction," 44.

31. Warren, *Equitable Commerce* (1852), x.

32. On early nineteenth-century critiques of the market economy, see Wilentz, *Chants Democratic*; Thompson, *Politics of Inequality*; Blau, *Social Theories of Jacksonian Democracy*.

33. Warren, *Equitable Commerce* (1852), 42, 48.

34. On the Ricardian socialists, see King, "Utopian or Scientific?"; Harrison, *Quest for the New Moral World*.

35. Thomas Skidmore, quoted in Pessen, *Most Uncommon Jacksonians*, 119.

36. Warren, *Equitable Commerce* (1852), 46.

37. On Owen's and other mid-nineteenth-century reformers' proposals for labor notes, see Martin, *Men against the State,* chap. 1; Poovey, *Genres of the Credit Economy,* chap. 3. In early accounts of the idea of equitable exchange, Warren proposed that different kinds of labor should not be valued differently; he later modified his stance, saying that more onerous forms of labor should be valued more highly.

38. Warren designed this system to be introduced gradually. Customers at the time store at first would pay for the cost value of goods with legal tender, using labor notes only to pay the storekeeper for his time. Eventually, once the cooperative became large enough and was well established, it could operate on labor notes alone. Warren's account of the opening of the first time store is rather comical. To get it under way, he asked a friend to come and make a purchase. "The keeper was there in waiting, but he never came!" Warren asked another friend, and then a third, neither of whom showed up. "Desperate with disappointment and chagrin," he prevailed on a relation (probably his brother) to come and purchase some coffee, sugar, and paper for $1.50 plus fifteen minutes of labor. The name "time store" was apparently invented by the public (in reference to the clock measuring the merchant's time) rather than by Warren himself. Warren, *Practical Details,* 14–17.

39. In the 1880s, Peter Kropotkin accused such labor note schemes of not going far enough, since they attempted to reconcile the interests of capital and labor while leaving the system of private property ownership intact. See Kropotkin, *Revolutionary Government,* 2–3. Warren, of course, was resolutely opposed to combination of property after his experience at New Harmony.

40. Warren started Equity in Tuscarawas County, Ohio, in 1835 with six families. James Martin has called this the first anarchist community in America. See Martin, *Men against the State,* chap. 2. The village was done in by disease, probably malaria, and abandoned shortly after its founding. Warren tried again with Utopia (also known as Trialville), which he founded in 1847 in partnership with veterans of the recently dismantled Clermont phalanx, a Fourierist community outside Cincinnati. The residents of Utopia operated a time store, a labor exchange, a steam mill, and a grist mill. Warren also started a music school. At its height, in 1852, the community may have numbered nearly one hundred. For details of these colonies, see Warren, *Practical Applications*.

Notes to Chapter 5

41. On the history of Modern Times, see Wunderlich, *Low Living*; Codman, "Brief History of 'The City of Modern Times.'" On Andrews, see Stern, *Pantarch*. Andrews was an abolitionist, spiritualist, free love radical, and spelling and language reformer who translated and orchestrated the first American publication of *The Communist Manifesto* in 1871.

42. Wunderlich, *Low Living*, 32–33. Wunderlich quotes settler Henry Edger's description of the main building in Modern Times: a "square brick building, thirty-two feet each way, containing two stories and attics. The ground floor is occupied by the time store and several workshops—a smithy, carpenter's shop and printing Press. The upper part is dwellings." This and other structures in the town were reported to be poorly built.

43. Dame was a carpenter from Boston. The second floor of his octagon house was apparently used as an assembly room and was named Archimedian Hall. In 1904, the mayor of New York City visited Modern Times (by then Brentwood) and asked Dame why he had built an eight-sided house. Dame responded, "Economy of space, no space being lost in acute angles." Wunderlich, *Low Living*, 37. Both the house and the school are still standing today, although the school has been moved.

44. Warren, *Practical Applications*, 17.

45. Warren, *Practical Applications*, 17, 18, 19, 24.

46. Warren's preference for action over words anticipated the later anarchist notion of "propaganda by the deed" rather than through traditional political channels, though without the implication of violence.

47. Warren, *Practical Applications*, 45.

48. Warren's 3-to-5-acre plots were too small to sustain a family farm yet too large to produce any kind of urban density. His quasi-urban, quasi-agrarian scheme may have been influenced by Lewis Masquerier's notion of a "rural city," which I discuss in chapter 2.

49. Warren, *Equitable Commerce* (1852), 99.

50. See my discussion of the links between settler colonialism and utopianism in chapter 2 and in the Epilogue.

51. This phrase comes from Bey, *T.A.Z.*

52. Warren, *Practical Applications*, 45–46.

53. Bestor, "Patent-Office Models."

54. Warren, *Practical Applications*, 45.

55. Warren, *Practical Applications*, 16.

56. On the relationship between nineteenth-century anarchism and the critique of representation, see Cohn, *Anarchism and the Crisis of Representation*.

57. Warren, *Equitable Commerce* (1852), 52.

58. Josiah Warren, in *Peaceful Revolutionist*, February 5, 1833, in *Practical Anarchist*, 103.

59. Gustafson, *Representative Words*; Kramer, *Imagining Language in America*; Cmiel, *Democratic Eloquence*; Gustafson, *Eloquence Is Power*. See also Simpson, *Politics of American English*.

60. Madison, "Federalist No. 37," 225.

61. Quoted in Gustafson, *Representative Words*, 323.

62. "Extract from Dr. Howe's Report," 76–77.

63. Tocqueville, *Democracy in America*, 482. My thanks to Sarah Whiting for sharing this reference with me.

64. Josiah Warren, "Improvement in the Machinery of Law," *Free Enquirer*, July 17, 1830, in *Practical Anarchist*, 222–25. Warren was here expressing an attitude of disdain toward party politics typical of many Jacksonian-era radicals, who saw politicians as the puppets of the wealthy. According to Edward Pessen, "Without exception the labor leaders regarded the American political system as a hoax." Pessen, *Most Uncommon Jacksonians*, 124.

65. Warren further described the "singular coincidence of my own views" with Johnson's and claimed that he used "language with a constant regard for its principles as developed by Mr. Johnson. . . . I do not intend to enter into any argument where the language does not refer to some sensible phenomena." Josiah Warren, "Individuality," *Peaceful Revolutionist,* April 5, 1833. On Johnson, see Todd and Sonkin, *Alexander Bryan Johnson.*

66. Johnson, *Philosophy of Human Knowledge,* 191–92.

67. Johnson, *Treatise on Language,* 152. On Johnson's "hard-money" approach to language, see Agnew, "Banking on Language."

68. On the long history of the relationship between money and language, see Shell, *Money, Language, and Thought.* On the relationship between literary genres and finance in Britain, see Poovey, *Genres of the Credit Economy.*

69. Emerson, *Nature,* 38.

70. Mihm, *Nation of Counterfeiters*; Sklansky, *Sovereign of the Market*; Greenberg, *Bank Notes and Shinplasters.*

71. Sklansky, *Sovereign of the Market,* 11. For a provocative alternative interpretation that highlights the essentialism that linked monetary and racial discourses, see O'Malley, "Specie and Species."

72. David Simpson argues that Emerson's and Johnson's theories of language are fundamentally opposed. Emerson and the transcendentalists advocated a return to "things" and the natural world but ultimately ended up returning to metaphysical generalizations, whereas Johnson remained more consistently critical of the abstractions of language. See Simpson, *Politics of American English,* chap. 7.

73. Johnson, *Philosophy of Human Knowledge,* 56, 193.

74. Johnson, *Philosophy of Human Knowledge,* 124.

75. Warren, *Equitable Commerce* (1852), 67. The miniature portrait was a popular metaphor for political representation in the early republic. See Slauter, *State as a Work of Art,* chap. 3.

76. Warren, *Equitable Commerce* (1852), 68.

77. For a detailed analysis of one of Warren's notes, see Greenberg, "Josiah Warren's Labor Notes."

78. Greenberg, *Bank Notes and Shinplasters,* chap. 3. On the role of geometric lathe-engraved ornament in signifying authenticity and value in nineteenth-century banknotes, see Roberts, "Currency of Ornament."

79. Warren, *Principle of Equivalents,* 16; Warren, *Equitable Commerce* (1852), 116–17.

80. Josiah Warren, *Gazette of Equitable Commerce* 1, no. 2 (September 1842): n.p., Indiana Historical Society. (The spacing in the word "artificial" appears in the original.)

81. Rosenfeld, *Revolution in Language.* See also Knowlson, *Universal Language Schemes*; Dawson, *Locke, Language, and Early-Modern Philosophy*; Lauzon, *Signs of Light*; Eco, *Search for the Perfect Language.*

82. On the history of spelling and language reform in the United States, see Lepore, *A Is for American*; Simpson, *Politics of American English*; Kramer, *Imagining Language in America.*

83. Gitelman, *Scripts, Grooves, and Writing Machines,* chap. 1.

84. Pitman, *Stenographic Sound-Hand,* 1, 10.

85. Allen, *Natural Alphabet,* 1. Like Pitman, Allen built his system on the notion of creating a more transparent correspondence between sign and sound.

86. Warren, *Equitable Commerce* (1852), 21.

87. Warren, *Written Music Remodeled,* 9. See also Warren, *New System of Notation.*

88. Peirce, "Logic as Semiotic," 102–13, 115.

89. Warren, *Written Music Remodeled,* ii, 4.

Notes to Chapter 5

90. Warren, *Equitable Commerce* (1852), 67.

91. Mitchell, *Iconology*, 43.

92. Warren, *Practical Applications*, 33.

93. The earlier patent included several drafts executed in the typical style of nineteenth-century machine drawing: two full-figure isometric drawings, as well as partial plan and section views. For a comparative history of technical drawing in the United States, Britain, and France, see Peter Booker, *History of Engineering Drawing*. Booker notes that in nineteenth-century Britain, technical drawings were viewed on at least two or three levels: ordinary artisans saw them "more or less as pictures or true shape views," as opposed to scholars, who approached orthographic projections more theoretically. Warren was certainly in the first category.

94. Warren, *Elements of Machine Construction*, 1–2. This author, S. Edward Warren, was a professor of descriptive geometry at the Rensselaer Polytechnic Institute. On the relationship between descriptive geometry and perspective drawing at the École des Beaux-Arts, see Thomine-Berrada, "Pictorial versus Intellectual Representation."

95. Warren, *Equitable Commerce* (1852), 3.

96. Warren, *Practical Applications*, 8.

97. Warren, *Practical Details*, 67–68. Warren's analogy of society to a machine continues over two more pages.

98. Warren, *Equitable Commerce* (1852), ix.

99. Warren, *Practical Details*, 14.

6. MODELS, MACHINES, AND MANIFESTATIONS

1. Simon Crosby Hewitt, "Architecture of the Future—Designs for Homes of Harmony, Transmitted from the Spirit World," *Robert Owen's Millennial Gazette*, July 1, 1856, 3–4. See also the descriptions of the new spiritual architecture in Newton, *The Educator*, 311–15, 342–50.

2. Newton, *The Educator*, 65, 88, 349–50.

3. *Equitable Commerce*, 4. Throughout this chapter, I cite this 1855 pamphlet, published by the New England Association of Philanthropic Commercialists. Note that this work is distinct from the two earlier publications by Josiah Warren of the same title.

4. Newton, *The Educator*, iv.

5. Hardinge, *Modern American Spiritualism*, 222.

6. Estimates of the number of spiritualists in the United States in the 1850s range from a million to eleven million, which would have been more than a third of the population of the country. For an overview of the disparate estimates, see Albanese, *Republic of Mind and Spirit*, 220–21.

7. Modern, *Secularism in Antebellum America*, 248. Erhard Schüttpelz has described spiritualism as a "boundary object" between religious and secular worldviews in the mid-nineteenth century. Schüttpelz, "Trance Mediums," 72.

8. Bennett, *Enchantment of Modern Life*.

9. Morgan, *Images at Work*.

10. My formulation of these questions is influenced by Alison Winter's analysis of Victorian mesmerism in *Mesmerized*, chap. 12.

11. Braude, *Radical Spirits*, 2.

12. Albanese, *Republic of Mind and Spirit*, 6–16.

13. Evans, *Shakers*, vi. On Shaker gift drawings, see Promey, *Spiritual Spectacles*; Morin, *Heavenly Visions*.

14. Emerson, *Representative Men*. Emerson admired Swedenborg but criticized his "exces-

Notes to Chapter 6   295

sive determination to form"—his predilection toward concrete descriptions and pictures of heaven—as a vulgarization in contrast to his more abstract philosophical meditations (120).

15. On the links between Universalism and spiritualism, see Buescher, *Other Side of Salvation*; Buescher, *Remarkable Life*; Lehman, "Life of John Murray Spear," 54–59. Lehman notes that a high percentage of early editors and lecturers on Swedenborgianism and spiritualism in the United States were Universalists. Besides Spear, Hewitt, and Adin Ballou, these included Thomas Lake Harris, William Fishbough, and Samuel Brittan.

16. Ann Braude recounts how in 1842, when Samuel Morse visited the U.S. Congress to discuss the development of his telegraph, various congressmen mocked the new technology, comparing it to mesmerism. Braude, *Radical Spirits,* 4–5. On the links between spiritualism and the telegraph, see Sconce, *Haunted Media*; Peters, *Speaking into the Air*.

17. Stolow, "Salvation by Electricity," 676.

18. Davis, *Present Age,* 76.

19. Stolow, "Salvation by Electricity," 681.

20. Kaplan, *Strange Case of William Mumler*; Chéroux, *Perfect Medium*; Gunning, "Phantom Images."

21. Lause, *Free Spirits*; Braude, *Radical Spirits.*

22. Carroll, *Spiritualism in Antebellum America*; Castronovo, *Necro Citizenship.*

23. Ferguson, *Determined Spirits.*

24. Albanese, *Republic of Mind and Spirit,* 266. This paradox of spiritualist politics relates to a broader quandary in the relationship between theology and politics in early America; namely, if one believed, as most Christians did, that a superior heavenly realm existed, did this logically lead one to renounce the earthly world, with its material concerns and debates? Or did it lead one to try to remake earthly society in the image of heaven? See Morgan, *Protestants and Pictures,* 29–30. The literary scholar Carrie Hyde makes a related distinction between what she calls "Christian estrangement" and "Christian nationalism" in *Civic Longing.*

25. For Spear's biography, see Buescher, *Remarkable Life*; Lehman, "Life of John Murray Spear."

26. Lehman, "Life of John Murray Spear," 80–82. According to Lehman, the attack was not related directly to Spear's stand on slavery but was a response to a statement he made at a gathering defending freedom of speech.

27. Lehman, "Life of John Murray Spear," 88.

28. Davis was also an admirer of Spear, as evidenced by an 1851 address in which Davis praised Spear as an exemplar of reform. Quoted in Buescher, *Remarkable Life,* 67.

29. These "messages" were recorded, edited, and collected by his associates into a handful of volumes. See Hewitt, *Messages from the Superior State*; Newton, *The Educator.*

30. Newton, *The Educator,* 42.

31. On Hewitt's early activities, see Foner, "Journal of an Early Labor Organizer."

32. Buescher, *Remarkable Life,* 155.

33. Newton, *The Educator,* 300, 302–3.

34. Newton, *The Educator,* 58.

35. Newton, *The Educator,* 42.

36. Webster, *American Dictionary* (1841).

37. Newton, *The Educator,* 248. See also the description in Davis, *The Penetralia,* 227–29.

38. "Convention of Spiritualists," *New York Daily Times,* May 26, 1857, 5.

39. Newton, *The Educator,* 239.

40. High Rock Tower was a consecrated site for spiritualism, since it was the site of Spear's first communications from the spirits as well as of a famous revelation to Davis.

Notes to Chapter 6

41. Newton, *The Educator*, 240.

42. Newton, *The Educator*, 245. See also Andrew Jackson Davis's appreciative yet skeptical firsthand account, "The New Motive Power," *The Spiritual Telegraph*, June 10, 1854, 23.

43. See Hardinge, *Modern American Spiritualism*, 225; "Reply to Davis," *The New Era*, June 28, 1854, 139.

44. Newton, *The Educator*, 247.

45. Quoted in Hardinge, *Modern American Spiritualism*, 223.

46. Newton, *The Educator*, 208–9.

47. John Buescher has analyzed Spear's edits to a manuscript description of the episode at High Rock Tower and has concluded that it consisted of a sexual rite, probably entailing *coitus reservatus* and possibly involving Paschal Beverly Randolph, an African American trance medium and writer on sexual magic who was an associate of Spear's and later a founder of the Rosicrucian order in the United States. Buescher, *Remarkable Life*, 128–33. On Randolph, see Deveney, *Paschal Beverly Randolph*.

48. Newton, *The Educator*, 252.

49. Hewitt presented a model of the machine at a spiritualist convention in New York in 1857. "Convention of Spiritualists," 5.

50. "Spiritual Machine," *Scientific American*, February 3, 1855, 162. On Koons, see Everett, *Book for Skeptics*.

51. Buescher, *Remarkable Life*, 326n14.

52. Malm, *Fossil Capital*, 206, 208.

53. Davis, *The Penetralia*, 230.

54. Ord-Hume, *Perpetual Motion*.

55. Etzler, *Paradise within the Reach*. On Etzler, see Stoll, *Great Delusion*; Claeys, "Ecology and Technology"; and Henry David Thoreau's review of Etzler's book, "Paradise (to Be) Regained," *United States Magazine, and Democratic Review* 8, no. 65 (1843): 451–62.

56. Darius Davison, "Davison's New Engine and Motor," *Scientific American*, July 25, 1852, 354. For another example, see "New Motive Power," *New-York Daily Tribune*, July 27, 1846.

57. Ord-Hume, *Perpetual Motion*, chap. 8.

58. Davis, *The Penetralia*, 228.

59. See also John Lardas Modern's illuminating reading of the Electric Motor episode in the epilogue of *Secularism in Antebellum America*. Although my interpretation takes a different path, I have been influenced by Modern's general interpretation of spiritualism and by his specific argument that the machine offered Spear a way to feel, firsthand, the phenomenon of being "haunted" by technology, of existing as part of a networked society in which agency is diffuse (297–99).

60. Peters, *Speaking into the Air*, 64, 75.

61. Newton, *The Educator*, 241.

62. On the ship and the sewing machine, see Buescher, *Remarkable Life*, 142–44, 235–45.

63. On correspondence as a central feature of all esoteric religions, see Faivre, *Access to Western Esotericism*.

64. Newton, *The Educator*, 418.

65. Newton, *The Educator*, 50–51, 54.

66. Morgan, *Images at Work*, 19.

67. "Movements of Spiritualists," *New York Times*, October 14, 1858.

68. Buescher, *Remarkable Life*, 167. On Kiantone, see also Duino, "Utopian Theme with Variations."

69. Newton, *The Educator*, 135.

Notes to Chapter 6   297

70. Newton, *The Educator,* 52. On model colonies as a strategy of social reform, see Bestor, "Patent-Office Models."

71. Simon Crosby Hewitt, "The Circular City, or Home of Symmetry and Peace," *The New Era,* May 3, 1854, 106. A diagram of the circular city was apparently subsequently drawn up and published. In the May 10, 1854, issue of *The New Era,* Hewitt announced that an artist friend had volunteered to make a drawing. The July 5, 1854, issue references a diagram published "week before last." Sadly, I have been unable to locate a surviving copy.

72. Simon Crosby Hewitt, "The Circular City, Etc.," *The New Era,* July 5, 1854, 142.

73. "Convention of Spiritualists," 5.

74. Hewitt, "Architecture of the Future," 3–11. Owen, the famed socialist, had by this time converted to spiritualism.

75. Chase, "Kiantone Movement," 829. One room was apparently devoted to the shattered remains of the Electric Motor. Some structures were reported to have been built on glass rollers so that they could be rotated to maximize the sunlight reaching the interiors.

76. Hewitt, "Architecture of the Future," 4.

77. "Convention of Spiritualists," 5.

78. Alcott, *House I Live In.*

79. Fowler, *Home for All* (1853). Hewitt met Fowler while the latter was on a phrenological lecture tour. In his diary, Hewitt recorded that Fowler was sympathetic to the workingmen's cause and promised to take up "the matter of labor and its perfection" in his next lecture. Foner, "Journal of an Early Labor Organizer," 217.

80. Newton, *The Educator,* 350.

81. Davis, *The Penetralia,* 232.

82. Newton, *The Educator,* 343.

83. Baker, *Cottage Builder's Manual.*

84. Adams, *Eye of Thomas Jefferson,* 295. Whereas all of these precedents contained oval or wedge-shaped rooms within perfect geometric volumes, Hewitt's plan allowed the shapes of the rooms to be articulated in the exterior form, which would have produced a more dynamic volume.

85. Morgan, *Images at Work,* 20.

86. As discussed in chapter 1, this classical tradition influenced Thomas Jefferson's fascination with octagons.

87. Swedenborg had developed a theory of forms that posited a hierarchy of shapes, with the angular at the lowest end and the circular above that, followed by the spiral, the vortical, the celestial, and the spiritual. Emerson, *Representative Men.*

88. Chandler, *Visible Hand,* 1.

89. A few of their ideas anticipate the science of psychophysics—work on the impact of environmental and sensory stimuli and human perception that was just beginning to make its way from German laboratories to the United States. On the relationship between psychophysics and spiritualism at a slightly later period, see Fretwell, *Sensory Experiments.* On the impact of psychophysics on modern art and architecture, see Alexander, *Kinaesthetic Knowing.*

90. Newton, *The Educator,* 347.

91. Hewitt, "Architecture of the Future," 11. Hewitt also thought the public might find the oval form more acceptable than the "baldly round."

92. Newton, *The Educator,* 346–47.

93. Newton, *The Educator,* 347.

94. "Human Chemistry—What Is It?," September 24, 1858, quoted in Buescher, *Remarkable Life,* 184.

298   *Notes to Chapter 6*

95. Newton, *The Educator,* 117.

96. Noyes and Foster, *Free Love in Utopia*; Carol Faulkner, *Unfaithful.*

97. On the links between spiritualism and eugenics, see Ferguson, *Determined Spirits.*

98. The key ideas in *Equitable Commerce* were repeated in Newton, *The Educator,* 27–38. Spear and colleagues also lectured on the subject and published a prospectus for an earthly organization, the New England Association of Philanthropic Commercialists, to promote their ideas. On the history of the association, see Buescher, *Remarkable Life,* 163–64.

99. *Equitable Commerce,* 4.

100. Andrews spoke in favor of Spear's Electric Motor at the 1857 spiritualist convention.

101. In 1856, Warren's wife wrote him a letter in which she discussed the spiritualists' oval homes of harmony. Caroline Warren to Josiah Warren, July 20, 1856, Josiah Warren Papers, Labadie Collection, University of Michigan Library.

102. *Equitable Commerce,* 8–9, 26–27.

103. Newton, *The Educator,* 86.

104. *Equitable Commerce,* 11, 13, 15, 32. Spear's friend Thaddeus Sheldon was to be the Leading Mind and Orvis the "agent" or "messenger."

105. In 1848, telegraph lines had reached Chicago, a burgeoning hub of commodity exchange. Ten years later, the Chicago Board of Trade began posting telegraph messages from New York about current grain prices. Scharlott, "Communication Technology," 14; Hochfelder, *Telegraph in America,* chap. 4; Cronon, *Nature's Metropolis,* 120–22.

106. Fourier, "Angels in the Market!," 92.

107. *Equitable Commerce,* 12, 21–22, 25.

108. *Equitable Commerce,* 16, 20. Numerous other details were given, down to descriptions of the shelves for arranging goods and specifications for the steam pipes that were to pass all around the structure.

109. Quoted in Burrows, *Finest Building in America,* 87. Just a few years earlier, A. T. Stewart had built a "Marble Palace"—one of the earliest department stores on Broadway in Manhattan.

110. Hawthorne, "Hall of Fantasy."

111. Scharlott, "Communication Technology," 7.

112. Belden, *New-York,* 62.

113. Chandler, *Visible Hand,* 211.

114. Abramson, *Building the Bank of England,* 70.

115. Abramson, *Building the Bank of England,* 70. On the typology of the exchange, see also Pevsner, *History of Building Types,* 204.

116. Benjamin, "Paris, Capital of the Nineteenth Century." See also Marx's comparison of the commodity fetish to spiritualist "table-turning" in Marx, *Capital,* 163.

117. *Equitable Commerce,* 17.

118. "Equitable Commerce," *The Liberator,* September 14, 1855, 146.

119. Newton, *The Educator,* 85.

120. John Orvis, "Equitable Commerce," *The Liberator,* September 28, 1855, 154.

121. *Equitable Commerce,* 36.

122. Newton, *The Educator,* 184.

123. Morgan, *Images at Work,* 2.

124. Winter, *Mesmerized,* chap. 12.

125. Bennett, *Enchantment of Modern Life,* esp. introduction and chap. 7.

126. Newton, *The Educator,* 30–31.

127. *Equitable Commerce,* 6.

128. *Equitable Commerce,* 4, 34.

Notes to Epilogue

129. Newton, *The Educator,* viii, 54.

130. *Equitable Commerce,* 34.

131. Newton, *The Educator,* 103.

EPILOGUE

1. On post–Civil War utopias, see Roemer, *Obsolete Necessity*; Prettyman, "Gilded Age Utopias"; Walker, *Victorian Visions.* Although there was a marked shift toward larger-scale utopian visions at the end of the century, small experimental colonies continued to be attempted, including several devoted to Fourierist, socialist, and anarchist principles.

2. Ben-Joseph and Gordon, "Hexagonal Planning."

3. Howard issued a revised edition four years later with the title *Garden Cities of To-Morrow.*

4. On the links between Howard and mid-nineteenth-century American communitarianism, see Aalen, "English Origins," 41–42.

5. The best sources on Howard and the garden city are Buder, *Visionaries and Planners*; Fishman, *Urban Utopias*; Beevers, *Garden City Utopia.*

6. On Howard's use of Esperanto, see Buder, *Visionaries and Planners,* 120. For the patents, see Howard, Shorthand Machine, U.S. Patent 1,542,455, filed August 13, 1923, issued June 16, 1925; and Howard, Type Writing Machine, Patent 346,104, filed July 24, 1885, issued July 27, 1886.

7. Quoted in Buder, *Visionaries and Planners,* 218n11. On spiritualism's influence on Howard, see Emmons, "Reading What Is Written"; Buder, *Visionaries and Planners,* 8–11.

8. On the transformation of the garden city concept from a social reform to an urban design proposal, see Ward, "Garden City Introduced"; Beevers, *Garden City Utopia*; Hall, *Cities of Tomorrow.*

9. Howard, *To-morrow,* 143.

10. George himself did not support land nationalization but instead advocated a tax on land values, which would be large enough to provide a minimum income and social benefits.

11. Buder, *Visionaries and Planners,* chap. 2.

12. In the second edition of his book, Howard prominently added the words "Diagram only: Plan cannot be drawn until site selected."

13. On earlier cobweb cities produced by advocates of land nationalization in Howard's orbit, see Buder, *Visionaries and Planners,* 59, 68, 228n4.

14. Hall et al., "Introduction," 6.

15. Pemberton, *Happy Colony.*

16. Emmons, "Reading What Is Written." Emmons's argument regarding the general influence of spiritualism on Howard is convincing, but the specific influence of spiritualism on the circular plan of the garden city is slightly less conclusive, and whether Howard was familiar with Spear's diagrams is far from clear.

17. Swift, "Garden City—II," 138, 137, emphasis added.

18. Buder, *Visionaries and Planners,* 65.

19. As we saw with the group led by John Murray Spear, discussed in chapter 6, spiritualists believed that magnetic forces were polar—positive and negative, male and female—and that they must be joined and harmonized to unleash cosmic energies. These beliefs are echoed in Howard's words: "The two magnets must be made one. As man and woman by their varied gifts and faculties supplement each other, so should town and country." And again later: "Town and country *must be married,* and out of this joyous union will spring a new home, a new life, a new civilization." Howard, *To-morrow,* 10, 11.

20. Newton, *The Educator,* 182.

21. "The Ideal City Again," *Traction and Transmission* 9 (1904): 135, emphasis added.

22. Lears, *Fables of Abundance*.

23. Hall, *Cities of Tomorrow*, 93; Roemer, *Obsolete Necessity*, 161.

24. Hardy, "Garden City Campaign."

25. Buder, *Visionaries and Planners*, 78.

26. Buder, *Visionaries and Planners*, 80.

27. Engels, "Socialism"; Marx and Engels, "Manifesto of the Communist Party."

28. Jacoby, *Picture Imperfect*, chap. 4.

29. Harvey, *Justice, Nature*, 239. See also Pinder, "In Defence of Utopian Urbanism." Colin Rowe makes a similar point, though without defending utopianism. He criticizes the idea of utopia for implying a static, hermetically sealed, end condition, and condemns it as a "monstrosity" and a "flagrant sociological or political nightmare." Rowe, "Architecture of Utopia," 216.

30. As Pier Vittorio Aureli puts it, "The power of the diagram is its ability to evoke the reshaping of an entire situation with one simple gesture." Aureli, "After Diagrams," 7. See also Vidler, "Diagrams of Utopia"; Bender and Marrinan, *Culture of Diagram*.

31. Arneil, *Domestic Colonies*; Puthoff, "'To Make Discoveries.'"

32. In *To-morrow* Howard cites the ideas of Edward Gibbon Wakefield, developer of an influential theory of systematic colonization and a major figure in the establishment of New Zealand as a settler colony.

33. Veracini, *World Turned Inside Out*, 9.

34. Estes, *Our History Is the Future*, 252, 256.

SELECTED BIBLIOGRAPHY

Aalen, Frederick H. A. "English Origins." In Ward, *Garden City,* 28–51.

Abelove, Henry. "From Thoreau to Queer Politics." *Yale Journal of Criticism* 6, no. 2 (1993): 17–27.

Abramson, Daniel M. *Building the Bank of England: Money, Architecture, Society 1694–1942.* New Haven, Conn.: Yale University Press, 2005.

Ackerman, James S. *The Villa: Form and Ideology of Country Houses.* Princeton, N.J.: Princeton University Press, 1990.

Adams, William Howard. *The Eye of Thomas Jefferson.* Charlottesville, Va.: Thomas Jefferson Memorial Foundation; Columbia: University of Missouri Press, 1992.

Adams, William Howard, ed. *Jefferson and the Arts: An Extended View.* Washington, D.C.: National Gallery of Art, 1976.

Agnew, Jean-Christophe. "Banking on Language: The Currency of Alexander Bryan Johnson." In *The Culture of the Market: Historical Essays,* edited by Thomas L. Haskell and Richard F. Teichgraeber III. Cambridge: Cambridge University Press, 1996.

Ahmed, Sara. *Queer Phenomenology: Orientations, Objects, Others.* Durham, N.C.: Duke University Press, 2006.

Albanese, Catherine L. *A Republic of Mind and Spirit: A Cultural History of American Metaphysical Religion.* New Haven, Conn.: Yale University Press, 2007.

Alcott, William A. *Essay on the Construction of School-Houses.* Boston: Hilliard, Gray, Little and Wilkins, 1832.

Alcott, William A. *The House I Live in; or, Popular Illustrations of the Structure and Functions of the Human Body for the Use of Families and Schools.* London: J. W. Parker, 1841.

Alcott, William A. *Vegetable Diet Defended.* London: J. Chapman, 1844.

Alexander, Zeynep Çelik. *Kinaesthetic Knowing: Aesthetics, Epistemology, Modern Design.* Chicago: University of Chicago Press, 2017.

Allen, James Madison. *Figs or Pigs? Fruit or Brute? Shall We Eat Flesh?* Springfield, Mo.: J. M. and M. T. Allen, 1896.

Allen, James Madison. *The Natural Alphabet, for the Representation, with Types or Pen, of All Languages.* Blue Anchor, N.J.: the author, 1867.

Allen, James Madison. *Normo-graphy (Normal, or Natural Writing): Full Style, for Beginners.* Ancora, N.J.: J. M. & S. S. Allen, 1872.

Allen, James Madison. *The Pan-norm-alpha.* Ancora, N.J., 1872.

Allen, James Madison. *The Panophonic Printing Alphabet, for the Philosophical*

Representation of All Languages, Based upon an Original and Comprehensive Classification of the Elementary Sounds. Rutland, Vt.: McLean & Robbins, 1867.

Anderson, Benedict. *Imagined Communities: Reflections on the Origin and Spread of Nationalism.* London: Verso, 1983.

Anderson, Patricia. *The Printed Image and the Transformation of Popular Culture, 1790–1860.* Oxford: Oxford University Press, 1991.

Appleby, Joyce Oldham. *Liberalism and Republicanism in the Historical Imagination.* Cambridge, Mass.: Harvard University Press, 1992.

Archer, John. *Architecture and Suburbia: From English Villa to American Dream House, 1690–2000.* Minneapolis: University of Minnesota Press, 2005.

Arneil, Barbara. *Domestic Colonies: The Turn Inward to Colony.* Oxford: Oxford University Press, 2017.

Arneil, Barbara. *John Locke and America: The Defence of English Colonialism.* Oxford: Oxford University Press, 1996.

Aureli, Pier Vittorio. "After Diagrams." *Log,* no. 6 (Fall 2005): 5–9.

Aureli, Pier Vittorio. "Appropriation, Subdivision, Abstraction: A Political History of the Urban Grid." *Log,* no. 44 (Fall 2018): 139–67.

Bailie, William. *Josiah Warren, the First American Anarchist: A Sociological Study.* Boston: Small, Maynard, 1906.

Baker, Jennifer J. *Securing the Commonwealth: Debt, Speculation, and Writing in the Making of Early America.* Baltimore: Johns Hopkins University Press, 2005.

Baker, Zephaniah. *The Cottage Builder's Manual.* Worcester, Mass.: Z. Baker, 1856.

Baker, Zephaniah. *Modern House Builder, from the Log Cabin and Cottage to the Mansion.* Boston: Higgins, Bradley, & Dayton, 1857.

Banner, Stuart. *How the Indians Lost Their Land: Law and Power on the Frontier.* Cambridge, Mass.: Belknap Press, 2007.

Bannister, Turpin C. "The Architecture of the Octagon in New York State." *New York History* 26, no. 1 (1945): 43–50.

Baridon, Laurent. "The Fourierist Phalanstère: Building a New Society through Architecture?" In *The Companions to the History of Architecture,* vol. 1, *Nineteenth-Century Architecture,* edited by Martin Bressani and Christina Contandriopoulos, 365–84. Chichester: John Wiley, 2017.

Barkun, Michael. *Crucible of the Millennium: The Burned-over District of New York in the 1840s.* Syracuse, N.Y.: Syracuse University Press, 1986.

Barnum, Phineas Taylor. *The Life of P.T. Barnum.* New York: Redfield, 1855.

Barrett, George. *The Poor Man's Home, and Rich Man's Palace; or, The Application of the Gravel Wall Cement to the Purposes of Building.* Cincinnati: Applegate, 1854.

Barthes, Roland. *Sade, Fourier, Loyola.* Berkeley: University of California Press, 1989.

Bear, James A., Jr. *Old Pictures of Monticello: An Essay in Historical Iconography.* Charlottesville: University of Virginia Press, 1957.

Beckert, Sven. *Empire of Cotton: A Global History.* New York: Vintage Books, 2014.

Beecher, Catharine, and Harriet Beecher Stowe. *The American Woman's Home; or,*

Principles of Domestic Science; Being a Guide to the Formation and Maintenance of Economical, Healthful, Beautiful, and Christian Homes. New York: J. B. Ford, 1869.

Beevers, Robert. *The Garden City Utopia: A Critical Biography of Ebenezer Howard.* London: Macmillan, 1988.

Belden, E. Porter. *New-York: Past, Present, and Future: Comprising a History of the City of New-York, a Description of Its Present Condition, and an Estimate of Its Future Increase.* New York: G. P. Putnam, 1849.

Bender, John B., and Michael Marrinan. *The Culture of Diagram.* Stanford, Calif.: Stanford University Press, 2010.

Benjamin. Walter. "Paris, Capital of the Nineteenth Century." In *Walter Benjamin: Selected Writings,* vol. 3, *1935–1938,* edited by Marcus Bullock and Michael W. Jennings, 32–47. Cambridge, Mass.: Harvard University Press, 2002.

Benjamin, Walter. "The Work of Art in the Age of Its Technological Reproducibility." In *Walter Benjamin: Selected Writings,* vol. 3, *1935–1938,* edited by Marcus Bullock and Michael W. Jennings, 101–33. Cambridge, Mass.: Harvard University Press, 2002.

Ben-Joseph, Eran, and David Gordon. "Hexagonal Planning in Theory and Practice." *Journal of Urban Design* 5, no. 3 (2000): 237–65.

Bennett, Jane. *The Enchantment of Modern Life: Attachments, Crossings, and Ethics.* Princeton, N.J.: Princeton University Press, 2001.

Bergdoll, Barry. *European Architecture, 1750–1890.* Oxford: Oxford University Press, 2000.

Berkhofer, Robert F., Jr. "Jefferson, the Ordinance of 1784, and the Origins of the American Territorial System." *William and Mary Quarterly* 29, no. 2 (1972): 231–62.

Bermingham, Ann. *Landscape and Ideology: The English Rustic Tradition, 1740–1860.* Berkeley: University of California Press, 1986.

Bernard, L. L., and Jessie Bernard. *Origins of American Sociology: The Social Science Movement in the United States.* New York: Russell & Russell, 1965.

Bernstein, David. *How the West Was Drawn: Mapping, Indians, and the Construction of the Trans-Mississippi West.* Lincoln: University of Nebraska Press, 2018.

Bestor, Arthur E. *Backwoods Utopias: The Sectarian and Owenite Phases of Communitarian Socialism in America, 1663–1829.* Philadelphia: University of Pennsylvania Press, 1950.

Bestor, Arthur E. "The Evolution of the Socialist Vocabulary." *Journal of the History of Ideas* 9, no. 3 (1948): 259–302.

Bestor, Arthur E. "Patent-Office Models of the Good Society: Some Relationships between Social Reform and Westward Expansion." *American Historical Review* 63, no. 3 (1953): 505–26.

Bey, Hakim. *T.A.Z.: The Temporary Autonomous Zone.* New York: Autonomedia, 1991.

Bhandar, Brenna. *Colonial Lives of Property: Law, Land, and Racial Regimes of Ownership.* Durham, N.C.: Duke University Press, 2018.

Bigg, Charlotte. "Diagrams." In *A Companion to the History of Science,* edited by Bernard Lightman. Chichester: Wiley-Blackwell, 2016.

Bindman, David. *Ape to Apollo: Aesthetics and the Idea of Race in the 18th Century.* London: Reaktion Books, 2002.

Bittel, Carla. "Testing the Truth of Phrenology: Knowledge Experiments in Antebellum American Cultures of Science and Health." *Medical History* 63, no. 3 (July 2019): 352–74.

Bittel, Carla. "Unpacking the Phrenological Toolkit: Knowledge and Identity in Antebellum America." In *Working with Paper,* edited by Carla Bittel, Elaine Leong, and Christine von Oertzen, 91–107. Pittsburgh: University of Pittsburgh Press, 2019.

Bittel, Carla. "Woman, Know Thyself: Producing and Using Phrenological Knowledge in 19th-Century America." *Centaurus* 55, no. 2 (2013): 104–30.

Black Hawk. *Life of Ma-ka-tai-me-she-kia-kiak or Black Hawk.* Edited by J. B. Patterson. Cincinnati: J. B. Patterson, 1833.

Blackmar, Frank W. *Kansas; a Cyclopedia of State History, Embracing Events, Institutions, Industries, Counties, Cities, Towns, Prominent Persons, Etc.* Chicago: Standard Publishing, 1912.

Blau, Joseph L. "Introduction: Jacksonian Social Thought." In Blau, *Social Theories of Jacksonian Democracy,* ix–xxviii.

Blau, Joseph L., ed. *Social Theories of Jacksonian Democracy: Representative Writings of the Period 1825–1850.* Indianapolis: Bobbs-Merrill, 1954.

Bloch, Ernst. *The Principle of Hope.* 3 vols. Cambridge: MIT Press, 1986.

Blomley, Nicholas. "Law, Property, and the Geography of Violence: The Frontier, the Survey, and the Grid." *Annals of the Association of American Geographers* 93, no. 1 (2003): 121–41.

Booker, Peter Jeffrey. *A History of Engineering Drawing.* London: Chatto & Windus, 1963.

Boorstin, Daniel J. *The Americans: The Democratic Experience.* New York: Vintage Books, 1974.

Branson, Susan. "Phrenology and the Science of Race in Antebellum America." *Early American Studies* 15, no. 1 (2017): 164–93.

Braude, Ann. *Radical Spirits: Spiritualism and Women's Rights in Nineteenth-Century America.* Boston: Beacon Press, 1989.

Bray, John Francis. *Labour's Wrongs and Labour's Remedy; or, The Age of Might and the Age of Right.* Leeds: David Green, 1839.

Breton, Rob. "Ghosts in the Machina: Plotting in Chartist and Working-Class Fiction." *Victorian Studies* 47, no. 4 (2005): 557–75.

Breton, Rob. *The Oppositional Aesthetics of Chartist Fiction: Reading against the Middle-Class Novel.* London: Routledge, 2016.

Bridges, William. *Map of the City of New York and Island of Manhattan.* New York: William Bridges, 1811.

Bronstein, Jamie L. *Land Reform and Working-Class Experience in Britain and the United States, 1800–1862.* Stanford, Calif.: Stanford University Press, 1999.

Brown, C. Allan. "Thomas Jefferson's Poplar Forest: The Mathematics of an Ideal Villa." *Journal of Garden History* 10, no. 2 (1990): 117–39.

Brownlee, Peter John. *The Commerce of Vision: Optical Culture and Perception in Antebellum America.* Philadelphia: University of Pennsylvania Press, 2018.

Brownson, Orestes A. "The Laboring Classes." *Boston Quarterly Review,* 1840. Reprinted in Blau, *Social Theories of Jacksonian Democracy,* 301–19.

Bruce, Susan. "Utopian Justifications: More's 'Utopia,' Settler Colonialism, and Contemporary Ecocritical Concerns." *College Literature* 42, no. 1 (2015): 23–43.

Brückner, Martin. *The Geographic Revolution in Early America: Maps, Literacy, and National Identity.* Chapel Hill: University of North Carolina Press, 2006.

Brückner, Martin. *The Social Life of Maps in America, 1750–1860.* Williamsburg, Va.: Omohundro Institute; Chapel Hill: University of North Carolina Press, 2017.

Buck-Morss, Susan. "Aesthetics and Anaesthetics: Walter Benjamin's Artwork Essay Reconsidered." *October* 62 (1992): 3–41.

Buck-Morss, Susan. "Envisioning Capital: Political Economy on Display." *Critical Inquiry* 21, no. 2 (1995): 434–67.

Buder, Stanley. *Visionaries and Planners: The Garden City Movement and the Modern Community.* New York: Oxford University Press, 1990.

Buescher, John B. *The Other Side of Salvation: Spiritualism and the Nineteenth-Century Religious Experience.* Boston: Skinner House Books, 2004.

Buescher, John B. *The Remarkable Life of John Murray Spear: Agitator for the Spirit Land.* Notre Dame, Ind.: University of Notre Dame Press, 2006.

Bullock, John. *The American Cottage Builder.* New York: Stringer & Townsend, 1854.

Burrows, Edwin G. *The Finest Building in America: The New York Crystal Palace, 1853–1858.* New York: Oxford University Press, 2018.

Butler, Ann. "Josiah Warren: Notebook 'D.'" PhD diss., Ball State University, 1968.

Calhoun, Craig. *The Roots of Radicalism: Tradition, the Public Sphere, and Early Nineteenth-Century Social Movements.* Chicago: University of Chicago Press, 2012.

Carlyle, Thomas, and Ralph Waldo Emerson. *The Correspondence of Thomas Carlyle and Ralph Waldo Emerson 1834–1872.* 2 vols. Boston: J. R. Osgood, 1883.

Carroll, Bret E. *Spiritualism in Antebellum America.* Bloomington: Indiana University Press, 1997.

Carson, Gerald. *Cornflake Crusade.* New York: Arno Press, 1976.

Casper, Scott E., Jeffrey D. Groves, Stephen W. Nissenbaum, and Michael Winship, eds. *A History of the Book in America.* Vol. 3, *The Industrial Book, 1840–1880.* Chapel Hill: University of North Carolina Press, 2007.

Castiglia, Christopher. *Interior States: Institutional Consciousness and the Inner Life of Democracy in the Antebellum United States.* Durham, N.C.: Duke University Press, 2008.

Castoriadis, Cornelius. *The Castoriadis Reader.* Cambridge, Mass.: Blackwell, 1997.

Castoriadis, Cornelius. *The Imaginary Institution of Society.* Cambridge: MIT Press, 1987.

Castronovo, Russ. *Necro Citizenship: Death, Eroticism, and the Public Sphere in the Nineteenth-Century United States.* Durham, N.C.: Duke University Press, 2001.

Cayleff, Susan E. *Wash and Be Healed: The Water-Cure Movement and Women's Health.* Philadelphia: Temple University Press, 1987.

Chambers, S. Allen. *Poplar Forest and Thomas Jefferson.* Forest, Va.: Corporation for Jefferson's Poplar Forest, 1993.

Chandler, Alfred D. *The Visible Hand: The Managerial Revolution in American Business.* Cambridge, Mass.: Belknap Press, 1977.

Chaney, Michael A. *Fugitive Vision: Slave Image and Black Identity in Antebellum Narrative.* Bloomington: Indiana University Press, 2008.

Chase, Malcolm. *Chartism: A New History.* Manchester: Manchester University Press, 2007.

Chase, Oliver F. "The Kiantone Movement." In *The Centennial History of Chautauqua County.* Jamestown, N.Y.: Chautauqua History Company, 1904.

Cheng, Irene. "Race and Architectural Geometry: Thomas Jefferson's Octagons." *J19: The Journal of Nineteenth-Century Americanists* 3, no. 1 (Spring 2015): 121–30.

Cheng, Irene, Charles L. Davis II, and Mabel O. Wilson, eds. *Race and Modern Architecture: A Critical History from the Enlightenment to the Present.* Pittsburgh: University of Pittsburgh Press, 2020.

Chéroux, Clément, ed. *The Perfect Medium: Photography and the Occult.* New Haven, Conn.: Yale University Press, 2005.

Chrostowska, S. D., and James Ingram, eds. *Political Uses of Utopia: New Marxist, Anarchist, and Radical Democratic Perspectives.* New York: Columbia University Press, 2017.

Claeys, Gregory. "Ecology and Technology in Early Nineteenth Century American Utopianism: A Note on John Adolphus Etzler." *Science & Society* 50, no. 2 (1986): 219–25.

Claeys, Gregory. "Lewis Masquerier and the Later Development of American Owenism, 1835–1945." *Labor History* 29, no. 2 (2007): 230–40.

Clark, Christopher. *Social Change in America: From the Revolution through the Civil War.* Chicago: Ivan R. Dee, 2006.

Clark, Clifford Edward. *The American Family Home, 1800–1960.* Chapel Hill: University of North Carolina Press, 1986.

Clark, Elizabeth B. "'The Sacred Rights of the Weak': Pain, Sympathy, and the Culture of Individual Rights in Antebellum America." *Journal of American History* 82, no. 2 (1995): 463–93.

Clawson, Marion. *The Land System of the United States: An Introduction to the History and Practice of Land Use and Land Tenure.* Lincoln: University of Nebraska Press, 1968.

Clubb, Henry S., ed. *The Illustrated Vegetarian Almanac for 1855.* New York: Fowlers and Wells, 1855.

Clubb, Henry S. *The Maine Liquor Law: Its Origin, History, and Results, Including a Life of Hon. Neal Dow.* New York: published for the Maine Law Statistical Society by Fowler and Wells, 1856.

Clubb, Henry S. "Octagon and Vegetarian Settlements of Kanzas." *Life Illustrated,* May 24, 1856.

Clubb, Henry S. "Origin of the Word 'Vegetarian.'" *Vegetarian Messenger,* November 1901.

Clubb, Henry S. "Recollections of the Concordium and Alcott House." *Herald of Health* 29, no. 341 (1906): 88.

Clubb, Henry S. *Results of Prohibition in Connecticut, Being Special Returns Received from Every County as to the Effects of the Maine Liquor Law.* New York: Fowler and Wells, 1855.

Clubb, Henry S. *Thirty-Nine Reasons Why I Am a Vegetarian.* Philadelphia: Vegetarian Society of America, 1903.

Clubb, Henry S. "The Vegetarian Principle." *Vegetarian Advocate,* March 1, 1850.

Clubb, Henry S. "Vegetarians for Kanzas." *Water-Cure Journal* 19, no. 4 (April 1855).

Clytus, Radiclani. "'Keep It before the People': The Pictorialization of American Abolitionism." In *Early African American Print Culture,* edited by Lara Langer Cohen and Jordan Alexander Stein, 290–317. Philadelphia: University of Pennsylvania Press and the Library Company of Philadelphia, 2012.

Cmiel, Kenneth. *Democratic Eloquence: The Fight over Popular Speech in Nineteenth-Century America.* New York: W. Morrow, 1990.

Codman, Charles A. "A Brief History of 'The City of Modern Times' Long Island, N.Y. and a Glorification of Some of Its Saints." Circa 1905. Brentwood Public Library, Brentwood, New York.

Cohen, I. Bernard. *Interactions: Some Contacts between the Natural Sciences and the Social Sciences.* Cambridge: MIT Press, 1994.

Cohen, I. Bernard. *Science and the Founding Fathers: Science in the Political Thought of Jefferson, Franklin, Adams and Madison.* New York: W. W. Norton, 1995.

Cohen, Joanna. *Luxurious Citizens: The Politics of Consumption in Nineteenth-Century America.* Philadelphia: University of Pennsylvania Press, 2017.

Cohen, Joanna. "Promoting Pleasure as Political Economy: The Transformation of American Advertising, 1800–1850." *Winterthur Portfolio* 48, nos. 2–3 (2014): 163–90.

Cohen, Patricia Cline. *A Calculating People: The Spread of Numeracy in Early America.* Chicago: University of Chicago Press, 1982.

Cohn, Jesse S. *Anarchism and the Crisis of Representation: Hermeneutics, Aesthetics, Politics.* Selinsgrove, Pa.: Susquehanna University Press, 2006.

Colbert, Charles. *Haunted Visions: Spiritualism and American Art.* Philadelphia: University of Pennsylvania Press, 2011.

Colbert, Charles. *A Measure of Perfection: Phrenology and the Fine Arts in America.* Chapel Hill: University of North Carolina Press, 1997.

Coleman, Nathaniel. "The Problematic of Architecture and Utopia." *Utopian Studies* 25, no. 1 (2014): 1–22.

Collens, T. Wharton. *The Eden of Labor; or, The Christian Utopia.* Philadelphia: Henry Carey Baird, 1876.

Colt, Miriam Davis. *Went to Kansas: Being a Thrilling Account of an Ill-Fated Expedition* to That Fairy Land, and Its Sad Results: Together with a Sketch of the Life of the Author, and How the World Goes with Her. Watertown, N.Y.: L. Ingalls, 1862.

Colton, J. H. The Western Tourist; or, Emigrant's Guide through the States of Ohio, Michigan, Indiana, Illinois, and Missouri, and the Territories of Wisconsin and Iowa. New York: J. H. Colton, 1839.

Combe, George. The Constitution of Man Considered in Relation to External Objects. Boston: Allen and Ticknor, 1833.

Conkin, Paul Keith. Prophets of Prosperity: America's First Political Economists. Bloomington: Indiana University Press, 1980.

Connolly, Brian. Domestic Intimacies: Incest and the Liberal Subject in Nineteenth-Century America. Philadelphia: University of Pennsylvania Press, 2014.

Cook, James W. The Arts of Deception: Playing with Fraud in the Age of Barnum. Cambridge, Mass.: Harvard University Press, 2001.

Cooter, Roger. The Cultural Meaning of Popular Science: Phrenology and the Organization of Consent in Nineteenth-Century Britain. Cambridge: Cambridge University Press, 1984.

Cosgrove, Denis. "Measures of America." In Geography and Vision: Seeing, Imagining and Representing the World, 87–103. London: I. B. Tauris, 2008.

Cosgrove, Denis. Social Formation and Symbolic Landscape. Madison: University of Wisconsin Press, 1984.

Craig, Robert William. "Temples of Learning: Octagon Schoolhouses in the Delaware Valley." MA thesis, Columbia University, 1988.

Crain, Patricia. The Story of A: The Alphabetization of America from "The New England Primer" to "The Scarlet Letter." Stanford, Calif.: Stanford University Press, 2000.

Crawford & Stearns. "The Octagon House: A Report on the History and Preservation of the Wilcox Octagon House." Syracuse, 1992.

Creese, Walter. "Fowler and the Domestic Octagon." Art Bulletin 28, no. 2 (1946): 89–102.

Cronin, Deborah K. Kiantone: Chautauqua County's Mystical Valley. Bloomington, Ind.: AuthorHouse, 2006.

Cronon, William. Nature's Metropolis: Chicago and the Great West. New York: W. W. Norton, 1992.

Cross, Whitney R. The Burned-over District: The Social and Intellectual History of Enthusiastic Religion in Western New York, 1800–1850. Ithaca, N.Y.: Cornell University Press, 1950.

"The Cultivation of Land." Vegetarian Messenger, January 1851.

Curran, Kathleen. The Romanesque Revival: Religion, Politics, and Transnational Exchange. University Park: Pennsylvania State University Press, 2003.

Cutter, Martha J. The Illustrated Slave: Empathy, Graphic Narrative, and the Visual Culture of the Transatlantic Abolition Movement, 1800–1852. Athens: University of Georgia Press, 2017.

Dabakis, Melissa. Visualizing Labor in American Sculpture: Monuments, Manliness, and the Work Ethic, 1880–1935. New York: Cambridge University Press, 1999.

Dahl, Adam. *Empire of the People: Settler Colonialism and the Foundations of Modern Democratic Thought.* Lawrence: University Press of Kansas, 2018.

Dalzell, Robert F., Jr. "Constructing Independence: Monticello, Mount Vernon, and the Men Who Built Them." *Eighteenth-Century Studies* 26, no. 4 (1993): 543–80.

Daston, Lorraine, and Peter Galison. *Objectivity.* New York: Zone Books, 2010.

Davies, John. *Phrenology: Fad and Science.* New Haven, Conn.: Yale University Press, 1955.

Davis, Alexander Jackson. *Rural Residences.* New York: Alexander Jackson Davis, 1837.

Davis, Andrew Jackson. *The Penetralia: Being Harmonial Answers to Important Questions.* Boston: Bela Marsh, 1856.

Davis, Andrew Jackson. *The Present Age and Inner Life: A Sequel to "Spiritual Intercourse"; Modern Mysteries Classified and Explained.* New York: Partridge & Brittan, 1853.

Davis, David Brion. *Ante-bellum Reform.* New York: Harper & Row, 1967.

Dawson, Hannah. *Locke, Language, and Early-Modern Philosophy.* Cambridge: Cambridge University Press, 2007.

Deleuze, Gilles. *Foucault.* Translated and edited by Seán Hand. Minneapolis: University of Minnesota Press, 1988.

Denning, Michael. *Mechanic Accents: Dime Novels and Working-Class Culture in America.* 2nd ed. London: Verso, 1998.

Deveney, John P. *Paschal Beverly Randolph: A Nineteenth-Century Black American Spiritualist, Rosicrucian, and Sex Magician.* Albany: State University of New York Press, 1997.

Devyr, Thomas Ainge. *The Odd Book of the Nineteenth Century; or, "Chivalry" in Modern Days: A Personal Record of Reform—Chiefly Land Reform, for the Last Fifty Years.* New York: the author, 1882.

A Diagram, Illustrative of the Formation of the Human Character: Suggested by Mr. Owen's Development of a New View of Society. London: Wheatley and Adlard, 1824.

Dinius, Marcy J. *The Camera and the Press: American Visual and Print Culture in the Age of the Daguerreotype.* Philadelphia: University of Pennsylvania Press, 2012.

Doggett's New York City Directory. New York: John Doggett Jr., 1848.

Douglass, Frederick. "Pictures and Progress." In *Picturing Frederick Douglass: An Illustrated Biography of the Nineteenth Century's Most Photographed American,* edited by John Stauffer, Zoe Trodd, and Celeste-Marie Bernier. New York: W. W. Norton, 2015.

Downing, Andrew Jackson. *The Architecture of Country Houses.* New York: D. Appleton, 1850.

Downing, Andrew Jackson. *Cottage Residences.* New York: Wiley and Putnam, 1842.

Drucker, Johanna, and Emily McVarish. *Graphic Design History: A Critical Guide.* Upper Saddle River, N.J.: Pearson, 2008.

Du Bois, W. E. B. *Black Reconstruction: An Essay toward a History of the Part Which*

Black Folk Played in the Attempt to Reconstruct Democracy in America, 1860–1880. New York: Harcourt, Brace, 1935.

Duino, Russell. "Utopian Theme with Variations: John Murray Spear and His Kiantone Domain." *Pennsylvania History* 29, no. 2 (1962): 140–50.

Dunbar-Ortiz, Roxanne. *An Indigenous Peoples' History of the United States.* Boston: Beacon Press, 2014.

Dwyer, Charles P. *The Economic Cottage Builder; or, Cottages for Men of Small Means, Adapted to Every Locality, with Instructions for Choosing the Most Economical Materials Afforded by the Neighborhood.* Buffalo: Wanzer, McKim, 1856.

Eco, Umberto. *The Search for the Perfect Language.* Oxford: Blackwell, 1995.

Egbert, Donald Drew. *Socialism and American Art in the Light of European Utopianism, Marxism, and Anarchism.* Princeton, N.J.: Princeton University Press, 1967.

Ehrlich, Heyward. "A Walk Up Nassau Street: Poe's Literary New York in the 1840s." *Edgar Allan Poe Review* 19, no. 2 (2018): 233.

Eisinger, Chester E. "The Freehold Concept in Eighteenth-Century American Letters." *William and Mary Quarterly* 4, no. 1 (1947): 42–59.

Elkins, James. *The Domain of Images.* Ithaca, N.Y.: Cornell University Press, 1999.

Elkins, James. "What Does Peirce's Sign Theory Have to Say to Art History?" *Culture, Theory and Critique* 44, no. 1 (2003): 5–22.

Emerson, Ralph Waldo. "English Reformers." *The Dial* 3, no. 2 (October 1842): 227–41.

Emerson, Ralph Waldo. *The Essential Writings of Ralph Waldo Emerson.* Edited by Brooks Atkinson. New York: Random House, 2000.

Emerson, Ralph Waldo. *Nature.* Boston: J. Munroe, 1836.

Emerson, Ralph Waldo. *Representative Men: Seven Lectures.* Boston: Phillips, Sampson, 1850.

Emmons, Paul. "Intimate Circulations: Representing Flow in House and City." *AA Files,* no. 51 (Winter 2005): 48–57.

Emmons, Paul. "Reading What Is Written between the Lines: The Esoteric Dimension of Ebenezer Howard's *Garden Cities of To-Morrow.*" In *Architecture's Appeal: How Theory Informs Architectural Praxis,* edited by Marc J. Neveu and Negin Djavaherian, 33–46. London: Routledge, 2015.

Engels, Friedrich. "Socialism: Utopian and Scientific" (1892). In *The Marx–Engels Reader,* translated and edited by Robert C. Tucker, 683–717. New York: W. W. Norton, 1972.

Epstein, James. "Radical Dining, Toasting and Symbolic Expression in Early Nineteenth-Century Lancashire: Rituals of Solidarity." *Albion* 20, no. 2 (1988): 271–91.

Equitable Commerce: A Proposal for the Abolition of Trade, by the Substitution of Equitable Exchange, with Full Plans and Details, in a Series of Papers Communicated from the Spirit-Life. Boston: New England Association of Philanthropic Commercialists, 1855.

Estes, Nick. *Our History Is the Future: Standing Rock versus the Dakota Access Pipeline, and the Long Tradition of Indigenous Resistance.* London: Verso Books, 2019.

Etcheson, Nicole. *Bleeding Kansas: Contested Liberty in the Civil War Era.* Lawrence: University Press of Kansas, 2004.

Etzler, J. A. *Emigration to the Tropical World, for the Melioration of All Classes of People of All Nations.* Ham Common, Surrey: Concordium, 1844.

Etzler, J. A. *The Paradise within the Reach of All Men, without Labour, by Powers of Nature and Machinery: An Address to All Intelligent Men.* London: John Brooks, 1836.

Evans, Frederick William. *Shakers: Compendium of the Origin, History, Principles, Rules and Regulations, Government, and Doctrines of the United Society of Believers in Christ's Second Appearing.* New Lebanon, N.Y.: Auchampaugh Brothers, 1859.

Evans, George Henry. "To the Working Men of the United States." *The Radical,* February 1841.

Evans, Robin. "Bentham's Panopticon: An Incident in the Social History of Architecture." *Architectural Association Quarterly* 3, no. 2 (1971): 21–37.

Evans, Robin. *The Fabrication of Virtue: English Prison Architecture, 1750–1840.* Cambridge: Cambridge University Press, 1982.

Evans, Robin. *Translations from Drawing to Building.* Cambridge: MIT Press, 1997.

Everett, J. *A Book for Skeptics: Being Communications from Angels, Written with Their Own Hands: Also, Oral Communications, Spoken by Angels through a Trumpet and Written Down as They Were Delivered in the Presence of Many Witnesses; Also, a Representation and Explanation of the Celestial Spheres, as Given by the Spirits at J. Koons' Spirit Room, in Dover, Athens County, Ohio.* Boston: Osgood & Blake, 1854.

"Extract from Dr. Howe's Report on Laura Bridgeman." In *Sixteenth Annual Report of the Trustees of the Perkins Institution and Massachusetts School for the Blind.* Cambridge, Mass.: Metcalf, 1848.

Faivre, Antoine. *Access to Western Esotericism.* Albany: State University of New York Press, 1994.

Faulkner, Carol. *Unfaithful: Love, Adultery, and Marriage Reform in Nineteenth-Century America.* Philadelphia: University of Pennsylvania Press, 2019.

Ferguson, Christine. *Determined Spirits: Eugenics, Heredity and Racial Regeneration in Anglo-American Spiritualist Writing, 1848–1930.* Edinburgh: Edinburgh University Press, 2012.

Ferguson, Robert A. "'What Is Enlightenment?': Some American Answers." *American Literary History* 1, no. 2 (1989): 245–72.

Fischer, David Hackett. *Liberty and Freedom: A Visual History of America's Founding Ideas.* Oxford: Oxford University Press, 2005.

Fisher, Philip. "Democratic Social Space: Whitman, Melville, and the Promise of American Transparency." *Representations,* no. 24 (1988): 60–101.

Fishman, Robert. *Urban Utopias in the Twentieth Century: Ebenezer Howard, Frank Lloyd Wright, and Le Corbusier.* New York: Basic Books, 1977.

Fliegelman, Jay. *Declaring Independence: Jefferson, Natural Language, and the Culture of Performance.* Stanford, Calif.: Stanford University Press, 1993.

Fogarty, Robert S. *All Things New: American Communes and Utopian Movements, 1860–1914.* Chicago: University of Chicago Press, 1990.

Foner, Eric. *Free Soil, Free Labor, Free Men: The Ideology of the Republican Party before the Civil War.* New York: Oxford University Press, 1995.

Foner, Philip S. "Journal of an Early Labor Organizer." *Labor History* 10, no. 2 (1969): 205–27.

Formisano, Ronald P. "The Concept of Political Culture." *Journal of Interdisciplinary History* 31, no. 3 (2001): 393–426.

Forty, Adrian. *Words and Buildings: A Vocabulary of Modern Architecture.* New York: Thames and Hudson, 2000.

Foster, Amber. "Nancy Prince's Utopias: Reimagining the African American Utopian Tradition." *Utopian Studies* 24, no. 2 (2013): 329–48.

Foucault, Michel. *Discipline and Punish: The Birth of the Prison.* Translated by Alan Sheridan. New York: Pantheon Books, 1977.

Foucault, Michel. *The History of Sexuality.* Vol. 1. Translated by Robert Hurley. New York: Pantheon Books, 1978.

Foucault, Michel. *"Society Must Be Defended": Lectures at the Collège de France, 1975–1976.* Edited by Mauro Bertani, Alessandro Fontana, and Arnold Davidson. Translated by David Macey. New York: Picador, 2003.

Foucault, Michel. "Technologies of the Self." In *Ethics, Subjectivity, and Truth,* edited by Paul Rabinow, 223–51. New York: New Press, 1994.

Fourier, Charles. "Angels in the Market!" *The Una,* June 1855, 92.

Fowler, J. A. "In the World of Endeavor: Men and Women of Talent." *Phrenological Journal and Science of Health* 118, no. 12 (December 1905): 379–88.

Fowler, Orson S. *Home for All; or, A New, Cheap, Convenient, and Superior Mode of Building.* New York: Fowlers and Wells, 1848.

Fowler, Orson S. *A Home for All; or, The Gravel Wall and Octagon Mode of Building New, Cheap, Convenient, Superior and Adapted to Rich and Poor.* Rev. ed. New York: Fowlers and Wells, 1853.

Fowler, Orson S. *Life: Its Science, Laws, Faculties, Functions, Organs, Conditions, Philosophy, and Improvement.* Boston: O. S. Fowler, 1871.

Fowler, Orson S. *Maternity; or, The Bearing and Nursing of Children; Including Female Education and Beauty.* New York: Fowlers and Wells, 1848.

Fowler, Orson S. *Matrimony: As Taught by Phrenology and Physiology.* New York: O. S. Fowler, 1859.

Fowler, Orson S. "Notes and Queries." *American Phrenological Journal,* May 1854, 19.

Fowler, Orson S. *Sexual Science: Including Manhood, Womanhood, and Their Mutual Interrelations; Love, Its Laws, Power, Etc.* Philadelphia: National Publishing, 1870.

Fowler, Orson S., and Lorenzo N. Fowler. *The Illustrated Self-Instructor in Phrenology and Physiology.* New York: Fowler and Wells, 1857.

Fowler, Orson S., Lorenzo N. Fowler, and Samuel Fowler. *Phrenology Proved.* New York: printed for the authors by W. H. Coyler, 1837.

Fox-Amato, Matthew. *Exposing Slavery: Photography, Human Bondage, and the Birth of Modern Visual Politics in America.* New York: Oxford University Press, 2019.

Francis, Richard. *Fruitlands: The Alcott Family and Their Search for Utopia.* New Haven, Conn.: Yale University Press, 2010.

Francis, Richard. *Transcendental Utopias: Individual and Community at Brook Farm, Fruitlands, and Walden.* Ithaca, N.Y.: Cornell University Press, 1997.

Fretwell, Erica. *Sensory Experiments: Psychophysics, Race, and the Aesthetics of Feeling.* Durham, N.C.: Duke University Press Books, 2020.

Gambone, Joseph C. "Kansas—a Vegetarian Utopia: The Letters of John Milton Hadley, 1855–56." *Kansas Historical Quarterly* 38, no. 1 (2008): 65–87.

Gates, Paul Wallace. *Fifty Million Acres: Conflicts over Kansas Land Policy, 1854–1890.* Norman: University of Oklahoma Press, 1997.

Gates, Paul Wallace. *History of Public Land Law Development.* Washington, D.C.: Government Printing Office, 1968.

Gibbons, Michelle G. "'Voices from the People': Letters to the *American Phrenological Journal,* 1854–64." *Journalism History* 35, no. 2 (2009): 72–81.

Gikandi, Simon. *Slavery and the Culture of Taste.* Princeton, N.J.: Princeton University Press, 2011.

Gilmartin, Kevin. "Popular Radicalism and the Public Sphere." *Studies in Romanticism* 33, no. 4 (1994): 549–57.

Gilmartin, Kevin. *Print Politics: The Press and Radical Opposition in Early Nineteenth-Century England.* New York: Cambridge University Press, 1996.

Gilpin, R. Blakeslee. *John Brown Still Lives! America's Long Reckoning with Violence, Equality, and Change.* Chapel Hill: University of North Carolina Press, 2011.

Gitelman, Lisa. *Scripts, Grooves, and Writing Machines: Representing Technology in the Edison Era.* Stanford, Calif.: Stanford University Press, 1999.

Goddu, Teresa A. "Anti-slavery's Panoramic Perspective." *MELUS: Multi-Ethnic Literature of the United States* 39, no. 2 (2014): 12–41.

Goddu, Teresa A. "Reform." In Zboray and Zboray, *Oxford History of Popular Print Culture,* 5: 597–610.

Goddu, Teresa A. *Selling Antislavery: Abolition and Mass Media in Antebellum America.* Philadelphia: University of Pennsylvania Press, 2020.

Goldstein, Jan. *The Post-revolutionary Self: Politics and Psyche in France, 1750–1850.* Cambridge, Mass.: Harvard University Press, 2008.

Gombrich, E. H. *The Uses of Images.* London: Phaidon, 1999.

Gonzalez, Aston. *Visualizing Equality: African American Rights and Visual Culture in the Nineteenth Century.* Chapel Hill: University of North Carolina Press, 2020.

Goodrich, Carter, and Sol Davison. "The Wage-Earner in the Westward Movement I." *Political Science Quarterly* 50, no. 2 (1935): 161–85.

Goodrich, Carter, and Sol Davison. "The Wage-Earner in the Westward Movement II." *Political Science Quarterly* 51, no. 1 (1936): 61–116.

Goodwin, Barbara. *Social Science and Utopia: Nineteenth-Century Models of Social Harmony.* Atlantic Highlands, N.J.: Humanities Press, 1978.

Gordon-Reed, Annette. *The Hemingses of Monticello: An American Family.* New York: W. W. Norton, 2008.

Gourevitch, Alex. *From Slavery to the Cooperative Commonwealth: Labor and Republican Liberty in the Nineteenth Century.* New York: Cambridge University Press, 2015.

Govan, Thomas P. "Agrarian and Agrarianism: A Study in the Use and Abuse of Words." *Journal of Southern History* 30, no. 1 (1964): 35–47.

Graeber, David. *The Democracy Project: A History, a Crisis, a Movement.* New York: Spiegel & Grau, 2013.

Graham, Sylvester. *The Philosophy of Sacred History Considered in Relation to Human Aliment and the Wines of Scripture.* New York: Fowler and Wells, 1855.

Grant, Jill. "The Dark Side of the Grid: Power and Urban Design." *Planning Perspectives* 16, no. 3 (2001): 219–41.

Greenberg, Joshua R. *Advocating the Man: Masculinity, Organized Labor, and the Household in New York, 1800–1840.* New York: Columbia University Press, 2008.

Greenberg, Joshua R. *Bank Notes and Shinplasters: The Rage for Paper Money in the Early Republic.* Philadelphia: University of Pennsylvania Press, 2020.

Greenberg, Joshua R. "Josiah Warren's Labor Notes." *Commonplace* 13, no. 1 (2012). http://commonplace.online.

Greenough, Horatio. "American Architecture" (1843). In *Form and Function: Remarks on Art, Design, and Architecture,* edited by Harold A. Small. Berkeley: University of California Press, 1947.

Gregory, James. "A Michigander, a Patriot and Gentleman: H. S. Clubb, President of the American Vegetarian Society." *Voices* (Kansas Collection online magazine), Summer 2001. https://www.kancoll.org/voices.

Gregory, James. *Of Victorians and Vegetarians: The Vegetarian Movement in Nineteenth-Century Britain.* New York: Tauris Academic Studies, 2007.

Grier, Katherine C. *Culture and Comfort: Parlor Making and Middle-Class Identity, 1850–1930.* Washington, D.C.: Smithsonian Institution Press, 1997.

Griffin, Sean. "Antislavery Utopias: Communitarian Labor Reform and the Abolitionist Movement." *Journal of the Civil War Era* 8, no. 2 (2018): 243–68.

Griffin, Sean. "A Reformers' Union: Land Reform, Labor, and the Evolution of Antislavery Politics, 1790–1860." PhD diss., City University of New York, 2017.

Griswold, A. Whitney. "The Agrarian Democracy of Thomas Jefferson." *American Political Science Review* 15, no. 4 (1946): 657–81.

Groseclose, Barbara. *Nineteenth-Century American Art.* New York: Oxford University Press, 2000.

Gross, Robert A., and Mary Kelley, eds. *A History of the Book in America.* Vol. 2, *An Extensive Republic: Print, Culture, and Society in the New Nation, 1790–1840.* Chapel Hill: University of North Carolina Press, 2010.

Grounds, Richard A. "Tallahassee, Osceola, and the Hermeneutics of American Place-Names." *Journal of the American Academy of Religion* 69, no. 2 (2001): 287–322.

Guarneri, Carl. *The Utopian Alternative: Fourierism in Nineteenth-Century America.* Ithaca, N.Y.: Cornell University Press, 1991.

Gunning, Tom. "Phantom Images and Modern Manifestations: Spirit Photography,

Magic Theater, Trick Films, and Photography's Uncanny." In *Fugitive Images from Photography to Video,* edited by Patrice Petro. Bloomington: Indiana University Press, 1995.

Gura, Philip F. *Man's Better Angels: Romantic Reformers and the Coming of the Civil War.* Cambridge, Mass.: Harvard University Press, 2017.

Gustafson, Sandra M. *Eloquence Is Power: Oratory and Performance in Early America.* Williamsburg, Va.: Omohundro Institute; Chapel Hill: University of North Carolina Press, 2000.

Gustafson, Thomas. *Representative Words: Politics, Literature, and the American Language, 1776–1865.* Cambridge: Cambridge University Press, 1993.

Guyatt, Mary. "The Wedgwood Slave Medallion: Values in Eighteenth-Century Design." *Journal of Design History* 13, no. 2 (2000): 93–105.

Habermas, Jürgen. *The Structural Transformation of the Public Sphere: An Inquiry into a Category of Bourgeois Society.* Cambridge: MIT Press, 1989.

Hafertepe, Kenneth. "An Inquiry into Thomas Jefferson's Ideas of Beauty." *Journal of the Society of Architectural Historians* 59, no. 2 (2000): 216–31.

Hafertepe, Kenneth, and James F. O'Gorman, eds. *American Architects and Their Books, 1840–1915.* Amherst: University of Massachusetts Press, 2007.

Hafertepe, Kenneth, and James F. O'Gorman, eds. *American Architects and Their Books to 1848.* Amherst: University of Massachusetts Press, 2001.

Hall, Peter. *Cities of Tomorrow.* 3rd ed. Malden, Mass.: Blackwell, 2002.

Hall, Peter, Dennis Hardy, and Colin Ward. "Introduction." In *To-Morrow: A Peaceful Path to Real Reform,* by Ebenezer Howard, edited by Peter Hall, Dennis Hardy, and Colin Ward, 1–8. London: Routledge, 2003.

Halttunen, Karen. *Confidence Men and Painted Women: A Study of Middle-Class Culture in America, 1830–1870.* New Haven, Conn.: Yale University Press, 1982.

Halttunen, Karen. "Humanitarianism and the Pornography of Pain in Anglo-American Culture." *American Historical Review* 100, no. 2 (1995): 303–34.

Hamer, David. *New Towns in the New World: Images and Perceptions of the Nineteenth-Century Urban Frontier.* New York: Columbia University Press, 1990.

Hamilton, Alexander. "The Federalist No. 31." In *The Federalist Papers,* edited by Clinton Rossiter, 189–93. New York: Penguin Books, 1961.

Hamilton, Alexander. "Public Lands: Report of a Uniform System for the Disposition of the Lands, the Property of the United States." In *The Works of Alexander Hamilton,* vol. 8, edited by Henry Cabot Lodge. New York: G. P. Putnam's Sons, 1904.

Hamilton, Cynthia S. "Hercules Subdued: The Visual Rhetoric of the Kneeling Slave." *Slavery and Abolition* 34, no. 4 (2013): 631–52.

Hammond, Bray. *Banks and Politics in America, from the Revolution to the Civil War.* Princeton, N.J.: Princeton University Press, 1957.

Handlin, David P. *The American Home: Architecture and Society, 1815–1915.* Boston: Little, Brown, 1979.

Hardinge, Emma. *Modern American Spiritualism: A Twenty Years' Record of the Communion between Earth and the World of Spirits.* New York: the author, 1870.

Selected Bibliography

Hardt, Michael. "Jefferson and Democracy." *American Quarterly* 59, no. 1 (2007): 41–78.

Hardy, Dennis. "The Garden City Campaign: An Overview." In *To-Morrow: A Peaceful Path to Real Reform,* by Ebenezer Howard, edited by Peter Hall, Dennis Hardy, and Colin Ward, 187–209. London: Routledge, 2003.

Hardy, Karl. "Unsettling Hope: Contemporary Indigenous Politics, Settler-Colonialism, and Utopianism." *Spaces of Utopia: An Electronic Journal* 2, no. 1 (2012): 123–36.

Harley, J. Brian. "Maps, Knowledge, and Power." In *The Iconography of Landscape,* edited by Denis Cosgrove and Stephen Daniels, 277–312. Cambridge: Cambridge University Press, 1988.

Harris, Cheryl I. "Whiteness as Property." *Harvard Law Review* 106, no. 8 (1993): 1707–91.

Harris, Neil. *Humbug: The Art of P. T. Barnum.* Boston: Little, Brown, 1973.

Harrison, J. F. C. *Quest for the New Moral World: Robert Owen and the Owenites in Britain and America.* New York: Charles Scribner's Sons, 1969.

Hartman, Saidiya V. *Scenes of Subjection: Terror, Slavery, and Self-Making in Nineteenth-Century America.* New York: Oxford University Press, 1997.

Harvey, David. *Justice, Nature and the Geography of Difference.* Oxford: Blackwell, 1996.

Haskell, Thomas L. *Objectivity Is Not Neutrality: Explanatory Schemes in History.* Baltimore: Johns Hopkins University Press, 1998.

Hawthorne, Nathaniel. "The Hall of Fantasy" (1843). *The New Atlantis,* no. 37 (Fall 2012). https://www.thenewatlantis.com.

Hawthorne, Nathaniel. *The House of the Seven Gables.* Boston: Ticknor, Reed, and Fields, 1851.

Hayden, Dolores. *The Grand Domestic Revolution: A History of Feminist Designs for American Homes, Neighborhoods, and Cities.* Cambridge: MIT Press, 1982.

Hayden, Dolores. *Seven American Utopias: The Architecture of Communitarian Socialism, 1790–1975.* Cambridge: MIT Press, 1976.

Hazen, Craig. *The Village Enlightenment in America: Popular Religion and Science in the Nineteenth Century.* Urbana: University of Illinois Press, 2000.

Heath, Barbara J. *Hidden Lives: The Archaeology of Slave Life at Thomas Jefferson's Poplar Forest.* Charlottesville: University Press of Virginia, 1999.

Heisner, Beverly. "Harriet Morrison Irwin's Hexagonal House: An Invention to Improve Domestic Dwellings." *North Carolina Historical Review* 58, no. 2 (1981): 105–24.

Henkin, David. *City Reading: Written Words and Public Spaces in Antebellum New York.* New York: Columbia University Press, 1998.

Hermann, Janet Sharp. *The Pursuit of a Dream.* Jackson: University Press of Mississippi, 1999.

Hewitt, S. C., ed., *Messages from the Superior State, Communicated by John Murray through John M. Spear, in the Summer of 1852, Containing Important Instruction to the Inhabitants of the Earth.* Boston: Bela Marsh, 1852.

Hickman, Russell. "The Vegetarian and Octagon Settlement Companies." *Kansas Historical Quarterly* 2, no. 4 (1933): 377–85.

Higgins, Hannah B. *The Grid Book.* Cambridge: MIT Press, 2009.

Higgins, Jerome S. *Subdivisions of the Public Lands.* St. Louis: Higgins, 1887.

Hill, Charles A., and Marguerite Helmers, eds. *Defining Visual Rhetorics.* Mahwah, N.J.: Routledge, 2004.

History of the Philadelphia Bible-Christian Church for the First Century of Its Existence, from 1817 to 1917. Philadelphia: J. B. Lippincott, 1922.

Hochfelder, David. *The Telegraph in America, 1832–1920.* Baltimore: Johns Hopkins University Press, 2012.

Horowitz, Helen Lefkowitz. *Attitudes toward Sex in Antebellum America: A Brief History with Documents.* Boston: Bedford/St. Martin's, 2006.

Horowitz, Helen Lefkowitz. *Rereading Sex: Battles over Sexual Knowledge and Suppression in Nineteenth-Century America.* New York: Alfred A. Knopf, 2002.

Howard, Ebenezer. *Garden Cities of To-Morrow.* London: Swan Sonnenschein, 1902.

Howard, Ebenezer. *To-Morrow: A Peaceful Path to Real Reform.* London: Swan Sonnenschein, 1898.

Howard, Hugh. *Thomas Jefferson, Architect: The Built Legacy of Our Third President.* New York: Rizzoli, 2003.

Howe, Daniel Walker. *Making the American Self: Jonathan Edwards to Abraham Lincoln.* New York: Oxford University Press, 1997.

Howe, Daniel Walker. *What Hath God Wrought: The Transformation of America, 1815–1848.* Oxford: Oxford University Press, 2007.

Howe, John R. *Language and Political Meaning in Revolutionary America.* Amherst: University of Massachusetts Press, 2004.

Hubbard, Bill. *American Boundaries: The Nation, the States, the Rectangular Survey.* Chicago: University of Chicago Press, 2009.

Hugins, Walter. *Jacksonian Democracy and the Working Class: A Study of the New York Workingmen's Movement, 1829–1837.* Stanford, Calif.: Stanford University Press, 1960.

Huston, Reeve. *Land and Freedom: Rural Society, Popular Protest, and Party Politics in Antebellum New York.* New York: Oxford University Press, 2000.

Huston, Reeve. "Land Conflict and Land Policy in the United States, 1785–1841." In *The World of the Revolutionary American Republic: Land, Labor, and the Conflict for a Continent,* edited by Andrew Shankman, 324–45. New York: Routledge, 2014.

Hvattum, Mari, and Anne Hultzsch, eds. *The Printed and the Built: Architecture, Print Culture and Public Debate in the Nineteenth Century.* London: Bloomsbury, 2018.

Hyde, Carrie. *Civic Longing: The Speculative Origins of U.S. Citizenship.* Cambridge, Mass.: Harvard University Press, 2018.

Iacobbo, Karen, and Michael Iacobbo. *Vegetarian America: A History.* Westport, Conn.: Praeger, 2004.

Ivey, Zida C. "The Famous Octagon House at Watertown." *Wisconsin Magazine of History* 24, no. 2 (1940): 167–73.

Jackson, John Brinckerhoff. "The Order of a Landscape: Reason and Religion in Newtonian America." In *The Interpretation of Ordinary Landscapes: Geographical Essays,* edited by D. W. Meinig. New York: Oxford University Press, 1979.

Jackson, Kellie Carter. *Force and Freedom: Black Abolitionists and the Politics of Violence.* Philadelphia: University of Pennsylvania Press, 2019.

Jacoby, Russell. *The End of Utopia: Politics and Culture in an Age of Apathy.* New York: Basic Books, 1999.

Jacoby, Russell. *Picture Imperfect: Utopian Thought for an Anti-utopian Age.* New York: Columbia University Press, 2005.

Jacques, Daniel Harrison. *The House: A Pocket Manual of Rural Architecture.* New York: Fowler and Wells, 1859.

Jaffee, David. "The Village Enlightenment in New England, 1760–1820." *William and Mary Quarterly* 47, no. 3 (1990): 327–46.

Jameson, Fredric. *Archaeologies of the Future: The Desire Called Utopia and Other Science Fictions.* London: Verso, 2005.

Jameson, Fredric. "Cognitive Mapping." In *Marxism and the Interpretation of Culture,* edited by Cary Nelson. Urbana: University of Illinois Press, 1988.

Jameson, Fredric. *Postmodernism, or, The Cultural Logic of Late Capitalism.* Durham, N.C.: Duke University Press, 1991.

Jay, Martin. *Downcast Eyes: The Denigration of Vision in Twentieth-Century French Thought.* Berkeley: University of California Press, 1993.

Jefferson, Thomas. *Notes on the State of Virginia.* In *Thomas Jefferson: Writings,* 123–326.

Jefferson, Thomas. *The Papers of Thomas Jefferson.* Princeton, N.J.: Princeton University Press, 1958. http://founders.archives.gov.

Jefferson, Thomas. *Thomas Jefferson: Writings.* Edited by Merrill D. Peterson. New York: Literary Classics of the United States, 1984.

Johnson, Alexander B. *The Philosophy of Human Knowledge; or, A Treatise on Language: A Course of Lectures Delivered at the Utica Lyceum.* New York: G. & C. Carvill, 1828.

Johnson, Alexander B. *A Treatise on Language; or, The Relation Which Words Bear to Things, in Four Parts.* New York: Harper & Brothers, 1836.

Johnson, Hildegard Binder. *Order upon the Land: The U.S. Rectangular Land Survey and the Upper Mississippi Country.* New York: Oxford University Press, 1976.

Johnson, Nan. *Nineteenth-Century Rhetoric in North America.* Carbondale: Southern Illinois University Press, 1991.

Johnson, Walter. *River of Dark Dreams.* Cambridge, Mass.: Harvard University Press, 2013.

Johnson, Walter R. "On the Utility of Visible Illustrations." *American Annals of Education* 3, no. 3 (1833): 67–85.

Johnston, Norman Bruce. *Forms of Constraint: A History of Prison Architecture.* Urbana: University of Illinois Press, 2000.

Johnston, Norman J. *Cities in the Round.* Seattle: University of Washington Press, 1983.

Jones, Buford. "'The Hall of Fantasy' and the Early Hawthorne-Thoreau Relationship." *PMLA* 83, no. 5 (1968): 1429–38.

Jordan, Winthrop D. *White over Black: American Attitudes towards the Negro, 1550–1812.* Baltimore: Penguin Books, 1969.

Kamensky, Jane. *The Exchange Artist: A Tale of High-Flying Speculation and America's First Banking Collapse.* New York: Viking Press, 2008.

Kanter, Rosabeth Moss. *Commitment and Community: Communes and Utopias in Sociological Perspective.* Cambridge, Mass.: Harvard University Press, 1972.

Kaplan, Amy. *The Anarchy of Empire in the Making of U.S. Culture.* Cambridge, Mass.: Harvard University Press, 2005.

Kaplan, Louis. *The Strange Case of William Mumler, Spirit Photographer.* Minneapolis: University of Minnesota Press, 2008.

Kasson, John F. *Civilizing the Machine: Technology and Republican Values in America, 1776–1900.* New York: Grossman, 1976.

Kaufmann, Emil. *Architecture in the Age of Reason: Baroque and Postbaroque in England, Italy, and France.* New York: Dover, 1968.

Kaufmann, Emil. "Three Revolutionary Architects, Boullée, Ledoux, and Lequeu." *Transactions of the American Philosophical Society* 42, no. 3 (1952): 431–564.

Kazanjian, David. *The Colonizing Trick: National Culture and Imperial Citizenship in Early America.* Minneapolis: University of Minnesota Press, 2003.

Kennedy, Roger. "Jefferson and the Indians." *Winterthur Portfolio* 27, nos. 2–3 (1992): 105–21.

Kimball, Fiske. "Jefferson and the Public Buildings of Virginia: I. Williamsburg, 1770–1776." *Huntington Library Quarterly* 12, no. 2 (1949): 115–20.

Kimball, Fiske. "Jefferson's Designs for Two Kentucky Houses." *Journal of the Society of Architectural Historians* 9, no. 3 (1950): 14–16.

Kimball, Fiske. *Thomas Jefferson, Architect.* Boston: Riverside Press, 1916.

King, J. E. "Utopian or Scientific? A Reconsideration of the Ricardian Socialists." *History of Political Economy* 15, no. 3 (1983): 345–73.

Kirkbride, Thomas Story. *On the Construction, Organization, and General Arrangements of Hospitals for the Insane.* Philadelphia: Lindsay & Blakiston, 1854.

Knowlson, James. *Universal Language Schemes in England and France, 1600–1800.* Toronto: University of Toronto Press, 1975.

Kolmerten, Carol. *Women in Utopia: The Ideology of Gender in the American Owenite Communities.* Syracuse, N.Y.: Syracuse University Press, 1998.

Kramer, Michael P. *Imagining Language in America: From the Revolution to the Civil War.* Princeton, N.J.: Princeton University Press, 1992.

Kropotkin, Peter. *Revolutionary Government.* London: Freedom Press, 1923.

Kumar, Krishan. *Utopia and Anti-utopia in Modern Times.* Oxford: Blackwell, 1987.

LaCroix, Alison L. "The Labor Theory of Empire." *Commonplace* 12, no. 3 (2012). http://commonplace.online.

Lancaster, Clay. "Jefferson's Architectural Indebtedness to Robert Morris." *Journal of the Society of Architectural Historians* 10, no. 1 (1951): 3–10.

Lancaster, Clay. "Some Octagonal Forms in Southern Architecture." *Art Bulletin* 28, no. 2 (1946): 103–11.

Landy, Joshua, and Michael T. Saler, eds. *The Re-enchantment of the World: Secular Magic in a Rational Age.* Stanford, Calif.: Stanford University Press, 2009.

Langsdorf, Edgar. "S. C. Pomeroy and the New England Emigrant Aid Company, 1854–1858." *Kansas Historical Quarterly* 7, no. 2 (1938): 227–45.

Lapsansky, Phillip. "Graphic Discord: Abolitionist and Antiabolitionist Images." In *The Abolitionist Sisterhood,* edited by Jean Fagan Yellin and John C. Van Horne, 201–30. Ithaca, N.Y.: Cornell University Press, 1994.

Larson, John Lauritz. *The Market Revolution in America: Liberty, Ambition, and the Eclipse of the Common Good.* Cambridge: Cambridge University Press, 2009.

Latham, J. E. M. *Search for a New Eden: James Pierrepont Greaves (1777–1842), the Sacred Socialist and His Followers.* Madison, N.J.: Fairleigh Dickinson University Press, 1999.

Latour, Bruno. "Visualization and Cognition: Thinking with Eyes and Hands." In *Knowledge and Society: Studies in the Sociology of Culture Past and Present,* vol. 6, edited by H. Kuklick, 1–40. Greenwich, Conn.: JAI Press, 1986.

Laurie, Bruce. *Artisans into Workers: Labor in Nineteenth-Century America.* Urbana: University of Illinois Press, 1997.

Lause, Mark A. *Free Spirits: Spiritualism, Republicanism, and Radicalism in the Civil War Era.* Urbana: University of Illinois Press, 2016.

Lause, Mark A. *Young America: Land, Labor, and the Republican Community.* Urbana: University of Illinois Press, 2005.

Lauzon, Matthew. *Signs of Light: French and British Theories of Linguistic Communication, 1648–1789.* Ithaca, N.Y.: Cornell University Press, 2010.

Lears, Jackson. *Fables of Abundance: A Cultural History of Advertising in America.* New York: Basic Books, 1994.

Lehman, Neil B. "The Life of John Murray Spear: Spiritualism and Reform in Antebellum America." PhD diss., Ohio State University, 1973.

Leonard, Thomas C. *The Power of the Press: The Birth of American Political Reporting.* New York: Oxford University Press, 1986.

Lepore, Jill. *A Is for American: Letters and Other Characters in the Newly United States.* New York: Alfred A. Knopf, 2002.

Levine, Caroline. *Forms: Whole, Rhythm, Hierarchy, Network.* Princeton, N.J.: Princeton University Press, 2017.

Levine, Lawrence W. *Highbrow/Lowbrow: The Emergence of Cultural Hierarchy in America.* Cambridge, Mass.: Harvard University Press, 1988.

Levitas, Ruth. *The Concept of Utopia.* Syracuse, N.Y.: Syracuse University Press, 1990.

Lewis, Michael J. *City of Refuge: Separatists and Utopian Town Planning.* Princeton, N.J.: Princeton University Press, 2016.

Linklater, Andro. *Measuring America: How an Untamed Wilderness Shaped the United States and Fulfilled the Promise of Democracy.* New York: Walker, 2002.

Linton, W. J. *The History of Wood-Engraving in America.* Boston: Estes and Lauriat, 1882.

Lippert, Amy K. DeFalco. *Consuming Identities: Visual Culture in Nineteenth-Century San Francisco.* New York: Oxford University Press, 2018.

Locke, John. *Some Thoughts Concerning Education, and Of the Conduct of the Understanding.* Edited by Ruth W. Grant and Nathan Tarcov. Indianapolis: Hackett, 1996.

Locke, John. *Two Treatises of Government.* Edited by Peter Laslett. Cambridge: Cambridge University Press, 1988.

Lueder, Christoph. "Diagram Utopias: Rota and Network as Instrument and Mirror of Utopia and Agronica." *Journal of Architectural Education* 67, no. 2 (2013): 224–33.

Lukasik, Christopher J. *Discerning Characters: The Culture of Appearance in Early America.* Philadelphia: University of Pennsylvania Press, 2010.

Lynch, Kevin. *The Image of the City.* Cambridge: MIT Press, 1960.

Lynd, Staughton. *Intellectual Origins of American Radicalism.* Rev. ed. Cambridge: Cambridge University Press, 2009.

Machor, James L. *Pastoral Cities: Urban Ideals and the Symbolic Landscape of America.* Madison: University of Wisconsin Press, 1987.

Macpherson, C. B. *The Political Theory of Possessive Individualism: Hobbes to Locke.* New York: Oxford University Press, 1962.

Madison, James. "The Federalist No. 37." In *The Federalist Papers,* edited by Clinton Rossiter, 220–27. New York: Penguin, 1961.

Malm, Andreas. *Fossil Capital: The Rise of Steam Power and the Roots of Global Warming.* New York: Verso, 2016.

Mannheim, Karl. *Ideology and Utopia: An Introduction to the Sociology of Knowledge.* Translated by Louis Wirth and Edward Shils. New York: Harcourt, Brace, 1936.

Markus, Thomas A. *Buildings and Power: Freedom and Control in the Origin of Modern Building Types.* London: Routledge, 1993.

Marshall, Peter. *Demanding the Impossible: A History of Anarchism.* London: HarperCollins, 1992.

Martin, James Joseph. *Men against the State: The Expositors of Individualist Anarchism in America, 1827–1908.* New York: Libertarian Book Club, 1957.

Martin, Reinhold. "Critical of What? Toward a Utopian Realism." *Harvard Design Magazine,* no. 22 (2005): 104–9.

Martin, Reinhold. "Drawing the Color Line: Silence and Civilization from Jefferson to Mumford." In Cheng et al., *Race and Modern Architecture,* 66–71.

Martin, Reinhold. *Knowledge Worlds: Media, Materiality, and the Making of the Modern University.* New York: Columbia University Press, 2021.

Martin, Reinhold. *Utopia's Ghost: Architecture and Postmodernism, Again.* Minneapolis: University of Minnesota Press, 2010.

Marx, Karl. *Capital: A Critique of Political Economy.* Vol. 1. Translated by Ben Fowkes. New York: Penguin Books, 1990.

Marx, Karl, and Friedrich Engels. "Manifesto of the Communist Party." In *The*

Marx–Engels Reader, 2nd ed., edited by Robert C. Tucker, 469–500. New York: W. W. Norton, 1978.

Masheck, Joseph. "The Meaning of Town and Davis' Octagonal Schoolhouse Design." *Journal of the Society of Architectural Historians* 25, no. 4 (1966): 302–4.

Masquerier, Lewis. *Appendix to Sociology; or, The Scientific Reconstruction of Society, Government and Property upon the Principles of the Individuality or Separateness of Ownership* [. . .]. New York: L. Masquerier, 1884.

Masquerier, Lewis. "Geohorticultural Fantasies: A Modest Proposal for Central Park" (1858). *Cabinet,* no. 6 (Spring 2002). https://www.cabinetmagazine.org.

Masquerier, Lewis. *The Phonotypic Spelling and Reading Manual, Applying the Thorough Principle of Writing the English Language According to the Single Sound Invariably Given to Each Vowel Letter and the Single Modification of Sound Always Given to Each Consonant Letter* [. . .]. New York: the author, 1867.

Masquerier, Lewis. *The Reformed Alphabet and Orthography, Applicable to All Languages; With Hints for the Combination of All Languages into One* [. . .]. St. Louis, 1834.

Masquerier, Lewis. *A Scientific Division and Nomenclature of the Earth, and Particularly the Territory of the United States into States, Counties, Townships, Farms and Lots* [. . .]. New York, 1847.

Masquerier, Lewis. *Sociology; or, The Reconstruction of Society, Government, and Property, upon the Principles of the Equality, the Perpetuity, and the Individuality of the Private Ownership of Life, Person, Government, Homestead, and the Whole Product of Labor* [. . .]. New York: the author, 1877.

Matteson, John. *Eden's Outcasts: The Story of Louisa May Alcott and Her Father.* New York: W. W. Norton, 2007.

Matthews, Richard K. *The Radical Politics of Thomas Jefferson: A Revisionist View.* Lawrence: University Press of Kansas, 1984.

Mayo, James M. "The American Public Market." *Journal of Architectural Education* 45, no. 1 (1991): 41–57.

McCarley, Rebecca Lawin. "Orson S. Fowler and *A Home for All*: The Octagon House in the Midwest." *Perspectives in Vernacular Architecture* 12 (2005): 49–63.

McCoy, Drew R. *The Elusive Republic: Political Economy in Jeffersonian America.* Chapel Hill: University of North Carolina Press, 1980.

McCoy, Drew R. "An 'Old-Fashioned' Nationalism: Lincoln, Jefferson, and the Classical Tradition." *Journal of the Abraham Lincoln Association* 23, no. 1 (2002): 55–67.

McDonald, Travis C. "Poplar Forest: A Masterpiece Rediscovered." *Virginia Cavalcade* 42, no. 3 (1993): 112–21.

McEwan, Barbara, and Peter W. Houck. *Thomas Jefferson's Poplar Forest.* Lynchburg, Va.: Warwick House, 1987.

McGill, Meredith L. *American Literature and the Culture of Reprinting, 1834–1853.* Philadelphia: University of Pennsylvania Press, 2002.

McLaughlin, Jack. *Jefferson and Monticello: The Biography of a Builder.* New York: H. Holt, 1988.

McLuhan, Marshall. *Understanding Media: The Extensions of Man.* 1964. Reprint, London: Routledge, 2001.

Mehta, Uday Singh. *Liberalism and Empire: A Study in Nineteenth-Century British Liberal Thought.* Chicago: University of Chicago Press, 1999.

Meinig, D. W. *The Shaping of America: A Geographical Perspective on 500 Years of History.* Vol. 2, *Continental America, 1800–1867.* New Haven, Conn.: Yale University Press, 1986.

Mignolo, Walter. *The Darker Side of the Renaissance: Literacy, Territoriality, and Colonization.* Ann Arbor: University of Michigan Press, 1995.

Mihm, Stephen. *A Nation of Counterfeiters: Capitalists, Con Men, and the Making of the United States.* Cambridge, Mass.: Harvard University Press, 2007.

Mill, John Stuart. "On Liberty" (1859). In *Utilitarianism, On Liberty, Considerations on Representative Government,* 69–185. London: Everyman, 1993.

Miller, Ernest C. "Utopian Communities in Warren County, Pennsylvania." *Western Pennsylvania Historical Magazine* 49, no. 4 (1966): 301–17.

Miller, Willis H. "The Octagon House at Hudson." *Wisconsin Magazine of History* 28, no. 1 (1844): 81–86.

Miner, Craig, and William E. Unrau. *The End of Indian Kansas: A Study in Cultural Revolution, 1854–1871.* Lawrence: University Press of Kansas, 1977.

Mintz, Steven. *Moralists and Modernizers: America's Pre-Civil War Reformers.* Baltimore: Johns Hopkins University Press, 1995.

Mirzoeff, Nicholas. *The Right to Look: A Counterhistory of Visuality.* Durham, N.C.: Duke University Press, 2011.

Mitchell, W. J. T. *Iconology: Image, Text, Ideology.* Chicago: University of Chicago Press, 1986.

Modern, John Lardas. *Secularism in Antebellum America: With Reference to Ghosts, Protestant Subcultures, Machines, and Their Metaphors; Featuring Discussions of Mass Media, "Moby-Dick," Spirituality, Phrenology, Anthropology, Sing Sing State Penitentiary, and Sex with the New Motive Power.* Chicago: University of Chicago Press, 2011.

Moore, R. Laurence. *In Search of White Crows: Spiritualism, Parapsychology, and American Culture.* New York: Oxford University Press, 1977.

Morgan, David. *Images at Work: The Material Culture of Enchantment.* New York: Oxford University Press, 2018.

Morgan, David. *The Lure of Images: A History of Religion and Visual Media in America.* London: Routledge, 2007.

Morgan, David. *Protestants and Pictures: Religion, Visual Culture, and the Age of American Mass Production.* New York: Oxford University Press, 1999.

Morin, France, ed. *Heavenly Visions: Shaker Gift Drawings and Gift Songs.* New York: Drawing Center; Minneapolis: University of Minnesota Press, 2001.

Morris, Robert. *Lectures on Architecture.* London, 1734.

Morris, Robert. *Select Architecture.* 2nd ed. London: Robert Sayer, 1757.

Morrison, Tessa. *Unbuilt Utopian Cities 1460 to 1900: Reconstructing Their Architecture and Political Philosophy.* Burlington, Vt.: Ashgate, 2015.

Mumford, Lewis. *The Story of Utopias.* New York: Boni and Liveright, 1922.

Mumford, Lewis. "Utopia, the City and the Machine." *Daedalus* 94, no. 2 (1965): 271–92.

National Reform Almanac for 1849. American Antiquarian Society, Worcester, Mass.

National Reform Association. *Vote Yourself a Farm.* New York: National Reform Association, 1845.

Neef, Joseph. *Sketch of a Plan of Education.* New York: Arno Press, 1808.

Nembhard, Jessica Gordon. *Collective Courage: A History of African American Cooperative Economic Thought and Practice.* University Park: Pennsylvania State University Press, 2014.

Neve, Richard. *The City and Countrey Purchaser, and Builder's Dictionary; or, The Compleat Builder's Guide.* London: printed for J. Sprint, G. Conyers, and T. Ballard, 1703.

Newton, A. E., ed. *The Educator: Being Suggestions, Theoretical and Practical, Designed to Promote Man-Culture and Integral Reform, with a View to the Ultimate Establishment of a Divine Social State on Earth.* Boston: Office of Practical Spiritualists, 1857.

Nichols, Frederick Doveton. *Thomas Jefferson's Architectural Drawings.* 5th ed. Boston: Massachusetts Historical Society; Charlottesville: Thomas Jefferson Memorial Foundation and University Press of Virginia, 1984.

Nichols, Robert. *Theft Is Property! Dispossession and Critical Theory.* Durham, N.C.: Duke University Press, 2019.

Nissenbaum, Stephen. *Sex, Diet, and Debility in Jacksonian America: Sylvester Graham and Health Reform.* Westport, Conn.: Greenwood Press, 1980.

Nord, David Paul. *Faith in Reading: Religious Publishing and the Birth of Mass Media in America.* Oxford: Oxford University Press, 2004.

Nordhoff, Charles. *The Communistic Societies of the United States.* New York: Harper & Brothers, 1875.

Noyes, George, and Lawrence Foster, eds. *Free Love in Utopia: John Humphrey Noyes and the Origin of the Oneida Community.* Urbana: University of Illinois Press, 2001.

Noyes, John Humphrey. *History of American Socialisms.* Philadelphia: J. B. Lippincott, 1870.

Nydahl, Joel. "Introduction." In *The Collected Works of John Adolphus Etzler, 1833–1844,* edited by Joel Nydahl. Delmar, N.Y.: Scholars' Facsimiles & Reprints, 1977.

The Octagon Settlement Company, Kanzas, Containing Full Information for Inquirers. New York, 1856. Kansas Historical Society.

Ogle, Maureen. *All the Modern Conveniences: American Household Plumbing, 1840–1890.* Baltimore: Johns Hopkins University Press, 2000.

Olson, Lester C. "Benjamin Franklin's Pictorial Representations of the British Colonies in America: A Study in Rhetorical Iconology." In Olson et al., *Visual Rhetoric,* 333–56.

Olson, Lester C. *Emblems of American Community in the Revolutionary Era: A Study in Rhetorical Iconology.* Washington, D.C.: Smithsonian Institution Press, 1991.

Olson, Lester C., Cara A. Finnegan, and Diane S. Hope, eds. *Visual Rhetoric: A Reader in Communication and American Culture.* Los Angeles: Sage, 2008.

O'Malley, Michael. "Specie and Species: Race and the Money Question in Nineteenth-Century America." *American Historical Review* 99, no. 2 (1994): 369–95.

Onuf, Peter S. *Statehood and Union: A History of the Northwest Ordinance.* Bloomington: Indiana University Press, 1987.

Ord-Hume, Arthur W. J. G. *Perpetual Motion.* London: George Allen & Unwin, 1977.

Ostler, Jeffrey. *Surviving Genocide: Native Nations and the United States from the American Revolution to Bleeding Kansas.* New Haven, Conn.: Yale University Press, 2019.

O'Sullivan, John. "Introduction." *United States Magazine and Democratic Review* 1, no. 1 (October 1837). Reprinted as "The Democratic Review: An Introductory Statement of the Democratic Principle." In Blau, *Social Theories of Jacksonian Democracy,* 21–37.

Owen, Robert. *A Development of the Principles and Plans on Which to Establish Self-Supporting Home Colonies; as a Most Secure and Profitable Investment for Capital, and an Effectual Means Permanently to Remove the Causes of Ignorance, Poverty, and Crime* [. . .]. London: Home Colonization Society, 1841.

Owen, Robert. *A New View of Society; or, Essays on the Formation of the Human Character Preparatory to the Development of a Plan for Gradually Ameliorating the Condition of Mankind.* London: printed for Longman, Hurst, Rees, Orme, and Brown, 1817.

Owen, Robert. *Outline of the Rational System of Society, Founded on Demonstrable Facts Developing the Constitution and Laws of Human Nature; Being the Only Effectual Remedy for the Evils Experienced by the Population of the World.* New York: printed by L. Masquerier, 1839.

Owen, Robert. *Robert Owen's Opening Speech, and His Reply to the Rev. Alex. Campbell, in the Recent Public Discussion in Cincinnati: To Prove That the Principles of All Religions Are Erroneous, and That Their Practice Is Injurious to the Human Race.* Cincinnati: published for R. Owen, 1829.

Paden, Roger. "Marx's Critique of the Utopian Socialists." *Utopian Studies* 13, no. 2 (2002): 67–91.

Paine, Thomas. *Agrarian Justice, Opposed to Agrarian Law, and to Agrarian Monopoly.* Paris: W. Adlard, 1797.

Palladio, Andrea. *The Architecture of A. Palladio; in Four Books.* London: John Darby, 1721.

Pattison, William David. *Beginnings of the American Rectangular Land Survey System, 1784–1800.* Chicago: University of Chicago, 1964.

Peabody, Elizabeth Palmer. *Chronological History of the United States, Arranged with Plates on Bem's Principle.* New York: Sheldon, Blakeman, 1856.

Pease, William Henry, and Jane H. Pease. *Black Utopia: Negro Communal Experiments in America.* Madison: State Historical Society of Wisconsin, 1963.

Peck, J. M. *A New Guide for Emigrants to the West, Containing Sketches of Ohio, Indiana, Illinois, Missouri, Michigan, with the Territories of Wisconsin and Arkansas, and the Adjacent Parts.* Boston: Gould, Kendall & Lincoln, 1836.

Peirce, Charles S. "Logic as Semiotic: The Theory of Signs." In *Philosophical Writings of Peirce,* edited by Justus Buchler, 98–119. New York: Dover, 1955.

Pemberton, Robert. *The Happy Colony.* London: Saunders and Otley, 1854.

Pérez-Gómez, Alberto. *Architecture and the Crisis of Modern Science.* Cambridge: MIT Press, 1983.

Pessen, Edward. *Most Uncommon Jacksonians: The Radical Leaders of the Early Labor Movement.* Albany: State University of New York Press, 1967.

Pessen, Edward. *Riches, Class, and Power before the Civil War.* Lexington, Mass.: D. C. Heath, 1973.

Pessen, Edward. "Thomas Skidmore, Agrarian Reformer in the Early American Labor Movement." *New York History* 35, no. 3 (1954): 280–96.

Pestalozzi, Johann Heinrich. *Letters on Early Education Addressed to J. P. Greaves, Esq.* London, 1827.

Peters, John Durham. *Speaking into the Air: A History of the Idea of Communication.* Chicago: University of Chicago Press, 1999.

Pevsner, Nikolaus. *A History of Building Types.* Princeton, N.J.: Princeton University Press, 1976.

Pickens, Buford. "Mr. Jefferson as Revolutionary Architect." *Journal of the Society of Architectural Historians* 34, no. 4 (1975): 257–79.

Picon, Antoine. "Notes on Utopia, the City, and Architecture." *Grey Room,* no. 68 (2017): 94–105.

Pinder, David. "In Defence of Utopian Urbanism: Imagining Cities after the 'End of Utopia.'" *Geografiska Annaler* 84, no. B (2002): 229–41.

Piola, Erika. "The Rise of Early American Lithography and Antebellum Visual Culture." *Winterthur Portfolio* 48, nos. 2–3 (2014): 125–38.

Pitkin, Hanna. *The Concept of Representation.* Berkeley: University of California Press, 1967.

Pitman, Isaac. *A Manual of Phonography; or, Writing by Sound: A Natural Method of Writing by Signs That Represent the Sounds of Language, and Adapted to the English Language as a Complete System of Phonetic Shorthand.* London: Samuel Bagster, 1845.

Pitman, Isaac. *Stenographic Sound-Hand.* London: Samuel Bagster, 1837.

Pitzer, Donald E. *America's Communal Utopias.* Chapel Hill: University of North Carolina Press, 1997.

Pocock, J. G. A. *The Machiavellian Moment: Florentine Political Thought and the Atlantic Republican Tradition.* Princeton, N.J.: Princeton University Press, 1975.

Poovey, Mary. *Genres of the Credit Economy: Mediating Value in Eighteenth- and Nineteenth-Century Britain.* Chicago: University of Chicago Press, 2008.

Popper, Karl R. "Aestheticism, Perfectionism, Utopianism." In *The Open Society and Its Enemies,* 147–57. Princeton, N.J.: Princeton University Press, 2013.

Prettyman, Gib. "Gilded Age Utopias of Incorporation." *Utopian Studies* 12, no. 1 (2001): 19–40.

Promey, Sally M. *Spiritual Spectacles: Vision and Image in Mid-Nineteenth-Century Shakerism.* Bloomington: Indiana University Press, 1993.

A Prospectus for the Establishment of a Concordium; or an Industry Harmony College. London: Strange, Paternoster Row, 1841.

Puerzer, Ellen L. *The Octagon House Inventory.* N.p.: Eight-Square Publishing, 2011.

Puthoff, David. "'To Make Discoveries in Those Latitudes': Utopia and Settler Colonialism in Equality; or, A History of Lithconia." *Utopian Studies* 32, no. 1 (2021): 73–89.

Ravenhill-Johnson, Annie. *The Art and Ideology of the Trade Union Emblem.* London: Anthem Press, 2013.

Reiff, Daniel. *Houses from Books: Treatises, Pattern Books, and Catalogs in American Architecture, 1738–1950.* University Park: Pennsylvania State University Press, 2000.

Reps, John W. *Cities of the American West: A History of Frontier Urban Planning.* Princeton, N.J.: Princeton University Press, 1979.

Reps, John W. *The Forgotten Frontier: Urban Planning in the American West before 1890.* Columbia: University of Missouri Press, 1981.

Reps, John W. *The Making of Urban America: A History of City Planning in the United States.* Princeton, N.J.: Princeton University Press, 1965.

Reps, John W. "Thomas Jefferson's Checkerboard Towns." *Journal of the Society of Architectural Historians* 20, no. 3 (1961): 108–14.

"The Rev. Henry S. Clubb." *Vegetarian Messenger,* January 1896.

"Rev. James Madison Allen." *Food, Home and Garden* 2, no. 16 (April 1898): 51–52.

Reynolds, David S. *John Brown, Abolitionist: The Man Who Killed Slavery, Sparked the Civil War, and Seeded Civil Rights.* New York: Alfred A. Knopf, 2005.

Reynolds, David S. *Waking Giant: America in the Age of Jackson.* New York: Harper, 2008.

Rice, Howard C., Jr. "A French Source of Jefferson's Plan for the Prison at Richmond." *Journal of the Society of Architectural Historians* 12, no. 4 (1953): 28–30.

Richardson, Albert D. *Beyond the Mississippi: From the Great River to the Great Ocean; Life and Adventure on the Prairies, Mountains, and Pacific Coast.* Hartford: American Publishing Company, 1867.

Rigal, Laura. *The American Manufactory: Art, Labor, and the World of Things in the Early Republic.* Princeton, N.J.: Princeton University Press, 2001.

Robbins, Roy M. *Our Landed Heritage: The Public Domain, 1776–1970.* 2nd ed. Lincoln: University of Nebraska Press, 1976.

Roberts, Jennifer L. "The Currency of Ornament: Machine-Lathed Anticounterfeiting Patterns and the Portability of Value." In *Histories of Ornament: From Global to Local,* edited by Gülru Necipoğlu and Alina Payne, 308–19. Princeton, N.J.: Princeton University Press, 2016.

Robertson, Andrew W. *The Language of Democracy: Political Rhetoric in the United States and Britain, 1790–1900.* Charlottesville: University of Virginia Press, 2005.

Robinson, Cedric J., and Elizabeth P. Robinson. Preface to *Futures of Black Radicalism,* edited by Gaye Theresa Johnson and Alex Lubin, 1–8. London: Verso, 2017.

Rockoff, Hugh. "The Free Banking Era: A Reexamination." *Journal of Money, Credit and Banking* 6, no. 2 (1974): 141–67.

Rodgers, Daniel T. *Contested Truths: Keywords in American Politics since Independence.* Cambridge, Mass.: Harvard University Press, 1998.

Rodgers, Daniel T. "Republicanism: The Career of a Concept." *Journal of American History* 79, no. 1 (1992): 11–38.

Rodgers, Daniel T. *The Work Ethic in Industrial America, 1850–1920.* Chicago: University of Chicago Press, 1978.

Roemer, Kenneth M. *The Obsolete Necessity: America in Utopian Writings, 1888–1900.* Kent, Ohio: Kent State University Press, 1976.

Rohrbough, Malcolm J. *The Land Office Business: The Settlement and Administration of American Public Lands, 1789–1837.* New York: Oxford University Press, 1968.

Rosen, Joel Nathan. *From New Lanark to Mound Bayou: Owenism in the Mississippi Delta.* Durham, N.C.: Carolina Academic Press, 2011.

Rosenberg, Daniel, and Anthony Grafton. *Cartographies of Time: A History of the Timeline.* New York: Princeton Architectural Press, 2012.

Rosenfeld, Sophia A. *A Revolution in Language: The Problem of Signs in Late Eighteenth-Century France.* Stanford, Calif.: Stanford University Press, 2001.

Rosenzweig, Roy, and Elizabeth Blackmar. *The Park and the People: A History of Central Park.* Ithaca, N.Y.: Cornell University Press, 1992.

Rothman, David J. *The Discovery of the Asylum: Social Order and Disorder in the New Republic.* Boston: Little, Brown, 1971.

Rowe, Colin. "The Architecture of Utopia." In *The Mathematics of the Ideal Villa, and Other Essays.* Cambridge: MIT Press, 1976.

Rowe, Colin, and Fred Koetter. *Collage City.* Cambridge: MIT Press, 1978.

Ryan, Mary P. *Cradle of the Middle Class: The Family in Oneida County, New York, 1790–1865.* Cambridge: Cambridge University Press, 1981.

Rykwert, Joseph. *The Dancing Column: On Order in Architecture.* Cambridge: MIT Press, 1998.

Saad-Filho, Alfredo. "Labor, Money, and 'Labour-Money': A Review of Marx's Critique of John Gray's Monetary Analysis." *History of Political Economy* 25, no. 1 (1993): 65–84.

Sandage, Scott A. *Born Losers: A History of Failure in America.* Cambridge, Mass.: Harvard University Press, 2005.

Sargent, Lyman Tower. "Colonial and Postcolonial Utopias." In *The Cambridge Companion to Utopian Literature,* edited by Gregory Claeys, 200–222. Cambridge: Cambridge University Press, 2010.

Sargent, Lyman Tower. "The Three Faces of Utopianism Revisited." *Utopian Studies* 5, no. 1 (1994): 1–37.

Sartwell, Crispin. "Introduction." In *The Practical Anarchist: Writings of Josiah Warren,* edited by Crispin Sartwell. New York: Fordham University Press, 2011.

Sartwell, Crispin. *Political Aesthetics.* Ithaca, N.Y.: Cornell University Press, 2010.

Scharlott, Bradford W. "Communication Technology Transforms the Marketplace: The Effect of the Telegraph, Telephone, and Ticker on the Cincinnati Merchants' Exchange." *Ohio History* 113 (Winter/Spring 2004): 4–17.

Schlereth, Thomas J. "The New York Artisan in the Early Republic: A Portrait from Graphic Evidence, 1787–1853." *Material Culture* 20, no. 1 (1988): 1–31.

Schlesinger, Arthur M. *Age of Jackson.* Boston: Little, Brown, 1953.

Schmidt, Carl F. *The Octagon Fad.* Scottsville, N.Y.: Carl F. Schmidt, 1958.

Schmidt, Carl F., and Philip Parr. *More about Octagons.* Rochester, N.Y.: Carl F. Schmidt, 1978.

Schneider, Birgit, Christoph Ernst, and Jan Wöpking, eds. *Diagrammatik-Reader: Grundlegende Texte aus Theorie und Geschichte.* Boston: De Gruyter, 2016.

Schulman, Vanessa Meikle. *Work Sights: The Visual Culture of Industry in Nineteenth-Century America.* Amherst: University of Massachusetts Press, 2015.

Schuster, Eunice Minette. *Native American Anarchism: A Study of Left-Wing American Individualism.* New York: Da Capo Press, 1970.

Schüttpelz, Erhard. "Trance Mediums and New Media: The Heritage of a European Term." In *Trance Mediums and New Media,* edited by Heike Behrend, Anja Dreschke, and Martin Zillinger, translated by Joel Golb, 56–76. New York: Fordham University Press, 2015.

Schuyler, David. *Apostle of Taste: Andrew Jackson Downing, 1815–1852.* Baltimore: Johns Hopkins University Press, 1996.

Schwartz, Vanessa R., and Jeannene M. Przyblyski, eds. *The Nineteenth-Century Visual Culture Reader.* New York: Routledge, 2004.

Sconce, Jeffrey. *Haunted Media: Electronic Presence from Telegraphy to Television.* Durham, N.C.: Duke University Press, 2000.

Scott, Felicity D. *Architecture or Techno-utopia: Politics after Modernism.* Cambridge: MIT Press, 2007.

Scott, James C. *Seeing like a State: How Certain Schemes to Improve the Human Condition Have Failed.* New Haven, Conn.: Yale University Press, 1998.

Scott, James C. *Two Cheers for Anarchism: Six Easy Pieces on Autonomy, Dignity, and Meaningful Work and Play.* Princeton, N.J.: Princeton University Press, 2012.

Sears, Clara Endicott, ed. *Bronson Alcott's Fruitlands.* Boston: Houghton Mifflin, 1915.

Segal, Howard P. *Technological Utopianism in American Culture.* Chicago: University of Chicago Press, 1985.

Sekula, Allan. "The Body and the Archive." *October* 39 (1986): 3–64.

Sellers, Charles. *The Market Revolution: Jacksonian America, 1815–1846.* New York: Oxford University Press, 1991.

Sennett, Richard. "American Cities: The Grid Plan and the Protestant Ethic." In *Gridded Worlds: An Urban Anthology,* edited by Reuben Rose-Redwood and Liora Bigon, 207–25. New York: Springer, 2018.

Shannon, Fred A. "A Post Mortem on the Labor-Safety Valve Theory." *Agricultural History* 19, no. 1 (1945): 31–37.

Sheehan, Tanya. *Study in Black and White: Photography, Race, Humor.* University Park: Pennsylvania State University Press, 2018.

Shell, Marc. *Money, Language, and Thought: Literary and Philosophic Economies from the Medieval to the Modern Era.* Baltimore: Johns Hopkins University Press, 1993.

Shi, David E. *The Simple Life: Plain Living and High Thinking in American Culture*. New York: Oxford University Press, 1985.

Short, John Rennie. *Representing the Republic: Mapping the United States 1600–1900*. London: Reaktion Books, 2004.

Shprintzen, Adam D. *The Vegetarian Crusade: The Rise of an American Reform Movement, 1817–1921*. Chapel Hill: University of North Carolina Press, 2013.

Simmel, Georg. *The Philosophy of Money*. Edited by David Frisby. London: Routledge, 1990.

Simpson, David. *The Politics of American English, 1776–1850*. New York: Oxford University Press, 1986.

Sinha, Manisha. *The Slave's Cause: A History of Abolition*. New Haven, Conn.: Yale University Press, 2016.

Skidmore, Thomas E. *The Rights of Man to Property! Being a Proposition to Make It Equal among the Adults of the Present Generation, and to Provide for Its Equal Transmission to Every Individual of Each Succeeding Generation on Arriving at the Age of Maturity*. New York: printed by A. Ming, 1829.

Sklansky, Jeffrey. *Sovereign of the Market: The Money Question in Early America*. Chicago: University of Chicago Press, 2017.

Slauter, Eric Thomas. *The State as a Work of Art: The Cultural Origins of the Constitution*. Chicago: University of Chicago Press, 2009.

Sloan, Herbert. "The Earth Belongs in Usufruct to the Living." In *Jeffersonian Legacies*, edited by Peter S. Onuf. Charlottesville: University Press of Virginia, 1993.

Sloan, Samuel. *The Model Architect: A Series of Original Designs for Cottages, Villas, Suburban Residences, Etc., Accompanied by Explanations, Specifications, Estimates, and Elaborate Details: Prepared Expressly for the Use of Projectors and Artisans throughout the United States*. Philadelphia: E. S. Jones, 1852.

Sloan, Samuel. *Sloan's Homestead Architecture, Containing Forty Designs for Villas, Cottages, and Farm Houses, with Essays on Style, Construction, Landscape Gardening, Furniture, Etc.* Philadelphia: J. B. Lippincott, 1861.

Smith, Caleb. *The Oracle and the Curse: A Poetics of Justice from the Revolution to the Civil War*. Cambridge, Mass.: Harvard University Press, 2013.

Smith, Henry Nash. *Virgin Land: The American West as Symbol and Myth*. Cambridge, Mass.: Harvard University Press, 1950.

Sokal, Michael M. "Practical Phrenology as Psychological Counseling in the 19th-Century United States." In *The Transformation of Psychology: Influences of 19th-Century Philosophy, Technology, and Natural Science*, edited by Christopher D. Green, Marline Shore, and Thomas Teo, 21–44. Washington, D.C.: American Psychological Association, 2001.

Sokolitz, Roberta. "Picturing the Plantation." In *Landscape of Slavery: The Plantation in American Art*, edited by Angela D. Mack and Stephen G. Hoffius, 30–57. Columbia: University of South Carolina Press, 2008.

Solan, Victoria Jane. "'Built for Health': American Architecture and the Healthy House." PhD diss., Yale University, 2004.

Spear, John Murray. *Twenty Years on the Wing.* Boston: William White, 1873.

Spurlock, John. "The Free Love Network in America, 1850 to 1860." *Journal of Social History* 21, no. 4 (1988): 765–79.

Stafford, Barbara Maria. *Artful Science: Enlightenment Entertainment and the Eclipse of Visual Education.* Cambridge: MIT Press, 1996.

Stanton, Lucia C. *"Those Who Labor for My Happiness": Slavery at Thomas Jefferson's Monticello.* Charlottesville: University of Virginia Press, 2012.

Starr, Paul. *The Creation of the Media: Political Origins of Modern Communications.* New York: Basic Books, 2005.

Stauffer, John, Zoe Trodd, and Celeste-Marie Bernier. *Picturing Frederick Douglass: An Illustrated Biography of the Nineteenth Century's Most Photographed American.* New York: W. W. Norton, 2015.

Stern, Madeleine B. "Every Man His Own Printer: The Typographical Experiments of Josiah Warren." *Printing History* 2, no. 2 (1980): 11–20.

Stern, Madeleine B. *Heads and Headlines: The Phrenological Fowlers.* Norman: University of Oklahoma Press, 1971.

Stern, Madeleine B. "Introduction." In *The Octagon House: A Home for All,* by Orson S. Fowler. New York: Dover, 1973.

Stern, Madeleine B. *The Pantarch: A Biography of Stephen Pearl Andrews.* Austin: University of Texas Press, 1968.

Stevens, Edward, Jr. *The Grammar of the Machine: Technical Literacy and Early Industrial Expansion in the United States.* New Haven, Conn.: Yale University Press, 1995.

Stewart, Watson. "Personal Memoirs of Watson Stewart." 1904. Kansas Collection, Kansas State Historical Society. http://www.kancoll.org/articles.

Stoll, Steven. *The Great Delusion: A Mad Inventor, Death in the Tropics, and the Utopian Origins of Economic Growth.* New York: Hill and Wang, 2008.

Stolow, Jeremy. "Salvation by Electricity." In *Religion: Beyond a Concept,* edited by Hent de Vries, 668–86. New York: Fordham University Press, 2008.

Stolow, Jeremy. "Wired Religion: Spiritualism and Telegraphic Globalization in the Nineteenth Century." In *Empires and Autonomy: Moments in the History of Globalization,* edited by Stephen Streeter, John Weaver, and William Coleman, 79–92. Vancouver: University of British Columbia Press, 2009.

Streeby, Shelley. *American Sensations: Class, Empire, and the Production of Popular Culture.* Berkeley: University of California Press, 2002.

Sweeting, Adam W. *Reading Houses and Building Books: Andrew Jackson Downing and the Architecture of Popular Antebellum Literature, 1835–1855.* Hanover, N.H.: University Press of New England, 1996.

Swift, Samuel. "The Garden City—II." *Indoors and Out* 1, no. 3 (1905): 137–45.

Sysling, Fenneke. "Science and Self-Assessment: Phrenological Charts 1840–1940." *British Journal for the History of Science* 51, no. 2 (2018): 261–80.

Tangires, Helen. *Public Markets and Civic Culture in Nineteenth-Century America.* Baltimore: Johns Hopkins University Press, 2020.

Tanke, Joseph J. "The Care of the Self and Environmental Politics: Towards a Foucaultian Account of Dietary Practice." *Ethics and the Environment* 12, no. 1 (2007): 79–96.

Taylor, Chloe. "Foucault and the Ethics of Eating." In *Foucault and Animals,* edited by Matthew Chrulew and Dinesh Joseph Wadiwel, 317–38. Boston: Brill, 2017.

Thomas, John L. "Romantic Reform in America, 1815–1865." *American Quarterly* 17, no. 4 (1965): 656–81.

Thomine-Berrada, Alice. "Pictorial versus Intellectual Representation." In *Perspective, Projections and Design: Technologies of Architectural Representation,* edited by Mario Carpo and Frédérique Lemerle, 141–50. London: Routledge, 2008.

Thompson, Dorothy. *The Chartists: Popular Politics in the Industrial Revolution.* New York: Pantheon Books, 1984.

Thompson, E. P. *The Making of the English Working Class.* New York: Vintage Books, 1966.

Thompson, Michael. *The Politics of Inequality: A Political History of the Idea of Economic Inequality in America.* New York: Columbia University Press, 2007.

Thoreau, Henry David. "Paradise (to Be) Regained." *United States Democratic Review* 13, no. 65 (1843): 451–62.

Thornton, William. *Cadmus; or, A Treatise on the Elements of Written Language: Illustrating, by a Philosophical Division of Speech, the Power of Each Character, Thereby Mutually Fixing the Orthography and Orthoepy* [. . .]. Philadelphia: R. Aitken & Son, 1793.

Titus, W. A. "The First Concrete Building in the United States." *Wisconsin Magazine of History* 24, no. 2 (1940): 183–88.

Tocqueville, Alexis de. *Democracy in America.* Edited by J. P. Mayer. Translated by George Lawrence. New York: Harper & Row, 1988.

Todd, Charles L., and Robert Sonkin. *Alexander Bryan Johnson, Philosophical Banker.* Syracuse, N.Y.: Syracuse University Press, 1977.

Todd, Sereno Edwards. *Todd's Country Homes, and How to Save Money to Buy a Home; How to Build Neat and Cheap Cottages; and How to Gain an Independent Fortune before Old Age Comes On.* New York, 1868.

Tomlinson, Stephen. *Head Masters: Phrenology, Secular Education, and Nineteenth-Century Social Thought.* Tuscaloosa: University of Alabama Press, 2005.

Toscano, Alberto, and Jeff Kinkle. *Cartographies of the Absolute.* Alresford, Hampshire: Zero Books, 2015.

Treat, Payson J. *The National Land System, 1785–1820.* New York: E. B. Treat, 1910.

Tufte, Edward R. *Envisioning Information.* Cheshire, Conn.: Graphics Press, 1990.

Tufte, Edward R. *The Visual Display of Quantitative Information.* Cheshire, Conn.: Graphics Press, 1983.

Tufte, Edward R. *Visual Explanations: Images and Quantities, Evidence and Narrative.* Cheshire, Conn.: Graphics Press, 1997.

Turner, Frederick Jackson. "The Significance of the Frontier in American History." In *The Frontier in American History,* 1–38. New York: Holt, 1920.

Twigg, Julia. "The Vegetarian Movement in England, 1847–1981: A Study in the Structure of Its Ideology." PhD diss., London School of Economics, 1981.

Upton, Dell. *Another City: Urban Life and Urban Spaces in the New American Republic.* New Haven, Conn.: Yale University Press, 2008.

Upton, Dell. *Architecture in the United States.* Oxford: Oxford University Press, 1998.

Upton, Dell. "Inventing the Metropolis: Civilization and Urbanity in Antebellum New York." In *Art and the Empire City: New York, 1825–1861,* edited by Catherine Hoover Voorsanger and John K. Howat, 3–45. New York: Metropolitan Museum of Art, 2000.

Upton, Dell. "Lancasterian Schools, Republican Citizenship, and the Spatial Imagination in Early Nineteenth-Century America." *Journal of the Society of Architectural Historians* 55, no. 3 (1996): 238–53.

Upton, Dell. "Pattern Books and Professionalism: Aspects of the Transformation of Domestic Architecture in America, 1800–1860." *Winterthur Portfolio* 19, nos. 2–3 (1984): 107–50.

Upton, Dell. "White and Black Landscapes in Eighteenth-Century Virginia." *Places Journal* 2, no. 2 (1984): 59–72.

"Vegetarian Company." *Water-Cure Journal* 20, no. 1 (July 1855).

Veracini, Lorenzo. *Settler Colonialism: A Theoretical Overview.* Basingstoke: Palgrave Macmillan, 2010.

Veracini, Lorenzo. "Suburbia, Settler Colonialism and the World Turned Inside Out." *Housing, Theory and Society* 29, no. 4 (2012): 339–57.

Veracini, Lorenzo. *The World Turned Inside Out: Settler Colonialism as a Political Idea.* London: Verso, 2021.

Vidler, Anthony. "Diagrams of Utopia." *Daidalos* 74 (2000): 6–13.

Vidler, Anthony. *The Scenes of the Street, and Other Essays.* New York: Monacelli Press, 2011.

Vidler, Anthony. *The Writing of the Walls: Architectural Theory in the Late Enlightenment.* New York: Princeton Architectural Press, 1987.

Vlach, John Michael. *Back of the Big House: The Architecture of Plantation Slavery.* Chapel Hill: University of North Carolina Press, 1993.

Vlach, John Michael. *The Planter's Prospect: Privilege and Slavery in Plantation Paintings.* Chapel Hill: University of North Carolina Press, 2002.

Waldstreicher, David, Jeffrey L. Pasley, and Andrew W. Robertson. "Introduction: Beyond the Founders." In *Beyond the Founders: New Approaches to the Political History of the Early American Republic,* edited by Jeffrey L. Pasley, Andrew W. Robertson, and David Waldstreicher, 1–28. Chapel Hill: University of North Carolina Press, 2004.

Walker, Nathaniel Robert. *Victorian Visions of Suburban Utopia: Abandoning Babylon.* Oxford: Oxford University Press, 2020.

Wallace, Anthony F. C. *Jefferson and the Indians: The Tragic Fate of the First Americans.* Cambridge, Mass.: Harvard University Press, 1999.

Wallace, Maurice O., and Shawn Michelle Smith, eds. *Pictures and Progress: Early*

Photography and the Making of African American Identity. Durham, N.C.: Duke University Press, 2012.

Wallenstein, Sven-Olov. *Biopolitics and the Emergence of Modern Architecture.* New York: Princeton Architectural Press and Buell Center/FORuM Project, 2009.

Walters, Ronald G. *American Reformers, 1815–1860.* New York: Hill and Wang, 1997.

Walters, Ronald G. *The Antislavery Appeal: American Abolitionism after 1830.* Baltimore: Johns Hopkins University Press, 1976.

Walters, Ronald G. *Primers for Prudery: Sexual Advice to Victorian America.* Englewood Cliffs, N.J.: Prentice Hall, 1973.

Ward, Stephen V. "The Garden City Introduced." In Ward, *Garden City,* 1–27.

Ward, Stephen V., ed. *The Garden City: Past, Present and Future.* London: Routledge, 2011.

Warner, Michael. *The Letters of the Republic: Publication and the Public Sphere in Eighteenth-Century America.* Cambridge, Mass.: Harvard University Press, 1990.

Warner, Michael. *Publics and Counterpublics.* New York: Zone Books, 2005.

Warren, Josiah. *Equitable Commerce: A New Development of Principles.* New Harmony, Ind.: Josiah Warren, 1846.

Warren, Josiah. *Equitable Commerce: A New Development of Principles, as Substitutes for Laws and Governments, for the Harmonious Adjustment and Regulation of the Pecuniary, Intellectual, and Moral Intercourse of Mankind.* New York: Fowlers and Wells, 1852.

Warren, Josiah. *Introduction to a New Printing Apparatus, Applied to the Wants and Capacities of Private Citizens.* 1836.

Warren, Josiah. *A New System of Notation Intended to Promote the More General Cultivation and More Just Performance of Music.* New Harmony, Ind.: J. Warren, 1843.

Warren, Josiah. *The Practical Anarchist: Writings of Josiah Warren.* Edited by Crispin Sartwell. New York: Fordham University Press, 2011.

Warren, Josiah. *Practical Applications of the Elementary Principles of "True Civilization," to the Minute Details of Every Day Life:* Princeton, Mass.: J. Warren, 1873.

Warren, Josiah. *Practical Details in Equitable Commerce, Showing the Workings, in Actual Experiment, during a Series of Years, of the Social Principles Expounded in the Works Called "Equitable Commerce."* New York: Fowlers and Wells, 1852.

Warren, Josiah. *The Principle of Equivalents.* 1861. Amherst College Library.

Warren, Josiah. *True Civilization an Immediate Necessity, and the Last Ground of Hope for Mankind.* Boston: J. Warren, 1863.

Warren, Josiah. *Written Music Remodeled, and Invested with the Simplicity of an Exact Science.* Boston: J. P. Jewett, 1860.

Warren, S. Edward. *Elements of Machine Construction and Drawing; or, Machine Drawing, with Some Elements of Descriptive and Rational Cinematics.* New York: John Wiley, 1870.

Webster, Noah. *An American Dictionary of the English Language.* New York: S. Converse, 1828.

Webster, Noah. *An American Dictionary of the English Language.* New York: White & Sheffield, 1841.

Webster, Noah. *Webster's Complete Dictionary of the English Language.* London: George Bell and Sons, 1886.

Webster, Noah. *Webster's International Dictionary of the English Language.* Springfield, Mass.: G. & C. Merriam, 1898.

Weisiger, Marsha, et al. "Grout Buildings of Milton." In *SAH Archipedia,* edited by Gabrielle Esperdy and Karen Kingsley (Charlottesville: University of Virginia Press, 2012). http://sah-archipedia.org.

Weitenkampf, Frank. "Our Political Symbols." *New York History* 33, no. 4 (1952): 371–78.

Wells, Samuel R., and Daniel Harrison Jacques. *How to Behave: A Pocket Manual of Republican Etiquette, and Guide to Correct Personal Habits.* New York: Fowler and Wells, 1857.

Wenger, Mark R. "Jefferson's Designs for Remodeling the Governor's Palace." *Winterthur Portfolio* 32, no. 4 (1997): 223–42.

Wenger, Mark R. "Thomas Jefferson, Tenant." *Winterthur Portfolio* 26, no. 4 (1991): 249–65.

Whately, Richard. *Elements of Logic.* Boston: James Munroe, 1843.

Whately, Richard. *Elements of Rhetoric.* Boston: James Munroe, 1839.

Whitwell, Stedman. *Description of an Architectural Model: From a Design by Stedman Whitwell, Esq. for a Community upon a Principle of United Interests, as Advocated by Robert Owen, Esq.* London: Hurst Chance and E. Wilson, 1830.

Whorton, James C. *Crusaders for Fitness: A History of American Health Reformers.* Princeton, N.J.: Princeton University Press, 1982.

Wilentz, Sean. *Chants Democratic: New York City and the Rise of the American Working Class, 1788–1850.* New York: Oxford University Press, 1984.

Williams, Raymond. *Keywords: A Vocabulary of Culture and Society.* 1976. Reprint, Oxford: Oxford University Press, 2014.

Williams, Raymond. *Marxism and Literature.* Oxford: Oxford University Press, 1977.

Wilson, Douglas L. "Dating Jefferson's Early Architectural Drawings." *Virginia Magazine of History and Biography* 101, no. 1 (1993): 53–76.

Wilson, Mabel O. "Notes on the Virginia Capitol: Nation, Race, and Slavery in Jefferson's America." In Cheng et al., *Race and Modern Architecture,* 23–42.

Winter, Alison. *Mesmerized: Powers of Mind in Victorian Britain.* Chicago: University of Chicago Press, 1998.

Witgen, Michael. "A Nation of Settlers: The Early American Republic and the Colonization of the Northwest Territory." *William and Mary Quarterly* 76, no. 3 (2019): 391–98.

Witgen, Michael. "Seeing Red: Race, Citizenship, and Indigeneity in the Old Northwest." *Journal of the Early Republic* 38, no. 4 (2018): 581–611.

Wittkower, Rudolf. *Architectural Principles in the Age of Humanism.* New York: W. W. Norton, 1971.

Wittman, Richard. *Architecture, Print Culture and the Public Sphere in Eighteenth-Century France.* London: Routledge, 2013.

Wolfe, Patrick. *Traces of History: Elementary Structures of Race.* London: Verso, 2016.

Wood, Charles B. "The New 'Pattern Books' and the Role of the Agricultural Press." In *Prophet with Honor: The Career of Andrew Jackson Downing, 1815–1852,* edited by George B. Tatum and Elisabeth B. MacDougall. Philadelphia: Athenaeum of Philadelphia; Washington, D.C.: Dumbarton Oaks Research Library, 1989.

Wood, Gordon S. *Empire of Liberty: A History of the Early Republic, 1789–1815.* Oxford: Oxford University Press, 2009.

Wood, Gordon S. *The Radicalism of the American Revolution.* New York: Alfred A. Knopf, 1992.

Wood, Gordon S. *Representation in the American Revolution.* Charlottesville: University of Virginia Press, 2008.

Wood, Marcus. *Blind Memory: Visual Representations of Slavery in England and America.* New York: Routledge, 2000.

Wood, Marcus. *The Horrible Gift of Freedom: Atlantic Slavery and the Representation of Emancipation.* Athens: University of Georgia Press, 2010.

Wright, Gwendolyn. *Building the Dream: A Social History of Housing in America.* Cambridge: MIT Press, 1983.

Wrobel, Arthur. *Pseudo-science and Society in Nineteenth-Century America.* Lexington: University Press of Kentucky, 1987.

Wunderlich, Roger. *Low Living and High Thinking at Modern Times, New York.* Syracuse, N.Y.: Syracuse University Press, 1992.

Wyhe, John van. *Phrenology and the Origins of Victorian Scientific Naturalism.* London: Routledge, 2004.

Wynter, Sylvia. "Unsettling the Coloniality of Being/Power/Truth/Freedom: Towards the Human, after Man, Its Overrepresentation—an Argument." *CR: The New Centennial Review* 3, no. 3 (2003): 257–337.

Yanni, Carla. *The Architecture of Madness: Insane Asylums in the United States.* Minneapolis: University of Minnesota Press, 2007.

Yirush, Craig. *Settlers, Liberty, and Empire: The Roots of Early American Political Theory, 1675–1775.* New York: Cambridge University Press, 2011.

Zagarri, Rosemarie. *The Politics of Size: Representation in the United States, 1776–1850.* Ithaca, N.Y.: Cornell University Press, 1987.

Zahler, Helene Sara. *Eastern Workingmen and National Land Policy, 1829–1862.* New York: Columbia University Press, 1941.

Zakim, Michael. "The Business Clerk as Social Revolutionary; or, A Labor History of the Nonproducing Classes." *Journal of the Early Republic* 26, no. 4 (2006): 563–603.

Zamalin, Alex. *Black Utopia: The History of an Idea from Black Nationalism to Afro-futurism.* New York: Columbia University Press, 2019.

Zboray, Ronald J. *A Fictive People: Antebellum Economic Development and the American Reading Public.* New York: Oxford University Press, 1993.

Zboray, Ronald J., and Mary Saracino Zboray, eds. *The Oxford History of Popular Print Culture.* Vol. 5, *US Popular Print Culture to 1860.* Oxford: Oxford University Press, 2019.

Archival Sources

American Antiquarian Society
Charles Codman Papers, Suffolk County Historical Society
Duke University Rare Book, Manuscript, and Special Collections Library
Ebenezer Howard Papers, Hertfordshire Archives and Local Studies Library
Fowler and Wells Families Papers, Cornell University Library
Gerritt Smith Papers, Syracuse University Library
Henry S. Clubb Papers, University of Michigan Bentley Historical Library
Historic American Buildings Survey, Library of Congress
Huntington Library
Indiana Historical Society
Indiana State Library
Josiah Warren Papers, Labadie Collection, University of Michigan Library
Kansas State Historical Society
National Archives
New Harmony Collection, Working Men's Institute Museum and Library
St. Croix County Historical Society
Suffolk County Historical Society
Thaddeus Sheldon Papers, University of Pittsburgh Library
Thomas Jefferson Papers, Albert and Shirley Small Special Collections Library,
    University of Virginia
Thomas Jefferson Papers, Massachusetts Historical Society
William L. Clements Library, University of Michigan
Wisconsin Historical Society
Younglove Family Papers, Steuben County Historical Society

INDEX

Page numbers in italics refer to illustrations.

Abramson, Daniel, 234

abstraction, 216; of diagrams, 12, 18, 92, 225, 258; of land grids, 31, 33, 83, 89

advertising, 256, 262

aesthetic, 25–26, 31, 39, 40, 42, 43, 44, 115, 117, 130; artisans', 15, 136; of circularity, 224–27; classical, 23, 26, 31; of efficiency, 114; Enlightenment, 164; functional, 24; of objectivity, 107; operational, 13, 109, 120, 131; political, 18, 22, 25–26; and race, 40; spiritualist, 200, 224, 225, 230, 233, 238, 240; of territorial possession, 44

African Americans, 19, 296n47; as abolitionists, 161, 162; as enslaved laborers, 47, 48; Thomas Jefferson on, 40, 41; relation to John Brown, 162–63; representations in antislavery imagery, 9, *10,* 162, *163;* and utopianism, 22–23, 269n73

agrarianism, 65, 81

Albanese, Catherine, 201, 207

Alcott, Bronson, 137, 138, 139, 284n18

Alcott, William Andrus, 218, *219*

Allen, J. Madison, 166, 167–68, 177–78, 185, *187,* 289n4

Allen, John, 208

American Anti-Slavery Society, 9, *10*

American Cottage Builder, The (Bullock), 123

American Phrenological Journal, 102, *103,* 117, 122, 126, 148

American Settlement Company, 150, *151*

American Tract Society, 9

anarchism, 24, 173, 177, 179, 243, 290–91n28

Ancora community, 166–67

Andrews, Stephen Pearl, 175, 230

angels, 213, 215, 225, 239; market facilitated by, 231–32

Anti-Federalists, 79, 181

antislavery, 5, 18, 95, 135–36, 142–43, 160–63; spiritualist involvement in, 206, 207; vegetarianism linked to, 135, 142–43; visual culture of, 9–10, *10,* 161–63

architecture: analogy to human body, 40, 218–19; capacity to shape subjects, 6–7, 30, 39; of exchanges, 233–34, *234, 235, 236;* as expression of cosmic order, 39–40; functionalist view of, 6–8, 18, 31, 111, 218; and health, 113, 218; of Thomas Jefferson, 30–31, 39–56; political dimension of, 26, 44; progress in, 96–97, 128, 195; of reform, 4–5, 6–7, 100; sensorial aspects of, 6, 43–44, 195, 200, 232–33; spiritualist, 195–99, 219–20, 232–33, 237; of utopias, 3, 5–6, 12

Arendt, Hannah, 35

association, 20, 135, 138, 147, 180, 206, 217, 254, 256; of spirits, 207. *See also* cooperation; phalanstery; phalanxes

atmosphere, spiritualist interest in, 25, 200, 205, 216, 227, 233, 238

Aureli, Pier Vittorio, 83, 300n30

Bacon, Francis, 182

Baker, Zephaniah, 123, 219–20, *220*

Bakunin, Mikhail, 174

Bank of England, 234, *235*

banks, 174, 182, 183, 185

Banneker, Benjamin, 272n42

Barbour, James, 47, *50*

Barnum, Phineas T., 101, 102, 111, 117, 121, 192, 205; and "Feejee mermaid," 109, *110;* operational aesthetic of, 109

Barrett, George, 120

Beecher, Catharine, 113

Beecher Bible and Rifle Colony (Union Emigrant Aid Company), 143

339

340 *Index*

Bellamy, Edward, 243
Bender, John, 12–13, 17, 92
Benjamin, Walter, 26, 233, 234
Bennett, Jane, 200, 238–39
Bentham, Jeremy, 6, *7,* 52, 53, 90, 236
Bestor, Arthur, 21, 179
Bewick, Thomas, 267n28
Bhandar, Brenna, 33–34, 46
Black Hawk (Sauk leader), 64–65
Blatchly, Cornelius, 64
Bleeding Kansas, 143–45, 159–61, *160*
Bloch, Ernst, 21, 22, 269n75
Boullée, Étienne-Louis, 3
Braude, Ann, 206
Bray, John Francis, 174
Bridgman, Laura, 181
Briggs, Charles W., 159, *160,* 162
Brook Farm settlement, 154, 208
Brooks, Preston S., 159, *161*
Brown, John, 136, 159, 162
Brownson, Orestes, 19
Buckingham, James Silk, 251
Buder, Stanley, 253
Buescher, John B., 211
Bullock, John, 123
Byllesby, Langton, 64

Cabell, Joseph, 34
Calhoun, Craig, 20
capitalism, 16, 23, 66, 137, 146, 148, 150, 180,
    233, 234, 243; and cognitive mapping, 16,
    279n101; critiques of, 16, 136, 137, 174; rep-
    resentations of, 16, *17,* 268n50; solutions
    for, 66, 68, 100, 246, 258
Carlyle, Thomas, 3
Carroll, Bret, 206
cartoons, 12, 16, 17, *17,* 65–66, *67,* 76, 159,
    278n71
Castiglia, Christopher, 104
Castronovo, Russ, 104, 206
cement. *See* gravel wall
Chandler, Alfred, 220
Channing, William, 66
Chartists, 66, 74, 140, *141,* 142, 150
Chase, Oliver, 217
Cherokees, 18, 66, 136
Chicago Board of Trade, 233

Chippewa (Ojibwe) Nation, 126
Christian Parlor Magazine, 122
chromolithography, 256
circles, 90, *91,* 178, 207, 217, 224–25, 232, 250;
    in architecture, 3, 6, *7,* 39–40, *41,* 52, 124,
    124, 130, 196, 217, 220, *221, 222, 223, 224,*
    225–27, 230, 232–36, *234, 235, 236*; in city
    plans, 38, 69, *72,* 195, 217, 243, 250–51, *251,*
    252, 253; in diagrams, *42,* 224, *226, 227,*
    228, 249–54, *251, 252, 255*; séance, 201, 202,
    204, 205, 225
Circleville, Ohio, 69, *72*
Clemens, Samuel, 233
Clubb, Henry S., 1, 133, 138, 147, 154, 163, 167,
    245; as Chartist, 140, 142, 150; early years
    of, 137–42; Indigenous land occupied by,
    18, 153, 288n87; octagonal city of, 6, 7, 24,
    133, 136, 148, 150–52, 159, 177; as short-
    hand advocate, 139, 168; as temperance
    advocate, 142, 153; vegetarian beliefs of,
    133, 135, 137–40
Clytus, Radiclani, 9–10
Cmiel, Kenneth, 181
cobweb cities, 69, 150–51, 251
cognitive mapping, 16, 92, 258, 268n49,
    279n101
Collens, T. Wharton, 16, *17*
colonization, 300n32; African American,
    21, 22, 66; of the Americas, 63, 64, 258,
    275n16; and utopia, 265n9, 265n10, 274n15.
    See also settler colonialism
Colt, Miriam Davis, 153–54, 157
Combe, George, 102
commodity exchanges, 233–34
communication, 139, 180, 215; commerce
    as, 231; with the dead, 200–201, 202;
    diagrams as means of, 258; Electric Motor
    as means of, 209–10; goal of transparency
    in, 168, 186, 192, 213; interplanetary, 199;
    telegraphic, 202, 215, 231; visual versus
    verbal, 13, 188
Comte, Auguste, 268n51
Concordium at Ham Common, 137–40, 154
concrete, 96, 118, 120, 121, 135. *See also* gravel
    wall
Condorcet, Jean-Antoine-Nicolas de Caritat,
    Marquis de, 90

Connecticut Kansas Colony (Beecher Bible and Rifle Colony), 143
Connolly, Brian, 105
Constitutional Convention (1787), 79, 181
Cook, James, 109
Cooley, Thomas, 234
cooperation, 19, 149, 152, 165, 173, 195, 213, 230, 249
Co-operative Land Company, 140, *141*
Cooter, Roger, 104
Cottage Builder's Manual, The (Baker), 123
Cottage Residences (Downing), *112*
Country Gentleman (periodical), 117, *118*
Crystal Palace, 233

Daguerre, Louis-Jacques Mandé, 8
daguerreotypy, 105
Dakota Access Pipeline, 259
D'Alembert, Jean le Rond, 13
Dame, William Upton, 176
Davis, Alexander Jackson, 111
Davis, Andrew Jackson, 202, *204*, 205, *205*, 206, 211, 213, 219, 225–26, *237*
Davis, David Brion, 20
Davis, Jefferson, 22
Davis, Joseph, 22
Davis Bend, Miss., 22
Davison, Darius, 213
Delaware Tribe, 136, 144
Deleuze, Gilles, 17
Democracy in America (Tocqueville), 182
Densmore, David, 215
department stores, 8
Désert de Retz, 220, *224*
Devyr, Thomas, 65–66, *67*
De Wolfe, Charles H., 152
diagrams, 9, 12–18, 90, 92, 101, 190, 258; abstraction of, 12, 18, 92, 225, 258; as cognitive maps of society, 16, 92, 258; of Ebenezer Howard, 243–57, *248, 255*; of human character, *91*; of machines, 190; mathematical, 15, 79, *80*; of the National Reform Association, 58, 62, 68, 74, 75, 92; of the Octagon Settlement Company, 1, 163–64; of Orson Fowler, 113–15, *115, 116,* 117, 129; pedagogical, 13–14, *14,* 79, *80*; published by Josiah Warren, 168,

177, 192–93; Shaker, 202, *202*; of Thomas Skidmore, 81–83, *82–83*; spiritualist, 225, *226, 227,* 232, 238; utopian, 4, 8, 12, 17, 24, 259; as visual rhetoric, 12–18, 25, 58, 62, 75, 81–83, 117, 167, 192–93, 258
Dickens, Charles, 155, *157*
Diderot, Denis, 13
Divine Revelations (Andrew Jackson Davis), 207
Douglass, Frederick, 95, 163
Downing, Andrew Jackson, 24, 111, *112*, 113, 130
Dreisbach, Daniel, 69
Dunbar-Ortiz, Roxanne, 35
Dwyer, Charles, 123

eccentricity, 130–31
Economic Cottage Builder, The (Dwyer), 123
Educator (Spear and Newton), 210, 215
Electric Motor, 209–13, 215, 216, 237, 296n59
emblems, 76–79, *77*
Emerson, Ralph Waldo, 126, 137, 202; on age of reform, 3; critique of reform, 135, 137, 138; on individualism, 19, 125, 126, 130, 131, 135, 138; on money and language, 183, 184
Emmons, Paul, 114, 251
enchantment, 212, 216, 220, 224, 237–39, 241; capitalism and, 233; definition of, 200; reform linked to, 200, 237–39
enclosure, 44
Engels, Friedrich, 6, 257
"English Reformers" (Emerson), 137
Enlightenment, 6, 13, 16, 23, 33, 58, 89, 93, 100–101, 136, 163, 256; universalism, 78
environmental determinism, 6–7
Epstein, James, 139–40
equitable commerce, 24, 25, 72, 149, 167, 174–75, 185, 196; spiritualist advocacy of, 230–33, 236, 237, 240
Equitable Commerce (Orvis et al.), 230, 231, 232, 236, 239–40
Equitable Commerce (Warren), 171, *172,* 176, 180, 186, 190, 192
Equity, Ohio, 175
Esperanto, 246
Estes, Nick, 259

eugenicism, 207, 238
evangelicals, 9, 11, 32, 122, 240
Evans, F. W., 201
Evans, George Henry, 23, 63, 65, 66, 80; on Indigenous dispossession and assimilation, 66
Etzler, John A., 139, 213, *214*

Fabians, 249
Farwell, Leonard, 128
Federalist, 15, 181
Federalists, 34, 79, 181
Ferguson, Christine, 206–7
feudalism, 44
formalism, 6, 18, 167
Forty, Adrian, 265–66n17
Fossett, Peter, 47–48
Foucault, Michel, 105, 280–81n28, 284n14
Fourier, Charles, 3, 10–11, 21, 90, 135, 231–32
Fowler, Charlotte, 102, 105–11
Fowler, Lorenzo, 102, 105–11
Fowler, Orson, 3, *4,* 56, 95–131, *97, 98, 100,* 133, 150, 176, 192, 220, 229; as advocate of individualism, 20, 24, 39, 131; aesthetic arguments of, 115, 117; as amateur and outsider, 111, 136; comparison to P. T. Barnum, 103; critical response to, 124; diagrams employed by, 113–15, *115, 116,* 117, 129; economic arguments of, 97, 118, 120, 123–24; as phrenologist, 96, 100, 101–2, 104–9, *108,* 111, 127–28; on progress in architecture, 96–97, 128; as proponent of octagon houses, 96–98, 100–1, 111–17, 121–22, 126–29, 131; sexual theories of, 105, 113. See also *Home for All, A*
Fowler and Wells (publishing house), 102, 105, 122, 130, 133, 142, 151, 167
Fox, Kate, 201
Fox, Margaret, 201
Fox-Amato, Matthew, 162
Fox Hill Bank Temperance Garden, 142
Franklin, Benjamin, 65, 76, *76,* 207, 209
Frederick, Christine, 114
free love, 3, 176, 177, 206, 229
Free Soil Party, 161
Fruitlands, 139, 154
Fugitive Slave Act (1850), 161

functionalism, 6–7, 18, 25, 31, 130, 266n19; octagon house as forerunner of, 100, 114

Gall, Franz Joseph, 101, 106
garden city, 25, 69, 243–57, *248, 249, 251, 252,* 258
Garrison, William Lloyd, 21, 143, 161, 207, 236
Gates, Paul W., 144
Genesee Farmer (periodical), 123
geometric utopianism, 2–8, 11–12, 15–18, 22–27, 167, 256, 257–58; decline of, 243; Ebenezer Howard's links to, 245, 254; Jefferson as predecessor of, 30; links between proponents of, 167
George, Henry, 246
Gillette, King Camp, 243, *244*
Gilmartin, Kevin, 15
Gitelman, Lisa, 186
Godey's Lady's Book (periodical), 123
Goldstein, Jan, 106
Gombrich, E. H., 77
Goodrich, Joseph, 120, *120*
government, 89, 181 185, 207; citizen participation in, 34–35, 72–74; critiques of, 15, 73–74, 81, 173, 174, 182; desire for small, 19
Graham, Sylvester, 136–37, 142; boardinghouses inspired by, 147
Grammichele, Italy, 69
gravel wall, 118, 120–21
Gray, John, 64, 174
Greaves, James Pierrepont, 137, 138
Greeley, Horace, 142
Greenberg, Joshua, 183
Greenough, Horatio, 114
grids, 16, 26, 34, 36–39, *38,* 57, 62, 79, 83, 89, 271n29; geographical, 84–89; of the land reformers, 30, *30,* 31, 56, 58, *60,* 62, 69, 70, 75, 76, 78, 92, 93; of Lewis Masquerier, 84–85, *85, 86, 87,* 89, 92; pedagogical, 14, 79, *80;* in popular imagination, 31, 36–38, 56, 58, 62, 74–83; of Thomas Skidmore, 80–83, *82, 83;* as symbols of equality, 16, 23, 26, 29–30, 34, 62, 69, 71; as tools for commodification of land, 23, 29–34, 62; as tools of settler colonialism, 23, 31, 33, 62, 89, 93; urban,

37–38, *38,* 71, 74, *145,* 150, *156,* 243. *See also* land ordinance grid
Guarneri, Carl, 21
Gustafson, Sandra, 181
Gustafson, Thomas, 181

Halle aux Blés, 234, *236*
"Hall of Fantasy, The" (Hawthorne), 233
Hamer, David, 150, 151
Hamilton, Alexander, 15, 34
Hangman (*Prisoner's Friend*; newspaper), 207
Harbinger (periodical), 124, *124*
Hardinge, Emma, 199–200
Hare, Robert, 205, *206*
Harmonia community, 206
harmonialism, 202, 206
Harpers Ferry Raid (1859), 136, 162–63
Harris, Neil, 13, 109
Harley, J. B., 89
Hartley, David, 34, *35*
Hartman, Saidiya, 22
Harvey, David, 257
Hawthorne, Nathaniel, 233
Hayden, Dolores, 3, 6, 21
hexagons: in architecture, 118, *119,* 120, *121,* 130; in city plans, 3, 24, 165–67, *166,* 168, 171, 177–79, 190, 192, 193, 243, *244, 245*
Hewitt, Simon Crosby, 195–96, 210, 231, 240; background in labor movement, 208; vision of circular city, 217; vision of homes of harmony, *196, 197, 198,* 217–20, 225–27, 229
Higgins, Jerome, 57
High Rock Tower, 210, *211*
Hinckley, Caroline, 229
Hobbes, Thomas, 182, 237
Holden's Dollar Magazine, 124
Holmes, James H., 159
Home for All, A (Fowler), 24, *98, 100, 115, 116,* 133; aesthetic arguments in, 115, 117; economic arguments in, 97, 118, 120, 123–24; phrenological undercurrents in, 127–28; racial themes in, 128; reception of, 96, 98, 117–29
homes of harmony, 196, *196, 197, 198,* 217–29
Homestead Act (1862), 63
Homestead Architecture (Sloan), 123

Hopedale community, 206
Horticulturist (periodical), 121, 122, 129
House, The (Jacques), 123
Howard, Ebenezer, *4,* 25, 69, 243–57, *247, 248, 249, 252, 255*; early years of, 246
Howard, Hugh, 47
Howard, John, 207
Howe, Samuel Gridley, 181–82
Howland, William, 128

immigration, 113
Indian Removal Act (1830), 64
Indigenous peoples, 1, 18, 35, 62, 66, 133; in Kansas, 135–36, 143–45; precarity of, 22, 64; U.S. government policies toward, 1, 22, 33, 64, 66, 144–45; utopians' dispossession of, 5, 31, 56, 68, 258–59
individualism, 18, 20, 56, 78, 124, 130–31, 138, 172–73, 176–80; grid geometry and, 16, 93; liberalism and, 19, 23, 76, 101, 135; markets and competition linked to, 19, 24, 39; octagon houses as symbol of, 129, 131
individual sovereignty, 55, 173–74, 176, 177, 185, 192
industrialization, 16, 25, 63, 69, 136, 212
Irwin, Harriet Morrison, 118, *119*

Jackson, Andrew, 182
Jackson, Kellie Carter, 161, 162
Jacoby, Russell, 257
Jacques, Daniel, 123, 130
Jameson, Fredric, 16, 92, 93, 265n9, 268n49, 279n101
Jay, John, 36
Jefferson, Isaac, 48
Jefferson, Thomas, *4,* 29–56, *49, 50, 53,* 173, 207; on African Americans, 40–42; on citizenship and reason, 44; city designed by, 37, *38*; on democracy and land ownership, 29–30, 34–35, 36–37, 131; design of Monticello, 42, 46–47, *46, 47, 48,* 50–51, *52,* 55, *55*; design for University of Virginia, 220, *223*; as egalitarian, 34; on Indigenous land sales, 33; land ordinance grid of, 16, 23, 29–33, 37, 55, 57, 58; new states proposed by, 31, 34, *35*; octagonal vision of, 23, 29–31, 35, 39–47, *40, 43, 47,* 53,

56, 115, 250; radicalism ascribed to, 35; retreat to private life, 52; rurality idealized by, 36, 69; utopianism of, 29–31; on ward-republics, 34–36, 38, 72; on western settlement as safety valve, 65
Johnson, Alexander Bryan, 182–83, 184
Johnson, Hildegard, 37
Johnson, Walter, 31

Kanza Nation, 135, 144
Kansas–Nebraska Act (1854), 1, 143–46
Kansas Territory, 133–47, 146, 152; land speculation in, 149–50, 155; removal of Indigenous people from, 135–36, 143–45
Kansas Vegetarian Settlement Company, 1, 18, 24, 131, 133–36, 147–54, 159, 167; failure of, 153–54; joint-stock structure of, 149; octagonal plan of, 1, 2, 6, 133, 134, 150–53; settlement on Indian land, 5, 18, 135–36, 288n87; sociality and, 6, 147–48. See also Octagon Settlement Company
Keywords (Williams), 25
Kiantone, N.Y., 216–17, 218, 229, 237, 241
Kickapoo Tribe, 135, 144
Koetter, Fred, 6
Koons, Jonathan, 211, 212
Kramer, Michael, 181
Kropotkin, Peter, 249

labor exchanges, 71–72, 174, 175, 185, 291nn37–39
labor notes, 171, 175, 175, 184–85, 188, 193, 230, 291nn37–38
labor theory of empire, 64
labor theory of property, 63–64, 68, 78
labor theory of value, 174
Lamb, Charles R., 243, 244
land ordinance grid, 16, 23, 29–33, 32, 37, 55, 57, 58, 148, 149, 273n1
land reform, 63–68, 100–101, 140–42, 150, 246; and Indigenous dispossession and assimilation, 66, 68
language, 15, 24, 167, 168, 293n72; ambiguity of, 79, 86, 168, 180–83, 192; and analogy to money, 183–84
language reform, 24, 86–90, 88, 167–68, 186, 188, 246
Lause, Mark, 206

Lawrence, Amos, 146
Leaves of Grass (Whitman), 102
Le Camus de Mézières, Nicolas, 234, 236
Ledoux, Claude-Nicolas, 3
L'Enfant, Pierre Charles, 69
Leonard, Thomas, 9
Letchworth (Hertfordshire, England), 250
liberalism, 19, 24, 39, 53, 68, 78, 131, 173–74, 268n60
Lippert, Amy K. DeFalco, 8
Literary Union (periodical), 124
lithography, 8, 256
Locke, John, 39, 41, 44; on the labor theory of property, 63–64, 81; on language, 181, 182
Loco Focos, 184
Looking Backward (Bellamy), 243
Lynd, Staughton, 35

machines, 13, 128, 182, 195, 202, 209, 212–13; cities as, 179; drawings as, 190, 192, 193; drawings of, 15, 109, 190, 191, 212, 214; for printing, 171, 191, 193, 246; for producing perpetual motion, 213; for producing political rhetoric, 182; for shorthand, 246, 247; society akin to, 190–91; spiritualist inventions for, 199, 200, 205, 206, 209–14, 212, 215, 216, 239, 240
Madison, James, 33, 34, 79, 181
Magee, John L., 159
magnetism, 135, 203, 237, 239, 253–54
Malm, Andreas, 212
manifest destiny, 5
Mann, Horace, 113
Mann, S. H., 117–18
Marienville, Pa., 69
Marrinan, Michael, 13, 17, 92
Martin Chuzzlewit (Dickens), 155, 157
Marx, Karl, 21, 81, 157, 234; critique of utopian socialists, 6, 257
Masquerier, Lewis, 62, 245, 276n37; on democratic governance, 73–74; as designer of republican village, 69–72; on diagrams, 58; as geographer, 84–86, 85, 86, 89, 90, 92; links to Josiah Warren, 72, 167; on rural cities, 68, 69, 72; as spelling reformer, 87, 88, 89, 90, 168
Massachusetts Society for the Abolition of Capital Punishment, 207

Matthews, Richard, 35
McCarley, Rebecca, 122
McCoy, Drew, 33
McLauren, John, 152
McLuhan, Marshall, 17
medium: diagram as, 8, 17, 190, 245; language as, 181, 192; machine as, 213; model as, 215; money as, 184, 188; print as, 3, 180, 239, 256; spiritualist, 201, 210, 211, 215, 219, 231, 239, 246, 254
merchants' exchanges, 233–34, *234*
Mesmer, Franz, 202
mesmerism, 201, 202, 237, *238*, 254
metaphysicalism, 201
Mexican–American War (1848), 66, 89
Miami Nation, 33
Mihm, Stephen, 183
Mill, John Stuart, 130–31, 174
millennialism, 2
Missouri Compromise (1820), 143
Mitchell, W. J. T., 188
models, 210; as vehicles of reform, 179, 200, 215–17, 239–40, 243
Modern, John Lardas, 200
Modern Times, N.Y., 165, 167, 175–76, *176*, 206, 230
Moffat, John S., 126, *127*
money, 135, 168, 188; analogy to language, 182–84; debates over paper versus metallic, 182–84, 232
"Monogram of Political Economy" (Collens), 16, *17*
Monroe Doctrine, 89
Montesquieu, Charles Louis de Secondat, Baron de, 34
Monticello, 46–47, *46, 47, 48*, 50–51, *52*, 55; octagonal forms in, 41, 46–47; privacy and publicity at, 50, 52, 55; quarters for enslaved people at, 54, *55*
More, Thomas, 5
Morgan, David, 9, 200, 217, 220, 237
Mormons, 3
Morris, Robert, 43–44, *45*
Morse, Samuel F. B., 202, 231
Mount Vernon, 55–56
Müller, Rudolf, 243, *245*
Muñoz, José Esteban, 21
music notation, 24, 186, 188, *188, 189*

My Bondage and My Freedom (Douglass), 95
mysticism, 201, 202

Nashoba colony, 21
National Land Company, 140
National Reform Association, 23, *59*, 149, 150, 246; on country versus city, 69; grid diagrams employed by, 18, 24, 57, 58, *60, 61, 62*, 83–84, 92–93; on Indigenous dispossession and assimilation, 66, 68; liberal individualism and, 78–79, 92–93; origins of, 63; on property, 63–65; "republican village" envisioned by, 69–74, *70*; safety valve theory reworked by, 65–66, 68; visual practices of, 74–80, 92–93
Natural Alphabet, The (Allen), 167
New Age movement, 201
New England Association of Philanthropic Commercialists, 230, 240
New England Emigrant Aid Company, 143, 150
"New England Reformers" (Emerson), 135
New Era (newspaper), 210, 217
New Harmony community, 11, *11*, 21, 70, 152, 165, 171
New Housekeeping, The (Frederick), 114
Newton, Alonzo E., 210–11, 215, 240
Newton, Sarah, 210
New York Merchants' Exchange, 233, *234*
New York State Kansas Aid Society, 150
Nichols, Mary Gove, 176
Nichols, Robert, 33
Nichols, Thomas Low, 176
Nord, David Paul, 9
Normo-graphy (Allen), 168, *187*
Northwest Territory, 31, *32*, 33
Notes on the State of Virginia (Jefferson), 40
Noyes, John Humphrey, 229
Nutt, Haller, 129, *129*

O'Connor, Feargus, 140
octagon house (Fowler): 3, *4*, 6, 7, 20, 23, 24, 56, 95–101, *98, 100*, 111, 113–18, *115, 116*, 120–28, 131, 135; criticisms of, 121, 130; as example of conspicuous consumption, 128–29; as expression of eccentricity, 130; houses influenced by Fowler, 95–96, *96, 97*, 98, *99*, 118, *119, 122, 123, 125, 127, 129*;

liberal subject linked to, 101, 131, 135; reception of, 117–31; visual rhetoric of, 111–21, 130, 131. *See also Home for All, A*

octagons: in architecture, 6, 43–44, *45*; in city plans, 1, *2*, 6, 35, 69–70, *69, 71*, 74, 133, *134*, 150–53; Thomas Jefferson's designs of, 23, 29–31, 39–41, *40, 43*, 44–56, *46, 47, 48, 49, 50, 51*, 52, 53, *54*, 55; as optical devices, 44, 47–48, 52–53

Octagon Settlement Company, *2*, 6, 147–48, 152–53. *See also* Kansas Vegetarian Settlement Company

Ojibwe (Chippewa) Nation, 126

"On Liberty" (Mill), 130–31, 174

operational aesthetic, 13, 109, 120, 131

orthography. *See* spelling reform

Orvis, John, 208, 230, 237

Osage Nation, 18, 135

Ostler, Jeffrey, 144

O'Sullivan, John, 19

Our History Is Our Future (Estes), 259

Ouseley, Gideon Jasper, 251

ovals: in architecture, 3, 26, 217, 218, 226–27; in city plans, 38

Owen, Robert, 2, 10–11, 22, 72, *73*, 139, 246; as founder of New Harmony community, 11, *11*, 21, 70, 152, 165, 171; as pioneer of labor exchange idea, 174; on the system of society, 90, 92

pacifism, 3, 136

Paine, Thomas, 64, 173

Palingenesia (Ouseley), 251

Palladio, Andrea, 39, *41*

Palmanova, Italy, 69

panics, 19, 63, 155, 183, 232

Pan-Norm-Alpha, The (Allen), 168, 186

Panophonic Printing Alphabet, The (Allen), 167–68

panopticon, 6, *7*, 53

panoramas, 8

Parker, Barry, 250

Peabody, Elizabeth Palmer, 14, *14*, 79

Peaceful Revolutionist (newspaper), 171

Peck, J. M., 152

Peirce, Charles Sanders, 12, 186, 188

Pemberton, Robert, 251

perpetual motion, 200, 213

Perryopolis, Pa., 69, *71*

Pestalozzi, Johann Heinrich, 13–14, 79, *80*, 137

Peters, John Durham, 213

phalanstery, 11, 21, 137, 267n39

phalanxes, 149, 269n73, 291n40

Philosophy of Human Knowledge, The (A. B. Johnson), 182–83

phonography. *See* shorthand

photography, 8, 9, 17, 105, 106, 256; of spirits, 205

phrenology, 3, 24, 96, 101–11, *103, 107, 108*, 135, 167; critiques of, 104; as discourse of self-improvement, 101–2, 104–5; racial determinism in, 102, 128

Phrenology, Proved, Illustrated, and Applied (O. Fowler), 102

phrenomagnetism, 203, 237

Picon, Antoine, 5

picturesque, 44, 11

Pierce, Franklin, 143

Pitman, Isaac, 168, 186

Plato, 180

Playfair, William, 13, *13*

politics, 159, 257–58: aesthetic dimension of, 25–26; as agonism, 159, 193; antislavery, 159, 161; enchantment as an element of, 238; form and, 6, 167, 257; language as a problem in, 181–82, 192; spiritualist circumvention of, 238; as temporary duty, 52; utopianism and, 21, 26, 257–58; Josiah Warren's disdain for, 182; workingmen's engagement in, 74

Poplar Forest, *4*, 53–54, *53, 54*

Popper, Karl, 84

Post, Amy, 206

Post, Isaac, 206

Potawatomi Nation, 135, 144

Pottawatomie Massacre, 136, 159

Practical Applications of the Elementary Principles of "True Civilization" (Warren), 24, 165–67, *166*, 177

Prairie Farmer (periodical), 130

preemption: Act of 1841, 64; frauds, 157, *158*

Present Age and Inner Life, The (Andrew Jackson Davis), 202, *204, 205*

print culture, 3, 8–12, 58

printing, 8, 22, *61*, 117, 139, 175, 246, 256;

importance to reform of, 56, 170, 193, 240, 288–89n107; Josiah Warren's innovations in, 168–71, *169, 170,* 177, 180, 190, *191,* 193

prison: design by Jeremy Bentham, 6–7, *7,* 52–53, 236; design by Thomas Jefferson, 39, 52–53; reform, 207

Prisoner's Friend (*Hangman;* newspaper), 207

Progress and Poverty (George), 246

property, 63–65, 68, 185; communalization of, 135, 165; conversion of Indigenous land to, 33, 38, 56, 57, 62, 63–64; equalization of, 1, 25, 33, 36, 81; Thomas Jefferson on link between property ownership and independence, 36, 131; labor theory of, 63–64, 68, 78; redistribution of, 31, 36, 55, 65, 69, 80–81, 83; Thomas Skidmore on right to, 80–81, 83, 92; usufruct right to, 36, 65, 81

Proudhon, Pierre-Joseph, 174

psychophysics, 297n89

railroads, 225, *228*

Randolph, Paschal Beverly, 296n47

Rappites, 11

Reconstruction, 22

Redheffer, Charles, 213

reform, 89, 90, 96, 100, 101, 124, 126, 135, 136, 137, 138, 139, 142, 171, 174, 177, 179–80, 200, 206; age of, 3, 5, 18–22, 237, 245–46; architecture of, 4–5, 6–7, 100; Ralph Waldo Emerson's views on, 135, 137, 138; environmental determinism and, 6–7; historiography of, 5; importance of printing to, 56, 170, 193, 240, 288–89n107; individual versus social, 137–38; mechanical metaphor for, 190–92; spiritualist approach to, 207, 208–9, 213, 215, 229, 230; use of diagrams by advocates of, 12–18; use of illustrated media by advocates of, 9–12; versus utopianism, 20–21

Reign of Terror in Kansas, The (Briggs), 159, *160*

reproduction, 105, 113, 229, 238; as means of reform, 229; and nationalism, 105. *See also* sexuality

Reps, John, 69–70

republicanism, 22, 34, 73, 181, 268–69n60

Republican Party, 143, 161

Reynolds, David, 146

rhetoric, 81–82; diagrams as, 15; enchantment linked to, 238; of Orson Fowler, 121; functionalism as, 130; geometric utopias as, 257–58; of Ebenezer Howard, 253–54; of land reformers, 58, 66; models as, 216; non-rhetorical form of, 193; phrenology as, 106; political, 182. *See also* visual rhetoric

Ricardian socialists, 64, 174

Ricardo, David, 174

Richards, John, 128

Richardson, Albert D., *144,* 146–47, 150, 155, *156,* 157, *158*

Richmond, Cora, 246

Rights of Man to Property!, The (Skidmore), 80–83, *82–83*

Ripley, George, 285n25

Ritchie, Thomas W., 117

Rittenhouse, David, 37

Robinson, Cedric, 269n76

Robinson, Enoch, 130, 220, *221, 222*

Rosenfeld, Sophia, 186

Rowe, Colin, 6

Rush, Benjamin, 207

safety valve theory, 57, 63, 65–66, *67,* 68, 142

Saint-Simon, Henri, Comte de, 90

Sandage, Scott, 105

Sargent, Lyman Tower, 265n10

Scientific American, 211, *212,* 213

Scientific Division and Nomenclature of the Earth, A (Masquerier), 84, *85, 86*

séances, 202, 210, 211, *211,* 225, 254

Second Bank of the United States, 183

Select Architecture (Morris), 43–44, *45*

self-improvement, 128, 131, 135, 137, 140, 142; octagon house and, 111, 128, 131, 135; phrenology and, 101–2, 104–5, 131

"Self-Reliance" (Emerson), 125

Seminoles, 66

semiotic utopianism, 87, 168, 186. *See also* language reform

sensationalism, 6, 31, 42–43, 226

settler colonialism, 23, 31, 33, 57, 62, 65, 89, 93, 131, 143; utopianism linked to, 5, 93, 258–59

Seven American Utopias (Hayden), 3

Seven Ranges map, *32,* 37
sexuality: Orson Fowler on, 105; proper and improper, 105; spiritualists on, 210, 229. *See also* reproduction
Shakers, 3, 201–2, *203,* 220
Shawnee, 33, 144
shorthand, 25, 139, 168, 186, *187,* 246; importance to social reform, 21, 139, 186; machine for, 246, *247*
Shprintzen, Adam, 137
Simpson, James, 139, 142
Six Nations, 33
Skidmore, Thomas, 80–83, *82–83,* 92, 174
Sklansky, Jeffrey, 183–84
slavery, 2, 3, 22, 131, 133. *See also* antislavery
Sloan, Samuel, 123, *123,* 129, *129*
smallpox, 144
Smith, Adam, 174, 225
Soane, John, 234
socialism, 3, 19, 25, 65. *See also* association
sociology, 16, 90, 268n51
Sociology (Masquerier), 90
Sojourner Truth, 206
Solan, Victoria, 113
Southern Home (periodical), 118
Spear, Charles, 207
Spear, John Murray, 195–96, 199–200, 207–17, 237, 239–40, 254; background as minister, 202; circular diagrams of, 25, 196, 207, *208,* 225–26, *227,* 232; early reform activity of, 207; "Electric Motor" and, 209–13, 215; Ebenezer Howard linked to, 251; models and, 215–17; on reproduction, 229; Warren's influence on, 167, 230
spelling reform, 19, 24, 86, 90, 166, 167–68, 181, 186
Spence, Thomas, 64
spiritualism, 3, *4,* 25, 135, 195–241, 243–54; circularity in, 224–30; "Electric Motor" and, 209–13, 215; enchantment in, 200, 216, 220, 224, 237–39, 241; history of, 200–202; models and, 215–17, 240; politics of, 238; telegraphy and, 200, 202, 213, 215, 231, 239
Spiritual Telegraph (newspaper), 202
Spurzheim, Johann Gaspar, 102
Standing Rock Reservation, 259
steam engine, 212

stereotyping, 8, 117, 175; Josiah Warren's innovations in, 168–70, *170,* 171, 177, 190
Stewart, Watson, 153, 154
Streeby, Shelley, 68
Sumner, Charles, 159, *161,* 162
surveillance, 6, 44, 47, 236
surveying, 13, 31, 33, 37, 57, 62, 89
Swedenborg, Emanuel, 202, 225
Swedenborgians, 136, 139, 201–2, 215, 225
symbols, 26–27, 76–77, 278n71; grids as, 58, 62, 72; Charles Peirce's theory of, 12, 186, 188. *See also* emblems
symmetry, 25–26, 40, 46, 95, 164, 255
Syslang, Fenneke, 106
systems, 90, 92, 167; reform of, 87, 89; of society, 16, 90, 92, 100; visualization of, 16, 92, 258

Taylor, Robert, 234, *235*
telegraph, 200, 202, *204,* 213, 215, 231, 239, 295n16, 298n105
temperance, 3, 7, 21, 142, 152–53
Temple of Vesta (Palladio), 39–40, *41*
Thayer, Eli, 146
Thirty-Nine Reasons Why I Am a Vegetarian (Clubb), 138
Thompson, William, 174
Thoreau, Henry David, 19, 130, 138, 228
Thornton, J. S., 120–21, 126–27
Thucydides, 180
time stores, 175, 177, 180, 184, 185, 192, 193, 195. *See also* labor exchanges
Tocqueville, Alexis de, 182
Todd, Sereno Edwards, 130
To-morrow (E. Howard), 243, 245, 246, *248, 250, 251, 252,* 253, *255,* 257
Trall, Russell, 152
transcendentalism, 137, 184, 202, 229
Treaty of Greenville (1795), 33
Tubman, Harriet, 289n112
Turner, Frederick Jackson, 275n24
Turner, Nat, 289n112
Twain, Mark, 233
Two Treatises of Government (Locke), 63–64

unemployment, 19, 63
Union Emigrant Aid Company, 143
Unitarianism, 202

United States Magazine and Democratic Review, 123
Universalism, 202
Unwin, Raymond, 250
Upton, Dell, 48, 50, 54, 55
urbanization, 69, 105, 136
urban plans, 3, 38,69–72, 155, 243; circular, 69, *72,* 195, 217, 243, 250–51, *251, 252;* cobweb, 69–70, 251; as cognitive maps, 16, 92; garden city, 250–51, *251, 252;* gridded, 37–38, *38,* 71, *145,* 150, *156,* 243; hexagonal, 165–67, *166,* 177–79, 243, *244, 245;* octagonal, *2,* 6, *69, 71,* 133, *134,* 150–53
usufruct, 65
utilitarianism, 4–5, 6
Utopia, Ohio, 165, 175
utopianism, 22; African Americans and, 21–22; architecture and, 3, 5–6, 12, 26; critiques of, 5–6, 26, 257; historiography of, 3, 5, 21, 26; settler colonialism linked to, 5, 93, 258–59; women and, 21. *See also* geometric utopianism

Veblen, Thorstein, 128
vegetarian colonies. *See* Concordium at Ham Common; Fruitlands; Kansas Vegetarian Settlement Company
vegetarianism, 3, 6, 105, 147, 154, 157, 167; antislavery linked to, 135, 142–43; history of, 136–140, 142; individualist ethos of, 135, 137; land reform linked to, 140, 142
Veracini, Lorenzo, 258, 275–76n30
Vidler, Anthony, 21
visual rhetoric, 12, 75–77, 101, 139, 159, 200, 216, 250, 257–58, 267n40; of antislavery, 163; geometric diagrams as, 8, 12–16, 56, 62, 192, 253–54; of Ebenezer Howard, 250, 253–54; of the octagon house, 111–21, 130, 131; of phrenology, 106–11; of spiritualists, 250
Vitruvian man, 40, *42*
Vitruvius Pollio, 218

Wakefield, Edward Gibbon, 300n32
Walden (Thoreau), 130, 228
Walker, David, 289n112
Wallace, Alfred Russell, 246
Ward, William G., 137

ward-republics, 34–36, 38, 72
Warren, Josiah, 4, *4,* 20, 21, 90, 165–93, 213, 215, 243, 245; "equitable commerce" envisioned by, 24–25, 72, 149, 165, 167, 171, *172,* 174–77, 180, 186; hexagonal city published by, 177–79, 192; as individualist, 172–73, 176–80; labor exchange system of, 174–75, *175,* 180, 184–85, 230; as language reformer, 167, 180–81, 182, 185–86; mechanical metaphors employed by, 190–92; music notation system of, 186, 188, *188, 189;* printing innovations of, 168, *169,* 170–71, 177, 180, 190, *191,* 193; as showman, 192–93
Washington, George, 55, 270n6
Water-Cure Journal, 102, 133
water cures, 3, 135, 148
Watt, James, 212
Webster, Noah, 90, 168, 181, 190, 195, 215
Wedgwood, Josiah, 162
Wells, Samuel, 102, 122, 130
Whately, Thomas, 81–82
Whitman, Walt, 102
Whitwell, Stedman, 278n88
Wilcox, Ann, 95, 101, 125
Wilcox, Isaiah, 95, 101, 125
Williams, Raymond, 23, 25, 131, 256
Winter, Alison, 237
women: health of, 113; spiritualist beliefs about, 229, 231; as trance mediums, 201; utopianism and, 21
women's rights, 3, 5, 18, 136, 206, 229
wood engraving, 9, 267n28
Wood, John, 128
Worcester County Kansas League, 143, 150
Working Man's Advocate, 29, *30,* 58, 64, 66, 75–76, *77. See also Young America*
Working Men's Party, 63, 65, 80
world's fairs, 8
Wotton, Henry, 44
Wren, Christopher, 69
Wright, Fanny, 21
Wright, Frank Lloyd, 69
Wyandot Nation, 33

Young America, 58, 68, 75, 78, *78. See also Working Man's Advocate*
Younglove, Timothy, 125–26

IRENE CHENG is associate professor of architecture at the California College of the Arts.